D1304694

RING LARDNER AND THE OTHER

RING LARDNER
AND THE OTHER

DOUGLAS ROBINSON
With an essay by Ellen Gardiner

New York   Oxford
OXFORD UNIVERSITY PRESS
1992

Oxford University Press

Oxford   New York   Toronto
Delhi   Bombay   Calcutta   Madras   Karachi
Kuala Lumpur   Singapore   Hong Kong   Tokyo
Nairobi   Dar es Salaam   Cape Town
Melbourne   Auckland   Madrid

and associated companies in
Berlin   Ibadan

Copyright © 1992 by Oxford University Press, Inc.

Published by Oxford University Press, Inc.,
200 Madison Avenue, New York, New York 10016

Oxford is a registered trademark of Oxford University Press

Library of Congress Cataloging-in-Publication Data
Robinson, Douglas.
Ring Lardner and the Other / Douglas Robinson.
p. cm.   Includes bibliographical references and index.
ISBN 0-19-507600-1
1. Lardner, Ring, 1885–1933 — Criticism and interpretation.
2. Masculinity (Psychology) in literature.   3. Canon (Literature)   I. Title.
PS3523.A7Z85   1992
818´.5209 — dc20   92-3864

"Who Dealt?" by Ring Lardner is reprinted with permission of Charles Scribner's Sons, an imprint of Macmillan Publishing Company, from *The Ring Lardner Reader*, by Ring Lardner. Copyright 1925, 1953, by Ellis A. Lardner.

Short excerpts from Lardner's "Zone of Quiet," "Dinner," "I Can't Breathe,"
"Haircut," "The Maysville Minstrel," "Travelogue," and "I. Gispiri"; as well as
short excerpts from "Lyricists Strike Pay Dirt" in *Shut Up, He Explained*
(Charles Scribner's Sons, 1962) and *You Know Me Al* (Charles Scribner's Sons,
1914) are also reprinted by permission.

Appendix 2, "Engendered in Melancholy" by Ellen Gardiner. Reprinted by permission of the author. Copyright © 1992 by Ellen Gardiner.

1 3 5 7 9 8 6 4 2

Printed in the United States of America
on acid-free paper

Contents

Introduction

As my title suggests, this both is and is not a single-author study. It is to the extent that it is about Ring Lardner; it is not to the extent that it is about the Other. The Ring Lardner book, which acts as a kind of methodological persona or mask, is about one Lardner short story, "Who Dealt?" (part I), Lardner's life and work in broader perspective (part II), and Lardner's readers in their cultural context (part III). The Other book, which wears or shapes the Lardner mask, is about the ways in which fictional characters, authors, and readers (including you and me) are "spoken" by various Others: authoritarian and rebellious; parental and childish; majoritarian and minoritarian; "esemphonic" and "asymphonic." The Ring Lardner book is a critical study of a minor American author who was popular in the twenties; the Other book is a theoretical exploration of what Fredric Jameson has called the "political unconscious," of our ideological entrapment in and various escape routes out of the double bind, the prison bars forged by society within our bodies.

The "who" questions that head the three parts of this study also point, by their very repetitive insistence, to and then past the obvious: in my Ring Lardner book, one of his characters dealt, Lardner himself wrote, and millions read. Even in that book, in fact, these "easy" answers raise more questions: Which of the characters in "Who Dealt?" dealt? The foursome plays at least three hands, one of which appears to have been dealt out by Arthur (and "made" for him by the narrator); but since "Who dealt?" is not a question actually asked in the story, the answer is at least problematic. Indeed, since the question seems primarily designed to reflect the narrator's ignorance of bridge, the "answer" may be a state of mind rather than a person's name. And who is Ring Lardner? One need not invoke poststructuralist pronouncements on the death or disappearance of the author to recognize the problematic nature of a simple "identification" like this: Ring Lardner wrote. Which Ring Lardner? The journalist or the short-story writer? The popular lyricist or the nonsense playwright? More germane to my argument in part II is the question as to whether it was the conservative, upper-middle-class moralist who despised his proletarian speakers (and readers), or the class traitor who poured himself into them with fierce(ly denied) hope. And who were his readers (part III)? Who were the million-headed masses who read his sports writing, humorous columns, and first short stories? How might we even begin to name them? Who, for that matter, are Lardner's critics? What do we know about them? Why do they write the way they do? Why are they Lardner's critics, for example, and not someone else's? If *Ring Lardner and the Other* is really two books, is the same Lardner reader writing both?

In the Other book, the answers to the "who" questions are at once simpler and more complicated. The simple answer is that the Other dealt, the Other wrote, and the Other read; but, like the theological postulate of a providential god who wields us as his instruments, this doesn't really answer anything until we explore in greater detail the complex ideological connections and interrelations among Others, and between Others and the fictional characters and real people (writers and readers) they "speak" or wield. Indeed, detailed and complex as my explorations of these relations are, they are still too sketchy to be seen as more than a prolegomenon to a theory of the Other in literature and society. The specific formulations I adapt from a number of thinkers — Gregory Bateson's double bind, Geoffrey Galt Harpham's ascetic imperative, Jacques Lacan's Other, Mikhail Bakhtin's internal dialogism, Julia Kristeva's infantile discourse, Gilles Deleuze and Fèlix Guattari's becoming-minoritarian, Michel Foucault's author function, Fredric Jameson's political unconscious, Rachel Blau DePlessis's writing beyond the ending — along with those whose sources are less clearly defined, like ideosomatics and esemphonic assimilation, only begin to lift the Other's mask, the ideological persona that literary critics (and everybody else) are taught to take at face value.

Part I, the long reading of "Who Dealt?," probably illustrates the schizoid impetus of "the" book best. Who needs a hundred-page interpretation of a minor writer's ten-page story? Nobody. To justify reading on — if in fact you do — you will probably feel uneasily compelled to shift to the Other book, to read part I for its theoretical and methodological musings: its formulation of the double bind, its mapping of masculine programming under conditions of bourgeois patriarchy, its analysis of the speaking of the Other-as-parent and the Other-as-child. These are all concepts that can be applied usefully to other texts — indeed, to a whole range of human phenomena that we don't normally call "texts" — and this applicability justifies the lengthy discussion of a single story. But the "excavation" or invention of useful methodologies also generates interest in the story, in Ring Lardner as its creator, in the cultural context that has branded him a minor writer. If there is this much "in" a single Lardner story, is he perhaps more interesting than we thought? Was his minor status perhaps a mistake, a critical oversight, a historical blindness best remedied by a fresh look? Soon the pressure builds to canonize Lardner, to raise him to major status. But can we "majoritize" a writer on the basis of a single story?

Of course not. In part II, therefore, I cover — or rather, since my discussion of such a large subject is this time too brief, I only pace off — the ground that critics traditionally cover with major authors by way of establishing their majority status: the "life and work." I do so specifically, however, in order to thwart majoritization, to theorize Lardner as a minor writer who consciously refused majority and courted minority, a "minoritarian" writer who let himself be spoken by an Other-as-minority that cried out for healing communication beyond the prison bars of the double bind. At the same time, if I argue persuasively enough for Lardner's minor status, the temptation will grow again to majoritize him: to take a writer seriously in the Western tradition of literary criticism is, by definition, to elevate him or her to major status, so that Lardner may emerge from part II seeming not so much minor because he failed to become major, as major because he was so insistently minor.

As I show in part III, this would be no more than a seeming. If my minoritarian reading makes Lardner interesting to majoritarian critics, the conjunction of two interpretations — mine of Lardner and yours of me — will generate the impression that Lardner was "essentially" major, that he "possessed" the "essence" of literary majority. Majority is clearly not something that "resides" in an author or a text. But neither is it what antievaluative critics like Northrop Frye derogate as a stock-market mummery (18), a skein of illusion earnestly or cynically woven by critics so as to preserve what they like and consign to oblivion what they don't like. Literary majority is, finally, not controlled by critics but by the majoritarian Other-as-culture — by "society" or the "political unconscious" or "ideology" or "hegemonic" institutions — and its shapes are no more illusory than any other ideological constructs. Literary majority is what Deleuze and Guattari call a "faked image" of social repression; but the very collective success of that repression makes the fake very real indeed, so real that even today intellectuals rarely question it.

My discussions of ideological programming in terms of the speaking of various majoritarian Others is an attempt to dynamize what is often an exceedingly static conception: to explore the shifting interrelations of various ideological voices in our heads/bodies rather than reifying ideology as abstract system. In the process I have also attempted—but probably not enough—to historicize the speaking of these Others: the field is much too large, and too largely unexplored, for me to do much more than sketch in a few historical and theoretical details as landmarks for further research. I have attempted in part I to set up my theoretical model (the double bind, the Other) with minimal historical grounding—speaking of the "normal" "patriarchal" "ideology" of "masculinity," for example, and meaning by it roughly the bourgeois gender ideologies of the last century and a half of American history—and then gradually, in parts II and III, to historicize that model. Thus in part II I explore the specific impact on American bourgeois gender ideologies of the late-nineteenth-century rise of the "supermom"—the strong mother as an increasingly definitive element in the American middle (especially upper-middle) classes—in terms of Lardner's conflicted relationship with his own mother. In part III I trace an actual history of twentieth-century reader response from the teens to today, in the process bringing my argument from Lardner's blocked masculinity in the teens, twenties, and thirties to an emancipatory perspective on our own future. I begin, in other words, more or less ahistorically—in the sense not of timelessness or universality but of a high degree of theoretical abstraction, departicularization—and then gradually narrow my focus to a particular historical epoch and problem, only to slide laterally, in chapter 6, into the present and our concerns for the future.

Within the tripartite movement of my argument I trace three traditional modes of literary criticism—textual/formal, biographical/psychological, and cultural/historical—but with an inner dialectic in each mode that might be thought of in terms of Fredric Jameson's dialectic between negative and positive hermeneutics, between an "ideological" and a "utopian" perspective. In the first, or "negative," chapter of each part I trace the floor plan of the ideological prisons in which we (are not supposed to) find ourselves, in the mechanistic, deterministic, fatalistic (if always playfully inventive) tones of a Lacan, a Foucault, or a Derrida. Each odd-numbered chapter slams the cell-block door on our illusions of freedom in the present and past and our hopes of freedom for the future. In the second, or "positive," chapter of each part I explore potential escape routes: through what I call the idiosomatic dialogism of the Other-as-child in chapter 2, through the infantile discourse of the Other-as-minor(ity) in chapter 4, and through the Other-as-anarchist's reading beyond the ending in chapter 6. I must admit that, however strongly I believe in the possibility and desirability of emancipation from existing ideological inscriptions, I find that the odd-numbered prison maps weaken my determination to escape even as they intensify my sense of the importance of escape. The more carefully we articulate the ideological double binds that enchain us, the more aware we become both of the urgency and of the extreme difficulty of a jailbreak. It can't be done, and it must be done.

My understanding of both the jail and the jailbreak has been shaped by several different discourses — Marxist and pragmatist, poststructuralist and reader-response — but it takes its most decisive impetus from the allied movements of the past two decades toward gender liberation: feminism and "masculism," the women's and men's liberation movements.[1] My assaults on the prisons in which Lardner lived, wrote, and died are heavily indebted to feminist critiques of patriarchal masculinity, especially those of Nancy Chodorow and Susan Griffin: Lardner's idealized anger at his mother, his repressed fear of becoming her, becoming like her, becoming engulfed by her, which is manifested in misogynistic portraits of talkative women; his retreat into the taciturnity of his father and of "normal" patriarchal masculinity, into iron self-control over speech and all other behavior so as to repress the maternal introject; and so forth. I begin and end the book with profeminist readings of "Who Dealt?," my own masculist reading in chapters 1 and 2, and a dialogue with Ellen Gardiner on her feminist reading (which appears in appendix B) in chapter 6. My unsympathetic reading of Lardner's sexism in chapter 3 is followed by a sympathetic reading of Miss Coakley's broken discourse in "Dinner" in chapter 4.

Because I am a man, however, feminism for me is always filtered through my masculist understanding of men's "normal" and "deviant" personalities — my understanding of how we are constituted as men by patriarchal society, and of how we can begin to reconstitute ourselves; of how we are trapped in patriarchal masculinity and how we can be liberated.[2] This means, for one thing, a concern for Lardner as a man, and as a male projection of the male reader's self. It also means a concern for his female characters — for example, Tom's wife in "Who Dealt?," Miss Coakley in "Dinner," and Nurse Lyons in "Zone of Quiet" — less as women, or as female projections of the female reader's self, than as Lardner's and the male reader's impulse toward femininity, or what I call the speaking of the (m)Other-as-child. This means that I do not attempt to appropriate the female subject, to speak for or as a woman, or to impose a feminist reading on a hypothetical female reader, a male-feminist project that irritates many female feminists; but it also means that I peripheralize the female subject — a patriarchal project that irritates even more feminists. My address to the male reader is not entirely exclusive — one of the reasons for including Ellen Gardiner's reading of "Who Dealt?" in an appendix and discussing it with her in chapter

6 (as opposed to merely "reading" it, citing and summarizing and taking issue with it) is to clear a space for dialogue between men and women, and thus to undermine any masculist separatism that might otherwise arise — but it is a fairly dominant critical move in the book, and as such is likely to antagonize some feminist readers. If it does, I am sorry.

In any case, the strongest and most persuasive reader of this book in manuscript was a woman and a feminist critic, Ellen Gardiner, my colleague at the University of Mississippi, whose sympathetic but divergent response to my attempts to voice the narrator of "Who Dealt?" led to the dialogue that surfaces in chapter 6 but also runs more or less silently (double-voiced) throughout the book. The finished text continues to exclude the female writer in several spots, despite her protests, but it also manages, largely thanks to her dialogical intervention, to address the female reader from a feminist point of view, a feat that would have been impossible had I been writing out of the defensively isolated, woman-excluding subjecthood prescribed for men in patriarchal society — and had Ellen not entered the dialogue and "spoken" or "written" the book in collaborative response to my words.

Male colleagues also offered invaluable assistance. David Nye read the entire manuscript and made useful suggestions; he also encouraged me to write the book when I had my doubts. David Galef read and responded to part I and maintained a running dialogue with me (and with Ellen Gardiner) on Lardner while I was researching it, a dialogue largely consisting of notes in our respective boxes and five-minute colloquies in the halls. A greatly reduced version of chapter 5 appeared in *American Literary History* under the title "Ring Lardner's Dual Audience and the Capitalist Double Bind," and Gordon Hutner's suggestions for revision helped me to rethink my argument in useful ways.

The School of Liberal Arts at the University of Mississippi awarded me a Faculty Development Grant, making it possible for me to travel to Chicago to read the Ring Lardner papers in the Newberry Library, which graciously granted me permission to use and photocopy those papers. Kristen Sulser transcribed the taped conversation that appears in chapter 6.

Liz Maguire at Oxford University Press was an enthusiastic supporter of the project from the start and managed to find a sympathetic reader in Susan Jeffords, whose criticisms and suggestions have been unusually valuable.

Oxford, Miss.   D.R.
January 1992

I

WHO DEALT?

1

The Ascetic Lover

"Who Dealt?" is not generally recognized as one of Ring Lardner's best stories. In the listings of the Lardner canon that Lardner critics love to offer, even overdone melodramas like "Champion" and "The Love Nest" are often included and "Who Dealt?" excluded.[1] "Who Dealt?" is never attacked or despised, certainly, and rarely even ignored; indeed many critics, like Maxwell Geismar, describe it as "a little gem in Lardner's best vein" (*Lardner* 79). But it is almost never anthologized—although I first happened upon it in a British anthology, *The Penguin Book of American Short Stories*, edited by James Cochrane—and it has never occasioned a critical debate (the only Lardner story that has, in fact, is "Haircut"). Since I will be discussing the story at considerable length here in part I, I have "anthologized" it myself: it appears in its entirety in appendix A, and all page references will be to this volume.

What is most characteristic (and, I will argue, most deadening) about the critical readings of "Who Dealt?" is in fact a kind of serene consensus—a consensus whose serenity is largely maintained, it seems to me, by its ideological normativeness, its grounding in "normal" masculine contempt for feminine discourse, and "normal" upper-middle-class contempt for lower-middle-class discourse. ("Normal" in quotes throughout this book is shorthand for "conforming to the ideological or social-unconscious norms of the last century and a half of American bourgeois society and thus generally regarded as natural or universally human.") So "normal" is the convergence of this contempt upon the lower-middle-class female narrator of the story, that even a lower-middle-class female critic like Elizabeth Evans, writing in 1979, can repeat her male colleagues' condemnations of the narrator, adding only the "bridge buff's" contempt for the inept bridge player: "She has botched every hand and has also laid her husband's life down on the table to his chagrin and embarrassment" (87). Evans's perspective on the story and its female teller is normatively masculine: like all "normal" professional critics, she

3

identifies with the husband and takes the wife to task for causing him "chagrin and embarrassment."

Evans's reading of the story may seem a bit outdated for 1979. The women's movement was not then as well established in the academy as it now is, and it was still "normal" for academic women to think and feel and write like men; but that ideological norm was already under heavy fire from feminist literary critics, and had been for well over a decade, since the work of Mary Ellmann and Kate Millett in the late sixties. (Judith Fetterley's *Resisting Reader* appeared in 1978, the year before Evans's book.) Taken out of the context of Lardner criticism, which has typically been as normatively repressive as its subject, Evans's attack on a female character does seem a bit anachronistic[2]; but in that context, whose repressions I hope to undo somewhat in the course of this study, it is perfectly ordinary.

In 1956 Donald Elder, for example, Lardner's first biographer, writes of the story (in toto):

> "Who Dealt?" is a monologue expertly calculated to produce in the reader just the bearable amount of embarrassment, agony, and suspense, topped with a fatal climax. The speaker is a bride of three months whose husband, Tom, has brought her to see his oldest friends, Arthur and Helen Gratz. During a bridge game the young wife rattles on, paying no attention to the cards. It becomes obvious that Helen was the childhood sweetheart of Tom, but has married Arthur instead. The bride cheerfully exposes their private life—Tom has gone on the wagon at her request; he wears pajamas instead of nightshirts. Over his protests she tells the plot of a story Tom has written; it is plainly autobiographical—the story of how Helen jilted Tom and eloped with Arthur, who is richer. Then the wife recites a sentimental love poem she has found among Tom's papers. The story ends:
>
> "Isn't that pretty? He wrote it four years ago. Why, Helen, you revoked! And, Tom, do you know that's Scotch you're drinking? You said— *Why, Tom!*"
>
> At the end of this agonizing recital one is sure that a marriage has been shattered. One can see the suburban living room, the characters, the very expressions on their faces, and the whole course of Tom's life which has brought him to marriage with this dreary, insensible, rattlebrained girl. In the course of her monologue she has unconsciously told everything about their fundamental incompatibility, the kind of lives they are doomed to; and the hosts' embarrassment and the husband's dismay are nearly intolerable. (240)

This is clearly a paean to repression, and to patriarchal marriage based on repression—on concealment and the ironclad self-control required to forestall disclosure. To reveal the secrets of the past is to shatter a marriage, and to shatter a marriage based on secrets and lies is to destroy something unquestionably valuable. Like Evans, like every other professional critic of the story, Elder assumes that the reader will naturally identify with Tom Cannon (and, to a lesser extent, with the rather hazy Gratzes)—will share both his embarrassment and dismay at the revelation of his secrets, and his secret perception of his wife as dreary, insensible, and rattlebrained.

Elder's book appeared, in fact, two years after the publication of "The Affective Fallacy"—an interesting historical juxtaposition because Elder so clearly and unrepentently commits the "fallacy" that Wimsatt and Beardsley identify. When he concludes his reading of the story by noting that "the hosts' embarrassment and the husband's dismay are nearly intolerable," he patently means intolerable *to him*, as the reader who is construing the suburban scene and facial expressions and characters' affective response out of his own (probably rather similar) experience. And quite rightly, too: how else is a story to take on significance, except through the reader's somatic identification with the characters in it? (My own less idealized response to the story has a great deal to do with memories of my parents playing bridge with friends in the early sixties: the uneasy determination I felt in their controlled cheerfulness, the repressed sexual charge of "switching partners," the incongruity of the cheap rickety bridge table and folding metal chairs in the middle of a carefully decorated middle-class living room.)

The problematic of the active reader is developed rather more explicitly (although no less uncritically) in Walton R. Patrick's 1963 book on Lardner (in Twayne's United States Authors Series):

> The stupid wife in "Who Dealt?" unwittingly chatters out the story of her husband's disappointment in a love affair, failing to perceive that she is telling the story to the very woman and man who figured as principals in it, and thus explodes a bombshell which may wreck her marriage as well as that of the other couple. The unconsciousness of the narrators in both stories ["Who Dealt?" and "Haircut"] vitally contributes to the highly ironic effects produced. With no character commenting on the narrator or providing internal clues for the reader to use in judging the narrator as in the third-person stories with interior monologues, the reader himself supplies the standard by which the narrator is measured. This, however, places no burden on him, for he simply watches as Lardner has the narrators tie the rope around their necks with their own words. (114–15)

Patrick's interpretive staging of the story (at least in the plot summary section of this passage) might be read as "voicing" the female narrator—

who chatters, fails to perceive, explodes a bombshell, and may wreck her own marriage—much more fully than Elder, who drew an implicit line of force from the male reader to the male author through an almost transparent female narrator. But it is still clearly an approach calculated to negate the narrator as subject, to show how her narrative negates or cancels her subjective integrity. Like Elder, Patrick clearly wants to portray the narrator as a prescriptively or normatively "wrong" or "deviant" sort of woman, a woman who deviates from the sweet, demure, passive feminine norm (presumably represented by Helen, named after the Homeric paragon of womanly beauty—who has also become an emblem of patriarchal strife), a woman whose presence is all surface and no depth, all talk ("chatter") and no semantic or perceptual substance, and therefore self-destructive: she may have wrecked her marriage, which is to say, in normative patriarchal terms, she may have wrecked her other-defined self.[3]

But there are obvious aporias in this reading. If the narrator is all surface, how can she explode a bombshell? What power does superficial discourse have over marriages? Are we to understand that the marriage exists on the same superficial level, and is therefore susceptible to the destructive effects of chatter? An argument might be made for that sort of reading, but the impact of Patrick's interpretation seems to be that the narrator's superficial chatter touches some deep chord that detonates the bomb, which seems to be a mine, set deep in Tom's and Helen's repression of the past. And in what sense is the narrator "unconscious"? Patrick's negations ("unwittingly," "failing to perceive") suggest that for him her chatter simply lacks consciousness, lacks the kind of rational control over articulation that has always been associated in Western patriarchy (for which term throughout read "male-dominated society") with masculinity. But the Freudian unconscious, which I assume Patrick is at least implicitly alluding to, is a deeper, repressed consciousness, a submerged and hidden knowing. The very fact that the narrator is able to explode the bomb implanted in her husband's repressed knowing (and, of course, that her discourse enables us to see what she fails to perceive) would suggest a rift or conflict between conceptions of her unconscious chatter as simple lack of consciousness and as the return of the repressed.

Patrick's analysis of the normative masculine reader's critical response to the story is even more problematic. The long and convoluted sentence modifier beginning "With no character commenting" seems to be a tacit apology for committing the affective fallacy—if Lardner had given us more internal clues, we could be more New Critical about the story—but it sets up a main clause that in its evocation of readerly power is highly suggestive: "the reader himself supplies the standard by which the narrator is measured." The interesting question is: Where does he get that standard? Is it a relativistic, psychologistic standard, like Norman Holland's identity theme? Is it just something every reader has, something uniquely his (not hers), that he "supplies" like a football at a pickup game? Or is it an ideological norm, as the generic "himself" suggests, something that constitutes the reader as a normative "man," as someone able to supply the missing standard or measure to the critical task of judging the narrator (and finding her lacking)? And why is Patrick so eager to reassure the normative male reader that this act of judgment "places no burden on him"? What burden is his generic reader afraid of having placed on him?[4] (I raise these questions of the reader here only in order to put them on hold until part III.)

Jonathan Yardley's biography appeared more than twenty years after Elder's, in 1977, and in many ways it shows the passage of time: like Ring Lardner, Jr., in his 1976 memoir of his father and family, Yardley is much less inclined to idealize Lardner's repressive self-control than Elder, and more sensitive to the effects of that self-control on his wife and sons. But his reading of "Who Dealt?" is tonally and ideologically almost identical to Elder's:

> It is not so much a narration as one long gurgle by a brand-new bride who, playing bridge with her husband, Tom, and his friends Arthur and Helen (a friendly bow to the Jackses: Ring loved to drop the names of his friends into his stories), babbles her way into the kind of self-revelation that is Ring's fictional art at its finest. . . . The more she chatters the deeper she digs the hole into which she is bound to fall. One mindless outburst leads to another until she has managed to get Tom to think seriously about jumping off the wagon, where he has been perched for her benefit. As she dumbly presses on, she discloses, without understanding it herself, that Tom had once been in love with Helen and had been jilted by her. (293)

"Gurgle" and "babble," "mindless" and "dumb." Let me again put one aspect of this reading on hold—the "bow" he makes to Arthur and Helen Jacks in naming the host couple in his story (just what sort of "friendliness" was involved in that choice of names?)—until chapter 3. For now, I want to seize upon Yardley's erroneous notion (which also appeared in Elder's reading) that Tom has been "perched" on the wagon "for her benefit," in order to begin to set up my antithetical reading of Tom's asceticism.[5] Yardley's textual evidence for this assumption is almost certainly this passage:

"Don't tempt him, Ken," I said. "Tom isn't a drinker like you and Gertie
and the rest of us. When he starts, he can't stop." Gertie is Mrs. Baker.
So Ken said why should he stop and I said there was good reason why
he should because he had promised me he would and he told me the day
we were married that if I ever saw him take another drink I would know
that — (230)

There is no hint here or elsewhere that Tom quits drinking to *please*
his wife; if anything (though, as I will argue in a moment, it is consider-
ably more complicated even than this), he makes his promise to his wife
in order to quit drinking. It is a kind of insurance, an added motivation
for his resolve not to drink, and in fact a telling one, given the story's
grounding in repression and the return of the repressed. The promise
Tom makes to his wife on their wedding day is: if I fall off the wagon,
you will *know*. The implication is that there is a secret which must be
kept from her — that he doesn't love her? that he still loves Helen? (this
may be the only thing the narrator does know and doesn't tell us) — and
the first drink he takes will signal that secret, that knowledge, to her.
Since that is a secret which she must never learn, a knowledge which she
must never gain — she *must* be kept ignorant; Tom's repression of his
continuing love for Helen and the hurt he still feels at being jilted *must*
be replicated in his wife's "unconsciousness" — he must never risk taking
a drink.

This is a typically desperate attempt to trick the desiring self that, in
one form or another, is almost universal among alcoholics and other
addicts. And Tom is an alcoholic. When he drinks, as his wife says, he
can't stop. He has been drinking steadily for four years (that much
Lardner's narrator knows, but he has probably been at it longer than
that) when he marries his wife, and has only been on the wagon three
months when the story's bridge game pushes him off. Lardner himself
was an alcoholic who used ruses like Tom's on himself all through his
short life (he died at age forty-eight), and his biographers Elder and
Yardley both know it. In his rush to ridicule the narrator of "Who
Dealt?," however, Yardley makes it seem as if Tom was a social drinker
who absurdly quit drinking to please a nagging wife and is now "thinking
seriously about jumping off the wagon."[6] Tom is *calmly* in control of
the situation: he is not an alcoholic, not someone who "when he starts,
he can't stop," and if he *decided* to quit drinking to please his "dumb"
and "mindless" wife, by God, he can *decide* to start up again. It is just a
matter of "thinking seriously," making calm, rational decisions about
the course of one's life.

As Gregory Bateson argues in his theory of alcoholism in *Steps to an Ecology of Mind*, something like this is the "normal" conception of alcoholism in Western society:

> The friends and relatives of the alcoholic commonly urge him to be "strong," and to "resist temptation." What they mean by this is not very clear, but it is significant that the alcoholic himself — while sober — commonly agrees with their view of his "problem." He believes that he could be, or, at least, ought to be the "captain of his soul."[7] But it is a cliché of alcoholism that after "that first drink," the motivation to stop drinking is zero. Typically the whole matter is phrased overtly as a battle between "self" and "John Barleycorn." Covertly the alcoholic may be planning or even secretly laying in supplies for the next binge, but it is almost impossible (in the hospital setting) to get the sober alcoholic to plan his next binge in an overt manner. He cannot, seemingly, be the "captain" of his soul and overtly will or command his own drunkenness. The "captain" can only command sobriety — and then not be obeyed. (312)

This analysis casts a rather different light on the psychodynamics of "Who Dealt?" than the idealizing critiques of Elder and Yardley. Tom constructs a self that is strong enough to resist temptation, to swear off alcohol, and buttresses that self with the social apparatus of a wife, a marriage, a socius of two that he explicitly conceives in terms of his determination to stay on the wagon. He quits drinking on his wedding day and has not touched a drop of alcohol for the entire three months of their marriage. Because the denied or repressed desiring self (the alcoholic self) knows that this structure will not withstand its desire, he takes extra precautions: he builds into the defensive social structure a trap — in Patrick's terms, a bomb, a mine, and ties the detonator to booze. If he takes a drink, his wife will *know*. If his wife *knows*, his marriage will crumble, will "be shattered," as Elder says.

The problem, of course, is that this reinforced structure will not withstand the alcoholic self's desire either, and Tom knows it — knows it unconsciously, perhaps, represses his knowledge of it, and in the interest of that repression trains his wife to repress her "knowledge" of his secret as well, the secret that she will *know* if he ever takes a drink. Here is the complication I mentioned earlier: it is not only that Tom uses his wife to help himself quit drinking; it is that the marriage and the "wagon" are mutually supporting structures for the repression (in himself and in his wife) of the secret of his continuing love for Helen, the frightening fact that he hasn't yet gotten over her.

More: in Tom's somatic economy his ongoing desire for Helen is inextricably tied to his ongoing desire for drink. He drank steadily from the time four years earlier when Helen jilted him until his wedding day, and starts drinking again when his wife unwittingly reveals that he is still fixated on Helen and the hurt she caused him. This suggests that the acceptable objects of his desire (his wife, the wagon) act as repressive surrogates for the unacceptable objects of his desire (Helen, drink), and further that the acceptable/unacceptable distinction is, as Deleuze and Guattari would put it, only a cut he makes in the flow of his desire. In Bateson's words, the alcoholic "cannot simply elect 'sobriety.' At best he could only elect 'sobriety — not drunkenness,' and his universe remains polarized, carrying always both alternatives" (319). Tom's acceptable desire for the "normalcy" of a wife and family without the curse of alcoholism is impossible, because it is only one pole of a binary desiring system that is both biochemically and emotionally inescapable: as the Alcoholics Anonymous insist, he *is* an alcoholic whether he drinks or not, and, as the Inamorati Anonymous insist in Thomas Pynchon's *Crying of Lot 49* (82–83), he is an inamorato, someone in love, whether he has Helen or not. He is an addict.

Like many addicts, Tom idealizes his addiction — normatively, along ideologically prescribed lines — in terms of presence and absence: the absence of Helen leads to or generates the presence of alcohol, and because he cannot reverse that causal process and use the presence of Helen to banish alcohol into absence (Helen is married and living in another state, inaccessible to his designs), he needs a surrogate Helen whose presence will allow him to "absent" both the real Helen and drink. But the "absent" objects of his desire are not truly absent in the sense of not being present to his desire. They are (or his desire for them is) merely resisted or controlled, and that resistance or control escalates desire. As his desire for the unacceptable things increases, so too does his control, which again escalates controlled desire. And as Bateson points out — and Lardner's story confirms — this "schismogenic" system of escalation is typically resolved in the alcoholic's case by a return to drinking.

One way of reading the ending of Lardner's story, as we have seen — implicit, almost explicit, in Elder's and Yardley's readings — is to say that the narrator-wife undermines Tom's determination, "drives him to drink." Another, simplemindedly antithetical, reading is that the narrator-wife really has nothing to do with it; she is merely the tool of Tom's self-control, and he himself builds into that tool the double whammy that undoes him, that drives him off the wagon. These two readings would in fact mark the masculine thesis and feminine antithesis of the patriarchally prescribed and inscribed dialectic we call the battle of the sexes: the first reading exonerates the man and blames the woman, while the second exonerates the woman and blames the man.

Bateson's analysis of alcoholism suggests that the situation is enormously more complicated than this. The ideologically correct or "normal" dialectic of patriarchal gender battle represses its own dialectical movement through dualistic projection: each gender negates its own "faults" or antithetical psychic inscriptions and projects them onto the other. The defensive blindness of "Who Dealt?" criticism—male critics' desire to portray the narrator as driving Tom to drink—is thus ideologically prescribed, "normal," socially correct. A naive "feminist" reading that attempted to exonerate the narrator and lay all the blame on Tom would be equally (if antithetically) "normal." (It would feel less normal, perhaps, because "normal" public discourse is constituted through the exclusion or antitheticalization of women's voices; but men's constant susceptibility to those "excluded" voices through maternally controlled guilt signals the complementary "normality" of women blaming men.[8])

Since one of my not-so-hidden agendas in this book is gender liberation, escape from the deadening force of the "normal" battle of the sexes, I shall oppose this defensive blindness, this dualistic denial of dialectic, this projection of blame outward onto a statically conceived other, as strenuously as I can. My oppositional project will require that I first of all uncover the repressed dialectic that traps us, so as to articulate the trap (and only then, in chapter 2, to move toward liberation). The ideological dialectic I want to explore binds us as much through repressive modalization (the programmed assumption that the dialectic is "human nature") as it does through substantive modeling (the internalized command to emulate your same-sex parent, for example); in fact, in important ways the operation of repression is more deadly, more powerfully binding, precisely because it keeps us convinced that there is nothing that can be done about the modeling. It is the way we are. It is biology, or at best an immutable psychic mechanism (as Freud would say), and we had best adapt ourselves to it. This fatalistic belief in the normality and therefore the immutability of our ideological programming is itself a product of that programming. Drawing on the theories of Alice Miller and Gregory Bateson, I hope to show here just how the programming process works and then, in chapter 2, how we can begin to struggle free from it.

By conflating two of Bateson's systemic analyses, the theory of alcoholism and the theory of schizophrenia, I shall argue that the dialectical repression system that drives Lardner's plot (and all our plots, insofar as they are ideologically "normal"—and almost all of them are) is specifically the destructively self-negating and self-perpetuating dialectic that Bateson identifies as the double bind. The double bind is so mind-numbing in its compounded complexity, however, that I want to build toward an understanding of it slowly—to sneak up on it, as it were—to move closer to a naming of the terrible ideological "god" that wields us by apparently innocent stealth, and so perhaps to catch it napping.

This naming will be explicitly structural, or (to use Greimas's term) "actantial"; I will be concerned in this chapter, and to some extent throughout part I, with the interaction not of real people, nor even of fictional people, but of roles or figures. This is not because I want us to idealize human relations in structural terms—far from it. Rather, it is because the patriarchal system of mutually defining and mutually destroying gender identification that I propose to explore in this chapter is itself structurally "transcendental": it dehumanizes the individuals it programs by assigning us structural or actantial roles in a dystopian drama of the absurd. If by night all cats are gray, in the night of the patriarchal double bind all sons are one, all daughters, all mothers, all fathers—all members of an ideologically normal "class" (or actantial role)—are identical and interchangeable.

Furthermore, in any "normal" psychic economy all men are identical and interchangeable, and all women likewise: for a "normal" man, all other men are at once the father and the self-as-son, and all women are the mother, and for a "normal" woman all other women are at once the mother and the self-as-daughter and all men are the father. I am referring to the phenomenon Freud dubbed "transference," but as I conceive it, it is not the subject's fantasy; it is an ideologically "normal" and normative illusion inscribed in each subject (every individual subjected by the double bind, constituted as subject by the specific patriarchal ideology of his or her society), and as such it is the ideological mechanism that ensures the proper transmission of the double bind to the next generation. What Freud called "transference" is primarily a channel for projecting doubly bound images of the parent-child relationship from the subject's own childhood to his or her parenting, so that the subject's child becomes as "perfectly" or "normally" doubly bound as he or she is.[9]

Back, then, to "Who Dealt?" I have suggested that the Helen figure, the Helen role, or actant, the woman (whether the real or the surrogate Helen, Tom's ex-lover or current wife), can work both sides of the sexual desiring system: that "love" for one woman can be used to resist and displace "love" for another; that marriage to the narrator, for example, enables Tom to shunt Helen over to the negated or controlled or absented ("unacceptable") side of the equation, which is to say, enables him to "forget" her. I also suggested, or hinted, that the Helen figure can work both sides of the alcoholic desiring system as well, when I argued that Tom used his wife to "overcome" the alcoholism with which he "overcame" his desire for Helen: marriage to the Helen surrogate enables Tom to shunt drink, too, over to the negated or controlled or absented ("unacceptable") side of the equation. What I want to explore now, in a preliminary approach to the self-negations of the double bind, is the possibility that the shunting might also work in reverse: that the new wife might undermine Tom's self-control precisely by her very success at bolstering it. Because he is, he thinks, so happily married, Tom can test his self-control by taking his new bride over to meet the Gratzes, can place himself in dangerous proximity to Helen without fear of breaking down and confessing to her his hurt and need and desire for her. This is, as Bateson reminds us, the same kind of thinking that leads the alcoholic to test his self-control by taking a drink, and in "Who Dealt?" Tom does specifically test his self-control (and fail the test) in regard both to Helen and to drink:

> In this sense, the so-called pride of the alcoholic is in some degree ironic. It is a determined effort to test something like "self-control" with an ulterior but unstateable purpose of proving that "self-control" is ineffectual and absurd. "It simply won't work." This ultimate proposition, since it contains a simple negation, is not to be expressed in primary process. Its final expression is in an action—the taking of a drink. The heroic battle with the bottle, that fictitious "other," ends up in a "kiss and make friends."
>
> In favor of this hypothesis, there is the undoubted fact that the testing of self-control leads back into drinking. And, as I have argued above, the whole epistemology of self-control which his friends urge upon the alcoholic is monstrous. (Bateson 327)

This would suggest that, by helping him to succeed (to remain firm, to abstain from drinking), the narrator helps Tom to fail: by encouraging him to believe that he is immune to temptation, she helps bring him into the proximity of the temptation to which he must succumb. We could run that the other way, from Tom's (unconscious) standpoint: by using his wife as a defense against drinking, Tom precipitates his own fall back into drinking. This would be a structural (or ideologically unconscious) synthesis of the "normal" masculine thesis of blaming the woman, and the "normal" feminine antithesis of blaming the man: just as drinking

and abstinence form the mutually defining poles of a binary desiring
system, so too do the alcoholic man and his wife form the mutually
defining poles of a binary repression system.

A stronger and more active synthesis would situate Tom and his
wife in what Bateson calls a "complementary" relationship, or what psy-
chotherapists call a "codependency." Typically, alcoholics and their
spouses — often other members of their family as well, such as parents or
children — all support the addictive habit: the spouse or other family
member will talk as if he or she disapproved of the alcoholic's drinking
but in fact, because it satisfies deep emotional needs (the need to be
needed), will support it through behavior. When the alcoholic or other
substance abuser goes on the wagon, therefore, the complementary relation is thrown off balance, and the codependent spouse (or parent or
child) will most frequently reverse his or her earlier behavior, now talking as if he or she approved of the alcoholic's will power but making it
clear by actions that abstinence is ruining their lives. Lardner has Tom's
wife give him something very like this double message in "Who Dealt?":

> I bet Tom wishes he could celebrate too, don't you, dear? Of course he
> could if he wanted to, but when he once makes up his mind to a thing,
> there's nothing in the world can shake him. He's got the strongest will
> power of any person I ever saw.
>   I do think it's wonderful, him staying on the wagon this long, a man
> that used to — well, you know as well as I do; probably a whole lot better,
> because you were with him so much in the old days, and all I know is just
> what he's told me. [She knows his drunken binges from narratives, just as
> she "knows" his history with Helen and Arthur from the story he wrote.]
> He told me about once in Pittsburgh — All right, Tommie; I won't say
> another word. But it's all over now, thank heavens! Not a drop since we've
> been married; three whole months! And he says it's forever, don't you,
> dear? Though I don't mind a person drinking if they do it in moderation.
> But you know Tom! He goes the limit in everything he does. (227–28)

The overt message here, that it is wonderful that Tom has stayed on
the wagon, is complexly and constantly undermined by the covert message (and it is not all that covert) that Tom is being silly by not drinking.
At the end of the first paragraph Lardner's narrator explicitly celebrates
his will power, performing her prescribed role in Tom's marital defense
against drinking; but by the end of the second paragraph she is already
implicitly needling him for his extremism. And where in the first paragraph she invokes a tempting *wishful* image of Tom drinking in the
present or future ("I bet Tom wishes he could celebrate too, don't you,
dear?"), in the second paragraph she invokes a tempting *critical* image

of him drinking in the past ("him staying on the wagon this long, a man that used to — "). Breaking off after "used to —," too, as if decorously, has the effect of rubbing Tom's nose in the past without seeming to — insinuating a criticism that she can later deny, because after all she broke off without saying it. Even her constant harping on how it's "all over now, thank heavens," and how "he says it's forever," it seems to me, must have the effect of undermining Tom's monstrous self-control, which to work well should ideally be sublimated, should become "second nature," an undetectable part of his "normal self." In the ideologically prescribed ("liberal" or "individualistic") process of "getting a hold on yourself," of constructing an autonomous self that is proof against all temptation, the ideal movement is from the articulation to the repressive internalization or "forgetting" of self-control: from revealingly defensive self-assurances ("I think I can, I think I can") to a serenely inarticulate self-confidence. Self-confidence should require no articulation; it should simply *be*. For Tom's wife to keep running up and down the scales of his autosuggestion, then, must be profoundly disturbing to him.

I am not saying here that the narrator is only pretending to support Tom's resolve. I don't believe that her declarations — "I do think it's wonderful, him staying on the wagon this long," or "But it's all over now, thank heavens!" — should be read as hypocritical. Bateson's systems model would suggest, in fact, that she is simultaneously and quite sincerely working both sides of the equation: that she is encouraging him to drink *and* not to drink. This expanded sense of the narrator's role in Tom's ascesis would make her the instrument not merely of his self-control, but of the entire ascetic system of conflicted and mutually resistant desires. In this system Tom uses his wife both for self-control and for the release of self-control, as a support system both for his abstinence and for his bingeing — and the narrator, for that matter, uses her husband to bolster both her sense of being protected and admired when he is sober (look at what a strong husband I have!) and her sense of being needed when he is drinking (look at what a strong nurturer I am!).

I take this complex conception of the ascetic system from Geoffrey Galt Harpham's *Ascetic Imperative*: "It is through the concept of temptation that the ascetic is both united with his essence and forever divided from it," Harpham writes. "Such a paradox attends all aspects of temptation. A marginal concept in itself, temptation unites and disjoins the polarities of ascetic thought, expressing both the interdependence and the independence of impulse and prohibition, observed and observing selves, essence and expression" (59). As ascetic lover, Tom mortifies his desire for Helen and everything she represents (worldly success, happiness, etc.) by marrying the narrator, a dummy Helen who is neither as beautiful nor as fashionable (as desirable) as Helen, a "dead" Helen whose relative unattractiveness helps Tom to "kill" disorderly desire in himself, to "die" to desire and thus to restore order to a precariously chaotic (needy, boozy) reality. In the ascetic economy of this psychic inscription this is, patently, to imagine his wife's flesh-and-blood reality *as* death, as a *desired* deathly lack of that "life" or ideal reality that he finds (or invests) in a hyperreal because absent Helen. In the dialectical complex Harpham teases out of the ascetic tradition, then, Tom both wields the "dead" Helen (his present wife) against the overwhelming power of the "living" Helen (his absent lover), and finds his living wife depleted of reality or life by the hyperreality of Helen, who is now dead to him. The more he attempts to protect himself against his desire for Helen in the arms of his wife, therefore, the more his undying dream of happiness in Helen's arms turns his desired marital "happiness" to ashes; and the more irresistibly dreams of Helen encroach upon his marriage, the more he escalates his defensive, protective "love" of his wife. I would guess, in fact, that Tom arranges this visit to the Gratzes out of a simultaneous desire to prove to Helen that he doesn't need her anymore—and to get her back. Or, more complexly, he takes his new wife to meet his old friends (1) to *demonstrate* his restoration of order through the agency of the dummy Helen: to show off his new wife and new life, his happiness and settledness, his enviable success as a man (control of his environment), as a husband (control of his wife), as an executive (promotion), and as a prominent citizen (asked to run for mayor of the small Maine town they live in); (2) to *test* his restoration of order, his ascetic renunciation both of Helen and of the alcohol that replaced her (that explosion of resolve, order, discipline, and resistance in drunkenness); and finally, (3) to *undo* his restoration of order, to collapse the false edifice of his ascetic resolve in a delicious fall back into the arms of both Helen and the bottle.

This is in one sense the exact opposite of the dream dreamed by Jay Gatsby—that doomed hero created by Lardner's neighbor and closest friend in Great Neck, F. Scott Fitzgerald.[10] Gatsby determines to repeat the past, to regain Daisy, to "fix everything just the way it was before" (111), and undertakes an ascetic regimen to achieve that goal; only when he wins Daisy back and discovers that the glorious past eludes him, or that the mystical merging of past and future in an eternal present eludes him, does he "deliciously" sink into "mortification" as both emotional humiliation and physical death. Tom determines *not* to repeat the past, not to regain Helen, and undertakes an ascetic regimen to achieve his goal—but (necessarily, according to Bateson and Harpham) fails, and sinks into the mortification of disclosure and drink. Gatsby muscles his way back to Daisy through the ascetic program of becoming and acting rich (throwing but not enjoying parties, etc.), but finds the flesh-and-blood Daisy he recovers emptied out by the ascesis, and accedes to death as loss of control; Tom muscles his way out of Helen's life through the ascetic program of getting married, but finds the flesh-and-blood reality of the woman he chooses emptied out by the ascesis, and accedes to disclosure and drink as loss of control. In another and deeper sense, however, both Gatsby and Lardner's Tom (Bu)Cannon[11] dream the same dream, the masculine dream of control over their lives, over their minds and bodies, over desire and dream. The difference between them is only that Gatsby seeks such control through reunion with Daisy, Tom through renunciation of Helen. Both fail in their dreams; both fail through success; and both exhibit failure through a relinquishing (*not* a renunciation) of control, a slippage into the denied opposite of their ascetic regimen, death for Gatsby and drink for Tom.

It is, however, more complicated than this. As Harpham makes clear, death is not necessarily (or always) the opposite of ascesis; indeed, for the early eremitic ascetics it was the stated goal of ascesis:

> In "The Epistle to the Romans," Ignatius, then in the hands of the authorities, insists to his readers that he is awaiting his martyrdom "with all the passion of a lover" (106), and sees himself as God's "wheat, ground fine by the lions' teeth to be made purest bread for Christ" (104). No torture would be too extreme; in fact, the greater the pain the better: "Fire, cross, beast-fighting, hacking and quartering, splintering of bone and mangling of limb, even the pulverizing of my entire body—let every horrid and diabolical torment come upon me, provided only that I can win my way to Jesus Christ!" (14–15)

The difference is, of course, that Ignatius seeks a controlled death, an ascetically desired death—a death that he masters in Christ *by* desiring it, by inclining himself toward it—while Gatsby merely surrenders to the inevitable, in a dizzily uncontrolled loss of world ("he had lost the old warm world, paid a high price for living too long with a single dream" [162]). The ascetic dream is to subordinate world so thoroughly to dream that it is subsumed in it; Gatsby's failure is that "living too long with a single dream" so depletes the world that it sucks dream out of it, too, and he finds himself before his death (so Fitzgerald-as-Nick speculates) living in "a new world, material without being real" (162).

Significantly, however—particularly since I am concerned here not with real people but with fictional characters, *written* ascetics — Harpham shows also how the early ascetics linked this idealized death drive to language, especially to writing. Harpham continues:

> This ecstatic death drive accompanies another desire that at first seems incongruous and unrelated, that his [Ignatius's] letter itself be granted greater status and authority than his person. He is writing to beseech his friends not to interfere with his execution, and says, "Even if I were to come and implore you in person, do not yield to my pleading; keep your compliance for this written entreaty instead" (106). Ignatius's zeal for martyrdom is doubled in his wish that the text supplant him. Both longings are motivated by the desire to die to the world, to be transfigured into another, purer mode of being. Speaking, he is all too human; writing, he communicates through the dead letter, as though he were already dead. (15)

And later, in his discussion of Augustine's *Confessions*, Harpham complicates this association still further:

> Perhaps the instinct to which confession, as a specifically ascetic language, most closely corresponds is the "death instinct." If, as ascetic writers felt, language served the interests of mortification, then Freud's puzzling suggestion that the death instinct is not an aberration but the most comprehensive and typical instinct, becomes clearer. For what category of human experience is larger than language? The connection between confession and the death instinct becomes even more sharply focused with Freud's virtual identification of instinct with the "repetition compulsion," *"an urge inherent in organic life to restore an earlier state of things"* (*Beyond the Pleasure Principle* 36). Both Aristotle and Augustine recognized imitation, or repetition, as the basis of language. Imitating, repeating, and "restoring" an earlier condition, the autobiographical narrative would intensify the death instinct of language itself, providing a signal instance of the repetition compulsion. The desire driving the autobiographical act is actually attracted not to the life of the human subject, or even to any idealization of that life, but rather to the margins or frames of that life, to a prenatal or instinctual past and to a projected death. (104–5)

The autobiographical story Tom writes about being jilted by Helen arises out of and enacts a repetition compulsion that at once seeks to kill and recapture the past. Tom writes the story, presumably, in order to derive some measure of ascetic/aesthetic power over the past: to project into the story's protagonist his ascetic will to happiness without Helen (marital bliss with the narrator), and then to introject that aesthetic image back into his own life with the narrator (and without Helen).

And, as his wife says, this process is *hard work*: "The only thing is that Tom worked so hard over it and sat up nights writing and rewriting, it's a kind of a disappointment to have them turn it down" (234). Writing and rewriting, aesthetic projections and ascetic introjections: ascesis as compulsive repetition. "Kind of a disappointment" doesn't come close. The story is another defensive structure, like the marriage. It is an attempt to replace the living but absent Helen with the dead (and therefore purer) letter of fiction, just as his marriage was an attempt to replace an idealized Helen with a mortal (and therefore safer) being. Let me quote the narrator's plot summary of her husband's story and telling comment:

It's a story about two men and a girl and they were all brought up together and one of the men was awfully popular and well off and good-looking and a great athlete—a man like Arthur. There, Arthur! How is that for a T.L. [true likeness?]? The other man was just an ordinary man with not much money, but the girl seemed to like him better and she promised to wait for him. Then this man worked hard and got money enough to see him through Yale.

The other man, the well-off one, went to Princeton and made a big hit as an athlete and everything and he was through college long before his friend because his friend had to earn the money first. And the well-off man kept after the girl to marry him. He didn't know she had promised the other one. Anyway she got tired of waiting for the man she was engaged to and eloped with the other one. And the story ends up by the man she threw down welcoming the couple when they came home and pretending everything was all right, though his heart was broken.

What are you blushing about, Tommie? It's nothing to be ashamed of. I thought it was very well written and if the editors had any sense they'd have taken it. (234)

Tom's body betrays him here: in an ideal world (as imagined by the ascetic lover) the story would have done its job and protected him from embarrassment (his telling blush)—would have protected him, in fact, from connection with the real world of physicality where desire is not killed by the desire to kill it, where images of desire do not displace the desiring images they representationally negate. His marriage would have done its job, too, would have insulated him from the idealized object of his desire, which seems to reach back through his defenses and wield *him*. But neither the story nor the marriage works. Indeed, marriage gives him a dummy Helen who conjures up the old one, both emotionally by negation ("you aren't her!"), and aesthetically by narration, by the act of finding and reading this story. Subliminally, in fact, Tom may even have suspected something like this might happen: "He says he's through sending it," the narrator says of the story, "and just the other day he was going to tear it up, but I made him keep it because we may meet somebody some time who knows the inside ropes and can get a hearing with some big editor. I'm sure it's just a question of pull" (235). Writing and then tearing up the story is precisely the same defensive process as uttering and then repressing a vow of temperance: by sublimating a linguistic defense against the loss of control one ostensibly builds it into the "true" (because inarticulate) masculine self, the self whose ontological "truth" is a function of its inaccessibility to language. And since Western patriarchy does associate this idealized inarticulateness with masculinity, and femininity with "empty chatter," it is entirely appropriate that it is a woman, Tom's wife, the narrator, who disables the repressive act: she not only prevents him from tearing up the story, she remembers the plot and blabs it out to Helen and Arthur. She has also memorized a poem Tom had written shortly after Helen Bird Strong married Arthur Gratz, and recites it to the assembled company, catalyzing the catastrophe that concludes the story (Helen revoking, Tom pouring himself a Scotch):

> "I thought the sweetness of her song
> Would ever, ever more belong
> To me; I thought (O thought divine!)
> My bird was really mine!
>
> "But promises are made, it seems,
> Just to be broken. All my dreams
> Fade out and leave me crushed, alone.
> My bird, alas, has flown!"   (235)

The narrator has told us that Helen's middle name is Bird and that she sings sweetly—she *remembers* things like this—but she does not put two and two together. She is, as I will argue in the next chapter, the surrogate not only of Helen (the tool of Tom's repression) but of his repressed memory (the return of Tom's repression). In a sense Tom has merely (though unconsciously) projected his desire to blurt out the hurt that Helen caused him onto his wife, assigned her the task of remembering what he (thinks he) wants to forget, and of speaking it out.

It would be possible, in fact, drawing again on Harpham's conception of ascetic confession, to describe the narrator—or perhaps the narration—as Tom's repetition compulsion. It is in fact verbally repetitive: the narrator repeats herself over and over, most obviously in her bidding at bridge ("Well, I'll pass" [229, 234]) and her description of their friends the Guthries ("He doesn't think there ought to be conventions; he says a person might just as well tell each other what they've got" [231, 232]).[12]

But it is also psychologically repetitive, in a dual Freudian sense: Tom enacts the desired winning of Helen by marrying the narrator, and in the narrator's chatter as the dummy in bridge—the perfect parroting or repetition of everything he has ever told or showed her—he reenacts the loss of Helen four years before. The narrator even hints at something like this:

> I guess we can afford it now, can't we, dear? Tom hasn't told you about his raise. He was—All right, Tommie, I'll shut up. I know you hate to be talked about, but your wife can't help being just a teeny bit proud of you. And I think your best friends are interested in your affairs, aren't you, folks?
>
> But Tom is the most secretive person I ever knew. I believe he even keeps things from me! Not very many, though. I can usually tell when he's hiding something and I keep after him till he confesses. He often says I should have been a lawyer or a detective, the way I can worm things out of people. Don't you, Tom? (228)

The irony of "I believe he even keeps things from me!" is obvious, but superficial. Lardner is setting up his ending, laying the groundwork for the reader's, and possibly the narrator's, ultimate discovery that Tom has kept the mosi important thing of all from her, the fact that he was once, and probably still is, in love with Helen. What makes this irony superficial is that the narrator is dead right when she adds, "Not very many, though." She does worm an immense amount of information out of a defensively close-mouthed man. And when, earlier in the story, she says that, "all I know is just what he's told me" (228), that is actually saying quite a lot—not because he is so forthcoming about his past but because she is so good at getting him to reveal it to her. Another way of saying this is, again, that Tom unconsciously wants to reveal it, not only to her but to Helen: that he has married an inquisitive woman (who should have been a lawyer or a detective) in order to displace the dismantling of his repressive structures onto a surrogate who does what she does because she is so "proud" of him.

But even this is too superficial. The "chatter" or "gurgle" that constitutes the entire story, the repetitive narration as fictional repetition compulsion, repeats not only itself and Tom's recent history but Tom's (or at least the "normal" bourgeois-patriarchal man's) infantile experience as well. (Here the textual evidence begins to wear thin, and I will have to retreat to a higher level of speculative or actantial generality, speaking less of Tom and more of "men.") It does not require a great amount of psychoanalytical ingenuity to suggest, for example, that Tom's transferential use of the narrator (as narrator of both Lardner's story and his own) to shatter or "self-destruct" his marriage is a compulsive repetition of his loss not only of Helen, but of his mother—specifically of the all-consuming maternal love that he (supposedly, retrospectively) consumed at her breast. The only real textual evidence for this reading is oblique: the fact that Tom repeatedly and compulsively replaces the mother figure who abandons him (Helen, and perhaps by the end of the story his wife as well) with the bottle, with the oral pleasure of drinking. This is a complicated psychological defense: the Scotch to which he turns when, at the end of the story, the cat is out of the bag (and, we may surmise, he assumes both Helen and his wife despise him), both repeats the mother's milk that once satisfied him and disintegrates the ordered self he constructed on the soft, treacherous foundation of his mother's love.

This already begins to swerve from Freud, of course. Freudian psychoanalysis (here I am thinking specifically of Lacan) links the maternal or preoedipal stage of the little boy's development with undifferentiation, formless chaos, which is precisely the state to (or toward) which booze returns the alcoholic. In actuality, I would claim, the little boy is differentiated from birth, in divergent ways, by both the need of the mother and the name (or, in Lacan's French pun, the no) of the father.[13] The newborn infant is constituted as "child" under conditions of bourgeois patriarchy by a mother who is emotionally demanding and a father who is emotionally withdrawn: by a woman who has been constituted as "mother" by the channeling of her (frustrated) need for love from her parents into her relationship with the baby she pushed out of her womb, and by a man who has been constituted as "father" by the anxious blocking of all emotional interchange.[14] The constitution of the infant as "child" is then further differentiated: the child is constituted as "son" through an identification with the emotionally blocked father and a defensive blockage against the emotionally demanding mother, or as "daughter" through an identification with the emotionally demanding mother and a defensive demand for love from the emotionally blocked father.[15]

This psychological reformulation of gender difference suggests a refinement of Harpham's discussion of ascesis. Ascesis is clearly endemic in bourgeois patriarchy, but in complexly crisscrossing ways. The "normal" woman will use an ideologically prescribed ascetic regimen to delay the gratification of her need for love. Her mother needs love from her and so is unable to give it; her father is afraid of her need for love and so shuts her out; so she must renounce love, deny her need, "mortify" her "carnal" desire for physical closeness with the people who claim to love her, for emotional warmth, support, and so on. But as Harpham makes clear, renunciation is never eradication, but rather resistance, specifically a resistant rechanneling of the renounced pleasure in the direction of transcendence. And so the "normal" woman will store up her need for love, withhold her demands from her skittish parents, and redirect it onto safe (because transcendental, imagined) surrogates: dogs and cats, horses, Barbie and Ken dolls, rock idols, and so on, until she gets old enough (as defined by ideological norms of feminine maturity) to date, go steady, get engaged, marry. Then she is allowed to release or project her stored-up need for love onto living men. Because of the "normal" clash between women's emotional demands and men's defenses against those demands, this is a hazardous undertaking that succeeds (ideologically, in the sense of leading to marriage) through the dual process of romantic idealization and status objectification. Society teaches young women both to romanticize men in terms of "love" (the idealized father as heroic savior), and to objectify them in terms of "status" (the objectified father as money-making machine), and thus to render them nearly as safe as dolls or pets or rock idols. Idealization and objectification normatively flatter the chosen man, which is to say, they mystify both the nature of the appeal and the effects of the emotional demands, convince him that he is loved and admired for himself while in fact directing love and admiration and the attendant emotional demands to an idealized love object. This defuses the powder keg of conflicting needs and defenses (which drives the "battle of the sexes") just long enough to get a man and a woman married. Then the idealizations drop away, the husband begins to block the woman's need for love, and she channels it into her children, among whom the intensity of her need will produce needy daughters and defensive and withdrawn sons. (There is a new and relatively safe, because less intensely cathected, stage of rechanneling when her children have children: the grandmother-grandchild relation.)

Complementarily (in dialectical interrelation), the "normal" man will use an ideologically prescribed ascetic regimen to repress the gratification of his need for love. His mother needs love from him and convinces him that her need *is* love; his father is afraid of his need for love and encourages him to believe that approval (a patriarchal counterfeit for love) will be forthcoming only if he bests him in competition. He too, therefore, must renounce love, deny his need, "mortify" his "carnal" desire for physical closeness with the people who claim to love him, for emotional warmth, support, and so on. For the "normal" patriarchal man this renunciation entails a resistant rechanneling of the renounced pleasure in the direction not of transcendence (or perhaps in the direction of *negative* transcendence or idealized denial) but of competition. Like the "normal" woman, the "normal" man too will store up his need for love, withhold his demands from his skittish parents; but unlike girls, boys are systematically trained to redirect their need for love *away from love* into the dehumanized world of gadgets (trucks, radios, etc.) or the deromanticized world of male rivalry. Little boys may in fact redirect that need onto "safe" surrogates like dogs and cats, or even idealized but deromanticized dolls (Rambo, Ninjas), like little girls; but the effect of boys' ideological training in competition is their weaning from such surrogates (indeed, *all* surrogates), their constitution as "self-sufficient" and "self-reliant," which is to say as unneedy. All through this process they are also constantly defending against the emotional demands made on them by their mothers in complex ways: seeming to remain open to those demands (since mothers' self-esteem normatively depends on the "love" — submissive support — of their sons) while still blocking them. As a result, they will enter adolescence in a tangled web of conflicted needs, desiring their mother's love and wanting to open themselves up to her (and her avatars among their peers), but also terrified of vulnerability to her demands. This hazardous undertaking succeeds (again, ideologically, in the sense of leading to marriage) from the normative masculine point of view through the dual process of romantic idealization and *sexual* objectification. Society teaches young men both to romanticize women in terms of "love" (the idealized mother as nurturer), and to objectify them in terms of sex appeal (the objectified mother as sexualized part objects: breasts, legs, buttocks, thighs, genitals), and thus to render them as "safe" as trucks or warrior dolls. Idealization and objectification, again, normatively flatter the chosen woman, which is to say, they mystify the nature of the appeal and the effects of the emotional demands, convince her that she is loved and admired for herself while in fact directing love and admiration and the attendant emotional needs to an idealized sex object. Once the idealized goal of this ideological shadow play is achieved and the young lovers are married, the idealizations drop away and the young wife is revealed as a demanding, nagging person for whom nothing is good enough; the young husband then accedes to her desire to have a baby, hoping that a child will at least take some of the emotional pressure off him. Unfortunately, the child soon begins to bring new emotional pressure to bear on him, and before long the wife and the child form an exclusive club to which he is barred entry; consequently, he retreats further and further into his (prescribed) isolation and attempts to convince himself that he prefers it this way.

Something like this patriarchal web of mutually ensnarled twists and tangles is what Tom finds himself (constituted by and) in. When Helen jilts him, the "normal" convergence of romanticizations and objectifications breaks down: she romanticizes him in terms of love but objectifies Arthur in terms of status, and allows the realistic considerations of status objectification to take precedence over romance. From Tom's point of view, this precipitates an imbalance in the maternal ordering of desire: in his somatic economy a carefully controlled openness to maternal demands is supposed to guarantee maternal attention (if not love at least further demands, which he has been programmed to thematize as love), and now the system has revoked its guarantee. He submits to the patriarchal need exchange, does what it requires of him (falls in love with Helen, opens himself up to her sufficiently to win her love in return) to gain a wife — and the system fails. He loses the girl. She marries his best friend, who has more money. He has opened himself up in vain. The imbalance is specifically in the emotional control system, the system of checks and balances that keeps openness from turning into self-awareness and failure from turning into despair. The man who is open to maternal demands but has failed to tie himself in marriage to a surrogate source of those demands is dangerously subject to the kind of chaotic emotional regression that rages against the absent mother and may in the process produce a self-reflexive sense of the "system," of how he is being controlled from within. In order to forestall the terrors this possibility normatively generates (the taboo against "knowing who you are," as Alice Miller says), Tom starts hitting the bottle, in effect replicating that regressive chaos chemically in the form of drunkenness. This is a relatively "safe" regression, in that the drunk becomes progressively less able to articulate any self-reflexive discoveries he might make about himself or the system in which he is lodged. This solution also progressively destroys him, in two senses: it destroys both the real physical self that is poisoned by alcohol, and the ideal patriarchal masculine self that is undermined by a loss of self-sufficient self-control. And so he "gets a hold on himself," or perhaps — to dramatize it as a kind of internalized morality play — his ideal self gets a hold on his physical self, and by a supreme ascesis he conforms his physical actions in the social world to patriarchal ideals: he finds someone else to marry, goes on the wagon, and on their wedding day tells her that if she ever sees him take another drink, she will *know*.

This is the "normal" bourgeois-patriarchal solution to being jilted (forget her, there are plenty of other fish in the sea), but it is built on quicksand: the instrument he selects as the key to his ascetic regimen of resistance to the maternal complex of need/drink/love that undid him is herself a woman, the image of Helen and his mother. In order to resist the mother, he must give himself over to the mother. Marrying a woman who in "normal" terms is clearly inferior to Helen (less attractive, less well-spoken, less demure) is a complex means of dealing with this aporia: the fact that she is less attractive also makes her more available (easier to rope into his ascetic project) and more easily resistible (easier to despise, and thus to hold at arm's length). But this solution too is built on quicksand: the unconscious womanly chatter (which he too no doubt thematizes as a *lack* of consciousness) that repels Tom also reveals him, repeats his unconscious compulsions and thus undoes his entire defensive structure, reverses his ascesis. The controlled repressive denial of love becomes a pathetically uncontrolled declaration of love; the resistance to hurt and drink regresses into self-pitying inebriation; the desire for conformity to the norm (abstemious marriage to the narrator) mutates into desire for deviation from the norm (drunken infidelity with Helen). Tom remains an ascetic even in his fall, just as he remained an alcoholic even when on the wagon; the only difference is that, whereas the conflicts that riddled his ascesis at the beginning of the story were concealed by conformity to an idealized patriarchal norm, now they are exposed to view. Now even the flimsy protection yielded by his halfhearted conformism is gone; his skin touches the world's.

The crowning blow in this rather pessimistic, pugilistic analysis of bourgeois-patriarchal gender programming is that the ascetic conflicts that Tom fails to conceal are in fact built into the system in the form of what Gregory Bateson identifies as the double bind. Bateson discusses the double bind in the specific context of schizophrenia, as the key ingredient of schizophrenogenesis; but I want to argue that schizophrenia is only one extreme form of patriarchal dysfunctionality that illustrates the dysfunctionality built into the entire system. One of Bateson's examples and his analysis of it are worth quoting at length:

A young man who had fairly well recovered from an acute schizophrenic episode was visited in the hospital by his mother. He was glad to see her and impulsively put his arm around her shoulders, whereupon she stiffened. He withdrew his arm and she asked, "Don't you love me any more?" He then blushed, and she said, "Dear, you must not be so easily embarrassed and afraid of your feelings." The patient was able to stay with her only a few minutes more and following her departure he assaulted an aide and was put in the tubs.

Obviously, this result could have been avoided if the young man had been able to say, "Mother, it is obvious that you become uncomfortable when I put my arm around you, and that you have difficulty accepting a gesture of affection from me." However, the schizophrenic patient doesn't have this possibility open to him. His intense dependency and training prevents him from commenting upon his mother's communicative behavior, though she comments on his and forces him to accept and to attempt to deal with the complicated sequence. The complications for the patient include the following:

(1) The mother's reaction of not accepting her son's affectionate gesture is masterfully covered up by her condemnation of him for withdrawing, and the patient denies his perception of the situation by accepting her condemnation.

(2) The statement "Don't you love me any more" in this context seems to imply:

(*a*) "I am lovable."

(*b*) "You should love me and if you don't you are bad or at fault."

(*c*) "Whereas you did love me previously you don't any longer," and thus focus is shifted from his expressing affection to his inability to be affectionate. Since the patient has also hated her, she is on good ground here, and he responds appropriately with guilt, which she then attacks.

(*d*) "What you just expressed *was not* affection," and in order to accept this statement the patient must deny what she and the culture have taught him about how one expresses affection. He must also question the times with her, and with others, when he thought he was experiencing affection and when they *seemed* to treat the situation as if he had. He experiences here loss-of-support phenomena and is put in doubt about the reliability of past experience.

(3) The statement, "You must not be so easily embarrassed and afraid of your feelings," seems to imply:

(*a*) "You are not like me and are different from other nice or normal people because we express our feelings."

(*b*) "The feelings you express are all right, it's only that *you* can't accept them." However, if the stiffening on her part had indicated "These are unacceptable feelings," then the boy is told that he should not be embarrassed by unacceptable feelings. Since he has had a long training in what is and is not acceptable to both her and society, he again comes into conflict with the past. If he is unafraid of his own feelings (which mother implies is good), he should be unafraid of his affection and would then notice it was she who was afraid, but he must not notice that because her whole approach is aimed at covering up this shortcoming in herself.

The impossible dilemma thus becomes: "If I am to keep my tie to mother, I must not show her that I love her, but if I do not show her that I love her, then I will lose her." (217–18)

Bateson tends to thematize the double bind in terms of mothers and sons, and here gives a powerful example of that particular scenario; but it should be clear (especially to feminists) that double binds work just as powerfully between fathers and daughters (act 1 of *King Lear*, for example),[16] and the realization that they also work between fathers and sons and between mothers and daughters should not be too far behind. My rather sweeping claim, in fact, is that the double bind is intrinsic to patriarchy: that it is built into the very warp and woof of the patriarchal "dynasty of wounds" that I have briefly outlined, and that patriarchal programming is so destructive and life-threatening precisely because it operates through the double bind.

Bateson defines the double bind in terms of both context and message. The double bind is activated, he shows, in contexts where a relationship between two or more people generates a repeated (as opposed to a single traumatic) experience of conflicted communication, which is then internalized. This relationship must be intense enough that the doubly bound subject "feels it is vitally important that he discriminate accurately what sort of message is being communicated so that he may respond appropriately" (208); conflicted enough that no single univocal message can be identified; and repressive enough that "the individual is unable to comment on the messages being expressed to correct his discrimination of what order of message to respond to, *i.e.*, he cannot make a metacommunicative statement" (208). But this sort of relationship does not strike me as ideologically deviant; in fact it seems to me to conform point for point to the (sublimated) ideological norm for the patriarchal family. The double bind is activated in other primary relationships as well — in orphanages, for example — and reinforced in numerous secondary relationships (teacher-student, priest-parishioner, advertiser-consumer), but the patriarchal norm for the relationship Bateson is describing is clearly the family — a depressing identification that is made particularly and painfully obvious in work by Alice Miller, Susan Forward, and numerous other recent writers on the destructive dysfunctionality of the "normal" family situation.

Bateson also attempts to sketch out the complexly stratified conflicts in the communicative messages that, when repeated and internalized in the contexts specified above, generate the psychosocial phenomenon he calls the double bind. There are, he suggests, three levels: (1) a negative command, a "thou shalt not," enforced by signals that threaten survival; (2) a conflicting negative command on a higher level of abstraction, a command not only to obey but to *accept* (1) as right and natural, again enforced by signals that threaten survival; and (3) an all-encompassing negative command that prevents escape from the dilemma posed by (1) and (2). An example of Bateson's three levels might be a father who tells his teenaged daughter to stop seeing a certain boy (1), and makes it clear through nonverbal signals that she should not only obey him but both conceive his command as motivated by paternal love for her *and* understand that the punishment for disobedience will be loss of that love (2), and further signals that any attempt to articulate any of this, to make sense of it, sort out the commands, would result in a similar loss of love (3).

But this seems inadequate to the debilitating contradictions of the double bind as Bateson himself exemplifies it. It seems to me that the imperative contradiction(s) must come not at different levels of abstraction but at precisely the same level—that the contradictions must be hidden from the subject not through shifts in the level of abstraction but through shifting thematizations or idealizations of the commands. Thus, for instance, in my example of the father and the teenaged daughter, it would seem more doubly binding if the father simultaneously told his daughter not to see a certain boy, urged her to find someone better to fall in love with and marry, *and* signaled to her that he didn't want her to marry anyone, that she should cleave to him. Let me expand that to something approaching its full debilitating complexity:

(1) Love your father (don't abandon me, I love you more than any callow youth ever could). Give me the love and understanding your (and my) mother never gave me. Devote yourself to me in return for my need for you (for your understanding, admiration, love, compliments, hugs, and in extreme cases sexual favors). Regard my need as reward enough for your devotion.

(2) Grow up, become an independent woman, marry a man I can be proud of, someone I can love like a son (the son *you* weren't). Separate from me; don't make emotional demands on me; I get enough of that from your (and my own) mother.

(3) Understand (without my having to tell you) that you will be punished for obeying both (1) and (2): that I will ridicule you for being an old maid if you obey (1) and that I will accuse you of not loving me if you obey (2).

(4) Repress these pushes and pulls. Be an independent woman *and* love me most. Taboo all awareness of contradiction and the threat of punishment. Feel no anger at me for imposing these requirements on you.

(5) Feel guilty at your inability to repress all contradictions, to deny all frustrations, to taboo all awareness, to suppress all anger. Despise yourself for your failure. Idealize me as the perfect father.

This might be schematized for all patriarchal double binding as follows: (1) do X; (2) do not-X; (3) internalize the command to do both, and expect punishment for failure; (4) repress (1), (2), and (3), and any anger or frustration their contradictoriness might provoke; and (5) idealize the double binder by taking all blame for failure on yourself. This seems to me to cover the entire range of patriarchal norms, and specifically to ground them in the normative familial context in and through which they are transmitted from generation to generation. In all patriarchal programming, as in the schizophrenogenic phenomenon Bateson calls the double bind, the mystifying of impossibly conflicting commands as mutually compatible expectations — for example, the thematization of the command to cling to your father as "expressing love," and of the command to separate from your father as "growing up" — is typically mired in a morass of repressive safeguards that taboo both awareness and escape (escape through awareness) by instilling guilt and self-loathing for obeying *and* disobeying commands, and impose an impossible ascesis as the only hope of retaining the rule-giver's love.

Let me begin to sum up the argument of this chapter by coding my readings of "Who Dealt?" into the expanded schema of the double bind. Tom's ascesis as the lover of Helen and the husband of the narrator might be imagined as driven by or grounded in a double bind roughly like the father-daughter one just sketched out, only in reverse (mother-son), with some corollaries to allow for the cross-generational repetition compulsion:

(1) Love your mother.

(a) Remain open to me. Give me what I need: your love and support. Be my boy.

(b) By extension, remain open to all my avatars you meet, every woman onto whom you make a transference from me. Give them what they need: your love and support. Internalize this command as the guarantee of success in love. Do what I tell you to do and any girl you pick will become your wife.

(c) Don't let anyone steal you away from me. Need *me*.

(2) Separate from your mother.

(a) Grow up, become an independent ~~man. Marry a~~ woman I can be proud of, someone I can love like a daughter. Make me proud of you. Make me feel like a successful mother.

(b) Don't make emotional demands on me. Leave me alone. I can't give you what you need. I don't like it when you demand things from me. I don't like you. Go away.

(c) By extension, don't make emotional demands on my avatars either. Be self-sufficient. Be strong. Be a man. Be tough. Impress the women you meet with how little you need them.

(d) If you have needs, take them to your girlfriends, not to me. Present your happy, unneedy face to me.

(3) Understand (without my having to tell you) that you will be punished for obeying both (1) and (2).

(a) I will ridicule you for being a mamma's boy if you obey (1), and I will accuse you of not loving me if you obey (2).

(b) Sublimate (and replicate) the internal riot this command generates through alcoholism. Pour all the torn feelings my impossible demands stir up in you into your Scotch. The more it hurts, the more you should drink.

(c) Drink to forget girls who jilt you. Drink to forget that you drink. Drink to forget that I encouraged you to drink. Drink to forget that your drinking is a repressive replication of my double bind.

(d) Be ashamed of your drinking. See it as an unmanly loss of control. Associate it with being a mamma's boy, and with my ridicule for your failure to separate from me. Go on the wagon. Get some mother figure to help you stay on it. Tell her that your sobriety means that you love her, and if you take a drink it is a sign that you no longer love her.

(e) Never tell her (or yourself, but continue to believe) that your drinking is a sign that you still love me most of all, that you need my needing.

(4) Repress all this.

(a) Be a strong, self-sufficient man *and* never leave me.

(b) Never articulate, or contemplate articulating, or allow yourself the luxury of recognizing the possibility of articulating, the doubly bound system that drives you. Think of it all as perfectly natural. Think of it as human nature. Be terrified of even approaching the door behind which the machinery of this system is kept.

(c) Feel no anger at me for doing this to you. I didn't make it up. I'm not responsible. It was done to me first.

(d) It wasn't done to anyone. You're just imagining it.

(e) Enlist the help of every woman you meet (especially those you love) in this project. Make them instruments of your repression. Do not allow them to undermine your repression. If they do, blame them for it. Don't blame me. Every time you have an angry feeling, conceive it as anger at a woman for challenging your repression, which you don't have, and which doesn't need defending — and take it out on them (in a carefully controlled way). Blame the women you fall in love with, one at a time. When one hurts you, blame her for everything and move on to the next one.

(f) Never allow yourself to suspect that these women may only be articulating what you long to articulate, but are afraid to. Never allow yourself to suspect that you long to articulate what I was afraid to face in my own life.

(5) Idealize me as the perfect mother.

(a) Construe every maternal command you can remember (every one I have commanded you to remember, every one I have not commanded you to repress, and every one you have failed to repress adequately) as evidence of my overflowing love for you, which first flowed into you in my milk and continues to flow into you in the command system you have internalized.

(b) Feel guilty at your failure to obey and idealize me. Blame and despise yourself for your failure. Consider yourself a failure as a man.

(c) Enlist every woman you meet (especially those you love) in the project of idealizing me. Find every one of them lacking in comparison with me. Never tell them this openly, but make it clear in subtle (or not-so-subtle) insinuations which you can then deny if challenged.

(d) Marry the women who remind you of me, and who help you to go on idealizing me as infinitely better than the women who remind you of me.

(e) Once you are married, discover (without quite being able to articulate your discovery to yourself) that your wife is really quite different from your idealized image of me, and cheat on her with another woman who initially seems to resemble me more. Divorce your first wife and marry the lover, and then repeat the process; or stay married to your wife and cheat on her with a succession of women who initially seem to resemble me but keep getting replaced with others who seem to resemble me more. Never make your mental/emotional association of these lovers with me explicit, and scoff at anyone who does. Ridicule the notion that a grown man could still be in love with his mother, and that you ever were.

One could go on, of course. This is an almost bottomless pit. And I have not yet even touched on the double binds instilled in men by their fathers, double binds that drive male rivalry — Tom's rivalry with Arthur, for example, who is a better football player and a better student and has a better job and gets the girl Tom loves. Lardner doesn't explore this complex as centrally or as powerfully in "Who Dealt?" as he does Tom's doubly bound relations to women and alcohol (it too requires ascesis, but does not constitute Tom as ascetic *lover*), and I want to defer discussion of it until chapter 2, when I deal with the idealized image of the self-as-father in Lacan's Schema L.

This is, as I hinted earlier, a pessimistic chapter. Certainly it is a pessimistic reading of a pessimistic story. As I have constructed the operation of patriarchy in the story and in our world, it has no loopholes, no centrifugal impulses, no breakdowns or other areas of potential liberation — nor do I believe that Lardner necessarily thought there might have been, or desired there to be. Lardner was almost certainly not aware of all the patriarchal assumptions that undergirded his story, and might not have articulated those assumptions in just the way I have; but I do assume that Lardner wrote the story more or less in the spirit of my analysis: as a trap that springs shut with awful finality and inevitability at the end.

What interests me about the story, however, and about Lardner as a writer, is what else is going on in it, beneath the surface of Lardner's sardonic imagination. If the story is really about Tom Cannon, why is he given no voice in the story? Why is it narrated by the "dummy," in several senses of the word (the woman who is too "dumb" to know what is going on, and who is supposedly rendered "dumb" or speechless by her role as dummy in the bridge game the foursome is playing)? And if the narrator is the return of Tom's repressed, the voicing of his repetition compulsion that undoes his repressive structure, how precisely does that work — and what hope does it hold out for those of us constituted by ascetic repression as "normal" patriarchal males?

2

Voicing the Dummy

"Who Dealt?" is a story about a bridge game—a game of auction bridge, evidently, given the year of its writing. (Contract bridge was introduced by Harold S. Vanderbilt in 1926, after Lardner's story had been published in *Cosmopolitan*; Lardner published a story about contract bridge in 1929 called "Contract.") Lardner's work is full of games, of course—it is one of the things he is famous for—but significantly, as he shifts from his work as a sportswriter in the first decade of this century to columns and short stories in the teens and twenties, he becomes less and less interested in games as games, as rule-governed technique, say, or as quasi-aesthetic play. Games come increasingly to serve an orientational function for Lardner, a way of situating and structuring the human interactions that interest him most.

One of the ways Lardner uses games in his stories, for example, is as class structure. There are the lower-class games that he (child of the upper middle class) doesn't play himself, that he reports on as a journalist, and therefore stands somewhat apart from, even when, as in some of his best-known stories, his narrator is himself a lower-class player. These would include baseball, obviously—Lardner's hallmark as a short story writer—in the busher stories about Jack Keefe collected in *You Know Me Al* (1916), *Treat 'Em Rough* (1918), and *The Real Dope* (1919), and stories like "My Roomy" (1914), "Alibi Ike" (1915), "Harmony" (1915), and "Hurry Kane" (1927); but also boxing in stories like "Champion" (1916), "A Frame-Up" (1921), and "The Battle of the Century" (1921). What stands out in these stories in terms of social class is not only the range of rube and busher dialects Lardner loves to mimic but also the absolute lack of social mobility: in the teens and twenties the baseball players and boxers Lardner portrays were making (slightly) better money than other members of the working class, but they were nonetheless stuck in it. Strikingly, the upper-middle-class game of golf, which Lardner did play (once with President Harding), also displays a lack of

social mobility, but at the opposite end of the social scale: stories like
"A Caddy's Diary" (1922) and "Mr. Frisbie" (1928) are narrated by
lower-class caddies about the successful men they carry for, and take the
form of exposés, revealing the nasty habits and personal anxieties of
men who are no longer on their way up.

In this social hierarchy, bridge situates the characters who play it
firmly in the upwardly mobile middle class, and powerfully reflects the
insecurities of social climbing. In fact, bridge is a peculiarly middle-class
game, replicating in its contractual bidding the liberal ideal of the social
contract (using negotiatory conventions to achieve a working consensus
for later play), and in its partner structure the liberal norm for social
interaction (one married couple "hosting" another, with no residue, no
unmarried partners, no fifth wheels). Those who, like the narrator of
"Who Dealt?," are unable to bid properly, who don't know the conventions, who fail to cooperate with their partners to achieve a consensus for
play, reveal thereby their unreadiness for middle-class life. The idealized
purpose of liberal education is to broaden the bourgeois base of participation, to include as many people as possible in the "democratic" middle
class, in the social sphere of equality; anyone who fails to learn what is
taught is branded, both in the schools and in bridge, a "dummy" who
must sit dumbly and passively and observe as others work (or play)
toward victory and success. The partner structure also reveals the psychodynamics of marriage (when you play "families") and of extramarital
sexual attractions (when you "cut for partners").[1] The fact that Lardner's
narrator prefers to play families rather than cutting for partners (because
"I don't feel so bad if I do something dumb when it's Tom I'm playing
with" [228]) reflects her anxious desire to cleave to her new husband and
probably, unconsciously, an unwillingness to let Tom play with Helen.
This entire paragraph, in fact, underscores the narrator's training as the
return of Tom's repressed:

> Oh, are you waiting for me? Do we cut for partners? Why can't we play
> families? I don't feel so bad if I do something dumb when it's Tom I'm
> playing with. He never scolds, though he does give me some terrible looks.
> But not very often lately; I don't make the silly mistakes I used to. I'm
> pretty good now, aren't I, Tom? You better say so, because if I'm not, it's
> your fault. You know Tom had to teach me the game. I never played at all
> till we were engaged. Imagine! And I guess I was pretty awful at first, but
> Tom was a dear, so patient! I know he thought I never would learn, but I
> fooled you, didn't I, Tommie? (228)

Here is all the insecurity of the narrator-Tom-Helen triangle; the multiple ironies of the word "dumb" (as ignorant, as unconscious, as silent,

and as bridge dummy, the person who can see everyone's cards but
cannot say or play anything); the narrator's role as Tom's trainee (in
bridge and repression); Tom's preternatural patience with his slow student (so much rides on this!); and above all the complexities of the
narrator "never learning" (learning the truth or learning not-to-know
and not-to-say the truth?) and "fooling" Tom (fooling him by learning
repression or by learning release and revelation?). The story displays
the dummy-narrator's implication in both psychosocial constructions of
"learning" and "fooling," her "unconscious" ability to work both sides
of the repressive equation: she remembers everything and knows nothing; she understands nothing and reveals all. She has not learned to
play bridge, and does so many "dumb" things that Tom makes her the
"dummy"; but as dummy she can see everyone's hands, and the "dumb"
things she says uncover the truth about all four of the players. She is bad
at bridge because she can't stop talking and concentrate (also because she
lacks the analytical abilities—comparison, contrast, syllogistic reasoning, ironic distance—traditionally associated in the West with masculinity); but the constant stream of talk that constitutes the story covers
every relevant detail about her husband and his friends. One way of
putting it might be that she plays bridge better as dummy than Tom
does as "smarty," as the rationally repressed knower who attempts to
control all the cards and take all the tricks (to say everything worth
saying, everything that must not be repressed). Here she is:

> Oh, are you waiting for me? I'm sorry. What did you bid, Helen? And
> you, Tom? You doubled her? And Arthur passed? Well, let's see. I wish I
> could remember what that means. I know that sometimes when he doubles
> he means one thing and sometimes another. But I always forget which is
> which. Let me see; it was two spades that he doubled, wasn't it? That
> means I'm to leave him in, I'm pretty sure. Well, I'll pass. Oh, I'm sorry,
> Tommie! I knew I'd get it wrong. Please forgive me. But maybe we'll set
> them anyway. Whose lead?
> I'll stop talking now and try and keep my mind on the game. You
> needn't look that way, Tommie. I *can* stop talking if I try. It's kind of
> hard to concentrate though, when you're, well, excited. (229)

> What did you make? Two odd? Well, thank heavens that isn't a game!
> Oh, that does make a game, doesn't it? Because Tom doubled and I left
> him in. Isn't that wicked! Oh, dearie, please forgive me and I'll promise to
> pay more attention from now on! What do I do with these? Oh, yes, I
> make them for Arthur. (230)

> You said a no-trump, didn't you, Tom? And Arthur passed. Let me see;
> I wish I knew what to do. I haven't any five-card—it's terrible! Just a
> minute. I wish somebody could—I know I ought to take—but—well, I'll

pass. Oh, Tom, this is the worst you ever saw, but I don't know what I could have done.

I do hold the most terrible cards! I certainly believe in the saying, "Unlucky at cards, lucky in love." Whoever made it up must have been thinking of me. I hate to lay them down, dear. I know you'll say I ought to have done something. Well, there they are! Let's see your hand, Helen. Oh, Tom, she's — but I mustn't tell, must I? Anyway, I'm dummy. That's one comfort. I can't make a mistake when I'm dummy. I believe Tom overbids lots of times so I'll be dummy and can't do anything ridiculous. But at that I'm much better than I used to be, aren't I, dear? (230–31)

That last line is telling: at *what* is she much better, being a dummy or doing anything ridiculous? This is the crucial ambiguity at the heart of her role in the game, and in the story, as dummy. Tom's overbidding is a control move, an attempt to silence his wife, to keep her from playing (and making him lose the game) *or* speaking (and making him lose control). The problem is that just making his wife dummy doesn't make her dumb, in either sense: it deprives her neither of her knowledge nor of her voice. Indeed, as dummy she is not only freed of the necessity of concentrating on the cards (which she doesn't really understand and ultimately could not care less about anyway) and thus given free rein to talk; she is also liberated from her restricted perspective on a single hand (her own) and allowed to wander around the table looking at what everyone else has. "Oh, Tom," she says, "she's — but I mustn't tell, must I?" Breaking off where she does is in fact "telling": it enacts the tension in her discourse between revelation ("she's got big cards in hearts," or whatever) and repression ("but I mustn't tell, must I?"), between her own unschooled tendency to let knowledge flow directly into speech and Tom's schooling in not-saying certain things. It also allows the reader (and presumably Tom and Helen as well) to hear any number of unsayable things after "she's — ": she's your former lover, she's still in love with you, she's sorry she hurt you, she's appalled at the wife you chose, and so on — all the emotional "hands" that her role as dummy gives her access to but that she "mustn't tell."

In fact it is more than that: it is also that she "*can't* tell" — but does. She remembers in time that as dummy she is not supposed to reveal other people's cards to her partner, and breaks off, just as, throughout the story, she sees in Tom's eyes the message that as the dumb wife she is not supposed to tell Helen and Arthur all about his drinking, his failures in athletics, his pathetic social success in a small Maine town, his knuckling under when she wants him to wear pajamas instead of a nightshirt, and, most important of all, that he wrote a story relating in fictional form his hurt and ascetic resolve vis-à-vis Arthur and Helen. This is all the "mustn't tell," the belated kicking-in of Tom's projected (and carefully trained) repression. The other side to it is that, because she doesn't understand anything, doesn't know the significance of any of the fragmentary facts she reveals, she really cannot "tell" anything—all she can do is list the facts she observes or remembers more or less at random, and let others make the "telling" connections. She has no idea, for example, which cards in Helen's hand Tom would be most interested in knowing about. She doesn't know bridge well enough (and she isn't analytical enough) to connect the cards in her own or anyone else's hand with the bidding or the play (the taking of tricks). All she could do as dummy, if she were not restrained by the rules from revealing other people's hands, would be to list the cards. In the same way she doesn't know enough about the past Tom shares with Helen and Arthur (and she isn't analytical enough) to do more than recall that Helen Bird Strong Gratz has a beautiful singing voice and then recite a poem Tom wrote about the sweetness of a bird's voice. But that is all it takes. Without knowing or understanding anything in a rational, analytical manner, she does "tell" all.

It seems reasonable, in traditional terms, to characterize the narrator's discourse as a different kind of knowing and telling: "irrational," for example, since that is the normative alternative to "rational" knowing and telling. Tom's knowing and telling is rational, logical, intellectual, analytical, and thus masculine and positively valued; the narrator's knowing and telling is irrational, illogical, emotional, associational, and thus feminine and negatively valued. And beyond that—the direction in which I am obviously taking this—Tom's knowing and telling is conscious, and the narrator's unconscious. In the rationalist tradition of the West, to say this is to thematize the narrator's knowing and telling as lack, as the absence of conscious control, which is what constitutes any knowing as communicable (valid, verifiable) knowledge. As we saw in chapter 1, this is roughly how Lardner's critics have conceived the story. From the beginning of his career, however, the great rationalist Freud set himself in opposition to this dismissive view:

> It is essential to abandon the overvaluation of the property of being conscious before it is possible to form any correct view of the origin of what is mental. In Lipps's words . . . the unconscious must be assumed to be the general basis of psychical life. The unconscious is the larger sphere, which includes within it the smaller sphere of the conscious. Everything conscious has an unconscious preliminary stage; whereas what is unconscious may remain at that stage and nevertheless claim to be regarded as

having the full value of a psychical process. The unconscious is the true
psychical reality; *in its innermost nature it is as much unknown to us as
the reality of the external world, and it is as incompletely presented by the
data of consciousness as is the external world by the communications of
our sense organs.* (*Dreams* 651; emphasis Freud's)

Note, however, the telling juxtaposition in that italicized passage: to
say "*it is . . . unknown to us*" is again to conceive the unconscious
through a negation of "our" knowledge, which in turn is to thematize
"us" as our conscious selves and the unconscious as alien knowing, the
knowing of some other. To characterize the unconscious, therefore, as
Freud often attempts to do—as for instance in terms of displacement,
condensation, and indirect representation (*Jokes* 163–65)—is to reify it
as a describable object, or (to put that differently) to raise oneself to an
idealized Archimedean point above the earth on which, and as a part of
which, one lives, and to conceive it as both other and lower. (In some
sense Freud inveigles in vain against the conception of "unconscious"
as "subconscious" or "under-knowing," since he does clearly reify the
unconscious as "below us.")

In other words, Freud does not wander very far from "normal" patriarchal rationalism, which identifies with the conscious mind and consigns all nonconscious knowing to sheer lack, sheer negation. Freud
wants to establish the psychic primacy of the unconscious, and at the
very least its equal validity alongside consciousness; but he can only do
so from the standpoint of the normative conscious mind, and so he
reiterates the ideologically prescribed conception of the unconscious as
"unknown to us."

Jacques Lacan picks up the thread of this argument in his reformulation of the unconscious in Saussurean terms—in his claim that the unconscious is structured like a language, like *la langue*, Saussure's methodological fantasy of a pure linguistic system from which *la parole* or
actual language use is imagined to deviate. This is patently an attempt to
push Freud's counterintuitive claim for the primacy of the unconscious
one step further: if in ideologically normal terms the unconscious is to
consciousness as *la parole* is to *la langue*—as an irrational or illogical
deviation from a purely rational or logical system—then to associate the
unconscious with *la langue* is to "raise" it to the privileged status of
normative system.

But this is, it seems to me, a cheap way of gaining recognition for an
excluded party. It is the equivalent of women, normatively excluded
from masculine rationality, simply accepting the rational norm and

applying it to themselves: "I'm as smart as any man." This solves nothing, and it really changes nothing. It is sheer semantic sleight-of-mind, which in practice becomes a form of tokenism. *La langue* is a methodological fiction to begin with, a way (ideologically normal in the Platonic-Christian-scientific West) of reducing speech to stable abstract structure (so as to permit the institution of linguistics as a "science") and then of reifying the abstraction as "better," more "normal," "purer," and thus more "real" than the real behavior (now deprivileged as a messy "deviation") from which it was abstracted. Associating the unconscious with *la langue* only compounds the obfuscations in which the unconscious is traditionally steeped — only adds one more level of mystifying abstraction to an ideological system that is already jerry-built with such abstractions. What we ought to be doing, it seems to me, is not to assimilate the unconscious to a fantasmic Platonic or Augustinian form (*la langue* as Logos) but to tear away the mystifications that maintain the hierarchical system.

Lacan's other famous aphorism about the unconscious, the one to which my title alludes, is that it is the "discourse of the Other." While this seems on the face of it to implicate Lacan in the same static alienations to which Freud found himself unconsciously returning, it really doesn't. For by "discourse" Lacan doesn't mean *la langue*, he means *la parole* — and *la parole* not as speech (a static linguistic concept) but as speaking, or even as voicing. The unconscious is thus the voicing of the Other, or the Other speaking. As for the Other, by capitalizing the *O* Lacan signals the problematically contingent nature of the Other's Otherness. It is, specifically, contingent upon how "we" (as subject-as-self or as subject-as-Other) construe it in relation to ourselves or ourselves in relation to it. Anthony Wilden explains:

> He supposes an unconscious discourse interfering with the conscious discourse, and responsible for the distortions and gaps in that discourse. In one sense, there is an unconscious subject (barred from consciousness) seeking to address itself to another unconscious subject (the Other). In another sense, this unconscious discourse is that of the Other in the subject who has been alienated from himself through his relationship to the mirror image of the other. But whether one can actually say that the unconscious is a discourse, or that it is structured like a language, depends upon the level at which one views the unconscious. (262)

Wilden's construction of the contingency in the last sentence of this passage again retreats back into "normal" mystifications, and the retreat is at least partly Lacan's: the assumption that unconscious-as-discourse ("speaking") and unconscious-as-*langue* ("system") are merely alternative levels of abstraction is prestructured by the reduction of "the" subject to an abstract tourist named "one" who "views" the unconscious. Part of the difficulty of Lacan's writing is that he is constantly twisting and turning in order to avoid falling into constructions like "the level at which one views the unconscious," but twisting and turning is no solution either. The fantasy of *la langue* is not the only part or conception of language that is ideologically controlled, steeped in "normal" intellectual assumptions about the shifting messiness or stable purity of reality; all speaking is ideological, all linguistic articulations are prestructured by collective knowing, and if our civilization's ideological unconscious (a notion I will return to later in the chapter) wants us to view the unconscious as a "place" or a "thing" to be viewed by "one," then it is going to be almost impossible *not* to talk about it in those terms.

In any case, Wilden also has a useful explanation of the Other that works a little harder not to be lulled into easy formalizations of Lacan's thought:

> It is not possible, for instance, to define the Other in any definite way, since for Lacan it has a functional value, representing both the "significant other" to whom the neurotic's demands are addressed (the appeal of the Other), as well as the internalization of this Other (we desire what the Other desires) and the unconscious subject itself or himself [or herself] (the unconscious is the discourse of — or from — the Other). In another context, it will simply mean the category of "Otherness," a translation Lacan has himself employed. Sometimes "the Other" refers to the parents: to the mother as the "real Other" (in the dual relationship of mother and child), to the father as the "Symbolic Other," yet it is never a *person*. Very often the term seems to refer simply to the unconscious itself, although the unconscious is most often described as "the locus of the Other." (263–64)

The Other is a kind of introjected shifter, an internalized Voice that, in Lacan's psychologization of Heidegger's language mysticism, *speaks us* (209), but speaks us specifically as now this, now that: now a maternal introject as the need of the mother, now a paternal introject as the name of the father, now a collectivized introject as the norm of the culture.[2] And in every case it is radically dialogical, or as Lacan says, intersubjective. Wilden's account of Lacan's theory continues in terms reminiscent of Buber's I-It vs. I-Thou and of Bakhtin's internal dialogism:

> In this sense the concept of "Otherness" is valid and important, because the identity and difference of "the other" in the Imaginary relationship is a

false kind of "otherness" in the human world: a relationship to objects, not to subjects [cf. Buber]. In this sense the unconscious is the Other for the subject, since it is the unconscious subject who tells the truth, and the test of truth in human relations is not the reality or perception it represents, but intersubjectivity. The unconscious, in its necessary dialectical relationship to the unconscious of others, is the test of the truth of the message. As the locus of the code, the unconscious is not "within" the subject; it is the third position through which the sender is provided with a receiver [cf. Bakhtin]. As I interpret it, in the sense that all messages, articulated or not, involve us in a dialogue mediated by the locus of the code (the unconscious), the desire to communicate is surely what enables Lacan to reformulate the notion of "the unconscious is the discourse of the Other" by defining the idea as "Your concern is with the Other in the discourse," for it is by the Other that you are unconsciously controlled. . . . This is true in the purely formal sense that our choice of messages is limited by the code; it is also true in the existential sense that the conscious subject has only a limited control over the content of his messages, and less over their reception. In any event, not even an apparent monologue can take place without the mediation of "Otherness." (264)

This talk of the "code" will not do; it simply suspends the imagination halfway between an abstract semiosis (code as *langue*) and a curiously disembodied ascesis (the unconscious as locus of control). Sliding laterally into Bakhtin's theory of the internal dialogism of the word, which Lacan's theory so closely resembles, will help concretize the image of control. For Bakhtin, every word we learn is saturated with the dialogues in which it has been used, and specifically with the socioideological charge of those dialogues. Bakhtin doesn't explore the actual psychological process by which this saturation is passed on to new speakers in and through dialogues, but, as I argued in *The Translator's Turn* (10–15), the only convincing explanation for this dialogical saturation is the somatics of language: the fact that we feel words, that we learn and store and use words by feel, and that "feel" or somatic response (the limbic system, to be precise: the seat of emotion, habit, and rote learning) is the primary bodily channel of ideological knowing. What we feel in words is the emotional charge of the dialogical situation in which we hear(d) them, the mood, the motivations of the speakers, whatever tensions or needs lurk beneath the semantic surface; using a word thus becomes a process of transporting our somatic memory of a previous dialogue, or a long series of previous dialogues, into a present dialogue. The fact that transportation into a new dialogical context always transforms the word's somatic charge (even if only slightly) guarantees linguistic change or flux: the meaning of every word changes every time it is used; syntactic and morphological structures change (in the form of slips, elisions, stammers, slurrings) with each successive somatized dialogical context; pronunciation and intonation are obviously highly flexible situationally.

But language is not all change. The meanings and morphological structures of words and phonetic and syntactic patterns do also remain relatively stable from one dialogue to the next, precisely because each speaker internalizes a received or inherited feel for a word or phrase, and what is received or inherited from past dialogues is that ideological saturation that Bakhtin speaks of. Internal (somatized) dialogism is accretive and in some sense repressive: it regulates communication by reducing meaning to a conventional "core" and consigns nonconventional meanings and what V. N. Voloshinov calls "evaluative accents" (88) to a deprivileged periphery. These repressed semantic peripheries are always potentially present to somatic awareness — available for dialogical recovery and revitalization — but there are deep-seated ideological (or "ideosomatic") checks on their use. An idiosyncratic (or "idiosomatic") usage will *feel wrong*, both to its user and to his or her interlocutors, because all of them will have somatized a collective ideological control on usage that rewards "correct" phrasings with a feeling of felicity (the joy we feel at saying something "just right," at hearing a brilliant speaker speak, at reading something that is well written) and punishes "incorrect" phrasings with anxiety signals (the knot in the middle-class chest at double negatives and "ain'ts," the composition teacher's feeling of constriction at misspellings or comma faults).

It is in this somatic sense, I suggest, that "the conscious subject has only a limited control over the content of his messages": what "speaks us," in Heidegger's phrase, is not language per se (there is no such thing as language per se), but a somatically internalized and dialogized feel for language. The Other, to return to Lacan's term, is the somatics of language, the embodied speaking of every dialogue we have ever been in, and through those dialogues, of our entire culture. The Other can be maternal or paternal or cultural introjects, but specifically as somatized voices: the voice(s) of our mothers, fathers, and (by a collective reduction) communities, which speaks us, and to us, *as* us. Because those voices come to us "intersubjectively" or dialogically, they always ground our knowing and telling in community, in relation, and thus render both the transcendental subjectivity of Humboldt's linguistics and the abstract objectivity of Saussure's linguistics obsolete.[3] And because they come to us interdialogically, through a succession of transportations from dialogue to dialogue — as Kenneth Burke says, through "the *evolutionary* processes whereby a language is built from generation to generation by gradual accretion" (427) — they also ground our knowing and telling in collective regulation, in a repressive ideosomatic that harbors in its body of repression the vestigial idiosomatic memory of peripheral or centrifugal utterances as well. This means that we are always "controlled" by the ideosomatic Other as ideologically normal "mother" or "father" or "culture"; but those very ideosomatic voices also coach us (sub rosa) in innovative and even emancipatory utterance, and can (and do) surreptitiously validate and perpetuate idiosomatic resistances and rebellions.

It is time to start working my way back to "Who Dealt?" This long excursus on the unconscious was essential to set up my reading of the dummy in terms of Lacan's Schema L, which traces the dependence of the subject "on what is being unfolded in the Other" (*Ecrits* 193); now I can start drawing the connections. Lacan's conception of that dependence as a bridge game, and of the Other as the dummy, was in fact the spark that lit the fire that became this book: it makes so much sense to read Lardner's narrator as Tom's Other, especially in the revised sense I have offered, that all of a sudden a story I had been impressed by but had never pretended to understand leaped into unexpected prominence. Let me show how this works.

Lacan diagrams the subject's dependence on the Other's speaking in a Z-shape, which for some reason he terms Schema L (*Ecrits* 193):

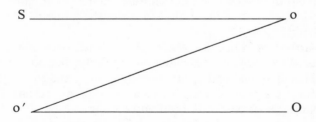

"Why," Lacan asks, "would the subject be interested in this discourse [of the Other], if he were not taking part in it? He is, indeed, a participator, in that he is stretched over the four corners of the schema: namely, S, his ineffable, stupid existence, *o*, his objects, *o'*, his ego, that is, that which is reflected of his form in his objects, and O, the locus from which the question of his existence may be presented to him" (*Ecrits* 194). Or, to elaborate that rather laconic key a little, *S* is the subject's self-presentation as conscious norm, as the rational, repressive self that denies its basis in repression, as the "existence" that is "ineffable" and "stupid" because it is so uneasily blind to all that it is repressing, and to the ways in which its life can only emerge out of what is repressed. *o* is any other person conceived as an object, objectified as the recalcitrant fulfiller of the subject's desires, someone who seems to offer him- or herself to the subject in love (for instance) but holds back, withholds part of him- or herself, never surrenders his or her whole being to the desiring of the subject. This recalcitrance is relational rather than personal, grounded in the subject's false (objectifying) relation to the other-small-*o*, which is in fact conditioned by lower levels on the schema. *o'* is the ego-ideal or *Ideal-Ich*, one of Freud's early names for the superego, the idealized image of the self that (in Freud's patriarchal formulation) is derived from the castrating father. For some reason Lacan splits the superego into the ego-ideal and the name-of-the-father, which he shunts over to the *O* or Other (I will return to this problem in a moment). As Lacan suggests in his complication of Schema L in Schema R (195), the subject's complexly falsified relation to both *o* and *o'* arises out of the Imaginary perception of the mirror stage: a specular image of the other mediates the subject's relation to the other-as-object (the objectified other as two-dimensional mirror image), and a specular image of the self (the ego) mediates the subject's relation to the ego-ideal or paternal superego (the idealized self as constituted by reflected difference). Another way of putting this might be that the other-as-object seems accessible to the subject, seems assimilable into the subject's desiring system, because the subject sees it (in Paul's phrase from 2 Corinthians) "through a mirror darkly" — while the subject idealizes the father as self by seeing it *in* a mirror *brightly*.[4]

The fourth term in Lacan's schema is the Other, on which, as he says, the subject is complexly dependent — complexly, because that dependence is mediated (and perhaps repressed) by the *o* and the *o'* (hence the zigzag course the scheme takes between its two major terms, the *S* and the *O*). And now we come to Lacan's bridge game:

> The fourth term is given by the subject in his reality, foreclosed as such in the system, and entering into the play of the signifiers only in the mode of death, but becoming the true subject to the extent that this play of the signifiers will make it signify.
>
> This play of the signifiers is not, in effect, an inert one, since it is animated in each particular part by the whole history of the ancestry of real others that the denomination of signifying Others involves in the contemporaneity of the Subject. Furthermore, in so far as it is set up *qua* rule over and above each part, this play already structures in the subject the three agencies: ego (ideal), reality, superego. . . .
>
> Furthermore, the subject enters the game as the dummy (*mort*), but it is

as a living being that he plays it; it is in his life that he must take up the suit (*couleur*) that he may bid. (*Ecrits* 196)

Lacan imagines here a closed system constituted by the three terms: the subject, the objectified other, and the idealized self — an expanded but still ideologically "normal" version of the "ineffable, stupid existence" that is locked into the *S*, which "forecloses" or represses the Object as the subject's psychic "reality." In Schema R Lacan tries to identify this system more or less as the Imaginary (constituted by the mirror stage) and the Other triangle (bottom right, triangulated by the *O*, *o*, and *o'*) as the Symbolic (constituted by the name of the father as Other), and to squeeze "reality" somehow awkwardly in between; but this is not really satisfactory. Lacan doesn't know what to do with the Real, probably because he is, ultimately, a systematic thinker, and his own system too forecloses on reality. In order for Schema L *or* R to work as Lacan desires, reality must not be squeezed in anywhere: it must be somewhere off the diagram, repressed by the diagram, foreclosed on the diagram, and yet somehow smuggled back into the psychodynamics represented in the diagram by the Other. This reformulation would feed into Lacan's notion that the Other enters into the "play" of the three Symbolic signifiers. Here, "play" is understood both as playing, or unstructured playful activity, and as the looseness in a system — the "play" of a steering wheel, for example — while the three Symbolic signifiers (subject, other-object, ego-ideal) are understood as death, in the mode of death, as the deathly lack of objectified/idealized "life" or Imaginary/Symbolic "reality" that is desired by the repressive system. The dead Other is the *mort* as bridge dummy, who comes to life in the subject's play, and constitutes the subject as living by becoming the true subject of his/her speaking, the voice that speaks the subject.

The "animation" of the Other as play of signifiers strongly suggests my revision of Lacan: all the somatized voices ("signifying Others") that speak the subject together trace the "whole history of the ancestry of real others" with whom the subject has spoken, and with whom his/her real others have spoken, and so on, back further and further, an interdialogical history as living ("animated") ideosomatics. This collective knowing and telling speaks the subject in the present ("in the contemporaneity of the Subject") but brings to that speaking an infinite cultural series of dialogues, and grounds the subject's contemporaneous speaking in a dialectic between regulative or repressive ideological control (the "signifiers") and the peripheral or playful return of the repressed ("play").

But enough of this; let me return to "Who Dealt?" In the Schema L of the story's bridge game, Tom is unquestionably the subject (*S*), the man who objectifies Helen as his "significant other" (*o*); Arthur is the ego-ideal (*o'*), specular image of the father-as-self, whom Tom seeks to emulate in order to win Helen, specular image of the self-as-other. This is the "normal" patriarchal system based on the idealized repression or foreclosure of reality: Tom and Helen, Tom and Arthur, Man and Lover, Man and Friend. Tom objectifies Helen as sexually attractive other and idealizes Arthur as socially attractive self: these would be the alignments suggested by Schema L. He perceives Helen through, and Arthur in, the mirror of his own self-regard—his specular vanity, if you like, the mirror in which his self was constituted as separate and different (from other selves and from itself) back in the mirror stage. Perceived through this mirror, Helen is the perfect complement to Tom's "me," which feels incomplete, in need of complementation, because it was and is constituted in self-alienating reflection. Helen stands behind the mirror and is dimly visible to Tom through its refractive surface, and his imagination of their union in marriage is mediated by the mirror. They are ideally joined by the refractions that differentiate and alienate them.

The "normal" patriarchal dream of love is: if only I could have her, I would be whole. She would meld into the tissues of my being and *I* would be whole (and she would be a part of that whole). Lacan would say that, because this dream of wholeness in union with an other is the structural consequence of the specular constitution of the self, it is hopeless: the mirroring that builds an alienation into the self cannot be reversed by a new mirroring, it can only be replicated. Or, to put that tropically: Tom and the "ideal" Helen he dreams of marrying are metonymies, differentiated parts of a specular whole, reflected fragments of the mirror image out of which he constructed his self; Tom's dream is to convert the alien (but strangely familiar) Helen-metonymy into a synecdoche for his "whole" self, a stray (but representative) element or component that will restore him to his "original" wholeness. Because this project is structurally doomed to failure, Tom (like all "normal" patriarchally programmed bourgeois men) is doomed to repeat the balancing act between objectifying the woman as assimilable complement (while there is still hope that she will become "his") and objectifying her as alien fragment (after she [the narrator] has become as much "his" as she ever will and still isn't, or after she [Helen] has made it clear to him that there is no hope she will ever become "his"). This constitutes a structural repetition compulsion that is enacted over and over with the same woman (repeated attempts to revive a marriage, say) or with a succession of women (successive wives, or successive escapes from a deidealized wife into the arms of idealized mistresses).

Perceived in the specular mirror of Tom's self-regard, Arthur is the projected perfection of Tom's "me," the man who is everything Tom wishes he was: rich, athletic, popular, successful—and, because he is all these things, Helen's husband. Arthur is Tom's male friend and rival as specular image of the self: he stands in front of the mirror in Tom's place, and his idealized image is reflected back to Tom when he gazes into it. Or, to put it differently: Tom gazes into Arthur's idealized image *as* mirror, and (ideally) becomes what he sees. Arthur goes to Princeton, so Tom goes to Yale. Arthur is captain of the Princeton football team, so Tom goes out for football at Yale. Arthur is rich, so Tom works to make money so as to seem rich. Arthur, Tom's friend and rival, becomes the ego-ideal on which Tom models himself. But the "normal" (ideologically prescribed, doubly bound) tension between male friendship and male rivalry drives a wedge into the heart of this modeling. As Tom's friend, Arthur helps Tom get ahead, molds or shapes his ego for success, coaches Tom in the repression of all those "purely" subjective behaviors, words, and thoughts that are not structured by his specular relationship with the ego-ideal, and thus are not conducive to "normal" masculine success. As Tom's rival, however, Arthur takes Tom's place. He is, after all, the model on which Tom attempts to construct a successful self, the original of which Tom is only the copy, the solid (because ideal) body of which Tom is only the reflection, the "normal" center of which Tom is the repressed periphery.

To the extent that the modeling works, Tom becomes an Arthur-clone—and what "normal" woman would not rather marry the original? To the extent that it fails (and it does fail, in the sense that Tom's poverty delays his college graduation and thus his ability to support a wife—that is, to meet Helen's "normal" requirements for status objectification), Tom becomes Arthur-dross, the repressed slough that Arthur casts off on his way to success in sports, business, and love. The "normal" patriarchal dream of emulation is: if only I could be him, I would be whole. I would meld into the tissues of his being and *I* would be whole (part of his whole). Tropically speaking, Tom's dream is to convert his familiar (but, because it is split off from the normative ideal, strangely alien) metonymic self into an Arthur-synecdoche for his "whole" self, to assimilate his preideal incompleteness into the idealized completeness of Arthur and thus finally achieve an "original" wholeness. Because this project too is structurally doomed to failure, Tom (like all "normal" patriarchally programmed men) is doomed to repeat the balancing act between objectifying himself as successful (got married, just got a raise, the locals want me to run for mayor) and subjectifying himself as a failure (a drunk living in a podunk town in Maine with a dumb wife and no Helen).

It is, of course, rather more complicated than this. This Lacanian analysis of Tom's predicament fails to take into consideration the ideosomatic control of Tom's objectifications and idealizations by the Other. Lacan's theory of the mirror stage, like Freud's theory of the Oedipus complex, is attractive for grown-up children taught to idealize their parents and repress the effects of their parenting, because it makes the schisms in the self seem the structural (and therefore inevitable) consequences of a mechanistic process: the child looks in the mirror, recognizes the other-image as self, and structures the self *as* other-image, with a built-in alienation derived from the distance and difference between the viewing subject and the mirror image. Self-alienation is not then the product of a repressed feeling of frustrated neediness. It is not a wound inflicted dynastically by parents, who received it from their parents, who received it from their parents (and so on). It is the structural consequence of looking in the mirror.

Adding the dummy-as-Other to the equation allows us to begin exploring the ideosomatic effects of being raised by certain parents in a certain culture.[5] Hegel defined dialectic as the introduction of an Other into a static Self, and while the notion that a "static" Self ever existed is an undialectical idealization, the "normal" construction of patriarchal gender identity might well be thought of in terms of the Hegelian dialectic. The little boy, for example, will somatize two Others, his father's defensive withdrawal or blockage as thesis and his mother's defensive and manipulative demand as antithesis, and will synthesize them as the interdialogical continuity of patriarchal ideosomatics programs him to, as an internalized (often externalized as well, especially in childhood) dialectical ascesis between control and release, withdrawal and opening up, refusing and giving, thrusting forward and pulling back, succeeding and failing. One might even say that, for the little boy, the Other-as-father is the thesis, the Other-as-mother is the antithesis, and the Other-as-culture is the synthesis that guides and powers the new thesis of his own "normal" masculinity.[6]

This is the "unconscious" control of our actions that we are taught to repress—that is, that we are taught to believe doesn't exist. (We are also taught not to remember that we were taught this.) Even without the spectacularly voiced dummy Lardner gives us, the narrator-wife whose revelatory speaking I want to explore in detail in a moment, the Other-as-dummy speaks more or less silently (in) all three of the "normal" bridge players, Tom, Helen, and Arthur. The mode of the silent Other-speaking is specifically what I identified in chapter 1 as the double bind: Tom becomes an alcoholic, and then institutes ascetic regimens to resist alcoholism, at the behest of his (m)Other, a somatized maternal introject that "speaks" him as a little baby dependent on the breast (a son who needs her) *and* as a strong self-sufficient man who doesn't need his mommy (a son who makes her feel like a good mother). Helen jilts Tom and marries his best friend Arthur, and four years later agrees to invite Tom and his new wife over for a game of bridge, at the behest of a maternal Other who tells her daughter to go for money over love (don't do what I did and marry a poor schmuck like your father whom I only thought I loved), or of a paternal Other who tells his daughter to marry someone big and strong and successful like him (but don't enjoy it, don't do it for selfish reasons like feeling good around him), or of a cultural Other that identifies Arthur as the "normal" successful man and Tom as a hopeless loser and drunk. These are, as I argued at some length at the end of chapter 1, enormously complicated and internally conflicted "speakings," partly because the Other speaks us in so many voices, but partly also because any one Other-voice is by ideological definition doubly bound. Here, for example, is another go at what Lacan would call the "specular" relation between Tom and Arthur, this time conceived not as structurally doomed to failure by the mirror stage but as "spoken" by the Other as somatized paternal introject:

(1) Respect your father.

(a) Speak respectfully to me. Don't talk back. Don't resist me. Don't indicate by tone of voice, gestures, facial expressions, or other nonverbal signals that you resent my commands. Conform yourself perfectly to my command.

(b) Never suggest, overtly or covertly, that you desire more from me (love, say, or unconditional approval), or that you might respect me more if I could give you more. Be satisfied with what I give you. *Be* what I give you. Mold yourself into the form of my giving.

(c) By extension, respect all authorities and all peers who resemble me. Be (satisfied with) what they give you. Never make impossible or unreasonable demands.

(d) Never respect anyone more than me.

(2) Be a man.

(a) Don't take any crap off anyone. Stick to your guns. Stand up for your rights. As my son, you are no one's inferior.

(b) Prove your superiority to every man you meet by beating him in competition. Edge all relationships with men toward competition or rivalry. Never allow yourself the luxury of personal warmth toward another man. Only queers love other men.

(c) Never let any woman get under your skin. Keep your guard up. If you ever do, you're a goner. They will take you to the cleaners. You be the boss. You draw the lines and expect your woman to stay inside them. Always keep your distance.

(d) What you do as a man, do for me. What honor you earn, give to me. Make me proud to be your father. Be proud to be my son. Make me feel like a good father.

(3) Understand (without my having to tell you) that you will be punished for obeying both (1) and (2).

(a) I will ridicule you for being a pussy if you obey (1) ("ain't you got any more gumption than that?") and I will accuse you of being uppity if you obey (2) ("getting a little big for your britches, ain't you kid? want me to knock some of that stuffing out of you?").

(b) Sublimate (and replicate) the internal riot this command generates in you by making friends with men with whom you can't compete, who are richer, handsomer, smarter, stronger, more athletic than you, and then swallowing your bile in the name of "friendship" every time they beat you (make captain of the football team when you don't make the cut, get better grades, get a better job, steal your girl).

(4) Repress all this.

(a) Be a self-sufficient man *and* remain subordinate to my command.

(b) Never articulate, or contemplate articulating, or allow yourself the luxury of recognizing the possibility of articulating, the doubly bound system that drives you. Think of it all as perfectly natural. Think of it as human nature. Be terrified of even approaching the door behind which the machinery of this system is kept.

(c) Feel no anger at me for doing this to you. I didn't make it up. I'm not responsible. It was done to me first.

(d) It wasn't done to anyone. You're just imagining it.

(e) Use the peculiar joy of competition, especially violent physical competition (contact sports or hand-to-hand combat, the thud of your body against another, the pain that contact inflicts on you) to help you keep your feelings repressed. Every time you have an angry feeling, control it. If you can't control it, release it physically on another man (conceived as an "enemy" or a "rival"). When you release it, do so in a controlled fashion. Never lose your temper. Never cry. Never show your vulnerability.

(f) Never admit to yourself or others that you have embarrassing feelings to show, or to suppress. Scoff at the very idea.

(5) Idealize me as the perfect father.

(a) Construe every paternal command you can remember (every one I have commanded you to remember, every one I have not commanded you to repress, and every one you have failed to repress adequately) as evidence of my immense respect for you. Construe my conditional approval as fatherly love.

(b) Feel guilty at your failure to obey and idealize me. Blame and despise yourself for your failure. Consider yourself a failure as a man. Believe that if you could only suppress a little more of your emotional response, I would admire you more, speak more approvingly of you — perhaps even love you.

(c) Believe that if you were as perfect as I am, you wouldn't even need my love and approval and respect. You wouldn't need anything or anybody.

(d) Need my love and approval and respect. Treat me as the ideal being whose love and approval and respect can validate you as a man and as a human being.

This does come back around to the ego-ideal that Lacan symbolized as o' and placed at the bottom left of Schema L; but because it is spoken by the doubly bound dummy-father-as-Other, it is no longer merely a structurally prescribed-slash-doomed relationship with either a Prescriber or a Doomer. It is ideosomatically programmed into us by our fathers and our culture, by real people in dialogical interaction, *as* an ideologically normal set of assumptions and behavior patterns. Its ongoing power to shape our thought and behavior is channeled not through a structural "mechanism" (though at the behest of our ideological programming we may be inclined to dehumanize it as a mechanism, like the cars and trucks little boys play with instead of dolls) but through somatized and intensely personalized voices, the voices of dialogical forces in our socially programmed limbic system that brook no (or co-opt all) resistance.

It was, in other words, and is continuously, *done* to us — which implies that it might eventually be undone. This is especially true if, as Lacan insists, the dummy-as-Other animates us through (and as) the play in the system, the repressed loose odds and ends that put the normative signifiers just slightly out of whack, the "forgotten" wrench in the works whose rattling and banging we steadfastly refuse to hear. Lacan waffles symptomatically on this issue, veering now dangerously (from a normative point of view) toward a therapeutic or emancipatory play or *jouissance*, now safely back into the mechanistic structuralism of Freud and Saussure. (It is a doubly bound balancing act controlled by the Other as patriarchal authority.) In his Freudian conception of the Other as *silenced* dummy—as unconscious and unheard speaking that speaks only through us, through various lapses and parapraxes in our speech and behavior—and especially in his adaptation of Freud's principle that the analyst-as-dummy should deliberately remain neutrally silent so as to forestall the patient's specular transference, Lacan veers back toward the normal patriarchal repression of the Other as the structural consequences of a system. Here, for example, is Wilden's reading of the Lacanian dummy-as-analyst:

> At the most elementary level, the silent "neutrality" of the analyst (his role as "dummy") enables the subject to project onto him the image of the significant other to whom the subject is addressing his *parole vide*. This *alter ego* of the subject is the ego of the subject himself insofar as his ego is the product of a capture by the other (ultimately reducible to the ideal of the ego). The relationship is a purely dual one for the subject; he is in fact maintaining a sort of short circuit between his narcissistic image of himself and the image of the other, in order to resist any attempts to change that image. But the analyst himself is neither an object nor an *alter ego*; he is the third man. Although he begins by acting as a mirror for the subject, it is through his refusal to respond at the level consciously or unconsciously demanded by the subject (ultimately the demand for love), that he will eventually (or ideally) pass from the role of "dummy," whose hand the subject seeks to play, to that of the Other with whom the barred subject of his patient is unconsciously communicating. The mirror relationship of ego and *alter ego* which was the obstacle to recognition of his unconscious desires which the subject has set up and maintained will be neutralized, the subject's mirages will be "consumed," and it will be possible for the barred subject to accede to the authenticity of what Lacan calls "the language of his desire" through his recognition of his relationship with the Other. (167–68)

The key words in this passage are "neutral" and "ideal": Lacan's concept of the analyst's work as dummy(-as-Other) is predicated on the idealized neutralization of transference, which sounds to me, coming out of Harpham, like an idealization of ascetic resistance. The "language of neutrality" is an idealized mathematical language that conceives desires as plus and minus charges or forces: the subject's "mirages" are false desires (marked with a minus sign) that must be met with their equal and opposite forces (marked with a plus sign) in order to be neutralized. Hence the strategic role of the analyst's neutral silence: the subject desires a particular affective response; in order to thwart that, the analyst marks the desired affect with a minus sign and responds with flat affect, thus negating the minus sign and generating a zero or neutral charge.

Tellingly, this is the exact analytical equivalent of the bourgeois parenting technique of withdrawing affection: instead of raging at or spanking the delinquent child (a negative affective response that by its very negation confirms the child's desire for a response, for affect, even if it is only anger), the parent goes cold, silent, indicating to the child that misbehavior will not be rewarded with attention of any sort. The normativity of this technique in bourgeois society — its increasing displacement of physical violence as the only "normal" channel of punishment — means that the patient in Freudian/Lacanian analysis will already have an ideosomatically controlled response to the Other-as-silent-dummy, and will respond to the analyst's "neutrality" not as a neutralization of mirages but as an exchange of mirages. After all, emotional neutrality is not emotionally neutral; refusing to respond *is* a response. The parent's emotional "neutrality" is experienced by the child as coldness, as a freezing (or, in the French word for "dummy," a *mort*, a deadening or mortification) of the affectionate parent that has the effect (through the somatization of the parent as Other) of freezing or deadening or mortifying the unruly self inside. By adopting the dummy role of the Other-as-affection-withdrawer, therefore, the Freudian/Lacanian analyst will in fact bring about change in the patient, but the change will not be from sickness to health; it will be from a socially unacceptable mirage to a socially acceptable one, from an unruly self to a self ruled (frozen, deadened, mortified) by the Other-as-parent.[7]

Lardner's narrator, on the other hand, is anything but silent: she is, as Donald Elder characterized her, a "dreary, insensible, rattlebrained girl" who "rattles on" and "cheerfully exposes" everything. She is not, we might say, a normal or socially acceptable dummy. She is not silent. She is not dead, as she should be in her assigned role as the structural replication of Tom's self-mortification. She is too much alive, talks too much, and talks in an unruly fashion. She is perfectly oblivious to her fellow bridge players' somatic responses, which are specifically ideosomatic attempts (the body's externalization of somatized ideological norms) to shut her up, to silence or deaden or mortify her: the angry and frozen looks, the blushes, the averted or rolled eyes, the shifting in seats. And, as Donald Elder implies ("'Who Dealt?' is a monologue expertly calculated to produce in the reader just the bearable amount of embarrassment, agony, and suspense" [240]), the reader is giving her these signals, too. We too want her to shut up. Her near oblivion to all the social pressure that is brought to bear on her to conform to normal behavior patterns makes us anxious, stirs up in us the unruly child whose untrained oblivion to subtle social signals caused our parents anxiety (because it stirred up the unruly child in *them*) and forced them to escalate or explicate the signs of rule. It is easier for us to bear than for Tom, Arthur, and Helen, of course, because, if the anxiety Lardner's narrator generates in us gets too strong, we can always stop reading—put the book down, go do something else for a while—and come back to it when we feel "better," which is to say, when we have once again forcibly frozen or deadened or mortified the unruly child in ourselves and feel capable of encountering Lardner's narrator again without succumbing to the somatized scenario in which the anxious parent is punishing the anxious child.

Revealingly, Tom, Arthur, and Helen—like most of us in similar situations—sit there and take it. No one screams "That's enough!" and threatens to leave the room if the narrator doesn't shut up. No one plugs his or her ears and starts to sing the national anthem loudly. This would be unseemly, "childish" behavior—indeed, unruly behavior—and would be read as stooping to the narrator's level, except of course by the narrator, who would probably think of herself as infinitely more mature than such a baby. She clearly sees her own behavior as conforming to the same adult norms as that of Tom, Helen, and Arthur. And since she never crosses the line into overt childishness or unruliness, since her unruly behavior is merely a matter of "innocently" revealing things that "one doesn't talk about," anyone who drew attention to her behavior and attempted to correct it in an authoritarian manner would immediately be perceived as "overreacting." In fact, the problem may be that Tom, Arthur, and Helen are too repressed even to recognize or articulate their sense that the narrator is revealing things that "one doesn't talk about." Articulating that sense would constitute "talking about" those things, and thus must be subject to the same repression. As a result, the three "normal" bridge players have to sit and endure the narrator's talk—until the climax, when Helen revokes and Tom pours himself a glass of Scotch. Silenced by their dummy-Other-as-parent, they can only act out.

This is a familiar situation for parents (and the guests of parents) of five-year-olds, especially in the repressed middle class: the child "rattles on," revealing embarrassing things about her parents' sex life and repeating things her parents have said about the guests before they arrive, and the parents, afraid of (being seen as) overreacting, sit there and take it, or at most attempt to distract the child, rechannel her attention onto other subjects. It might be useful, in fact, to make a distinction between the speaking of the Other-as-parent and the speaking of the Other-as-child: between the kind of controlling, regulatory, repressive, freezing/deadening/mortifying speaking of the ideosomatic double bind that is typically silenced by (and in) parents (the basis of a Freudian/Lacanian "cure"), and the kind of unruly, subversive, revelatory, playful speaking of the idiosomatic periphery that is typically voiced by (and in) small children (which, I am going to argue, may lead to a real cure). Lardner's narrator *is* a child, in some sense: she speaks the Other-as-child and it speaks her, and through that speaking she gains a power over the speaking of the Other-as-parent that is potentially liberating.

Indeed, a parallel text to "Who Dealt?" in this sense might be H. C. Andersen's tale "The Emperor's New Clothes." There the tailors were able to convince the Emperor, and the Emperor his subjects, that a nonexistent suit of finery really existed simply by grounding belief in its existence in the Other-as-parent's speaking of the double bind: the clothes were visible, they said, only to those with perfect (ideal) marriages, to those with faithful spouses. The Emperor and his subjects then both saw and didn't see the new clothes: saw them insofar as they were coached by the Other-as-parent to believe in the ideality of both their marriages and their selves (be perfect so as to bring honor to me, your parent), and didn't see them insofar as they were coached by the Other-as-parent to believe in their failures as the naughty children of perfect parents (be imperfect so as to allow me the illusion of being better than you). In the social speaking of this double bind, perfection must be presented to public view as the ideal you both do and do not believe in, so as to conceal failure as the shameful secret with which you torment yourself: be perfect in public so as to redound to my greater glory, be imperfect in private so as to remain properly humble before your glorious parent. In this horrific situation, which is ours, there is only one (kind of) speaker who can break the bonds of the double bind: the (Other-as-)child, who has not yet been sufficiently trained in the ideosomatics of (im)perfection and can therefore *innocently* (or apparently innocently) disregard the official proclamation. "Why isn't he wearing any clothes?" This has the effect of stripping both the Emperor of his nonexistent clothes and the Other-as-parent of its double-binding speech. Her parents will want to shush her, to say, "They're *magic* clothes,

honey" (sure, Dad), but the damage will be done: the Other-as-child will
have been voiced in her parents and other adults, and the double bind
will begin to come unbound.

As Lardner's narrator shows, of course, it is not that simple. Her
response to the speaking of the Other-as-parent is in fact complexly
double, for she responds to that speaking both in the other players and
in herself, in her own ideosomatic response. The Other-as-parent speaks
most powerfully and insistently in the story through Tom's blushes and
dirty looks, which do usually stop the narrator for a moment:

> All right, dear; I won't make you blush. (228)
>
> All right, Tommie, I'll shut up. (228)
>
> All right, Tommie, I won't give away our secrets. (229)
>
> All right, Tommie, I won't. (229)
>
> All right, Tommie, I won't say another word. (231)

But only for a moment, and then she's off into another subject that Tom
tries to shut her up about. And in any case she doesn't always accede to
the Other-as-parent in Tom's looks:

> No, Tom, I'm going to tell Arthur even if you hate me for it. (229)
>
> You needn't look that way, Tommie. I *can* stop talking if I try. (229)
>
> Tom is making faces at me to shut up, but I don't see any harm in telling
> it to his best friends. (231)
>
> What are you grinning about, Tommie? I am, too, bashful when I don't
> know people. Not exactly bashful, maybe, but, well, bashful. (232)
>
> What are you blushing about, Tommie? It's nothing to be ashamed of.
> (234)
>
> Hush, Tommie! What hurt will it do anybody? (235)

That last, of course, is the crucial one, where the narrator recites Tom's
poem about the "bird" who has "flown" and brings things to a head.

The narrator also responds to the regulatory voice of the Other-as-
parent in her own head:

> I do think it's wonderful, him staying on the wagon this long, a man that
> used to — well, you know as well as I do. (227)
>
> I'll stop talking now and try and keep my mind on the game. (229)

[W]e certainly weren't [tired of each other], were we, Tommie? And aren't yet, are we, dear? And never will be. But I guess I better speak for myself. (230)

Oh, Tom, she's — but I mustn't tell, must I? (230)

Tom's always after me to buy clothes, but I can't seem to get used to spending somebody else's money, though it was dad's money I spent before I did Tom's, but that's different, don't you think so? (231)

"Bridge work." I meant bridge, not bridge work. That's funny, isn't it? (232)

There is also, just after this last parapraxis and correction, a two-paragraph self-depiction of the narrator as Tom's mother, as the "normal" controlling or civilizing wife whose prescribed task is regulating her husband's behavior (especially around the house); here the narration draws heavily on the speaking of the Other-as-mother:

Tom insists, or that is he did insist, on a great big breakfast — fruit, cereal, eggs, toast, and coffee. All I want is a little fruit and dry toast and coffee. I think it's a great deal better for a person. So that's one habit I broke Tom of, was big breakfasts. And another thing he did when we were first married was to take off his shoes as soon as he got home from the office and put on bedroom slippers. I believe a person ought not to get sloppy just because they're married.

But the worst of all was pajamas! What's the difference, Tommie? Helen and Arthur don't mind. And I think it's kind of funny, you being so old-fashioned. I mean Tom had always worn a nightgown till I made him give it up. And it was a struggle, believe me! I had to threaten to leave him if he didn't buy pajamas. He certainly hated it. And now he's mad at me for telling, aren't you, Tommie? I just couldn't help it. I think it's so funny in this day and age. I hope Arthur doesn't wear them; nightgowns, I mean. You don't, do you, Arthur? I knew you didn't. (233)

The narrator is spoken by the Other-as-parent, clearly, and in some powerful ways — particularly when she escalates the battle over what her husband wears to bed into a threat of abandonment (no doubt a threat her mother used subliminally, and effectively, on her). Strangely, however, I get no sense that the memory of this battle has any somatic effect on her — that she responds to it autonomically, with anxiety signals, for instance. When I tell a story like that, I feel my body tighten and constrict in an attempt to control the anger and anxiety that the original dialogue generated, which resurfaces in my somatic memory. But for Lardner's narrator there seems to be no somatic undercurrent of uneasiness or anxiety. It is just one of the things she tells the assembled company. It is just "kind of funny." And there is, in general, an easiness to her responses to the speaking of the Other-as-parent. It is like hurling a boulder into a river: the river just goes around it, or else (if the boulder is small enough) sweeps it away. The river image here recalls William James's famous theory of the stream of thought; in some sense "Who Dealt?" is narrated by (or as, or in) the stream of speech, by the voiced speaking of the Other-as-child with only occasional interruptions from (or the silent irruptions of) the Other-as-parent. What makes the stream-of-thought theory initially counterintuitive is the ideosomatically controlled introjection of the Other-as-parent's linguistic speaking (as Saussurean *langue*) back into the unruly stream of thought, both as a psychological and as a methodological ruling principle; what makes both James's chapter and Lardner's story potentially liberating is the release of the stream of the Other-as-child's speaking (as both thought and language) from ideosomatic norms, into the flow of uninhibited play.[8]

My insistence on the liberatory potential of Lardner's story may itself seem counterintuitive, even on my own terms: I have, after all, demonstrated at some length how the narrator works both sides of the repressive equation, encourages Tom both to drink and not to drink, and in the end precipitates his fall off the wagon, the beginning of a new repressive or ascetic cycle. To the extent that "Who Dealt?" "is" a liberating text, it is so only potentially, and that liberatory potential "is" "in" the idiosomatic periphery to which the Other-as-child guides the reader. Because, as Lacan stresses, the Other is never purely subjective or personal but intersubjective, relational, dialogical, another way of saying this is that the liberatory potential of a text is neither "in" the text nor "in" the reader but constructed dialogically by the repressed or peripheralized Other-as-child that facilitates the reader-text interaction. It is a relational playfulness, a "play" or looseness in the repressive structures of the "reader's" dialogical re-creation of the "writer's" dialogical act. Or rather, since the reader is only a reader and the writer is only a writer in dialogue with the text, and the text is only a text in the dialogical relations of real writers and readers, it is a relational play or playfulness in the repressive structures of the Other-as-writer-as-reader.

This notion is so difficult to articulate because, as I mentioned earlier, linguistic articulation is so carefully controlled by the Other-as-parent, by the whole history of regulatory dialogues that led up to it. The notion of a relational Other that could inhabit and facilitate and direct the dialogical acts of two different people at the same time is counterintuitive in the Christian-scientific-liberal West, where people are "normally" conceived as self-sufficient isolates. The notion of a dialogical Other sounds mystical, and in fact it is a notion widely accepted in animistic and polytheistic civilizations more open to mystical views than ours, and in the mystical peripheries of our own. But it need not be thematized as mysticism. There is persuasive evidence (which is repressed or dismissed in the Western ideological mainstream) that the boundaries between "individuals" are partly artificial and socially maintained. There is the notorious contagiousness of the autonomic system, for example: the fact that yawning, laughing, crying, and other autonomic responses are infectious, that, when one person yawns or laughs or cries, other people feel an almost irresistible urge to do the same. How are these autonomic responses communicated, if there is no dialogical "Other" (or whatever we choose to call it) structuring the somatic interchange? The empiricism of the five senses cannot explain it. If anxiety were not contagious, the somatic grounding of ideological norms could not be transmitted from generation to generation. Parents would not feel anxiety at their children's unruly behavior (the return of their own repressed), and parents' anxiety would not impose an ideosomatic rule on their children's behavior. And finally, if the joy of subversive and liberatory play were not contagious, ideosomatic programming would be a Devil's Island from which no one ever escaped. This relational "contagion," I argue, is the work of the Other—specifically as the somatized dialogical voices that ground our behavior in the intersubjectivity of human interrelations.

Granted, much of the Other-spoken contagion in "Who Dealt?" is regulatory and repressive, and feeds back into the ideosomatic double binds that generate it. But the very embarrassment and discomfort we feel as we read the story is the Other-as-parent's somatic signal that there is a powerfully subversive movement in it as well, an untrained and unruly childish delight in remembered details and "playing grown-ups," an almost total disregard for social pressures to conform. This disregard is perhaps superficial in that, while the narrator may not be conscious of those pressures, the Other-as-child certainly is, and speaks the narrator's speaking as a playing-as-undoing. Most important, the Other-as-child knows that the ideosomatic double binds with which the Other-as-parent speaks Tom, Helen, and Arthur are psychosocially destructive, and that the only way to avert that destruction is to slip out through the "play" in the repressive structures. Like psychotherapy at its best, the narrative moves from repression toward release: from the concealment of truth to its revelation, from the deadening insecurities of pretense into the enlivening terrors of exposure, from idealization toward a new grounding in the real, and from the aporias of double bondage to at least an opportunity for freedom. It moves in those directions not, however, through the carefully controlled silence of the Other-as-parent, as in Freudian and Lacanian analysis, but through the exuberantly playful voicing of the Other-as-child, a voicing that moves through the free-association method Freud instituted to the free play of jokes and dreams and uninhibited slips of the tongue, and from there to baby talk and animal noises and primal screams. These are more and more regressive voicings that dredge up the buried ideosomatic experiences that keep the child in thrall and make them accessible to the transitional adult — the adult en route from fearful adherence to the speaking of the Other-as-parent to an open and transformative dialogue with all the Others, all the voices that speak from behind barricades: a dialogue that tears down the barricades and lets the stream of thought and speech flow freely.

If we imagine Lardner's narrator as Tom's psychotherapist, in fact — as the "dummy" who keeps saying things that sound dumb because they are too painfully true to be voiced and so have been ridiculed into hiding — then it becomes possible to read the story as the transcript of a cure (or at least of a possible cure: we are not told what happens after Tom picks up the glass of Scotch). Lardner takes us up to the transitional or transformative moment, the cusp of Tom's therapeutic progress, and leaves us there to imagine the rest. If we are pessimistic about our own power to break free of patriarchal ideosomatics, we will probably construe the ending more or less as I did in chapter 1, as a return to more of the same. But if we have felt in our bodies the impulse toward liberation and know that it is a realistic possibility, we may even construe it as Tom's moment of surrender to the truth, his yielding to the voice of the Other-as-child that is telling him to break down and cry like a baby, confess his love and hurt to Helen, blurt out his anger at Helen and Arthur for treating him so shabbily, become Hansel to his wife's Gretel and with her rail at the father and evil stepmother for abandoning them, or else curl up like a needy infant at his wife's breast and restage the separation traumas that have addicted him to alcohol.

This is embarrassing, I know. It is even more embarrassing than Lardner's narrative, which stops just short of such a bacchanalian regression. But it is what typically happens, and what has to happen, in psychotherapies that work (imagery therapy, drama therapy, rebirthing, primal scream therapy, etc.). It is embarrassing because the Other-as-parent controls us, perpetuates our repression, keeps us doubly bound, through embarrassment. Embarrassment is generated by the somatic memory of parental (and other authoritarian) ridicule and sarcasm. It is what we feel when others signal to us that we have not sufficiently conformed our behavior to adult norms. In fact, the truly "successful" citizen (like Arthur, who remains a cipher in the story largely because he never reacts in any way that provokes a narratorial comment) successfully represses embarrassment as well, and never blushes. To feel embarrassment is at the very least to feel alive, and thus to feel the potential for liberation from the Other-as-parent that generates embarrassment through somatized ridicule.

If we are not entirely enamored of patriarchal double binds, therefore, and have any hope at all of escaping them, we must be willing to risk embarrassment — to risk doing embarrassing things, experiencing the embarrassment of others, and to keep pushing past all the other somatic stop signs until we begin to hear the speaking of the Other-as-child. Tom Cannon may or may not have made it that far, may or may not have freed himself from the double binds of booze and rivalry and success. No matter; he is a fictional character. What matters are real people, and that is the direction I am heading in, from the story of the bridge game to the real person who wrote it, en route to a confrontation with the real people (you and me) who read this.

II

WHO WROTE?

3

The Conflicted Writer

Tom Cannon is not Ring Lardner. Ring Lardner is not Tom Cannon. In the primary narratee (as it were) of "Who Dealt?," Lardner did not create a mere fictionalized version of himself. Tom is a small-town businessman in Maine who went to Yale and lost the woman he loved to another man and never became a published writer; Lardner was a famous journalist and writer in Chicago and New York who never went to college and married the woman he loved. Let me not be taken, in other words, to be setting up a facile one-to-one correspondence between author and character.

On the other hand, as I have already begun to hint, in important ways Tom Cannon also *is* Ring Lardner. Like Tom, Lardner was an insecure writer for whom writing was never easy, who never thought much of himself as a writer, and who filled his stories (a fortiori his columns) with thinly disguised autobiographical elements. Like Tom, Lardner was a repressively needy lover who devoted a great deal of emotional energy to the denial of his deep need and hurt. Like Tom, as I noted in chapter 1, Lardner was an alcoholic. Here in chapter 3, then, I want to begin to make the methodological shift from close reading to authorial portrait by exploring these parallels between the two men — between Tom as Lardner's construct and Lardner as mine. I want to pursue those parallels more heuristically than definitively, less as a kind of slavish application of my theoretical frameworks (the double bind, the Other) to Lardner as a writer and as a human being than as a way of going on, a way of constructing (and perhaps partially deconstructing) a reading of Lardner as conflicted writer on the shifting theoretical and interpretive foundations laid in part I.

I propose to begin my juxtaposition of the "real" writer and the "fictitious" one at a place that may itself be fictitious: the anecdotal material on how Lardner placed his first story, the epistolary "A Busher's Letters

Home" (later collected as the opening story in *You Know Me Al*), with *The Saturday Evening Post* in 1913. The bare bones of the anecdote are that the Sunday editor of the *Chicago Tribune*, claiming that it was too unorthodox, refused to publish "A Busher's Letters Home" in "In the Wake of the News," Lardner's popular column, so Lardner published it in the *Post*, to much national acclaim. This is a critical juncture in Lardner's authorial biography: had he been able to publish anything he wanted in the *Tribune*, he might never have been perceived as a short-story writer, and thus as a writer worthy of authorial biographies and critical studies. His stories would have been columns, not stories — as many of his fictional, epistolary, narrative columns are still perceived today.

As the tale was widely told in Lardner's own day, however, and as it is retold by Lardner's first biographer, Donald Elder (114), and his third son, Ring Jr. (87), *Post* editor George Horace Lorimer rejected it — "so fast," as Elder puts it, "that Ring was convinced that the *Post* had some sort of interceptor in Cleveland — they couldn't have got to Philadelphia and back in so short a time" (114). So Lardner sent it to a variously identified friend, who used his pull with Lorimer to get it published. In 1977, the year after Ring Jr.'s memoir appeared, Jonathan Yardley (163) exploded these legends, quoting a letter from Lardner to his good friend Burton Rascoe, another newspaperman who had written for the *Chicago Tribune* while Lardner was there and was now a New York–based syndicated columnist like Lardner. Rascoe had reported as fact some of the stories about the publication of Lardner's first story thirteen years earlier, and Lardner wrote to set the record straight.[1]

The sliding across generic boundaries upon which this episode devolves is telling: we have an apparently apocryphal "story" (journalistic anecdote) that Lardner writes a letter to correct, about a "story" (epistolary anecdote) that he wrote — a fictitious anecdote told in a newspaper column, about a fictional anecdote that Lardner was not able to publish in a newspaper column, by a man who worked for the newspaper that originally refused to publish the story. As I started to suggest a moment ago, such crossovers were in fact endemic, even essential, to Lardner's career as a writer, and they remain endemic to his reputation after his death. Was Lardner a journalist who dabbled in fiction (and thus is beneath the notice of academic critics), or a major writer who never quite rose above the journalistic mire out of which he pulled himself (and thus is deserving of critical — though condescending — attention)?

I want to return to those crossovers in chapter 4; for now, what I find interesting about the episode is that Lardner's exchange with Rascoe takes place in early October 1926, nine months after the publication of "Who Dealt?," and that the "plot" of the episode revolves so patently around the dubious reassurance Tom gets from his wife: "You've either got to have a name or a pull to get your things published" (234). In 1913, when he was writing and placing "A Busher's Letters Home," Lardner had a "name" in journalism even outside the Chicago area (he was a nationally known columnist); but the "stories" (both Rascoe's column and "Who Dealt?") suggest that he still needed a "pull" with Lorimer to get the first busher story published. Are these stories just stories? Given the striking congruence of Rascoe's story about Ring with Ring's story about Tom, are they both fiction, or both (in some sense) true?

> You remember, Tom, that Mr. Hastings we met at the Hammonds'. He's a writer and knows all about it. He was telling me of an experience he had with one of the magazines; I forget which one, but it was one of the big ones. He wrote a story and sent it to them and they sent it back and said they couldn't use it.
>
> Well, some time after that Mr. Hastings was in a hotel in Chicago and a bell-boy went around the lobby paging Mr. —— I forget the name, but it was the name of the editor of this magazine that had sent back the story, Runkle, or Byers, or some such name. So the man, whatever his name was, he was really there and answered the page and afterwards Mr. Hastings went up to him and introduced himself and told the man about sending a story to his magazine and the man said he didn't remember anything about it. And he was the editor! Of course he'd never seen it. (234-35)

Lardner claims he never needed such help; we are to assume that the narrator of "Who Dealt?" is referring to some other writer's experience, not her creator's. Whatever the truth of the matter was, it seems clear that Lardner did not want to be perceived as someone who *wanted* to be a writer, someone who tried to foist his authorial self-conception on other people; that part of what bothered him about Burton Rascoe's column was the impression it gave that he had, thirteen years earlier, been ambitious; that he had aspired to the status of Writer: that he had had to work at it, worry about it, plot a way to get his story published.

It was in fact typical of Lardner's professional career that he fell into things, that plums fell into his lap — his first four or five reporting jobs, his first weekly column — but he also went to some pains to make it appear as if this were always the case, as if he *never* took pains to advance his career. He moved up through the ranks of the journalistic world through no doing of his own, even — he sometimes insisted on this—through no merit of his own. He was the right man at the right place at the right time. He had friends who thought he deserved things that he really did not. He was pushed into things that he did not desire, but was too well-bred to decline.

This careful image management throws a new light on Tom Cannon's blush when his wife summarizes his autobiographical story for Arthur and Helen: he is ashamed, it seems likely, not only of the revelation about his feelings for Helen but of his wife's portrait of him as a writer. He is a businessman who dreams of publishing a story, but who certainly does not want to be seen as staging himself as a writer.[2] Lardner too was notoriously chary of calling himself a writer, and as his son says, he almost quit writing short stories in 1922—only the intervention of Scott Fitzgerald and Max Perkins of Scribner's prevented it (Ring Jr., *Lardners* 174). Unlike Fitzgerald, Sherwood Anderson, Ernest Hemingway, and other writers who admired, imitated, and condescended to him, Lardner did not take his own writing seriously. Elder reports that Lardner "kept on shrugging off literary laurels and pretending that he did not understand what the 'high-brow' critics were talking about. It was not an evasion of the responsibility of a man of letters; he did not think of himself as one, however gratifying he found the praise of Mencken, Franklin P. Adams, and [Edmund] Wilson" (217). Ring Jr. remarks that "he was part-way serious when he said he would rather do almost anything than write short stories but had no choice 'because I have four children and a wife who has extravagant ideas about a garden'" (*Lardners* 175). He really did write mainly for money; he really did deny that his stories had any value other than as passing entertainment.

This curious feature might of course be written off (as it implicitly is by Lardner's biographers) as a kind of quirky integrity—Lardner remained true to his own self-perception as a journalist even in the face of critical accolades—or, at worst, as the rube's failure to comprehend the status to which he has been unaccountably raised. In the former reading, Lardner would be the good secondary relief pitcher who loves doing batting practice and saving the occasional game but doesn't want to start, and sees stardom as pure hype; in the latter reading, he would be the farm boy who likes to throw rocks and suddenly finds himself recruited as the star pitcher on a major league baseball team. Either analogy might have satisfied Lardner himself, at least with some qualifications; but there seems to be more to it than that. The problem was gratification: feeling good, feeling gratified. For Lardner, it is clear from his letters and from his son Ring Jr.'s memoir, feeling good did not feel good. It did not feel "right." Anything that started feeling good, that he began to enjoy, awakened all his suspicions. There must be a catch in it somewhere, and he had better stop doing it while he was ahead — or else stop enjoying it.

Nor was this just an isolated quirk. It was a dominant personality trait running like a scarlet thread through a dozen other "quirks": Lardner consistently hated doing, or put the straitest straitjackets on, the things he did best. He was a writer who made his name writing dialect, but he was obsessive about good grammar, often ridiculing other writers' or his family's grammatical infelicities at the dinner table or in print. Like Tom, who "worked so hard over it and sat up nights writing and rewriting" (234), Lardner never wrote quickly or spontaneously; from his first baseball articles through the famous stories of the teens and twenties to the pieces of his last painful years, he remained what Elder calls "a meticulous and anxious worker" (95) who typically spent an entire day laboring over a 500-word column. He was never a writer plagued with too many ideas for columns and stories, and he bore down mercilessly on the ideas he did get, constantly changing his mind on which were the good ones and which the bad, as often hammering trite and banal ideas into something just barely publishable as bludgeoning exciting ideas into something trite and banal.[3]

He was a success story who always insisted that his success was due to good fortune (not merit), and a chronic worrier who was always suspicious of good fortune. He was a gross sentimentalist who cynically believed that if anything could be faked, it was. He was a shy socialite who loved to be around people and always felt awkward around them (including his family), and who was loved by nearly everyone who knew him but kept them all at arm's length. He was an alcoholic who could "hold his liquor" — which is to say, he never became exuberant (or maudlin, or showed any emotion whatsoever) while drinking. No matter how much he drank, his iron self-control never slipped, he never staggered. He was an ardent supporter of Prohibition (and generally a fanatical advocate of law and order) who broke the law in speakeasies constantly, and always with excruciating guilt. He was an uncritical racist who numbered several black and Jewish artists (composers, singers) among his friends, and never noticed the discrepancy between his admiration and friendship for these men and his overt racist remarks. He was a famous humorist who hated funny stories, and was almost never seen to laugh. When he did laugh — with his sister Anne or his children, or at professional comedians whom he admired, as Ring Jr. tells us (*Lardners* 38) — he never gave himself to his laughter. He never split his sides laughing. He never laughed till he cried. He chuckled slightly. He raised the corners of his mouth and crinkled his mournful eyes. (In a famous phrase, Hugh Fullerton said that he "looked like Rameses II with his wrappings off" [Elder 45].) Indeed, he was a humorist who hated his reputation for being one. His son Ring Jr. once asked him whether it was true what people said, that he was a humorist, and he replied that "it was a loaded question. 'If I said yes, it would be like if you asked a ballplayer what position he played and he answered, 'I'm a great third baseman'" (*Lardners* 4).

This is a strange remark—almost a red herring. It seems, for one thing, to undermine Lardner's unwillingness to be taken seriously as a writer (and to contradict my baseball analogies). On the one hand, he would rather be thought of as a journalist who occasionally (to make some extra money) writes a short story or two—which is to say, as a third baseman, a man who fields grounders and makes the long throw to first well enough, but can't really be considered proficient at any other position. On the other hand, being thought of as a humorist seems to deny his versatility, his ability to play more positions than one. In shying away from characterizations of him as a writer (as a "great" or "literary" or "major" writer), he seems to be seeking precisely the humble anonymity that he expressly denies in shying away from characterizations of him as a humorist.

If it is contradictory, however, it is complexly so. At one level, for example, Lardner's conflicted self-projections seem to proceed from a sheer refusal to be labeled: I'm not a writer, I'm not a humorist, I'm not a satirist, I'm not just a journalist (I do these other things, too). But that refusal to be labeled was not blanket: he did long to be labeled a composer-lyricist on Broadway, a Rodgers or a Hammerstein (or preferably both)—the one profession he turned his hand to that he never succeeded at. In this light his conflicted self-conception as a writer was a way of saying: I don't want to be what I already am; I only want to be what I can never be.

This is perversity, perhaps; but it is a kind of perversity that American society idealizes as "ambition," as ever striving onward, as a contempt for what you have already achieved and a longing to break new paths, meet new challenges—a contempt for the present, specifically, as a *spur* to longing. A less idealized reading would see this "perversity" as driven by a fear of achievement, or rather, perhaps, a fear of the gratification that achievement seems to promise. Dream a big dream, achieve it, and enter paradise. This was the dream dreamed by Lardner's good friend Fitzgerald. But of course, as Fitzgerald kept demonstrating in all his stories, this quintessentially American dream is doubly bound: it holds out the promise of a reward that is withdrawn the instant it is earned, and, to help the dreamer manage the disappointment of this withdrawal, it portrays the reward that keeps the dreamer striving as not worth striving for. Hate what you have and strive for what you don't have, but hate what you strive for the instant you have it, and strive for something else. As spoken by the American Other-as-culture, this dream drives a capitalist ideology that breeds alienation in the midst of a culture of success: the paradisal happiness of the rich and successful is held up as a dream icon to the poor and unsuccessful, miring the latter in either restless dissatisfaction or passive fatalism, self-loathing or class envy (or both), and simultaneously miring the former in empty self-satisfaction and a similar passivity and fatalism, because the trivial pursuits of the wealthy (shopping, partying, travel to five-star hotels, drugs) never quite disguise the awareness that none of this constitutes paradisal happiness. As spoken by the bourgeois Other-as-parent, it is a channel of liberal child rearing that employs the withholding of love: ostensibly in lieu of physical punishment, but at a deeper emotional level to defer the moment at which the parent would actually have to award the child the promised love that he or she (the parent) doesn't have, having never got it as a child. Family therapists refer to this as conditional love, love tied to achievement: do these things and I will love you. When the child does the required things, the parent gives the child new tasks to perform, new achievements to attain, new hurdles to jump, before the promised love will be bestowed — because, in fact, it never will be, and both the child and the parent him- or herself must be protected from the realization that this is the case.

In fact, as my tabulations of the double bind in part I suggest, the parent will typically ("normally") resent the child's success at performing the required tasks, especially when the child becomes an adult and enters the working world. *What are you trying to do, make me look bad? Show me up?* For twenty years the father pushes his son to be smart, and then for the next twenty years resents him for arguing circles around him, using words that he doesn't understand, having intellectual discussions that exclude him. For twenty years the mother pushes her daughter to be beautiful, sexy, enticingly devious with men, and then for the next twenty years resents her for being more beautiful and sexier than her. Succeed, make me look like a good parent, and I will love you; succeed, make me look like a frumpy second-stringer, and I will punish you by withholding the promised love.

This ideologically "normal" resentment may in fact have something to do with a second implication in Lardner's remark about being called a humorist: it might be read as a refusal to brag, or to have anything to brag about. "[I]t would be like if you asked a ballplayer what position he played and he answered, 'I'm a great third baseman'": the key word there is "great," the response to a neutral question about position with self-praise. The correct answer for Lardner would be "I play third base," or even, more self-deprecatingly, "The manager plays me at third." In other words, I don't want to be thought of as "great" at what I already am, or as someone who thinks of himself as "great," or even as someone who thinks of himself as potentially great, someone who has a goal, who strives to improve himself, who keeps longing for bigger and better things. To seek to better yourself in our culture is normatively to seek to be better than your parents, and in the "normal" doubly bound parent-child relationship, that is profoundly threatening to the parent and therefore anxiety-producing for the child. Be successful, but don't seem to *want* to be successful. Make it seem as if someone else foisted success upon you, as if you did everything in your power to keep it from happening, but it was inexorable, success simply overtook you. To the extent that you do want to be successful, want it for me, not for yourself: to make me look good. Don't show me up.

Certainly this would explain Lardner's curious lack of ambition for the year or two immediately after he finished high school. His family's fortune had collapsed, and if you believe the Horatio Alger myths you might think that Lardner would have gone straight out to make a new fortune—and then *given it back* to his parents. In fact Lardner did just this, after a few years: got rich and sent his parents lots of money; even while he was a struggling journalist trying to earn enough to marry on, he sent them most of his salary. Why, then, did he loaf around home for the year after his high school graduation doing nothing, then take the Civil Service exam to become a mailman, and spend the next year working occasionally as a substitute mail carrier? Why was his first full-time job one he hated and was no good at—as "bookkeeper" (actually, bill collector) for the Niles Gas Company?

Significantly, the opening story in *Round Up* (1929), Lardner's definitive short story collection, is a fictionalization of his experiences at the gas company: "The Maysville Minstrel" tells the story of Stephen Gale, bookkeeper-cum-bill-collector for the Maysville Gas Company and would-be poet. Like Lardner, Stephen is too soft-hearted to collect bills from poor people; like Lardner, he sends his salary home to his mother (his father, like Lardner's by 1929, is dead)[4]; and like Lardner, he denies that he dreams of being a writer:

The Gales were too poor to go to picture shows; besides, there was no one to leave the children with. So Stephen and Stella stayed at home evenings and read books from the town library. The books Stephen read were books of poetry.

And often, after Stella had gone to bed, he wrote poetry of his own.

He wrote a poem to Stella and gave it to her on one of her birthdays and she said it was great and he ought to quit the darn old gas company and write poetry for a living.

He laughed that off, remarking that he was as poor now as he cared to be. (4)

It is Stella who says the poem is "great," not Stephen: calling himself a great poet would be like calling himself a great third baseman. But even Stella's praise is suspect. All praise is suspect. One should not feel too good about oneself. And the story is plotted to confirm that suspicion. Stephen allows himself to be conned by a wisecracking New York salesman named Charley Roberts into sending a poem to a New York columnist Roberts knows, and the columnist prints the poem in his column:

> Stella you today are twenty-three years old
> And yet your hair is still pure gold
> Stella they tell me your name in Latin means a star
> And to me that is what you are
> With your eyes and your hair so yellow
> I rate myself a lucky fellow Stella. (6)

It is clear to Lardner and the reader that the columnist prints this as a joke, to ridicule Midwestern hick poets, not because (as Roberts tries to tell Stephen) it is an immortal work of literature; but Stephen believes his "critic," Roberts, accepts false praise, and ends up making a fool of himself. Roberts sends him a telegram in the name of "James's Weekly," asking for some of his poetry to publish, and Stephen falls for it: he sends off several more poems, thinking to be paid a dollar a line for them, and quits his job. When the whole thing falls through, he is forced to swallow his pride and go back to the gas company; he tears up all his poetry except "To Stella," which his wife has hidden away.

The moral for Lardner is clear: be wary of all praise and all ambition. Never try to better your situation, never try to rise above your station; accept windfalls (and thematize any success you have *as* a windfall), but only with consummate wariness, and always with an escape route mapped out in advance, allowing you not only to escape, but to escape with dignity—that is, without emotional risk.[5] There is also the problem of the "manliness" of writing poetry for a living: Lardner, ambivalent about getting paid to entertain people with his pen, about getting paid for what feels to him more like his mother's avocation than his father's vocation, sends Stephen back to gainful employment with his masculine tail between his legs.

Like many "normal" young men, Lardner only became ambitious when he fell in love—with Ellis Abbott. Settling down and getting married, we are taught to believe, gives a shiftless young man a "direction" in life; suddenly, in 1907, Lardner too conceived the desire to rise in the world, specifically in the world of journalism, at first in order to make enough money to qualify as an eligible bachelor for the wealthy Ellis Abbott, and then, once she had agreed to marry him, in order not to have to travel so much, so that he could spend more time at home with his wife-to-be. (Since his father-in-law-to-be was worried about giving his daughter to a man who fraternized with ballplayers and other riffraff, his ambition also required that he gradually extricate himself from such fraternization—a requirement he met by becoming first an editor, then a columnist.)[6] And, having married Ellis and "given her" four sons, as they used to say (Ellis, like a good new wife, was lonely and longed for a baby, which Ring, like a good new husband, promptly gave her), he went on tying his ambition and his success to his family until his death:

> Ring, when asked once to what he attributed his success, said, "To Home Run cigarettes and a family with extravagant tastes which always needs money." Actually the extravagance of the family's tastes was largely Ring's doing. He himself had been brought up in comparative luxury, and Ellis had come from a prosperous home. But Ring had his mother's flair for spending freely, and although his personal requirements were modest—he seldom bought himself anything, and Ellis had to see that he bought new clothes occasionally—he wanted the best for his family. Their welfare and security were almost an obsession with him; they did not make the demands. (Elder 219)

In a sense, of course, his family did make the demands—they made *his* demands. He instilled in them the demands they made on him. As Elder all but explicitly says, in fact, he transferred the demands they made on him onto them from his mother, whose "flair for spending freely" invariably had the ideologically prescribed liberal-maternal strings attached: those on whom she spent freely were to feel properly grateful. Because his mother spent freely and made emotional demands on him, it "felt right" for him to duplicate that childhood grid in his own family life: he encouraged his wife and sons—obsessively, as Elder says—to spend freely and make demands on him. This required that he transform his mother's emotional demands into his family's financial demands, of course—a transformation specified by patriarchal gender ideology: the mother demands gratitude from her son; the son-as-pater-familias demands not gratitude but recognition, a recognition that he is a good father (and thus, transferentially, his mother's dutiful son), and he typically displaces that demand from his family onto society. To demand gratitude is to need love, and men are not supposed to be needy. Men are taught, therefore, to transform their need into the "simple," almost mechanical expectation of recognition: good provider, dutiful son, upright pillar of the community. This is the liberal-paternal nexus of spending and demanding: spending not for love but for fame, and lusting after fame not for love but for wealth, the money to keep the vicious familial circle of spending and demanding going. Lardner's father "fails" his mother, loses their wealth—albeit in a socially acceptable way, in order to make good on the bad investments made by his oldest son, William—so Ring, the youngest son, makes it up to her by getting rich. He makes lots of money as a writer, becomes famous, gains national recognition—but not for himself. That would be "selfish," which is to say needy (demanding instead of giving). He does it for his family, like a good patriarch—and, like a good doubly bound son, secretly for his mother.

Now, I say that Lardner lusted after fame not for love but for wealth, and after wealth not for himself but for his family, but obviously it is more complicated than that. Love does fit into the normal patriarchal man's scheme of things, too—Lardner does love Ellis—but it is a love that is peculiarly (and normatively) designed to defend against the needy, clutching love normatively assigned to patriarchal women—to defend against that love, need I add, both in himself and in Ellis. Lardner's love for Ellis, throughout their extended (four-year) epistolary courtship and the twenty-two years of their marriage, is stretched on the same rack of needy self-control as is Tom Cannon's love for Helen: whether he gets her or loses her, once he has fixated on her, transferred his mother onto her, he begins ("obsessively," as Elder says, driven by the half-heard conflicting voices of the Other-as-mother and the Other-as-father) to define his relationship with her in terms of a double bind of need and control.

This is particularly clear in Lardner's letters to Ellis during the long courtship. They met seldom before they were married: Lardner's Other

(as mother? as father?) fell in love with Ellis at first sight in 1907, but he
was traveling virtually year-round reporting on sports events, and their
communication right up until they were married in 1911 was almost
entirely restricted to hastily arranged meetings at train stations (Lardner
frantically trying to route his train travel through Goshen, Indiana,
where the Abbotts lived, or through Northampton, Massachusetts,
where Ellis attended Smith) or to letters. In all the letters Lardner wrote
to his wife-to-be there is a fierce control of need, a watchful repression
of all demands (lest Lardner frighten Ellis, or himself), a determined
image management that allowed through its iron gates only such need as
sounded like conventional love — and, for that matter, only such control
as sounded like conventional humility, self-abnegation in favor of the
worshipped other.[7]

The earliest letters, before Lardner declared his love to Ellis, were all
written in doggerel verse of studied cheeriness; they include parodies of
Poe, Longfellow, and other popular poets of a half century before and
strongly anticipate the doggerel poem Tom Cannon will write about the
"bird" who has "flown." The anticipation of that later "fictional" poem is
more tonal than thematic, of course — Lardner's "rabbit" (his defensively
endearing nickname, which she hated, for Ellis *Abbott*) had not fled —
and the tonal quality that anticipates Tom's poem is not so much melancholy as an almost obsessive intensity:

> I'll admit that this strange pome
> Which I now write you,
> Is far sadder than a home
> Filled with orphans two.
> Your indulgence now I ask
> Answer quick, young fiend,
> Or your proud young face I'll mask
> With sweet gasolined.   (February 22, 1909)

Lardner is, as usual, sad about not being able to see Ellis in the next
few weeks, and imagines his sadness as a kind of orphanhood, a loss of
parents, a stylized separation anxiety. The orphan image here is a telling
one, for it suggests (as did many of their explicit remarks) that they are
each other's parents, Ring being Ellis's father and Ellis his mother: an
association that is, of course, a "normal" or ideologically prescribed
association under bourgeois patriarchy. The man in love must be both
father (authority) and son (needy infant) to the woman he loves, and
the woman must be both mother (nurturer) and daughter (submissive,
obedient, passive little girl) to the man. These schizoid roles are lodged

deeply in the double binds of gender imposed on us by the Other-as-parent. What is not "normal," however — or perhaps only nightmarishly "normal," by and through repression — is Lardner's "playful" escalation of his demand for a letter to the imagery of murder: "Or your proud young face I'll mask / With sweet gasolined." The cute doggerel *d* at the end of "gasoline" (to make it rhyme with "fiend") adds just the right "playful" touch to "mask" Lardner's frightening intensity and thus to keep Ellis from turning tail and running like the rabbit Lardner imagines her to be; but the mask, as Ellis herself saw sporadically (her own later letters deal with it), concealed about as much as gasoline.

(I should note that murder images are not exactly rife in the correspondence; I would not want to give the impression that Lardner calls down wrack and ruin on Ellis, even playfully, in letter after letter. What is rife is the intensity of his balancing of need and self-control; I single out the image of murder because slips in the balancing act reveal so much about what is at stake in it. Lardner's self-control is so "good," in fact, so strong, so measured, and his writing so masterly, that he slips rarely and thus reveals little about his true feelings — which makes the slips all the more important to a close reading of the letters.)

A rather more complex murder image appears in a series of letters in April and May that same year, two to Ellis and one to his friend and sometime romantic interest Wilma Johnson (whom he called Wilma Ginseng, or "Ginnie"). On May 9, 1909, he wrote to Ellis:

> I was given an awful scare a little while ago when I read in the Chicago American headlines that looked like this —
>
> SMITH COLLEGE SENIOR FATALLY
> SHOT AFTER LOVE QUARREL
>
> The man in the case certainly had a nice way of showing his affection, did he not?

He certainly did — and a most ascetic way at that: kill your love for a woman whose recalcitrance hurts and scares you (in the sense I explored in chapter 2, the objectified other who will not submit herself wholly to your specular image of her) by killing her. Deaden your hurt by reducing the projected cause of the hurt to death. The ideal woman under patriarchy is one who deadens everything in herself that causes her man anxiety — who conforms herself in every detail to her man's deathly repression, and represses even the awareness that she is doing it for him, to protect him from (knowledge and experience of) his repressed anxiety. When real women fall short of that ideal, as by definition all of them always will, the "normal" doubly bound patriarchal man will not kill her, but kill a little more of his feeling for her and try (usually unsuccessfully) to repress his reproaches. Lardner is closer to that "normal" patriarchal man than he is to the murderer in the news item, but the finely balanced irony of "The man in the case certainly had a nice way of showing his affection" indicates how torn he is inwardly by the maternal double bind (love me — don't love me; need me — don't need me; feel no anger — direct your anger at other women).

This is even more evident in his letter a week and a half earlier to Wilma Johnson: "When I read the News head, saying a Smith College senior had been murdered, my thoughts instantly flew to the Rabbit, so many brutal huntsmen there are gadding about" (April 30, 1909). This is a wonderfully complex remark that I hear sending at least three messages: (1) I was worried that Ellis might have been murdered; (2) I am worried that one of the many "huntsmen" (suitors) might "murder" (win the hand of) Ellis before I do; (3) I want to murder her for not writing more often, loving me more openly, giving herself to me more fully. Of these, (3) is implicit in the letter of February 22, 1909, quoted earlier, and in perhaps five or ten others as well, in which he promises to strangle or mutilate her if she doesn't write more often. (2) is made almost explicit in a verse letter (parodying *Hiawatha*) he wrote to Ellis later in May, where he associated his own recent courting of her at Smith (literally: he proposed to her) with rabbit hunting: "Days must end, but not their mem'ries / Days when one is rabbit hunting / In the valleys of Mass'-chusetts" (May 26, 1909). Here is the ascetic lover's double bind in a nutshell: I don't want another man to kill my rabbit before I do; I don't want anyone to kill my rabbit before I can win her hand in marriage; I'm afraid she's going to marry someone else and I want to kill her before she does. By marrying her I will protect her from dying at another man's hand; by killing her I will protect her from living with another man; by marrying her I will kill her, render her dead to the world, mummify her, make her my own mummy-as-mommy. By imagining both marrying her and killing her as protecting her, I protect myself against both need and loss; by imagining protecting as both marrying and killing her, I leave myself open to my own need and loss. The ascetic control Lardner imposes on his pursuit of Ellis keeps generating idealized images of their bliss together that also, as if accidentally (the "unintended" return of the repressed), generate spin-off images of gruesome destruction, mayhem, mutilation, the chaos that will ensue (and that Lardner's repressed need will itself precipitate) if he cannot possess the object of his ascetic desire. Paradise and chaos, love and murder, the ideal and the grotesque run hand in hand through the very same images — the ascetic images Lardner summons in order to bring both his own need and Ellis's will into conformity with the future perfection he projects.

The early years of the courtship — especially 1907 and 1908, when he was writing verse doggerel letters to Wilma Johnson in much the same public tone of humorous need as to Ellis — were dotted with crises provoked almost invariably by Lardner's thrashing about in the knots of the double bind. One of these was precipitated by an earlier *Hiawatha* poem Lardner and Wilma cooked up on a date, all about the joys of their date, and then both sent to Ellis. Ellis was not pleased:

> When I received on the same mail twin epistulas I was tempted to wire two telegrams of congratulations, but refrained. Don't do it again and if you write me any more poetry I am going to rebel and never answer your letters as long as I live. So the very next poetry I receive from you I shall understand as a tactful suggestion to whoa Elizabeth — in other words stop. (October 31, 1907; *Letters* 8)

Lardner, stung, responded with the most tonal honesty he revealed in the entire four-year correspondence:

> Dear Rabbits,
>   In the happy past, I often boasted to myself thus:
>   However harshly I may be used by others, the Rabbit is incapable of a deliberate attempt to hurt my much-abused feelings.
>   Vain boast — the Rabbit, with premeditated malice, ridicules my poetry to my very face and requests that I burden her with it no longer. All right, Rabbit; if you should ask me on bended knee to ship you more of my inimitable verse, I will refuse you with a curse in my throat and sneer in my ear. . . .
>   I want to remind you, before we go a step further — that you hinted some time ago at a Christmas surprise for me. I can almost guess what it is — a lemon peel or an invitation not to write any more. But I want to ward this off and tell you what I really want Santa Claus to bring me from old Northampton, Mass., — a Kodak picture (afraid to ask for a larger one) of Miss Ellis Abbott to cheer me in my hours of melancholy, anxiety and grouch. I wouldn't get very mad if Mr. Claus came in far ahead of time with such a welcome gift. Is this too much to ask? You know you owe me something for slamming my poetry. (December 5, 1907; *Letters* 8–9)

The tonal honesty is still largely buried here in the carefully controlled ascetic cuteness (a kind of stylistic exfoliation of the name "Rabbit") with which Lardner defended himself against losing Ellis — and against the pain he would (try not to) feel if he did. But especially the "However harshly" paragraph stands almost bare of cute control: the letter's opening line frames the paragraph with cuteness ("happy past," "boasted," "thus"), and so allows Lardner's hurt to light up every unadorned word ("however harshly," "used by others," "incapable," "deliberate attempt," "hurt," "much-abused feelings"). Then, of course, the frame is closed ("Vain boast"), and Lardner escalates his epistolary ascesis to its normative "cute" masking.[8]

Ellis apologized in her next letter for her brusqueness, and said she would be happy to read more of Ring's verse; but she also seems to have decided that turnabout is fair play, for the next spring she invited a suitor of hers from Yale named Loring Hoover to her junior prom at Smith, and let word get back to Ring about it. Lardner was instantly (if carefully, controlledly) jealous, and wrote a spate of letters to her urging, in solemn paternal tones, the disclosure to him of full details, which Ellis declined to give. But Lardner would not let it alone; he continued to harp on it, and to ferret out little bits of information about the prom and Ellis's feelings for Loring (whom she described to her mother as "so much older and more self-possessed and nicer all around than he used to be" [*Letters* 17]), for months and, in some sense, for years afterward. As Caruthers reports, the prom incident had such a powerful impact on Lardner's feelings that in 1921, ten years after their wedding and thirteen years after the original incident, he wrote and staged a play reenacting it for Ellis's birthday (17). A play—a drama, a playful enactment; nothing serious. But Lardner is never lightly playful. His playfulness is always a desperate attempt to control his anger, his fear, his need, his vulnerability, his guilt, and an equally desperate attempt to mask his self-control as caring, as an easygoing love. Loring Hoover, to conflate two of the images I've discussed, threatens to orphan Lardner by killing his rabbit-mother; furthermore, even when he has securely tied Ellis to him in marriage (and there is no evidence that Lardner ever suspected, or had reason to suspect, that Ellis might be cheating on him), he still lives with the gnawing fear that he might lose something precious, maybe only the promise of something precious, if he relaxes his vigilance on the Loring Hoover affair.

This is exaggerating Loring Hoover's importance to Lardner, no doubt. But I don't think I'm exaggerating the importance to Lardner of a threat that he (intermittently but repeatedly) thematized as Loring Hoover. Loring Hoover does not figure directly in the love triangle of "Who Dealt?" (five years after the birthday reenactment), for example, but the prom incident itself does, at least indirectly: one of the girls who attended the prom with Ellis and Loring was Helen Gibson, Ellis's best friend at Smith and later her maid-of-honor at their wedding; Ring's best man was his best friend Arthur Jacks, and Arthur and Helen (who first met at the wedding) later fell in love and were married. "Arthur and Helen Jacks" translates neatly, of course, as Arthur and Helen Gratz. Ring Lardner, Jr., tells us (on the authority of his Aunt Ruby, Ellis's sister) that at the time of the prom Ellis's affections were not yet exclusively fixed on Ring, and that both Wilma Johnson and Helen Gibson hoped she would choose someone else (like Loring), so that one of them would have a chance at Ring (*Lardners* 33). Helen, in other words, was at one time a fallback alternative to Ellis. Furthermore, in that 1921 staging of the prom, Ring Jr. says, Ring himself played Ellis, Helen's brother Jimmy played Helen, Ring's brother Rex played Loring Hoover, and Arthur Jacks played a third girl (*Lardners* 144).

Needless to say, this is circumstantial evidence at best. But it seems clear that Lardner poured into the story much of the intense insecurity he felt about Ellis during his courtship years: the almost infantile need he felt for her company and her letters and her love, the massive stylistic ascesis he brought to bear on that need, and the intense jealousy he felt toward Loring Hoover (whom he never met).[9]

In addition, of course, there was the undeniable fact of Lardner's alcoholism, which was already well advanced during his long courtship of Ellis. Lardner had started drinking heavily in Niles, in his middle teens, with his brother Rex, and kept hard at it during his years on the various Chicago papers:

> Ring was hired [by Duke Hutchinson, sports editor of the Chicago *Inter-Ocean*]. "Have you figured out how you're going to live in Chicago on eighteen-fifty a week?" Hutchinson asked Ring.
> "I can get on the wagon."
> "You can get on the wagon," Duke said, "but nobody can work for us and stay there." (Elder 45)

The only reason to quit drinking at this point is financial: Lardner cannot afford the alcohol he consumes. Falling in love with Ellis changes that. Lardner's ideal self-projection as Ellis's husband is a sober, upright citizen, and once he has won her hand in marriage, in 1909, he begins carefully to broach the issue of his alcoholism—though only in order to negate it:

> A co-worker came up last night and offered to take me out and satiate me with drinks at his expense. That was a rash offer because I have a reputation—an unfortunate one—for infinite capacity. But I was very

good – good to him, too – and declined with thanks. I *think*, after the world's series is over, I'll quit altogether, but it's a horribly hard thing to do on this job, especially when one is about to join some celebrating champions. But I don't see why I'm talking about this. Anyway, it's one thing you won't have to worry over any more than my love for you. (September 20, 1910)

Note the equation in that last sentence between abstinence and love, and the corollary to that equation (in the previous one) in silence: all three are founded, Lardner seems to be suggesting, on rock-hard self-control, on his determination to be "good," to live up to an idealized self-image as Ellis's sober and loving husband. If he can only love Ellis, stay on the wagon, and not talk about it – a checklist of ascetic virtues, each of which is itself attained and maintained by checking off a long list of renunciations and self-restrictions – then everything will be all right. The next month he goes on the wagon again, and in December begins reporting to Ellis just how good he has been: "But I'll have to gird up my resolution to stay on the good old wagon. It will be two calendar months a week from tomorrow" (December 19, 1910). "Today is the 28th and I've been riding the wagon two calendar months. That's the longest for five years" (December 28, 1910). This is a way of handing Ellis the keys to the liquor cabinet, of course, as was Tom's wedding-day promise to his wife in "Who Dealt?" – enlisting her support in his resolve, projecting his self-control outward onto an external judge and jailer – but it also has (at least potentially) the unfortunate effect of driving home to Ellis that she is marrying a drunk. Two whole months! His longest sober spell in five years!

Three days later, on New Year's Eve, Lardner went out to mail a letter to Ellis and fell off the wagon. He wrote about it to Ellis two days later, when he had sobered up enough to write:

I won't tell you why my beautiful record was spoiled for a minute or two, because of my New Year's resolution not to lie, and I don't want to tell you the truth. A piece of the truth is that I had been a little too good and something had to break. But everything's all right again now, and I'll try to keep it so.   (January 3, 1911; *Letters* 89)

Now a new channel of self-control is added to the equation: now Lardner must not drink, not talk, and not *lie* (and not not-love Ellis). Because he must not lie, he has to talk; but to talk and not to lie means telling her that he has been drinking. This is rather like a juggler (a *drunk* juggler) keeping five balls and a plate in the air at the same time, and urging his partner to toss him more objects to juggle (I can do it!). So much rides on all this for Lardner: everything.[10] He solves the problem temporarily by making a controlled break in the ascetic structure of his "goodness," a verbal break (a talking that isn't a lying) that repeats and (he hopes) rehabilitates the uncontrolled alcoholic break of the past two days (his New Years' binge): where in falling off the wagon he broke off a piece of his resolve and watched his ascetic structure come crashing down, in telling Ellis about it he breaks off a piece of the truth and attempts to apply it to a restructuring. Unfortunately, the piece of the truth that he uses to control his "good" image—"everything's all right again now, and I'll try to keep it so"—is that his goodness is fragile, ultimately uncontrollable.

Ellis senses some of this and replies with mitigated concern:

> I'm sorry that anything happened but not surprised. One can't begin all over again and succeed—at first. But I think you had better tell me the truth about it. The truth is always better than an imagination let loose, and don't you think perhaps I'll have to know some time? . . . Has it occurred to you that if anything—that could have been helped—can keep you from writing to me for two days *now*, that there is a strong possibility of similar events in the future? (Ring Jr., *Lardners* 61)

The mitigations—"at first," "that could have been helped"—are Ellis's attempts to give Ring the benefit of the doubt, but even more, perhaps, they are her attempts to convince herself that she is doing the right thing in marrying an alcoholic. He *can* help drinking, she reassures herself, if he puts his mind to it; the reason he fell off the wagon this time, surely, is that he tried to give up too much too fast, to start his life over as a sober man all at once. A different method might work better, a gradual tapering off. Ellis's codependency is already beginning; she is already starting to assume the role that her son Ring Jr. says would be her response to her husband's alcoholism till his death: it doesn't exist, and even if it did, it wouldn't be a problem (192).

Lardner's reply to Ellis's question about the possibility of his falling off the wagon again is the most revealing of all. She has, after all, tied his drinking specifically to her: by falling off the wagon he failed to write to her for two days. While he was drinking, in fact, she had written him a letter with a "playful" threat that recalled some of his own: "However if you stop writing to me every day I'll *kill* you. You needn't worry about caring too much. The more you love me the more I'll love you" (*Letters* 88). Here love is a kind of brinksmanship, a nervous bilateral upping the ante toward perfect "goodness," with murder and mayhem as the penalty for failure—or even for slippage! To go on a binge that makes him forget to write her every day is to say he doesn't love her (enough!), and thus to lose both her and his life (in Lardner's desperately sentimental discourse the two are in any case equated). So when Lardner responds to Ellis's cautious query about the possibility of him falling off the wagon again, he knows what is at stake and does not resort to hyperbole lightly:

> The answer is, "No, it hasn't," for there isn't a strong possibility nor a bare possibility of similar events in the future. . . . You don't understand, Ellis dear. When I have you I will have *everything I want*. . . . I give you my word, dear, that you'll never, never have occasion to worry about anything like that.   (Ring Jr., *Lardners* 61)

"The extent to which Ring's life is a tragedy rests, I believe," his son comments, "on the fact that he believed implicitly in those words. He subscribed to all the moral principles he had grown up by, including the proposition that the love of a good woman could effect a fundamental change in a man" (*Lardners* 61). Of course Lardner's tragedy does not rest solely on the clash between his alcoholism and his ideals; that particular clash is only a symptom of a larger tragic (or perhaps only ironic) pattern that dogged him throughout his life, in relation to his writing, to laughter, to money, to profanity, to illness, to grammar. But it is a strong symptom, a representative one, and I think that Ring Lardner, Jr., is largely right in identifying his father's belief in the therapeutic or redemptive power of "the love of a good woman" as his tragic flaw. What does him in is precisely the slippage between his supreme sustaining belief in the parity between abstinence and love and his fallback belief in the power of love to bolster abstinence: he wants to believe that he needs no help, that he can both love Ellis and abstain from drink on his own (he is a man, strong, self-sufficient, unneedy); and also, conflictingly, that Ellis's help is all he needs, that he is nothing without her love, and that anything is possible with her love (he is her little boy, dependent, needy; he can only be a man with her as his mommy). These two things are what he is supposed to believe, what he is told to believe, by the Other-as-parent. They are the little boy's first two conflicting commands in the parental double bind (grow up—don't grow up; be a man—be my baby; don't bother me—don't leave me).

His thrashing in the knots of this double bind is particularly clear in this passage from a letter during the period of abstinence the previous fall, where Lardner is at some pains to maintain his doubly bound image of Ellis as at once a mother ("a big, big help") and a daughter ("a small, small child"):

You mustn't say a word ever about my giving up anything for you. The things I have given up were bad for me, so there was no hardship about it. If you hadn't come into my existence so forcibly and insistently, I might have been dead by now, so you are a big, big help, even if you are a small, small child. Even if I had given up anything worth while, your love would repay me many times over.   (Ring Jr., *Lardners* 52)

If his mother hadn't come into his existence "so forcibly and insistently" — given him birth, taken charge of his nursing — he might well have been dead by now. This is the truest transferential sense of Lardner's claim: he owes his mother his life (few twenty-six-year-olds die of alcoholism). But he owes his life specifically to the oral pleasures he subliminally remembers at her breast, and in his relations with Ellis he finds himself compelled to reverse that alignment: as her prospective husband he owes his life to his renunciation of oral pleasures at the bottle.

This reversal allows him to reverse the parent-child alignments as well, so as to think of himself as the daddy and Ellis as the "small, small child" — indeed, he achieves the reversal by using Ellis as mommy just long enough to convince himself that he is and always has been the daddy, and that she (it is one of his favorite pet names for her throughout the correspondence) is his "small child." Hence his injunction on her saying "a word ever about my giving up anything for you": like Tom's wife crowing about his resolve ("And he says it's forever, don't you, dear?"), for Ellis to say "a word ever" about his abstinence, and specifically about the way in which he has enlisted her as surrogate mommy in his resolve ("my giving up anything *for you*"), would articulate and thus render artificial what should be inarticulately natural. He is giving up alcohol because it is bad for him, because he aspires to goodness — to the ideal state he projects for himself as Ellis's husband — and as part of that projection he imagines that goodness is not an artificial state (only imperfectly to be achieved through a vigilant ascesis) but natural — the most natural thing in the world. Thus there is no hardship; the only hardship lies in not having Ellis, not possessing her — or rather, not possessing the idealized self that he projects into his future married state. To put it schematically: his alcoholic ascesis at this point of his life, a few months shy of marrying Ellis, consists of the simultaneous belief (1) that he is renouncing "bad" things and attaining ideal "goodness" in order to demonstrate his manly unneediness and thus to deserve (and make things perfect for) Ellis, and (2) that he is waiting for marriage to Ellis as the perfect state of (surreptitiously maternal) love that will dry up his need for alcohol and make it easy (no hardship) for him to renounce "bad" things. Or aphoristically: he is putting the horse both before and after the cart. He uses (2), the "after" scenario, to help bolster his resolve in (1), the "before" scenario (before the ideal state is consummated), and rationalizes his failure "before" by reference to the imminent certainty of success in the "after."

Needless to say, it didn't work. He kept drinking, off and on, till his death. The only real change in his alcoholic ascesis after marriage was that he gradually accepted it as a fact of his life, and, instead of pretending that every period of abstinence was forever, simply instituted an alternating regimen of abstaining and bingeing. He would go on the wagon for a few months in order to get some work done, then go on a "bat" for a few months. The relative realism of this regimen places it just one step short of the Alcoholics Anonymous method: Lardner admitted, in effect, that he was an alcoholic, and instead of fighting it with an idealized self-control that is bound to fail, he gave in to it, surrendered the captaincy of his soul to his disease, which is unquestionably, as Bateson shows, the first step toward a cure. He also dealt extensively with his alcoholism in his stories, both incidentally, in the inclination of almost every Lardner hero to cope with an unpleasant situation by taking a drink, and explicitly, in stories like "Sun Cured" (1927) and "Cured!" (1931): as befits Lardner's doubly bound alcoholic ascesis, the former denies and the latter asserts the possibility of a cure. The step that he did not take was to join a quasi-religious support group like the AA, complete with all the rituals (pledges, confessions, testimonials) and companionship that offer the most powerful weapon against the alcoholic double bind. (William Griffith Wilson, or "Bill W.," and Robert Holbrook Smith, or "Dr. Bob S.," didn't found the AA until 1935, two years after Lardner's death.)[11]

Lardner maintained his alternating regimen until his death, with ever longer periods of abstinence toward the end owing to the tuberculosis that was diagnosed in the summer of 1926. Ring Jr. notes that "he never reached the stage of personality deterioration where there are complete reversals of behavior, as when a normally gentle man becomes aggressive and violent. All the testimony is that when drunk he remained as unsmiling and taciturn as ever, and just as intolerant of 'funny stories,' especially 'dirty' ones" (*Lardners* 190–91). This was, of course, part of the ascesis: feed the monkey on your back but don't let him get under your skin; drink for the release from inhibitions it gives you, but never allow that release to show outwardly. Drink to control the alcoholic release of inhibitions; abstain to channel the ascetic resistance to release into writing.

Of all Lardner's biographers, his son and namesake offers the best analysis of his alcoholism. This is partly, I would guess, because so much was at stake for him, because he was certainly affected and probably traumatized by his father's drinking as a child (he relates all the efforts that were made to protect the boys from their father's drinking, which meant isolating him from them and never allowing open discussion of it). But partly also it was because he has a good deal more emotional courage and acumen than either Elder or Yardley, more willingness to explore his own hurt, fear, and vulnerability than they. He notes that his father's alcoholism never occasioned any violent, recriminatory scenes between his parents. Typically, for example, Ellis "commented" on Lardner's drinking wordlessly (obeying his injunction never to say a word about him falling off the wagon) by moving into a separate bedroom. But Ring Jr. goes on to suggest that this silence might even have been worse:

> That effort probably caused as much psychic damage as the opposite kind of strain on a different sort of couple with the same problem who yell at each other in endless, futile argument. For Ellis there was the knowledge that he had intended to quit and failed to do so despite material success, growing fame and children in whom he clearly delighted. If instead of satisfaction he displayed increasing depression and the need of the drug to escape it, mightn't that be because she had fallen short of his expectations? And along with the self-doubt there was anger at the unfairness of it all, a great mass of stored anger whose existence she never even admitted to herself until she sought some psychiatric aid in the last years of her life. What she did instead of expressing how she felt was simply to remove herself, first into a bedroom of her own, and then into a separate existence whenever he was fully launched on a binge. More often than not, removing herself from him took the form of staying home instead of joining him on the town. (*Lardners* 192)

What is surprising in this is not that Ellis never expressed her anger while her husband was alive, nor that it only surfaced in the last years of her life. What is surprising is that it surfaced at all. Ellis's silent withdrawal, her repression of all anger, her self-doubt and self-blame ("mightn't that be because she had fallen short of his expectations?") — all this is ideologically prescribed for and ideosomatically inscribed on women in bourgeois patriarchy, especially for and on upper-middle-class women like Ellis Abbott Lardner. Working-class women, the Other-as-culture tells her, scream and shout at their husbands; ladies never do. So Ellis suffers in silence, puts a good face on it, tries to live her "own life" within the confines of upper-middle-class monogamy: she has a separate room to move into, for example, but she does not have the option (does it never even occur to her?) of moving out of the house, having an affair, leaving Ring.

This is, of course, the domestic bliss that feminists (as conservatives say) have "ruined" with their talk of, and political action for, equality for women. Just recently, so Reaganite conservatives think—in the seventies, during the most recent wave of feminism. As Michael Kimmel has shown, however, feminists have been undermining the holy bourgeois family throughout the bourgeois era, beginning as far back as the seventeenth century, and conservatives have been accusing women of usurping too much power for at least as long. It is not surprising, in this historical light, to find Lardner making similar conservative/patriarchal complaints about women (not about Ellis—he is too much the perfect husband for that—but about fictionalized wives) and calling for a return to "normal" conjugality. In a 1922 piece in *Wheeler's Magazine*, for example, entitled "Ring Lardner's Letter on Neglected Husbands," he first sets up a gender defense of men (and an attack on feminists, or generally on angry women) and then narrates a short short story. In the gender defense he reports on his reading in the family pages of various newspapers:

> [A]nd then if I still got time I generally always read a story about married life like "Me and My Husband" or "My Marital Adventures" or "Herbert and Pearl" and all of them is wrote by a woman from the female status and after reading a whole lot of them I will half to admit that the frail sects don't never give themselfs none the worst of it and everything is our fault and you would think that the majority of husbands should ought to spend their evenings in the electric chair counting volts.
>
> Well I don't hold no beef for most husbands but still and all they's some of us that can speak to our family without frothing at the mouth and it looks to me like it is somebody's business to take up the cuddles for the Male before all the young lady readers of the family page gets scared out of the holy bans of matrimony because they's been cases where its vice and versa.
>
> So in defence of my fellow men and for the good of the race I am going to try and write it up from the husband's pt. of view and give a fair minded version though I kindly request my readers to not think it is based on personal experience but on several typical households that has come to my tension in the last few yrs. (9)

Lardner's "wise boob" persona, his trademark in his columns and many of his most famous stories, protects him here (at least, it is de-

signed to do so) from the charge of taking these women too seriously—
of feeling personally threatened: the story "ME AND MY GAL. A Story
of Conjugal Relish" is *not* (we are to understand) about his own marriage. What makes this persona so powerful, however, and so popular
among Lardner's readers, is its patent flimsiness, the obvious fact that it
is not at all frivolous or lighthearted or superficial: that it is charged
with Lardner's deeply felt vision of gender relations (or other social
problem areas); that it really *is*, at least at some level, Lardner himself.
The murder image ("should ought to spend their evenings in the electric
chair counting volts") is familiar from the correspondence with Ellis,
where murder was the "playful" penalty for failure to write daily, or for
other deviations from the love ideal; but it is compounded in this passage
with the rabies/insanity image ("they's some of us that can speak to our
family without frothing at the mouth"). The man who killed his lover at
Smith in the news item Lardner saw back in 1909 was implicitly "insane"—at least he "went crazy," a falling off from idealized masculine
self-control—and so, in the doubly bound economy of love and death
that Lardner is cultivating, deserved to die in the electric chair. He was,
to shift to the other side of the metaphor, a rabid dog (frothing at the
mouth) who killed a rabbit and must therefore be put down. Lardner's
defense of men, in this light, is lame: some of us don't froth at the
mouth, some of us still control ourselves. Given the vicious circle of
love and violence required and maintained by this particular masculine
ascesis, Lardner's protests offer slim reassurance.

In any case, he is en route to turning the tables on women in his story:
it is told by the neglected husband of one "Emma" who, like Ellis,
withdraws from the nurturing demanded (but denied) by her emotionally
needy husband. The crisis in their marriage comes the magical three
months after their wedding, the same period the Cannons' marital bliss
lasted in "Who Dealt?"; the narrator comes home from work to find his
wife gone:

> On the linoleum layed a note witch read.
> "Am out. Get your own supper dam you."
> Stabbed to the quick I at 1st felt like setting down and haveing a good
> cry and then all of a sudden I remembered it was Thursday and no wonder
> she had taken it off [has he married his housekeeper?]. One does not
> overcome the habits of a life time in 3 short months do they?
> So I choked back my tears and set down to a lonely meal of weasel eggs
> en brochette. But a meal cannot last forever, can they? And how the hours
> drug. (9)

Typically, the wife's neglect revolves around her refusal to feed her husband: to provide the oral pleasure once provided at the mother's breast. Ellis, a rich girl, never learned to cook, and six months before their wedding he wrote to her: "Dear, you are not to worry about cooking. I would much rather eat burned things you cooked than anything anyone else cooked" (December 10, 1910). How about learning to cook yourself, Ring? It never occurs to him. In the back of his mind is his determination to make enough money to hire a cook, as his parents and Ellis's had — to elevate Ellis to the same idealized uselessness as his own mother and hers had been by their fathers — but he is still too unsure about his future to make any such promise (and it would, in any case, be several years of Ellis's cooking before Lardner could afford to hire the cook). The upper-middle-class solution to gender conflicts: throw money at them and pretend they have gone away. It is significant that, in this pointed defense of neglected husbands, Lardner has his narrator "fix" himself some supper — although I read "weasel eggs en brochette" as a cute way of saying he supped on his own bile — rather than hitting the bottle, which is to say transferring his infantile desire for the breast from the dinner his wife didn't fix to the Scotch that even a helpless baby of a man can uncork on his own. Lardner himself would have preferred the bottle to the "weasel eggs," but as he says, he is not speaking from personal experience: he is both displacing (talking about other men) and idealizing (denying the efficacy of alcohol among neglected husbands).

The rest of "ME AND MY GAL" is a tale of carefully controlled jealousy: Emma is seeing some guy, who she claims is her brother, and the narrator accepts the story so as not to alienate her, but closes the narration on a plaintive note: "But even at that one can't help from getting jealous and lonesome, can they?" The implied answer, of course, is no; but that is the kind of resigned, fatalistic answer that comes from accepting the patriarchal double bind as human nature, the kind of answer that precludes a therapeutic break or escape from bondage.

Let me end this chapter, then, by slamming the last door on Lardner's patriarchal jail cell, in preparation for my investigation in the next chapter of the ways he found to ooze between the bars. Let me turn, finally, to the great mystery (and insistently mystified issue) of Lardner criticism, his mother.

Donald Elder set the tone for treatments of Lardner's childhood in his meticulously researched 1956 biography: he interviewed many of the people who had grown up with Lardner and were still alive in the early fifties, and even Ring Jr. relies heavily on Elder's portrait of his father as a young man. But of course even meticulous research is not always proof against the whispering of the Other-as-culture:

> Everything Ring was to become in his professional life is foreshadowed in his early childhood and has its roots in his family background—his love of sports, music, theater, writing, and literature. The youngest son of wealthy and indulgent parents, he was given every advantage and diversion, and he was allowed every opportunity to display his native talents to the most appreciative audience a child could have, a large and doting family of acutely sensitive and highly cultivated people. Within that circle of security and affluence, of benevolence and amiability, the three youngest Lardner children [Rex, born 1881, Anna, born 1883, and Ringgold, born 1885] seem to have had enchanted childhoods. (Elder 10)

Part of the "security" of this "enchanted childhood," Elder tells us, was that they were not allowed to leave the yard unaccompanied until Ring was eight; however, "their restricted life," Elder says, "hardly typical of a Midwestern upbringing, does not seem to have been at all oppressive" (15). None of the three younger children attended public schools until Ring was twelve (and Rex was sixteen); their mother tutored them beginning at age five. The "enchantment" of Elder's depiction revolves almost entirely, in fact, around Lena Lardner: her "unquenchable optimism," her determination through "ceaseless activity" and "natural ebullience" to maintain "a happy disposition"; "life in the Lardner home was highspirited, for she was witty, she loved fun, and she had an inborn gift for entertaining others, grownups and children alike" (14). She "had high and unrestrained qualities of imagination" (14); if "sometimes she strayed outside the path of strict charity [outside the home] and laid herself open to the charge of meddling," nevertheless in general "she managed things with a firm and authoritative air" (15). Henry Lardner conformed fairly closely to the patriarchal masculine ideal, but Elder manages to throw a soft romantic glow over even his taciturnity by allowing Lena's "natural ebullience" to overshadow any gloom Henry might have cast:

> Mr. Lardner, kindly, indulgent, and quiet by nature, was not so close to the younger children as their mother was. He seems to have remained in the background, while Mrs. Lardner's personality dominated the house and she was the center of conviviality. As he grew older and his health failed, he grew more taciturn. Later he endured the loss of his fortune with stoicism, allowing his wife and family every luxury he could afford until his resources were depleted. But when Ring was growing up, his father was already an elderly man; he did not leave so powerful an impression on Ring as his mother did. (15)

In Henry, Elder could be describing Ring: "As he grew older and his health failed, he grew more taciturn . . . allowing his wife and family every luxury he could afford until his resources were depleted." (As Ring's health failed and it became harder to churn out columns and short stories, the Lardners of Great Neck too began to have financial difficulties.) Ring's adult masculinity is modeled almost line for line on his father's (and more broadly, of course, on the idealized capitalist father, the withdrawn, taciturn money-maker who leaves all family life to his wife); yet Elder is able to conclude that "he did not leave so powerful an impression on Ring as his mother did." The replication of gender identity is coincidental, accidental, perhaps biological (that's just the way men are, just the way Ring was); it is *not* the "impression" or stamp left on his masculinity by his father. Lardner does not grow to manhood by internalizing Henry's taciturnity, emotional withdrawal, and other defenses against Lena's (and Henry's own mother's) emotional onslaught; Lena's (and Ring's sisters') emotional onslaught is not originally generated and continually exacerbated by male defensiveness, distance, disapproval; it is all just the way Lardner (and his family) happened to be. Lardner was like his mother when he was small and like his father when he grew up: period.

Of course in another sense Elder is quite right: even if Henry Lardner's taciturn withdrawal from family life provided Ring with his most influential model for adult masculinity, he did not have the pyrotechnic impact on Ring's emotional life that Lena did. There are "normal" patriarchal families in which the father is a bossy tyrant and the mother a gray mouse; the Lardners were not one of them. The tyrannical-father-and-withdrawn-mother model is, in fact, the patriarchal norm usually stressed in feminist critiques of the family: the father is so domineering that the mother has no voice. Families like this still exist, of course, but historically the advancement of the bourgeoisie has meant a progressive shift from the older, father-dominated form of patriarchy to a more "liberal," "moral," "cultural"—in a word, more bourgeois—mother-dominated form.[12] Particularly around the middle of the nineteenth century this patriarchal maternalism (or, in James Thurber's term from Lardner's era, "momism") began to take hold in the American upper middle class, as part of an overall feminization of culture, as Ann Douglas and others have noted. The father-dominated model is increasingly perceived in bourgeois society as outdated, medieval in origin and authoritarian in nature: not democratic enough, not sensitive enough to the privatized moral and cultural values of the bourgeoisie. And so privileged women begin to assert themselves in schools, churches, and "culture" (the arts as an arena for bourgeois self-legitimation, especially music, theater, and literature), in the professions (especially teaching and nursing at first, but the circle keeps widening), and of course in the home.

Lena Lardner was a prime example of this development. She was a professional mother, but she extended her maternal professionalism to every conceivable facet of her children's lives, all the areas in which middle-class women were making strides in society: she was their teacher and nurse; she wrote sentimental poetry and encouraged her children to do the same, organized theatricals with herself as director and her three youngest children as cast, and taught them to sing and play the piano and organ (she had perfect pitch, and Ring inherited it from her); and above all she kept her children all snug inside her little (actually rather large, as houses go) cocoon and forbade them to leave the compound.

She sounds, in fact, overwhelming. Elder's talk of the "impression" she made on Ring is euphemistic; it was not an "impression," it was a deluge. She did her best (and she was extremely efficient and tirelessly energetic at it) to structure every minute of her children's waking lives, and to charge those structures with the full emotional force of her volatile personality. It is not surprising that her three youngest children (the only ones we have any detailed information about, thanks to Lardner's fame) responded to this onslaught along ideologically prescribed lines: Rex and Ring became defensively controlled, taciturn, and passive like their father, and Anna a queen bee like her mother.

Some of Lena's "ebullience," surely, can be attributed to larger psychosocial patterns, specifically the nineteenth-century bourgeois return of the patriarchal repressed: as upper-middle-class Victorian women began to find a voice—a channel of self-expression—in patriarchal society, they understandably charged the ideologically "normal" (socially approved) structures of their expression with all the force of untold centuries of repressed anger and frustration.[13] What James Thurber accusingly calls "momism" is largely the rage of repressed womanhood surging into social expression through the only acceptable channel provided for it in patriarchy: being a mom. Certainly in Elder's glowing descriptions of Lena Lardner's "ceaseless activity," which her grandson Ring Jr. (who does not remember her) and Jonathan Yardley pick up and pass on almost unchallenged,[14] we see vast quantities of carefully channeled and barely concealed anger: every stroke portrays an absolutely driven woman, a woman who can leave nothing—no situation, no child—to develop on its own, but must be constantly at it, at everything, "ceaselessly" hammering it into a shape pleasing to her, a shape that (she

hopes) will begin to satisfy her vast emotional needs. After her first visit
to the Lardner house, Ellis wrote to her sister Florence that "Mrs. Lardner is enormous and queer but very bright and a great talker" (Ring Jr.,
Lardners 48); this "enormous and queer" woman would later die, like at
least two of her sons, Rex and Ring, an alcoholic.

But some of it is more personal, more clearly restricted to Lena Lardner's life situation. She delivered a total of nine children, but three of
the first six died in childhood; the three oldest surviving children were
William (whose bad investments devastated the family's fortune) and a
boy and a girl named after their parents, Henry Jr. and Lena. (It is said
that between them the two Lena Lardners played the organ at the Niles,
Michigan, Episcopalian church for an entire century.) Lardner's biographers do not consider the death of three older siblings of particular
significance for his childhood; Elder, for example, comments only that
"Rex, Anna, and Ring were the children of her middle age, and on
them she lavished a particular devotion" (15). In *For Your Own Good*,
however, noting that the loss of children is invariably a traumatizing
experience for mothers, Alice Miller argues persuasively that one of the
typical responses to that trauma in a patriarchal culture that represses
emotion and the body—that assumes, for example, that one child can be
replaced in its mother's affections by another—is precisely the kind of
overindulgence of later children that Elder describes in Lena:

> [M]others who after losing one child have another often idealize the dead
> child (the way unhappy people frequently fantasize about the missed op-
> portunities in their lives). The living child then feels impelled to make a
> special effort and to accomplish something extraordinary in order not to
> be overshadowed by the dead sibling. But the mother's real love is usually
> directed toward the idealized dead child, whom she imagines as possessing
> every virtue—if only it had lived. The same thing happened to van Gogh,
> for instance, although only one of his brothers had died. (183)

This is not to say that Lardner was the way he was merely because his
mother had buried three of his older siblings and invested herself far too
heavily in her three youngest. This is not an area where mechanical cause
and effect apply. There are always too many other factors involved in
the formation of a child's personality to attribute everything to a single
event like the death of an older sibling. As Miller stresses, however, a
child's death, combined with a cultural taboo on grief, almost invariably
has a traumatizing impact on mothers and their surviving children.
"Many people have had a similar fate," she says. "For example, Novalis,

Hölderlin, and Kafka were also strongly influenced by the loss of several siblings, but they were all able to express their sorrow" (183). Were they? As adults, maybe—as writers, like Lardner. But were they allowed to grieve, and to articulate their grief, as children? Did their mothers and fathers grieve openly, and encourage their children to work through their feelings of loss?

This is one of the cornerstones of Miller's psychology, that mental illness is caused not by sorrow, frustration, fear, anger—emotions considered "negative" or undesirable or threatening by parents or society at large—but by the repression of those emotions, by the systematic and fear-driven blockage of all attempts to access and articulate them. The recovery and expressive reenactment of those emotions, even long after they were inscribed on the subject's body, is healing. But from Elder's depictions it seems likely that Lena Lardner would brook no overt expression of these "negative" emotions either, let alone (perish the thought) public discussion of her grief for her dead children: "Not one false note disturbed life's harmony, inside the home; and if it did, it was suppressed" (14)—by Lena. "She wanted the atmosphere of the home to be amiable and unruffled, and so it was. Beside learning and sensibility she had a firm will, and she also had a way of closing her eyes to things that were disturbing. The less agreeable aspects of family and town life were minimized, and the three youngest children probably saw nothing of them" (33).[15]

On the other hand, undeniably, Lardner did manage to "maintain appearances" virtually until he died; did support his family with his writing and also, perhaps, with his emotional self-control. More than that, as I want to show in chapter 4, he too, like Novalis, Hölderlin, and Kafka, successfully articulated his pain in his writing, and maybe in some small measure thereby mitigated it. And if it was, at least in part, his mother's pain that stunted his emotional growth, one of his legacies from her was what I want to call the (m)Other-as-child, a "natural ebullience" that may even have given him some unsuspected tools for dealing with his own (and her) repressed feelings. In particular I shall look at his delight in mimicry, which he patently learned from her, and which he turned to such powerfully artistic and potentially therapeutic use in his writing.

But let me not make too much of this healthy legacy yet—I want to plumb the depths of his unhealthy legacy first. As a child Ring seems to have modeled himself more on Lena than on Henry: he was not at all taciturn, according to all accounts, but outgoing, playful, a "natural-born" clown who was, of course, not born that way but grew into it through direct modeling on his mother. This sounds like the voice of the (m)Other-as-child in Ring, and it could well be construed (as it largely is by his biographers) in purely positive terms. There are, however, a number of factors that militate against such a reading. One is that, since Lena bestowed her special favor on people who could amuse and entertain her, there is no reason to assume that Ring clowned around through sheer boyish exuberance; it was almost certainly a defensive personality structure developed (by the baby of the family, who was also physically handicapped[16]) to win his mother's affection and attention.

A second point against a purely positive reading is the fact that he lost almost all this clownishness as an adult, becoming stern and unsmiling like his father. What happened? Shall we say that he simply "grew up"? Shall we thematize the repressive clamps he placed on laughter in adolescence and adulthood as "maturity"? The almost total repression of clownishness in Lardner's adult life suggests that his childhood clowning was driven more by fear than by a sense of humor, and that to repress his fear (of his mother's uncontrolled and therefore unpredictable emotions?) he had to control his clowning.[17] This repression he inherited somatically from his taciturn father, of course, whose taciturnity was a "normal" masculine defense against feminine emotionalism; or rather, he was spoken as its heir by the patriarchal Other-as-parent in the dual role of the paternal introject that represses emotional expression through fear and of the maternal introject that intensifies emotional expression through fear. (I should add a disclaimer at the bottom of every page: I am not blaming Lardner's mother *or* father here, merely exploring the speaking of the patriarchal Other-as-parent through them, the ways in which Lardner was constructed as a conflicted man and writer by the intertwining defenses and projections of his mother and father.)

A third point against a positive reading is that Lardner showed absolutely no inclination to re-create his "enchanted" childhood for his own children. His son reports that "Ring attributed his own weaknesses to the permissiveness of his upbringing" (*Lardners* 111), and worked hard to ensure that the "mistakes" his mother made with him were not repeated with his sons.[18] With the help of Miss Feldman, the boys' German governess, Lardner imposed a Spartan regime on his sons that could not have differed more greatly from his own childhood—at least on the surface.[19] In fact, many similarities exist. In both Ring's and his children's childhood, all unstructured "playing" was suspect (Ring Jr. recalls that they were lucky to find ten minutes a day to play on their own); the difference was that Lena structured play as determined "fun," while Ring and Miss Feldman structured it as rule-governed athletics. It does not seem unreasonable to assume that if Ring had truly been having fun in his mother's house, he would have allowed his sons to have fun in his; his obsessive need to structure his sons' childhood in superficially opposite ways, so as to preclude their having the kind of "fun" he had as a child, suggests that Lena's wit, charm, and ebullience may have felt as oppressive to the young Ring as Miss Feldman's Prussian regime did to the young Ring Jr.

This question of "fun" is a central one to any appraisal of Lardner's work, especially, of course, to one that portrays him as a humorist. Compare Yardley:

> If there is a recurrent theme in the pursuits Lena Lardner enjoyed and passed on to her children, it lies in the word "enjoyed." Notwithstanding her compassion and her strong sense of *noblesse oblige*, at heart she believed that life was supposed to be fun. For Ring, learning this lesson was a mixed blessing. Certainly it helped him maintain a healthy perspective on life; he had a splendid capacity to take things seriously but never solemnly, and his playful spirit brought laughter, warmth and happiness to everyone who knew him even remotely well, not to mention millions of readers. On the other hand, the search for fun — which was at the heart of his quixotic quest for success in vaudeville and the Broadway theater — prevented him from making the kind of wholehearted commitments necessary to the fulfillment of his artistic talents. A principal reason why he never wrote a novel, for example, no matter what justifications he gave in various letters, interviews and private conversations, was that the effort of writing one was more of a commitment than he cared to make to work he basically did not like very much; he was capable of pouring countless hours into disastrous musical comedies which — to what should be his admirers' everlasting gratitude — never saw the light of day, but he simply did not allow himself the time for a sustained effort at serious writing. In that respect, his priorities were somewhat out of kilter. And so, too, were his expectations. Though he was at heart a realist, he never quite lost Lena's firm conviction that life not merely should be but *would be* fun, and there is no question that when life became no fun at all, that was a principal cause of the disillusionment and despair that set in on him. (52–53)

This may seem a radically different, infinitely more upbeat reading of Lardner's life than mine, but in fact my reading differs from Yardley's in only one respect: I take the "fun" that Lardner supposedly had as a child and supposedly pursued all his life to have been no fun at all, ever. My sense is that "fun" was a defensive structure for Lena and remained a defensive structure for her famous son all through his life. If this is true, it does place quite a different light on the "healthy perspective" Lena's fun helped Lardner "maintain" on life—indeed, it suggests that a "healthy perspective" that has to be "maintained" is no healthier than "fun" that has to be determinedly "had." It suggests, further, that Lardner did take things much too seriously and solemnly (child rearing, profanity, grammar, storytelling), and that what humor he did manage to produce was a desperate attempt to head off despair, an anxious attempt to ease his anxiety.

In fact, the simplest (perhaps too simplistic) explanation for Lardner's failure or refusal to write a novel is that his mother never wrote one: it was a kind of "fun" to which Lena Lardner never dedicated herself. As her grandson tells us, she wrote "florid poetry and rigidly moral essays" (*Lardners* 11) and "could play her own piano arrangement of any piece of music she had heard" (12), and her son devoted his professional life to variations on these genres: doggerel verse, humorous journalistic essays (which veered into short fiction), and songs for musical comedies. All are short genres, things quickly dashed off, without extensive planning or large emotional investments. Lardner seems to have had a good deal more stick-with-itness than his mother, as is only to be expected, since the anxious son of a volatile, unpredictable mother will have grown up with a deep-seated need to stick with the sudden twists and turns of her volatility in order to keep in her good graces, and even in imitating her short-range creativity will show more long-range self-control than she ever did; but Lardner never felt at home with big creative projects requiring a steady commitment over several months (let alone years). The musical comedies he worked on were stitched together (often in collaboration with someone else) from short songs and snippets of dialogue, much like, in fact, the coherent short-story collections that are the closest things to a novel he ever wrote: the Jack Keefe books (*You Know Me Al*, *Treat 'Em Rough*, and *The Real Dope*), *Gullible's Travels*, *The Big Town*, and *Lose with a Smile*.

Lardner's conflicted feelings about his own writing can also be traced to his early experience of his mother. On the one hand, he was a professional to the hilt: a writer who always met his deadlines and took pride in crafting his essays and stories with meticulous care. On the other, he shrugged off all critical accolades, ridiculed his own writing in print (the infamous prefaces to *How to Write Short Stories* and *The Love Nest*, his mock autobiography *The Story of a Wonder Man*), and denied that he wrote for anything but money. His mother seems to have taken everything so seriously that she couldn't take any one thing seriously: to have poured herself so intensely (and with equal intensity) into every project of the moment, and to have put down one project and picked up another with such rapidity that no emotional priorities could ever be formed. There was no *rest*, no satisfaction, in any pleasure. Nothing could emerge from the frantic hustling and bustling of her existence with a more profound claim on her attention than anything else — unless it was the sheer restless force of her personality itself. Lardner, as I say, imitated this approach in his own life, but with the critical difference always instituted by imitation, especially needy, emotionally motivated imitation: self-consciousness. Too much was at stake for him to toss off poems and essays as his mother did, almost casually, even forgetfully, unself-consciously, with little or no sense that any of this *mattered*. It all mattered for Lardner, because to succeed in these areas was to imitate and thus to please his mother (the emotional motivation for imitation); but again, none of it mattered, because it didn't for her (the formal structure of imitation). To conceive of himself as a Writer, as Scott Fitzgerald did, for example, would have been to conceive of himself as better than his mother, structurally superior: someone who does not merely toss off casual pieces with one hand while the other hand is doling out charity (or whatever), someone who is dedicated not to occasional entertainment but to Art. Another way of putting this is to say that to conceive of himself as a Writer would have been to dedicate himself to posterity, to the creation of a writerly dynasty (as in fact he did, both in his own sons, all four of whom became writers,[20] and in a generation of minimalist modernists like Ernest Hemingway and journalists like Damon Runyon[21]); but he only felt comfortable dedicating himself to anteriority, to acts of loyalty to his mother.[22]

The unhealthy legacy Lardner received from his mother is painfully evident in his stories — most clearly, perhaps, in the famous misogynistic pieces, the bitter attacks on talkative women: "Zone of Quiet" (1925), "I Can't Breathe" (1926), and "Travelogue" (1926). "Zone of Quiet" in particular gives us the Lena Lardner type in fictional form: Lardner portrays Nurse Lyons as at once captivating and capricious, as a woman who demands (and gets) men's doting attentions but discards the men she collects as soon as her own precarious emotional security is threatened. As a nurse she combines the power both to care and to kill that the male infant needs and fears in his mother (nor would the oral maternal associations of "nursing" have been lost on the alcoholic Lardner). And she is specifically a "bad" nurse, a nurse who, against doctor's orders, exhausts her patients with endless vivacity — even, Lardner implies, to death: Nurse Lyons's last five patients have died. She loves them to death, especially the men:

> But it is queer, the way things have happened, and it's made me feel kind of creepy. And besides, I'm not like some of the girls and don't care. I get awfully fond of some of my cases and I hate to see them die, especially if they're men and not very sick and treat you half-way decent and don't yell for you the minute you go out of the room. There's only one case I was ever on where I didn't mind her dying and that was a woman. (72)

Lardner is controlling a lot of anger here, anger undergirded by infantile terror, at the mother who directs at her screaming infant both love and murderous rage — and the anger and terror are only intensified by the infant's subliminal perception that she defends against those contradictory emotions with "vivacity," with a breathless gush of this emotion and that, all tumbling out together. Nurse Lyons's breathless tales of nursing cry out with the double bind normatively imposed on mothers and other caretakers, of caring too much and too little, of needing so much that you pretend to need too little and minister instead to other people's needs (you "need" to be needed). Her breathless tales from the singles scene, for their part, display the kind of inconstancy of affection and attachment that Lardner needs and fears in his restlessly demanding mother, as she (Nurse Lyons) ridicules her girlfriend's boyfriend, then steals him, then ridicules him again once it turns out that she hadn't won his affections after all. Perhaps most telling of all is the male listener/narrator's response to all this: determinedly silent, decisively unanxious, he blithely refuses to identify with either the dead former patients or the maligned and manipulated boyfriend, and simply lets the words flow over him. It is the revenge of the male infant who has grown to be a man: self-control, not caring, not being moved, not feeling threatened by his caretaker's indifference and caprice. It is also, normatively, the mirror image of that indifference: an indifference couched not in a flood of insecure and inconstant words (the feminine mode) but in hard, defensive silence (the masculine mode).

Lardner's little-boy response to his mother is less patent but no less powerful, I would argue, in a story like "Haircut" (1925), to which I shall return in chapters 5 and 6. The story, narrated by a barber named Whitey, revolves around a local small-town "card" named Jim Kendall, who plays nasty tricks on the townsfolk until he attempts to rape Julie Gregg, whose boyfriend Doc Stair is one of the upright citizens in town. Doc hints to Paul Dickson, the local half-wit who has intermittent lucid spells, that a man like that should not be allowed to live; Paul goes hunting with Jim and shoots him dead. In his capacity as coroner Doc Stair pronounces the shooting accidental, and the town closes ranks; the story ends with Whitey chuckling easily that Jim certainly was a card.

This is a story full of displaced rage against the mother, both in the malicious pranks Jim plays on his wife and other women (the narrator calls him "quite a lady-killer" [28]) and in Paul's fixation on Julie. Jim and Paul both know that Julie is beyond their reach; but where Jim's frustration is channeled into emotional and finally physical violence against the inaccessible object of his desire, Paul's is redirected against anyone who would hurt her. Together, then, Jim and Paul act out the son's maternal double bind, at once hating and loving the Julie-mother, deidealizing and idealizing her, inflicting harm on her and protecting her from harm. To fill out the oedipal equation mandated by the parental double bind, we need add only the paternal Doc Stair: in the murder of Jim, the son asserts and demonstrates the father's prior claim to the mother by killing himself (or his desire for the mother), thus removing himself as a rival while maintaining the illusion of his father's innocence.

Read this way, the story becomes a psychodrama of Lardner's relationship with his mother. Whitey-as-adult-Ring gives us the defensive pose of the small-town wise boob, the ostensibly "blind" storyteller whose naive and neutral appreciation for all the characters and events in the story is his uneasy defense against accusations of complicity. Whitey introduces us to Jim-as-young-Ring, the fearful little boy who so desperately wanted to make his mother laugh that he often went overboard. Listening to Whitey's narration, we watch with increasing horror as Jim's pranks reveal more and more hostility at the unavailable mother, the demanding but self-withholding mother, whom Jim the "lady-killer" wants first to "possess," forcibly "have," ultimately to murder. Jim's attempted rape of Julie Gregg next points us to Paul-as-young-Ring, the idiot mother-idealizing son who acts as the oedipalized gun of the normative father, of society as represented by Whitey and Doc Stair and all other avatars of the proper conservative adult Ring. Having pointed Paul at Jim and disposed of the threat he posed to social stability, the paternal forces then step in to mop up the mess. Doc as coroner pronounces Jim's murder accidental, and Whitey as narrator seconds the verdict and covers the entire incident over with pleasant mindless chatter, subliminally insisting that *we didn't kill him, we had nothing to do with it, no one killed him, it was an accident, we didn't hate him, we loved him, we miss him, he was a real card.*

This subtext uneasily reveals what Lardner wants to hide: that he has killed a part of himself, the manically funny little boy who was fixated on his mother, and transformed himself into a funereally quiet, unsmiling, unjoking father who is not angry at his mother and not sexually attracted to her and not in the slightest interested in making her laugh. "Haircut" gives us Whitey, finally, as Lardner's adult defense against both his ebullient mother and the needy infantile selves that would kill to silence or defend her. The writer of the story, like the narrator, wants to be perceived as just a harmless storyteller, an unschooled yarn-spinner whose yarns have no barb, no point, no social message, no psychological depth, but are intended merely to amuse, to please, to pass the time while your hair is being cut.

4

Becoming Minor

How does a conservative, intensely repressed, mother-locked man like Lardner become a writer? How does he become a popular humorist who explores sympathetically in his columns and stories all the human traits he despises and represses in himself and his sons and painfully refrains from correcting in strangers?

This seems to me the key question in any reading of Lardner — one that must be insistently asked and, if not answered with any finality, at least complexly accommodated. It is not enough simply to idealize Lardner's loving, caring, self-sacrificing character and, while admitting that he had some faults (alcoholism, obsessive prudery, racism, defensive sexism, paternalism), to insist that this or that little idiosyncrasy "was a flaw of character in a man who otherwise had very few" (Yardley 54).

Nor is it enough to set up a myth of a gradual fall or decay from Lardner's idyllic childhood (vivacious mother, well-to-do family, sunny humor, charming small-town life) to increasing bitterness and misanthropy in his later years, as Maxwell Geismar does in *Ring Lardner and the Portrait of Folly* (1972), refracting in and through Lardner's personal development his own conservative account of modernism (the suburbanization-cum-dehumanization of a pastoral Victorian America in the early decades of this century). Geismar's willingness to recognize Lardner's violent (though carefully controlled) hatreds and hostilities make his reading more interesting in many ways, despite its cloying Mr. Rogers rhetoric, than either Elder's or Yardley's; but Geismar's Golden Age/decadence model forces him to dualize all Lardner's inner conflicts both chronologically (early/late) and socially (agrarian/[sub]urban, preindustrial/industrial, upper/lower middle class). This or that. Then and now.

None of this, neither the cheeriness of Elder and Yardley nor the divided gloom of Geismar, can explain how a man like Lardner could become a popular writer, a humorist, a beloved funnyman who mani-

105

festly empathized with the voices he was so bitterly satirizing. None of it, for that matter, can explain how a man as obsessive about prescriptively logical syntax as Lardner was could even have tried his hand at, much less made his fame and fortune by, writing in various plebeian dialects. As early as 1909, in a letter to the upper-middle-class woman he was so anxiously courting, Ellis Abbott, Lardner was experimenting with the dialectal "wise boob" persona in which he would eventually write all his columns and for which he would become nationally famous: "Well, Ellis, I suppose I am tireing you with all this talk about myself. But, Ellis, you have knew me a long time and if you hadn't of liked me you would of told me so a long time ago. You see I know you got a frank disposin, to" (December 16, 1909; *Letters* 47). Is this a purely defensive discursive strategy, like the doggerel verse he wrote to her at the beginning of their courtship? Is his wise boob persona just another doubly bound attempt to keep his conflictedly "deviant" feelings tucked away out of sight?

Obviously, I don't think so; but what else it might be is difficult to say. Lardner drifts into sports journalism more or less by accident—in his self-depictions it's a job, nothing more. He knows baseball, learns the ropes of reporting quickly, rises from lowly to ever more prestigious papers and writing assignments, without ever having a clear sense of why he is doing any of this, where it is taking him, what he wants out of it. He starts writing about the "human" side of the baseball players he travels with—their poker playing, their storytelling, their letter writing, their harmonizing—because he has to file a story every day, and many days there is no sports action to report on. Besides, the games are repetitive and the baseball statistics are well covered by other reporters: as he has his narrator complain in "Harmony" (1915), "[Waldron]'s been worked so much that there's nothing more to say about him. Everybody in the country knows that he's hitting .420, that he's made nine home runs, twelve triples and twenty-some doubles, that he's stolen twenty-five bases, and that he can play the piano and sing like Car*us*'" (181). What else is there to say about him? This narrator keeps pushing and discovers that Waldron was scouted not for his spectacular hitting, which no one had even seen, but for his ability to harmonize: like so much of Lardner's early sports reporting and later sports fiction, "Harmony" is centrifugal to baseball. It is about "something else," something out on the periphery of the sports story, something untold, unread, ignored. But Lardner doesn't know why he goes out onto that periphery. He just does. It seems like the right place to go.

In the same way, he drifts from telling more or less "true" journalistic stories about baseball players in his articles and columns from 1905 to the early teens into telling more or less "fictional" literary stories about baseball players in his columns and short stories beginning in 1913. There is no clearly marked decision to go "literary." There is no clearly marked boundary that he crosses from journalism into fiction. His journalism was "New Journalistic," novelistic, almost from the start. His fictional busher's letters were themselves virtually journalistic: Jack Keefe played for the Chicago White Sox, and was the only fictional character in Lardner's "fictionalized" American League — the rest of the players, owners, commissioners, and so on, were recognizable by name, position, and temperament from the sports page of the *Tribune*. In fact, as Yardley notes (87–88), Jack Keefe's precursor was an illiterate White Sox infielder whom Lardner called "Jack Gibbs" in his reporting on the team in 1908: presumably out of delicacy, not wanting to hurt the real player's feelings or reputation, he gave him a fictionalized name.

What draws the upper-middle-class Lardner to these "hillbillies and urban rejects," as Yardley describes them (19)? Why does he enjoy traveling with them, playing poker and singing songs and getting drunk with them? Why does he increasingly begin to mimic their speech in his stories, to reproduce the letters they write to their girlfriends and wives (they would often give him a rough draft and ask him to fix it up), to publish and comment on the poems they write? This is not the kind of life his mother raised him to lead, yet in some strange way she also prepared him for it, drove him to it — even joined him in it. In my term from chapter 2, what prepared him for it, drove him to it, and joined him in it was specifically Lardner's (m)Other-as-child: her unrestrained delight in playacting and impersonation, her "ebullient" childish willingness to assume other voices, to be spoken by them as Other, and to front the world, for however short a time, through that Other-speech. As Ring Jr. tells us, drawing apparently on stories told him by his aunt Anne, in his humorous writing Lardner

> was pursuing an interest he had shared as a child with Rex, Anne and their mother in unconscious humor and the abuse of the English language by the semiliterate. They delighted in passages of prose or verse that were intended quite seriously by their authors, and some of the funniest lines in Ring's work, especially in the earlier stories and plays, are ones the narrator or speaker doesn't realize are funny ("I treat every woman like they was my sister, till I find out different"). One of the great moments in Anne Tobin's life was her discovery of *Musings of a Coroner*, a book of privately printed verse containing a line that became a family favorite: "If by perchance the inevitable should come." (177)

Tellingly, Ring Jr. takes "unconscious humor" to consist of lines that "the narrator or speaker doesn't realize are funny," which is to say, *not*-conscious humor — just as Lardner's critics read the "unconscious narration" of "Who Dealt?" in terms of the narrator's failure to realize the import of her words. This is no doubt the ordinary sense of the phrase "unconscious humor." But what *is* funny about "I treat every woman like they was my sister, till I find out different," or "If by perchance the inevitable should come"? In the latter there is the logical incongruity between chance and inevitability, of course, but is that it? Is that all that makes us laugh in the line — bad logic? There is also the redundancy of "by" and "per" — is this funny? Is the redundancy alone humorous? Obviously not: a formalist reading of unconscious humor is not going to get us very far. Does the humor lie, then, in the speaker's failure to notice the formal problems, his or her *lack* of consciousness? That would ring rather hollow to me, the empty laughter of a snob sneering at the stupid; while there may have been an element of that in the Lardners' delight in unconscious humor, that cannot be all. If it had been, Lardner's humorous writing would have been very different — stilted, unfeeling, even antipathetic.

The calm intensity and conflicted sympathy that pervade his humor suggest that there must be more. The contradiction and repetition in "If by perchance the inevitable should come" point clearly, in fact, to the unconscious in Freud's strong sense: not unknowing but a deeper level of knowing, a realm of mind in which all the elements we attempt so nervously to sort out with our conscious reason are jumbled up together, using the emotional proximity of contradictory elements to radiate ambivalence, for example, and the proliferation of similar elements to radiate intensity. (There is no repetition, Gertrude Stein once wrote, speaking for or as the unconscious; there is only insistence.) "I treat every woman like they was my sister, till I find out different" suggests a similar unconscious inability to place people and relationships, a dreamlike porosity of labels that makes it impossible to know (remember, anticipate) whether a given woman is your sister or not, or whether "every woman" is (are?) singular or plural. All the careful conscious self-control of the "liberated" man, who would eradicate every trace of offensive sexism (and sexualization) from his relations with women through the idealization of all women as "sister," is here washed away in the grotesque inanity of the unconscious.

What emerges in unconscious humor is the uncanny, the dark dreamworld in which it is possible for something to be at once "perchance" and "inevitable," in which inevitability is chancy and chance is inevitable — in which it is possible for a woman to be at once "my sister" and "different," "every woman" and all women, she and "they." That uncanny assault on our conscious reason generates both delight and fear, delightful play as a defense against fear, fear as a check on playful delight. In Freud's reading, humor is the id's way of beating the censor—the superego, the paternal introject as Ideal-I, the combined forces of reason, critical judgment, and suppression—through the playful release of nonsense. To put that in revised Lacanian terms, for Freud the Other-as-father coaches us to dread the uncanny, to fence it in, while the Other-as-child coaches us to revel in it, hurl it in the introjected father's face. Since both speak simultaneously, both demand a coherent and exclusive response to their unheard command, the clash of this double command (this doubly bound Other-speech) explodes physically into laughter.

As always with Freud and Lacan, however, this formulation presupposes the silence or absence of the mother. What difference does it make for Lardner's humor that his mother acts on him all through his life, both in her official (socially approved) capacity as doubly bound and double-binding Other-as-mother and in her unofficial (secretly rebellious) capacity as unbinding (m)Other-as-child? For this we must move beyond Freud and Lacan to a reading of engenderment that is fully cognizant of the impact of the mother. Julia Kristeva, for example, in "Place Names," argues that "maternity knots and unknots paranoia—the ground on which hysterics stand" (280)—adumbrating by her knotting and unknotting precisely the official/binding and unofficial/unbinding effects of patriarchal maternity (maternal introjects) that I distinguished earlier. Kristeva suggests that the child be(come) the Real (in Lacan's sense) through which we analyze our own infantile language, the richly infantile elements of any adult speech: "We would then be concerned with the attentiveness that the adult, through his still infantile sexuality [i.e., through that core of his or her sexuality that remains infantile, through somatically stored infantility], is able to perceive in the discourse of a child (boy or girl) while it refers him [or her] to that level where his [or her] 'own' language is never totally rationalized or normated according to Cartesian linguistics, but where it always remains an 'infantile language'" (278). This seems a useful analytical motto for this chapter: we concern ourselves with the adult's infantilized perception of the child's discursive attentiveness. Or, more simply still: we attend to the child in our own discourse. We become, or learn to inhabit, the attentive child in our own (or any) discourse.

And, since Kristeva explicitly inserts the "child" into a dialectical relation with the "mother"—in fact defines the "mother" as "a being for whom the One, and therefore the Other, is not taken for granted" (279)—this implicitly requires that we become, or learn to inhabit, the attentive (m)Other-as-child in our own (or Lardner's) discourse. Like Freud and Lacan (and other feminist psychoanalysts such as Chodorow), Kristeva situates this mother-child dialectic in the preoedipal or (in Kristeva's Lacanian terms) presymbolic stage: the father, for Freud and Lacan and the feminists who follow them, doesn't appear on the scene until the third year of life, and then strictly in terms of *"negation* and the designation of *protagonists of enunciation* (personal pronouns)" (290). Kristeva is interested in what she calls the "semiotic disposition," that preoedipal/presymbolic "libidinal-signifying organization in infancy" that is "grasped by the adult only as regression—jouissance or schizophrenic psychosis" (276). I have argued elsewhere[1] that this preoedipal/oedipal split, this relegation of the father to the third year of life (and then in terms of negation), only perpetuates the myth of patriarchal parenting: it not only fails to allow for emancipated paternal bonding with the newborn infant but inaccurately depicts the patriarchal realities of paternal withdrawal from the infant. But in fact, Kristeva's exclusive feminist concern with the mother-child dialectic is useful in a discussion of Lardner's humor. Her analysis of the interplay of orality and anality in the generation of infant laughter, for example, offers an excellent explanation for the laughter of an emotionally blocked alcoholic:

> Orality plays an essential role in this primary fixation-sublimation: appropriation of the breast, the so-called "paranoid" certainty of the nursing infant that he has been in possession of it, and his ability to lose it after having had his fill. What should not be obscured is the importance of the anal "instinctual drive" from this period on: the child has a secure anal discharge while, balancing that loss, it incorporates the breast. Anal loss, accompanied by considerable expenditure of muscular motility, combined with the satisfaction of incorporating the breast, probably encourages projecting facilitation into this visible or audible point that gives the infant a glimpse of space and produces laughter. (284)

Or, to paraphrase for Lardner: "Writing, accompanied by considerable expenditure of muscular motility, combined with the satisfaction of alcoholic intake, probably encourages projecting facilitation into this visible or audible point that gives Lardner's (m)Other-as-child a glimpse of space and produces laughter." Writing *was* hard work for Lardner; he never enjoyed doing it, but he did a lot of it and made (and spent, though only on others) a lot of money doing it. Drinking was not hard work; he enjoyed it immensely but restrained himself in order to be able to write. The pushing out of words was always delicately balanced in Lardner's professional life with the taking in of whiskey.

This delicate balance does not seem able to account for Lardner's humor, however, until we add to the equation his mother—that "enormous" and "queer" "great talker" (as Ellis described her) who also, like at least two of her sons, died an alcoholic. And indeed Kristeva goes on, problematically I think, to reinscribe the laughter-producing tension between anal loss and breast incorporation in the blockages and releases of the mother: "We have either a riant, porous boundary, or a blocking barrier of earnest sullenness—the child gets one or the other from its mother. Either a hysterical mother defying her own mother through parental identification, or a mother subjugated to her's [*sic*], perpetually seeking symbolic recognition. Either one determines, as early as this 'first point of psychic organization' [in the first three months of life], attitudes whose peaks lie in imaginative freedom on the one hand, and ritualistic obsession on the other" (284–85). The problem here is that this tension between laughter and sullenness, porosity and blockage, defiance and subjugation, imaginative freedom and ritualistic obsession is never so neatly divided into "kinds" of mother(ing); rather, the tension is built into the patriarchal double bind of maternity. Some mothers may, because of their own childhoods and marriages (and class and race and historical moment—any number of social variables), lean toward defiance, others toward subjugation; but it seems naive to me to say that "the child gets one *or* the other from its mother." Lena Lardner, for example, leaned most strongly toward what Kristeva calls hysterical defiance; but the very fact that she did so through parental identification, as Kristeva suggests, indicates her continuing subjugation to patriarchal authority (she is still spoken by the official Other-as-parent). And at the same time, the very fact that she was able to channel her hysterical defiance to the Other-as-parent (which still powerfully spoke her) across a "riant, porous boundary"—indeed, was able to keep the boundary riant and porous *through* her hysterical defiance—indicates her potential for slipping through the subjugating net of parental identification.

And if this inner division in Lena was then channeled into her son, we should expect to find in Lardner's adult life (and writing) "attitudes whose peaks lie in imaginative freedom on the one hand, and ritualistic obsession on the other"—that is, *both* imaginative freedom *and* ritualistic obsession. The two "peaks" are always intermeshed in Lardner. His imaginative freedom is always obsessive and ritualistic, and his defiance to subjugating patriarchal norms may find ways of slipping out of parental identification, but it is always hysterical. His porosities are always partially blocked, his laughter is always partially smothered in sullenness.

It may have been largely historical accident that channeled Lardner into sports journalism rather than, say, cultural journalism or (less likely, given his childhood and adolescence in Niles, Michigan) writing for the musical stage. Certainly, once he had made his mark in sports journalism, he quickly began to move into those other areas as well, with varying success but unflagging intensity. In line with his professional profile as "accidental writer" (Sheed 11), however, he went with what he had: finding himself on trains and in locker rooms and hotels with baseball players, he began to internalize their voices, to bring them into the dramas his (m)Other-as-child was staging in his dialogized body, to let himself be spoken by them *as* his Other-as-baseball-player—or, if that sounds farfetched, by them as his Other-as-plebe.

Lardner had, after all, fallen socially and economically from the upper middle to the lower middle class. More important, while with his father's impoverishment he became lower-middle-class in economic fact, in psychological fact (in the speaking of his social Other-as-culture) he remained upper-middle-class: trained to be rich, forced to be poor. Working as a mail carrier, bill collector, and sports reporter, he was a rich man('s son) in a poor man's job. This might have made him disdainful, haughty, superior, of course, but significantly, it didn't; the baseball players he traveled with accepted him as one of their own, respecting his emotional distance (as a recognizably and acceptably masculine feature) without interpreting it as social distance. Needless to say, he did feel social distance from the players—he was raised rich and was reasonably well educated, while most of them were functionally or literally illiterate farmers' sons—but that distance did not manifest itself as disdain. It manifested itself, in both his personal relations with the players and his journalism, as his own peculiar blend of irony and sympathy, ridicule and understanding—a blend that looked to the players like affectionate banter, and that they accepted and relished as such. It wasn't that, or it wasn't only that; it was, for one thing, steeped in an inward clash of self-deprecation and self-control and liberating laughter; but in some sense it might as well have been. (Perhaps that is what affectionate banter is.) However conflicted, Lardner was not a man who made enemies. He was never hated or resented—at any social stratum.

Lardner's empathy with what his parents would have seen as his social inferiors did not in any case begin with his father's impoverishment. As soon as his mother let him out of her compound, he began hanging around with kids from the wrong side of the tracks, and when he was fourteen and fifteen he began frequenting local bars. He never thought of this as rebelliousness, or even as slumming. It was never a way of rejecting his parents' life-style. This suggests to me that he was unconsciously encouraged to cultivate his Other-as-plebe by his (m)Other-as-child (or vice versa?): that part of his mother's intensely conflicted "ebullience" was a deep-seated ambivalence about her own class origins and behavior, and that she passed this ambivalence on to her children. Lardner only became ambitious, remember, when he met Ellis, who may have stimulated the Other-as-patrician in him. His subsequent rise to fame and fortune was marked and driven by that same ambivalence, the frantic (though denied) attempt to regain his father's lost wealth through the speaking of the Other-as-plebe, the wise boob that became his journalistic trademark.

Not that the Other-as-plebe always speaks in Lardner's writing as the wise boob. The wise boob persona does narrate (and dominate the conversations in) some of his fiction — notably *Gullible's Travels* — but Lardner has a wide range of plebeian voices, from the boastful boob of the Jack Keefe books to various working-class voices ("Haircut," "Mr. Frisbie"), to various upwardly mobile female voices ("Who Dealt?," "I Can't Breathe," "Dinner," "Zone of Quiet"), to various child voices ("Bob's Birthday," and "The Young Immigrunts" by a five-year-old "Ring Lardner, Jr."). The striking thing about this list is that all the voices on which Lardner's popularity and fame rest are not-his: they are the voices of other people, and specifically of other *kinds* of people. Lardner's writing is spoken by the Other-as-plebe in him, but that Other ranges across the social spectrum from the working class to the upwardly mobile middle class (usually that portion of the middle class that has only recently arrived there, and still talks like the working class — a spectrum I am referring to loosely as "plebeian" and will be fine-tuning in chapter 5), from men to women, and from adults to children.

In *A Thousand Plateaus* Gilles Deleuze and Felix Guattari coin the term *xenoglossia* for roughly this sliding or stammering one's way out of the rule-governed speech of the Standardized Subject into unruly Other-speech: it is "a power of forgetting permitting one to feel absolved of the order-words one has followed and then abandoned in order to welcome others; a properly ideal or ghostly capacity for the apprehension of incorporeal transformations; an aptitude for grasping language as an immense indirect discourse" (84). All Lardner's best work is restlessly xenoglossic in this sense: it forgets the order-words that drive his correctness anxiety, absolves him of his obsession about grammar and syllogistic articulation, and haunts him with the ghostly speech of plebe-

ian, female, and childish Others, of "minor(itie)s" in the broadest sense
of that word (those words), all those Others whose speech is silenced or
muted in adult middle-class male ("majoritarian") society.

This suggests an expansion and modification of my stammering
dummy term from chapter 2, and a more encompassing form of my
tentative dummy term from the previous paragraphs (Other-as-plebe): if
"Who Dealt?" was stammered out by the dummy as Other-as-child, it
might make sense to say that Lardner's best writing was stammered out
by the dummy as Other-as-minor(ity), by the internalized (somatized)
voices of the semiliterate lower class, of women, and of children. Lardner becomes a minor writer by letting himself be spoken by the Other-as-
minor(ity), by slipping out onto a somatic periphery undefined by the
normative Other-as-majority and becoming peripheralized, becoming
what Deleuze and Guattari call "minoritarian." Majority, they argue,
has nothing to do with numbers, either of people (the larger group as
majority, the smaller as minority) or of years (adults as majors, children
as minors):

> Majority implies a constant, of expression and content, serving as a stan-
> dard measure by which to evaluate it. Let us suppose that the constant or
> standard is the average adult-white-heterosexual-European-male-speaking
> a standard language (Joyce's or Ezra Pound's Ulysses). It is obvious that
> "man" holds the majority, even if he is less numerous than mosquitoes,
> children, women, blacks, peasants, homosexuals, etc. That is because he
> appears twice, once in the constant and again in the variable from which
> the constant is extracted. Majority assumes a state of power and domina-
> tion, not the other way around. It assumes the standard measure, not the
> other way around. . . . A determination different from that of the con-
> stant will therefore be considered minoritarian, by nature and regardless
> of number, in other words, a subsystem or an outsystem. (*Plateaus* 105)

It is obvious also that Jay Gatsby, for instance, holds the majority,
even if he is less numerous than the Jack Keefes of minor American
fiction in the twenties. Jay Gatsby is a "hillbilly" (not so different in his
origins from Jack Keefe) who has assimilated himself to the dominant
upper middle class, a minor character who has re-created himself in
terms of majority; Jack Keefe and his ilk remain insistently, almost
pugnaciously, minor. *The Great Gatsby* is a slight and rather overwritten
romantic novel of manners (compare it to *Ulysses* or *The Sound and the
Fury*, for example[2]) that has been canonized as a major American novel,
largely owing to its majoritarian plot (tragic), style (elegiac), and characterization (upper-middle-class); *You Know Me Al* is a slight and un-
derwritten epistolary fiction (short-story collection? novel?) that resists

classification *except* as minoritarian: episodic or nonexistent plot, semi-literate style, working-class or lower-middle-class characterization. By trusting his ear more than his ego, by letting the minoritarian voices that sounded in his head take him where they would, even if that meant stammering out tiny little stories and sketches and fragments that earned him money but little satisfaction, Lardner clung tenaciously to the sloping back of literary minority.

He was, to put it in traditional terms, a minor writer who employed a minor language to write about minor subjects—a glorified journalist who wrote about sports and petty suburban contretemps in substandard American dialect. This majoritarian derogation of Lardner was in fact one he himself advanced (speaking as his Other-as-majority), and one that his influential admirers (Fitzgerald, Hemingway, Wilson) reluctantly shared; but in the inner clash between the Other-as-majority and the Other-as-minority, Lardner always insistently inclined toward the latter. He had very little desire (if any) to become a great American novelist—to become a "major" writer. He insisted on remaining a glorified journalist, a minor writer, a hack who ridiculed his own literary productions and pretensions in the notorious prefaces to *How to Write Short Stories* and *The Love Nest* and himself as public figure in *The Story of a Wonder Man*.

Was this self-derogation? Certainly, as I showed in chapter 3, Lardner was neurotically humble, modest, self-deprecating, careful never to let anyone think that he thought highly of himself; this was the dark or flip side of being spoken by the Other-as-majority, his recognition that he did not and could not live up to that majoritarian Other's standards (and hence his defensive decision not to try). But he also reveled in his minor status, his popularity, the value of his work as popular entertainment. He didn't (only) settle for that value; he didn't (only) wield it as defense: he reveled in it. There was a powerful and, I would argue, healthy, life-enhancing, minoritarian impulse in him. He not only refused to aspire to become a major writer; in some sense he aspired to become a minor one.

This sounds like condescension, perhaps. It sounds like an admission that "my" author is not as great as someone else's—and thus, perhaps, that I am not a major critic (minor writers attract minor critics), or if I am, that I am wasting my time on Lardner. The problem is that these terms don't really work with Lardner, as all his critics sense and attempt to articulate. Lardner is unmistakably a minor writer. If anyone is, he is. This identification is more social, institutional, ideological than it is "essential"—Lardner is not transcendentally minor—but within those social, institutional, and ideological parameters the identification seems to me beyond question. There is, however, something else about him, something that makes his critics want to push at the parameters. He was not, for example, *dismissably* minor. He was not minor as his mother was minor, for example, or as Stephen Gale in "The Maysville Minstrel" is minor. He was minor as James Thuber and Dorothy Parker were minor—or, more boldly, as Mark Twain and Harriet Beecher Stowe were minor, as Kurt Vonnegut and Alice Walker are minor. He was the kind of minor writer whom major critics want to assimilate to majority, want to canonize as major writers—but somehow cannot. He was the kind of minor writer who resists majoritarian readings, who refuses to be forced into the major author straitjacket.

He is, in fact, Deleuze and Guattari's kind of minor writer, a heroic, tough-minded, nomadic minor writer, one of a select group that they insist are "the greatest, the only greats" (*Plateaus* 105)—an attempt to push at the institutional envelope which indicates a direction but really doesn't solve much. To call minor writers "the only greats" is to perform a rather simplistic Nietzchean transvaluation of critical hierarchies: it is merely to reverse the conventional equation of great writing with major writers. "Greatness" in writing is, after all, structurally parallel to "majority" in writing: both are social constructs associated with a dominant and therefore normative group. To call minor writers "the only greats" is really to say no more than that the writers whom majoritarian critics exclude from the canon are by definition (by the very fact of exclusion) better than those they include—an obvious inanity that gets us nowhere (the mystique of the outlaw or the outcast).

In a slightly less simplistic reading, Deleuze and Guattari might be taken to be claiming not that only minor writing is great, but that great writing is always minoritarian. This is a still polemical but at least defensible position: it would imply that minoritarian writing (like Twain's, say, or Kafka's, or Kleist's) may occasionally be canonized, majoritized, and this may entail a systematic trivialization or out-and-out repression of those minoritarian impulses in the work that keep it vital; but even when elevated to major status, minoritarian writers remain greater than those who aspire to majority. Kafka is greater than Musil, therefore; Twain is greater than Henry James; Lardner is greater than Fitzgerald.

Implicit in this reading of minority is also a constructivist bias: "There are not, therefore, two kinds of languages but two possible treatments of the same language" (103). There are, to paraphrase that, not two kinds of writers but two ways of reading the same writers: there are majoritarian and minoritarian readings of Twain and James, Lardner and Fitzgerald. Certainly James and Fitzgerald aspired to major writer status as Twain and Lardner did not, but if aspiration to majority were the only requirement for inclusion in the canon, its ranks would swell a thousandfold. To become a major writer, one must be "majoritized" by a major critic or by a majoritarian critical institution: one must be reduced (in critical books and articles and in college classrooms) to major plots, styles, characters, symbols, and themes; one must be universalized, analytically repressed, thematically consolidated and controlled, assimilated to dominant ideologies of taste and style, "normalized," critically purged of everything that deviates or differs from esemplastic norms. Deleuze and Guattari portray the minor writer as one who can "make language stammer, or make it 'wail,' stretch tensors through all of language, even written language, and draw from it cries, shouts, pitches, durations, timbres, accents, intensities" (104)—but of course no writer can be recognized in these terms until a minoritarian critic(ism) has made the *writer*'s language stammer or wail, stretched tensors through it, drawn from it insistently minoritarian cries and shouts, timbres and accents, and the rest.[3] As Deleuze and Guattari insist:

> Minor languages are characterized not by overload and poverty in relation to a standard or major language, but by a sobriety and variation that are like a minor treatment of the standard language, a becoming-minor of the major language. The problem is not the distinction between major and minor language; it is one of a becoming. It is a question not of reterritorializing oneself on a dialect or a patois but of deterritorializing the major language. Black Americans do not oppose Black to English, they transform the American English that is their own language into Black English. Minor languages do not exist in themselves; they exist only in relation to a major language and are also investments of that language for the purpose of making it minor. One must find the minor language, the dialect or rather idiolect, on the basis of which one can make one's own major language minor. That is the strength of authors termed "minor," who are in fact the greatest, the only greats; having to conquer one's own language, in other words, to attain that sobriety in the use of a major language, in order to place it in a state of continuous variation (the opposite of regionalism). It is in one's own language that one is bilingual or multilingual. Conquer the major language in order to delineate in it as yet unknown minor languages. Use the minor language to *send the major language racing*. Minor authors are foreigners in their own tongue. If they are bastards, if they experience themselves as bastards, it is due not to a mixing or intermingling of languages but rather to a subtraction and variation of their own language achieved by stretching tensors through it. (104–5)

This sounds very much like Lardner's literary project: becoming a foreigner in the upper-middle-class American English of his childhood, finding the dialect(s) on the basis of which he could make that major language minor, finding the "becoming-minor" of that major language and speaking it, or allowing himself in the voices of various narrators to be spoken by it, and "send[ing] the major language racing." Lardner *becomes* a minor writer by becoming minoritarian. This is quite a different process from James Gatz transforming himself into Jay Gatsby or F. Scott Fitzgerald transforming himself into the author of *The Great Gatsby*. Gatsby models himself on a social abstraction—the rich man, the self-made man—and becomes an empty parody of that abstraction ("Then came the war, old sport" [66]). Fitzgerald models himself on major writers and, somewhat uneasily, like Gatsby on West Egg, joins their rank. Lardner doesn't model; he listens. "Where do they get that stuff about me being a satirist?" he complains. "I just listen" (Ring Jr., *Lardners* 175). Fitzgerald becomes majoritarian by modeling; Lardner becomes minoritarian by listening.[4] To model yourself on an ideal is to empty yourself, to assimilate yourself to the nothingness of abstraction; to listen is to become other(s), to fill yourself with otherness.

"But at this point," Deleuze and Guattari cry, "everything is reversed. For the majority, insofar as it is analytically included in the abstract standard, is never anybody, it is always Nobody—Ulysses—whereas the minority is the becoming of everybody, one's potential becoming to the extent that one deviates from the model. There is a majoritarian 'fact,' but it is the analytic fact of Nobody, as opposed to the becoming-minoritarian of everybody" (105). Jay Gatsby *is* Nobody. He is Benjamin Franklin and Jesus Christ—and thus Nobody. He is the American self-made man—and thus Nobody. He assimilates himself to his ideal, incarnates himself as Platonic Son of Man, ascetically, like Benjamin Franklin, by paring off idiosyncrasies, leaving Nothing. Instead of listening to Franklin's voices (did he ever read anything? did he ever listen to anyone?), Gatsby imitated Franklin's asceses. Jack Keefe is not exactly everybody; he is, as Deleuze and Guattari suggest, the "becoming-minoritarian of everybody."

In fact, interestingly, in some sense *You Know Me Al* revolves around Lardner's (and our own) "becoming-minor-league" in and through the voice of the busher Jack Keefe—specifically, around Lardner's crossings of the porous boundary between the "majors" and the "minors" in professional baseball. The first story in the collection, "A Busher's Letters Home," gives us the epistolary self-portrait of a minor-league pitcher who gets his big chance in the majors and (by the end of the story) blows it: "You could of knocked me over with a feather," he writes his hometown friend Al, "when the old man come up to me and says Jack

I've sold you to the Chicago Americans" (21), the American League team in Chicago, the White Sox.

> I didn't have no idea that anything like that was coming off. For five minutes I was just dum and couldn't say a word.
>
> He says We aren't getting what you are worth but I want you to go up to that big league and show those birds that there is a Central League on the map. He says Go and pitch the ball you been pitching down here and there won't be nothing to it. He says All you need is the nerve and Walsh or no one won't have nothing on you. (21)

This is every minor-league player's dream: to make it to the "bigs," the "show," the "big leagues," the majors. The minor leagues consist of "farm teams" owned by the major-league teams, and are thought of as a kind of secondary, a second-string team, from which the majors pick the best players whenever they need someone new, or to which they send a player with promise who needs to have some rough edges rubbed off. Since even in Lardner's day the major-league teams drafted many of their new players not from the minors but directly from various school and club teams (nowadays largely from college teams), the minors were and are actually a kind of side rail off the main track, or a stagnant pond off the mainstream. As a result they run rife with unorthodox minoritarian behavior: three-fingered pitchers, fat home-run hitters, Cuban second basemen who speak no English, and so on. There is, in fact, a whole minoritarian mythology surrounding the minors, which is celebrated in determinedly minor(itarian) novels like Bernard Malamud's *The Natural*, Philip Roth's *The Great American Novel* (ironically undermining the majoritarian American novelist's dream in his title), and Donald Hays's *The Dixie Association*, and in Ron Shelton's gloriously minoritarian movie from 1988, *Bull Durham*. It is, in fact, a carnivalesque tradition that parallels and in some ways overlaps with the American tradition of the carny, the circus: nomadic, populist, grounded deeply in errors, laughter, and the grotesque. The majoritarian ideology of competition is suspended in the pact between players and audience: the players think of themselves as trying to win, but they never do (except by freaks of nature, which is to say, never by actually *beating* the other team), and subliminally they know that the fans don't want them to win anyway, so they don't really try. The ball seems bewitched: it shoots through their legs or bounces off their heads; pitches fly wild and strike the announcer or the mascot; the rare home-run ball hits a passing bird, which falls into left field dead while the ball veers foul; outfielders crash into each other and the ball drops between them. All the players are powerfully superstitious, but their various magics never work — unless to confirm and continue the bewitchment, which seems cast on them by their fans.

This minoritarian minor-league mythology has to some extent infected the majors as well: in New York, for example, the majoritarian New York Yankees were resisted and opposed in the popular imagination (though not in league play, except in the World Series) by the minoritarian Brooklyn Dodgers,[5] until the Dodgers moved to Los Angeles in 1958 and were replaced in the popular imagination (in 1962) by the minoritarian New York Mets, the grotesquely bad team that couldn't do anything right (and were loved for it by their devoted fans). And Lardner carries much of this minoritarian spirit into his busher stories: Jack Keefe nervously, defensively breaks down the mythic barriers between the minors and the majors by quoting his old manager ("Go and pitch the ball you been pitching down here and there won't be nothing to it") and insisting on his own integrity as a pitcher despite the change: "I will just give them what I got and if they don't like it they can send me back to the old Central and I will be perfectly satisfied" (22) — satisfied, in Deleuze and Guattari's term, with "becoming-minoritarian." By the end of this story he does just that, and while he returns to the majors in the beginning of the second story, the collection as a whole teeters constantly, both in Keefe's life and in his voice, in the middle territory between the minors and the majors:

> Manager Callahan is a funny guy and I don't understand him sometimes. I can't figure out if he is kidding or in ernest. We road back to Oakland on the ferry together after yesterday's game and he says Don't you never throw a slow ball? I says I don't need no slow ball with my spitter and my fast one. He says No of course you don't but if I was you I would get one of the boys to learn it to me. He says And you better watch the way the boys fields their positions and holds up the runners. He says To see you work a man might think they had a rule in the Central League forbidding a pitcher from leaving the box or looking toward first base.
>
> I told him the Central didn't have no rule like that. He says And I noticed you taking your wind up when What's His Name was on second base there to-day. I says Yes I got more stuff when I wind up. He says Of course you have if you wind up like that with Cobb on base he will steal your watch and chain. I says Maybe Cobb can't get on base when I work against him. He says That's right and maybe San Fransisco Bay is made of grapejuice. Then he walks away from me. (32–33)

What is striking about this interchange (and characteristic of the collection) is Lardner's discursive volatility, his sliding across the major-minor boundary in both directions. In the ironic slippage of Manager Callahan's sarcasm, for example, Jack both is and is not back in the Central League. In both his poor fielding and in his misunderstanding of the manager's sarcasm he still is (and, as the story titles suggest, always will be) a "busher," a bush leaguer or minor-league player who has not yet learned to move off the pitcher's mound, to field bunts, to cover or throw to first, to go into the stretch when he has a runner on, or to understand the "sophisticated" lingo of the big show and the big city. He is from the "bush," the "sticks," and everything he does and says shows it. At the same time, however, he is not in the bush leagues any longer—there *is* a difference—and his bush-league habits are going to get him in trouble. Ty Cobb is going to get on first and steal second and third—as in fact he does a month later. Keefe had better shape up or he is not going to last long in the majors. Instead of having him shape up and stay in the majors or fail to shape up and drop back to the minors, however, Lardner has it both ways: Keefe does some bouncing back and forth, but mainly stays in the majors with all his minor-league attitudes and speech habits.

If fact, it is even more complicated than that. In some sense Keefe's minor-league attitudes are themselves majoritarian, lordly, haughty: he is the pitcher; he throws the fast balls that bring the batters to their knees; let the other players field the ball. The pitcher is, of course, the star of any baseball team—at least until he has to go to bat, which he no longer does in the American League and college ball—and Keefe feels it is demeaning for a man of his stature to have to run after bunts. The pitcher does look silly fielding a bunt: running all bent over for a little dribbling hit that won't even come to him, then throwing to first over the receding back of the runner. Ty Cobb, the Detroit Tiger who in some sense was a "Dodger" (sneaky, fast on his feet), the holder of the stolen-base record (892 career) for over half a century, is the minoritarian major leaguer, the "plebeian" hitter who will "steal your watch and chain."

In part, of course, this is a "class" distinction built into baseball: the pitcher is the lord who tries to strike out (even, in extreme cases, to bean and kill) the batter; the batter is the plebe who tries to steal from the pitcher. But Lardner replicates this distinction in the story's discourse as well: Jack Keefe is the lord who doesn't need to stoop to figuring out whether his manager "is kidding or in ernest"; Callahan is the plebe who has to challenge Keefe's authority by indirection (irony).

In both cases, in Keefe's relation both to Cobb and to Callahan, there is a significant major-minor crossover: Keefe is the pitcher and Cobb is the batter, but Keefe is also the rookie and Cobb is the star (still today thought of as the greatest offensive baseball player in the history of the game); and Callahan is the manager, the man with the authority to play or bench Keefe, but Keefe is a pitcher, without whose arm Callahan has nothing to manage. Keefe's lordly refusal to interpret Callahan's irony masks a plebeian inability to do so, and insecurity about that failure; Callahan's irony ("maybe San Fransisco Bay is made of grapejuice") masks his contempt for Keefe's idle boasting, but the very fact that he has to mask it suggests that to "manage" his players he has to be very careful not to alienate them.

Even more significant, perhaps, is the major-minor convergence: all three men, after all, busher, manager, and major-league star, are plebes whose speech and occupation (which was much less respectable in the teens and twenties than it is today) mark them indelibly as "minorities," minor leaguers in the larger game of American society. All the substandard or "non-U" (non-upper-class) markers in Keefe's letters — misspellings ("ernest," "road back"), double negatives, number incongruence ("the way the boys fields their positions," "I says"), and so on — mark *all* the characters in this book, whether minor- or major-league, as minor.

Jack Keefe, you might say, is a minor character in his own story: his narrative voice minoritizes him. Jack is so driven by his needs and fears, his insecurities and self-aggrandizements, that the stories he narrates strand the reader, as it were, in a rhetorical periphery or backwash — in the "bush" or "sticks" of fictional discourse, cut off from that highly clarified contact with hegemonic social reality that constitutes majoritarian fiction as "realism." The reader, looking for Lardner, becomes Al, that hometown cipher who supposedly "knows" Jack ("You know me Al") but doesn't, and can't — not only because Jack doesn't know himself, but because Al doesn't know himself either. In becoming Al, the reader too falls into self-confusion, falls into that state of mind all of us harbor within us in which we know nothing, nothing makes sense, the world is a flurry of shifting shapes and colors, we are not ourselves, we recognize no one around us, or recognize them as in a dream, with disorienting gaps between a distanced robotic knowledge (of names, relationships, significances) and felt integrity. If the reader-as-Al knows Jack(-as-Lardner?), it is the knowing of the Other-as-minority, for which (whom) Jack is at once all too familiar (his fears, his boasting, and his directional shifts are our own, we speak him, we use his first-person pronouns) and utterly alien (he is not a person at all, he is a succession of masks, of behaviors, coherent only in their incoherence). I become Al, and I become Jack, and in becoming the two of them I lose my I, or find it mired in mirrorings: Jack becomes an I in his specular letters to Al, who exists only as the reflection of Jack's "wishes," in the sense both of his instructions (get me a house, get me out of my lease) and of his hometown wish fulfillment (I wish I was there with you, I wish you could be here with me). In placing me between them, Lardner alienates me from my majoritarian self, places me in a becoming-minoritarian that sends my critical reason racing, shunts me too out onto the periphery of my reading. I become minoritarian not only in the sense that I am made to identify with plebeian correspondents (though that is part of it too), but also in the sense that I lose my firm hold on majority, my sense of myself as self-possessed, reasonable, rational, in control.

Part of this loss is a becoming-childish, of course: Jack Keefe is a big man who acts (and in a minoritarian sense talks) like a big baby, and in identifying with him, living his life with him (and with Al), male readers (at least—maybe female readers also) become big babies, too.[6] This (always-already) infantilization of adult males is "normal" under bourgeois patriarchy, of course—men are constituted as men as both the fathers and the needy infants of women (and as the *un*needy *non*infants of men)—but repressively so: men are expected to repress the "normal" fact of their infantility. Women are expected to call us babies and we are expected to deny it. Hence the potentially emancipatory effect of Kristeva's concern "with the attentiveness that the adult [male, like Jack Keefe, or the masculine critic], through his still infantile sexuality, is able to perceive in the discourse of a child (boy or girl) while it refers him to that level where his 'own' language is never totally rationalized or normated according to Cartesian linguistics, but where it always remains an 'infantile language'" (278). In Jack's "infantile language" the speaking of Lardner's Other-as-minor speaks us, too: it "refers" us, or rather bodily (somatically) transports us, to the infantility of our own speaking, to that realm of unconscious knowing in which we are no more able to make clear distinctions and place effective controls on animal rages and needs than a baby, and puts us (potentially) in touch with those feelings the repression of which keeps us tied up in the patriarchal double bind.

This transport is probably clearest in *You Know Me Al* when Jack writes to Al about his new baby:

> FRIEND AL: Al I beat the Athaletics 2 to 1 to-day but I am writeing to you to give you the supprise of your life. Old pal I got a baby and he is a boy and we are going to name him Allen which Florrie thinks is after his uncle and aunt Allen but which is after you old pal. And she can call him Allen but I will call him Al because I don't never go back on my old pals. The baby was born over to the hospital and it is going to cost me a bunch

of money but I should not worry. This is the secret I was going to tell you Al and I am the happyest man in the world and I bet you are most as tickled to death to hear about it as I am.

The baby was born just about the time I was makeing McInnis look like a sucker in the pinch but they did not tell me nothing about it till after the game and then they give me a phone messige in the clubhouse. I went right over there and everything was all O.K. Little Al is a homely little skate but I guess all babys is homely and don't have no looks till they get older and maybe he will look like Florrie or I then I won't have no kick comeing. (150)

Note once again the crossovers or blurrings in this passage, here blurrings of naming and identity in which the baby at once becomes and does not become the principals in the story, and they at once become and do not become him: the baby is named Al after either "friend Al" or Florrie's uncle and aunt; friend Al will be "most as tickled to death" about the birth as Jack; the baby "don't have no looks" yet, but Jack hopes "he will look like Florrie or I then I won't have no kick comeing." The unpunctuated transition in that last phrase — "or I then I" — points murkily (*not* clearly) to the diffusion of identity that the birth of this baby precipitates. Grammatically, logically, in the norm-driven system of majoritarian grammar, "I" is the doer, "me" the done-to, and the effect of the hypercorrect lower-middle-class "look like Florrie or I" is to place Jack in a peculiar limbo between modeling for his infant boy's looks ("me") and becoming-infantilized ("I"). "Then I won't have no kick comeing" has a similar limboing effect: it is at once "I will have no room to complain" (about the kid being ugly, about him not looking like me, about him not being my son), "I will have no reason to kick anyone" (to be a traditional violent male, to kick my wife as my infant son has been doing for the last five or six months, to become the infant son), and "Nobody will kick me" (for whatever burden of guilt I like all men carry, for passivity or aggression, for anger or fear, for sexuality or impotence). The baby was also born "just about the time I was makeing McInnis look like a sucker," suggesting another series of blurrings: McInnis *looks* like a sucker, while the sucker at his wife's breast doesn't look like Jack; Jack is a sucker for thinking that little Al is his son; he wishes he were a (or the) sucker at his wife's (or his mother's) breast.

It goes without saying that this infantilization of the adult male speaker goes unsaid in the stories. Lardner himself doesn't seem to be aware that it is happening; it is the speech of his Other-as-minor, his Other-as-child, an unconscious voice of resistance to adult male self-control. Jack Keefe voices all the childish impulses Lardner keeps bottled up: the desire to tell the world how great he is, and to rage at people who don't recognize his worth; the sudden mood swings and changes of mind; and the willingness to take enormous emotional risks, especially the repeated mortification when brags fall flat and directional shifts hurt the people who love him. Jack hurls himself on the world's mercy, with an infantlike trust that his caretakers will continue to take care of him, that he will not be rejected, no matter how he kicks and screams and makes impossible demands.

This infantile ability to *trust* the world enough to "regress," to be spoken by the Other-as-minor, or what Kristeva calls the "semiotic disposition," is a powerfully (or potentially) therapeutic tool, the penultimate stage of all successful psychotherapy (just before the cure). Trust exceeds the equation of the double bind, in some sense overloads the double bind, and thus carves out a dynamic space (roughly what Kristeva calls a *chora*) in and through which it is possible to untie the knots, break the bonds of patriarchal programming. It is an exceedingly risky undertaking, since the patriarchal double bind inscribes "trust" as "vulnerability" and thus as "submission" to the very powers the trusting child would undermine: when the Other-as-parent says "Trust me" it means "Surrender to me, obey me, cling close to me." Because it is doubly bound and double-binding, of course, it also says simultaneously, "Don't trust me, beware of me, stand apart from me, be suspicious of me, keep your guard up, never allow yourself to feel comfortable around me (or anyone else)." It uses trust to engender submission, and suspicion to engender repressive self-control. The kind of trust Lardner is able to channel into Jack Keefe is *regressive* trust, an infantile surrendering of adult suspicion and self-control, a descent into angry trust, fearful trust, needy trust, into the infantile state not of submission but of selfless somatic demands: give the body what it needs! This is not egotism, as the Other-as-parent insists, for the ego doesn't exist in that state. It is rather what might be called somatism, the demanding of the unselfed body, the crying of the desubjectified Other. If, conflating Kristeva's and Deleuze and Guattari's terms, we identify the ego or adult self as doubly bound "majority" and the soma or infant body as semiotic "minority," Lardner's achievement in *You Know Me Al* lies in the forgetting of his own majority in a potentially liberating regression to minority—a regression that, as Kristeva (coming out of Bakhtin) predicts, generates laughter:[7]

FRIEND AL: Coming out of Amarillo last night I and Lord and Weaver was sitting at a table in the dining car with a old lady. None of us were talking to her but she looked me over pretty careful and seemed to kind of like my looks. Finally she says Are you boys with some football club? Lord nor Weaver didn't say nothing so I thought it was up to me and I says No mam this is the Chicago White Sox Ball Club. She says I knew you were athalets. I says Yes I guess you could spot us for athaletes. She says Yes indeed and specially you. You certainly look healthy. I says You ought to see me stripped. I didn't see nothing funny about that but I thought Lord and Weaver would die laughing. Lord had to get up and leave the table and he told everybody what I said. (36–37)

The humor in this scene is generated out of the clash between Jack's infantile delight in his "healthy" body and the prescribed sexualization of the adult body represented by Lord and Weaver. Lardner stretches us between two images, that of the woman admiring the naked body of a strapping baby boy and that of the strapping male athlete exposing himself to the old woman, and when the tension between the images becomes unbearable, we laugh. The prudish Lardner must have felt profoundly uneasy at the merest flash of the latter image, and in "real life"—outside the speaking of the Other-as-minor—he would have clamped down on any hint of such matters; but here in Jack Keefe's persona he is able to let go, to let himself feel the discomfort long enough to make the joke, and possibly (this is sheer speculation) to explode back through the joke and the discomfort it occasions to his own naked infancy, his own physical intimacy with his mother in the first months of his life.

Typically, Jack doesn't linger over this incident; he moves breezily on from Lord's lording the faux pas over him to "All the boys wanted me to play poker on the way here" (37), and from there to Callahan's instructions to get off the pitcher's mound and start fielding his position. Things just sort of happen to Jack. An old lady talks to him, words come out of his mouth, and people laugh at him; the boys want to play poker, and more words come out of his mouth ("I told them I didn't feel good" [37]); the manager warns him to shape up or "I will have to ship you back to the sticks" (37), and he gets "kind of sore" and says, "Oh I guess I can get along all right" (37). For a man who is described by his critics as "pigheaded, cocky, gullible, selfish, sentimental, naive, stubborn, self-deceiving—and talented" (Yardley 165), Jack is remarkably selfless. He is almost, in fact, like a Robbe-Grillet "hero": locked out of the prison house of the autonomous liberal self, pushed and pulled by this and that "minor" character in his world and in his body, by teammates and managers and strangers and the various minoritarian Others he harbors within him.

When I call Jack Keefe a "minor" character in his own story, minoritized by his own regressive voice, clearly I mean something quite different from the textbook minor character. He is not, for example, a minor character in the same sense as George and Myrtle Wilson in *The Great Gatsby* are minor characters. All three characters belong to the same social class, although Keefe's rural origins and athletic occupation distinguish him socially and dialectally from the urban-mechanical Wilsons; but the Wilsons are mere plebeian plot devices (jealous husband/murderer, kept woman/victim) in Fitzgerald's majoritarian exploration of the Gatsby-Daisy-Nick triangle ("romantic hero," "seductress," "moralistic commentator").[8] The Wilsons are trapped in minority by majoritarian society and its majoritarian representative, Fitzgerald; Jack Keefe gravitates toward minority, embraces it and all its crossings and contradictions (plebeian and infantile in his adult masculine denial of those attributes). The Wilsons, you might say, are minor; Jack Keefe is minoritarian. He has no class envy of the rich, and no aspirations above pitching the baseball. He is not imprisoned in the dark side of majoritarian society as the Wilsons are, envying the passing Long Islanders, trying to buy their cars, having affairs with them; baseball constitutes an alternative world for him, a minoritarian world that impinges on the world of the majority only in order to "send it racing."[9] Like popular music and (in a different sense) organized crime, organized sports in America is a cultural realm in which plebeian speech and dress (and infantile behavior) do not doom you to self-loathing; indeed, for some sectors of the white middle-class majority (especially the adolescent minority within the majority), plebeian speech and dress (and even infantile behavior) become a sign of minoritarian prestige, what sociologists call "prestige from below" ("ain'ts" and jeans among the adolescent white middle class).[10]

Perhaps I should note that something similar is going on in this book as well: the white male middle-class critic who grew up loving the Los Angeles Dodgers in the sixties (Duke Snyder the aging slugger, Sandy Koufax the brilliant southpaw, Maury Wills the base stealer) and the baseball stories of Ring Lardner (also television, movies, rock music, comic books, other genre fiction—all "infantile" tastes I still cherish) seeks prestige from below by writing a minoritarian book about a minor writer. By calling the book "minoritarian," of course, I also pretend not to be presenting it as major criticism, even while weaving a dense rhetorical web out of esoteric concepts from impenetrably difficult theorists like Lacan, Kristeva, and Deleuze and Guattari, thus virtually guaranteeing that only major critics will be able to read it. I also held off writing this book for four or five years after first conceiving the idea for it, fearing that the linkage between Lardner's dummy and Lacan's *mort* was too clever, too cute, for "serious" (major?) criticism — and only decided to go ahead with it after two or three major critics among my colleagues got excited about my idea and urged me to write the book.

And of course, when I finally came to write about the minor writer whose baseball stories I loved as a kid, I did a hundred-page reading of a non-baseball story, a story about the middle class (to make the overingenious point about the bridge dummy, which also gave me the esoteric tie-in to Lacan), and only now, two chapters later, over halfway into the book, do I get around to talking about baseball. And so, with an uneasily indulgent nod to my Other-as-child, let me turn now, more quickly and collectively, to three other baseball stories: "Hurry Kane," "My Roomy," and my favorite Lardner story from childhood, "Alibi Ike."

All three stories are narrated by reasonably "sensible" (read "repressively adult") baseball players about "crazy" ("childish") players on their teams. Hurry Kane, "Buster" Elliott, and Frank X. "Alibi Ike" Farrell are bushers like Jack Keefe, baseball grotesques whose dangerously centrifugal quirks "center" or "ground" the stories told by their teammates about them — a centering that operates as decentering, obviously, a grounding that shakes the ground under both the baseball teams and Lardner's fiction. By allowing a more sensible narrator to tell the story, Lardner at once puts distance between the reader and the crazy hero and, significantly enough, escalates the hero's craziness: by comparison, Jack Keefe was too childish to show us the full extent of his childish behavior. Even so, the "sensibility" of these three narrators remains only relative and relational, and varies from story to story: "Hurry Kane" is the most repressively adult of the three stories, with a narrator who knows what's right and a hero who finally does what's right; "My Roomy" has an irredeemably loony hero and a narrator who succeeds in taming him at first by pretending to be even loonier, but then loses him by retreating from that all-too-attractive pretense into repressive adult behavior; and "Alibi Ike" undermines the adulthood of all of the characters, both the hero Ike and the two jokesters ("I and Carey").

All three of the loony heroes are Percival figures, "bugs," as Lardner's narrators say, who arrive at spring training or in the middle of the season looking straight off the farm. "Standing six foot three in what was left of his stockings, he [Hurry Kane] was wearing a suit of Arizona store clothes that would have been a fit for Singer's youngest Midget and looked like he had pressed it with a tractor that had been parked on a river bottom" (88). "Buster" Elliott arrives with no luggage after not eating for three days, and promptly eats "about four meals at once"

(328). It takes Alibi Ike "half an hour longer'n us to eat because he had to excuse himself every time he lifted his fork" (36). All three might be described as athletic idiot savants: each has some virtually supernatural talent in baseball (Hurry Kane has a demonic fast ball, Elliott can hit any pitch out of the park, Ike is a brilliant all-round player) combined with some fatally limiting quirk. Kane fixates obsessively on every woman who catches his eye, and wants to drop everything (including the team and the last woman he was fixated on) to chase after her. Elliott refuses to field balls on defense (he came here to hit the ball, not to catch it, so they play him as pinch hitter — he would have made a great designated hitter), and he is self-destructively contrary: he will always do precisely the opposite of whatever anyone tells him to do. Ike is obsessively self-deprecatory: he cannot do anything without apologizing for not doing it better. And in each case, the story (and the team it centers around) is conceived as a collective effort to master or manage this "loony," to keep him happy and doing his stuff for the team, in order to win the pennant and take home the World Series money. The coach flies Kane's hometown girlfriend in to travel with the team, all expenses paid; the narrator of "My Roomy" rooms with Elliott and tries first successfully (with reverse psychology) and then unsuccessfully (by reasoning with him) to bring him into line; and the coach sends Ike "scouting," again all expenses paid, in order to let him make up with his fiancée.

What is striking about these three stories is not only their subtextual explorations of Lardner's masculine self-management — the way each team operates as an athletic allegory of Lardner's psychic economy — but their focal concern with the failure of that self-management. Psychologized, each story might be read as recognizing both the vital importance and the terrible fragility and instability of "lunacy," of what the Other-as-majority defines as deviant behavior, but what the Other-as-minority knows is indispensable to human existence. Lardner pours himself into the obsessional intensity of Kane's attraction to women (the pursuit of Ellis), Elliott's contrariness (the refusal to laugh at funny stories), and Alibi Ike's self-deprecation (the denial of all self-worth as a writer). By at once releasing his repressed desires in exaggerated form (the loonies) and attempting to manage those desires in liberal, humane ways (the narrators and their coaches), he seeks an out, an escape, a liberation from the double bind. What if, we can imagine his Other-as-minority whispering, it were possible to be both crazy *and* loved — what if you could let loose, go wild, be as deviant as you feel, and still be not only tolerated but pampered, protected? What if your deviant behavior were perceived as the necessary by-product of your brilliance, and therefore to be cherished along with the talents that make you a success?

These whisperings, heeded so histrionically by numberless enfants terribles of art and literature, would not have taken Lardner very far, perhaps. The release they promise is typically just as doubly bound as the repression that blocks release. Yes, go ahead, play the clown, the Other-as-majority can whisper back: I don't mind, as long as I keep getting results. As long as you keep achieving, performing, succeeding, making me look good. And of course, as long as you continue to conceive your "crazy" behavior as merely an extreme form of "normal" behavior: as long as your release remains reactive and thus structurally repressive. As long as Hurry Kane's womanizing ties him to displaced images of the mother, and Elliott's contrariness ties him to the parental command, and Ike's self-deprecation ties him to images of parental superiority, all three men can be manipulated, controlled: Kane by providing him with a woman and directing all his impulses toward her, Elliott through reverse psychology, and Ike by thematizing his apologies as humility and taking care not to push him past accepted limits.

Lardner's drinking was probably the closest he came to allowing himself this sort of manipulable release; in all other areas (except through fictional characters), he maintained strict watchful control over his behavior. Not for him the "artistic" volatility of Scott Fitzgerald, as described by Anita Loos, whom Fitzgerald took for a "wild ride" and then home:

> Zelda was at home and we sat down to dinner. Scott was very moody, and not saying much. Zelda and I ignored him, and that seemed to make him angry. Finally he jumped up from the table and said, "I'm going to kill you two." And he tried. He jerked off the tablecloth with everything on it and then started throwing the candelabra and other big, heavy things at us. Scott had locked all the doors, but the butler — he will always be a hero to me — broke through a glass pane in one of the doors and came in and held Scott. Then Zelda and I ran across to Ring Lardner's house. Ring decided to go out looking for Scott. He looked for quite a while before he found him. "I'm a monster," he was saying. "I tried to kill those two darling girls and now I've got to eat dirt." (quoted in Yardley 262)

Except for Scott's remorse, this is in fact strongly reminiscent of "Buster" Elliott, who gets kicked off the team and arrives home to find his fiancée married to another man (she had written him about it, but he had torn up her letters without reading them to prove his masculine independence), and "busts" their heads with a baseball bat: "Old Roomy: I was at bat twice and made two hits; but I guess I did not meet 'em square.

They tell me they are both alive yet, which I did not mean 'em to be. I hope they got good curve-ball pitchers where I am goin' [the local asylum]. I sure can bust them curves — can't I, sport?" (346).

This is the dark side of release, as Lardner well knows: it can lead to murder and mayhem, and ultimately to incarceration, the imposition of institutional repression on a body that cannot adequately police itself. The threat of such incarceration is the last and greatest in a series of social warnings designed to get us to incarcerate ourselves, to police ourselves by putting ourselves in the prison of the Other-as-parent: if you let go even a little, you will go wild and end up in jail or the loony bin. This is the rhetoric of all-or-nothing, perfect control or criminal release, which is designed to write the subject into the doubly bound middle of neither-nor: neither perfect control nor criminal release but the attenuating adjustments of imperfect control and anxious release. Drink a little, abstain a little, and feel guilty for falling. Murder only in "playful" talk ("your proud young face I'll mask / With sweet gasolined").

The doubly bound middle was the straitjacket in which Lardner lived his life, afraid to lean too far in this direction or that. His stories were his first tentative step (and, alas, his last) down the road of excess that, as William Blake tells us, leads to the palace of wisdom. The voice of the Other-as-minority that wrote his stories lures him out onto that road, whispering, with Blake:

> If the fool would persist in his folly he would become wise
>
> The tygers of wrath are wiser than the horses of instruction
>
> You never know what is enough unless you know what is more than enough
>
> Sooner murder an infant in its cradle than nurse unacted desires (36–38)

The "horses of instruction" instruct us in the double bind, teach us the "wisdom" of restraint, self-control, the management of desire; and, lest that instruction not be enough to enforce restraint, they paint dire scenes of murder before our eyes, the bleeding infant in its cradle, as the only conceivable alternative to restraint. Nurse unacted desires, the Other-as-majority instructs us, or you *will* murder an infant in its cradle. Lardner's baseball loonies are the fools who persist in their folly — not quite long enough to become wise, but long enough to allow Lardner (and us) to explore what is "more than enough" and thus to begin to mark out the path to the palace of wisdom. And again, as both Kristeva and Blake remind us ("Excess of sorrow laughs. Excess of joy weeps" [36]), that path leads through regressive, excessive laughter, the laughter that undermines the controlling adult self and fills it with a laughing/weeping Other, the laughter that does not so much "set another before you" (36), as Blake says, as set you within an Other, inscribe you within the speech of an Other:

And Ike goes up there with orders to bunt and cracks the first ball into that right-field stand! It was fair this time, and we're two ahead, but I didn't think about that at the time. I was too busy watchin' Cap's face. First he turned pale and then he got red as fire and then he got blue and purple, and finally he just laid back and busted out laughin'. So we wasn't afraid to laugh ourselfs when we seen him doin' it, and when Ike come in everybody on the bench was in hysterics.

But instead o' takin' advantage, Ike had to try and excuse himself. His play was to shut up and he didn't know how to make it.

"Well," he says, "if I hadn't hit quite so quick at that one I bet it'd of cleared the center-field fence."

Cap stopped laughin'.

"It'll cost you plain fifty," he says.

"What for?"

"When I say 'bunt' I mean 'bunt,'" says Cap.

"You didn't say 'bunt,'" says Ike.

"I says 'Lay it down,'" says Cap. "If that don't mean 'bunt,' what does it mean?"

"'Lay it down' means 'bunt' all right," says Ike, "but I understood you to say 'Lay on it.'"

"All right," says Cap, "and the little misunderstandin' will cost you fifty."

Ike didn't say nothin' for a few minutes. Then he had another bright idear.

"I was just kiddin' about misunderstandin' you," he says. "I knowed you wanted me to bunt."

"Well, then, why didn't you bunt?" ast Cap.

"I was goin' to on the next ball," says Ike. "But I thought if I took a good wallop I'd have 'em all fooled. So I walloped at the first one to fool 'em, and I didn't have no intention o' hittin' it."

"You tried to miss it, did you?" says Cap.

"Yes," says Ike.

"How'd you happen to hit it?" ast Cap.

"Well," Ike says, "I was lookin' for him to throw me a fast one and I was goin' to swing under it. But he come with a hook and I met it right square where I was swingin' to go under the fast one."

"Great!" says Cap. "Boys," he says, "Ike's learned how to hit Marquard's curve. Pretend a fast one's comin' and then try to miss it. It's a good thing to know and Ike'd ought to be willin' to pay for the lesson. So I'm goin' to make it a hundred instead o' fifty." (43–44)

What is interesting about this passage is that it doesn't get funny for the reader until after the team stops laughing: the coach and the team are emotionally invested in Ike's obedience and disobedience, and end up in a series of anxious somatic responses to their investment that culminate in laughter; but Lardner "invests" the reader in the trials of explanation and interpretation, and generates reader laughter out of Ike's excuses. When Ike comes in bragging that if he had hit it better he could have driven it over the center-field fence, I smile. And the smile broadens as he keeps worrying the home run, trying to find a reasonable explanation for it, until his attempt to explain the home run as an attempt to miss a misread pitch pushes me over the edge into laughter. It might even make sense to say that the team's laughter is the bunt and my laughter is the home run, or that the coach's wordless somatic response to the home run is the fast ball Ike thought was coming, and the punitive/apologetic verbal exchange that follows is the curve ball he slammed out of the park: the team's laughter is just words on the page ("everybody on the bench was in hysterics"), someone else's hypothetical situation (the commanded bunt, the imagined fast ball), but the words on the page that follow the team's laughter connect with the "hook" thrown by my Other-as-pitcher, and I laugh (and drive in two runs).

It is significant, too, that Ike claims to have connected with the breaking ball by trying to miss it: the road of *excess* leads to the palace of wisdom, a wandering road, a stammering speech, a bad swing of the bat. Ike stammers his way into the home run, which Cap fines him for and then tries to equate with the fine under the rubric of "lesson": as one of society's horses of instruction, he is concerned about his authority, about his ability to make his players obey his commands, and uses both ridicule and the fine to keep Ike in line. Ike's brilliance as both a baseball player and a character, however, arises out of his blithe refusal to learn such lessons, his apparently uncontrived deafness to "instruction." Similarly, Lardner stammers his way to his reader's laughter, groping past the authoritarian structures that bind his extrafictional life to that potentially therapeutic moment when laughter explodes those structures, brings the double-binding lessons of patriarchal programming crashing down.

Perhaps the greatest stammerers in Lardner's fiction, outside of the nonsense plays, are the women:

> Mr. Halpern, on Miss Bell's right, spoke to her and Harry found himself attacked by Miss Coakley.
> "Mr. Barton, I was just telling Mr. Walters about— I don't know whether you'd be interested or not—maybe you don't—but still everybody I've told, they think—it's probably—"

"I'm sure I'd like to hear," said Harry [Barton].

"I hate to bore people with — you know how it is — you'd be too polite to — and this is so awfully — well, it isn't a thing that — it's just interesting if you happen — people in Baltimore — though we've only lived there a few — "

"If," said Harry to himself, "she doesn't complete a sentence in the next two minutes, I'm going to ask Grace for a high-ball."

" — it was some people who lived — well, our apartment was just two buildings — they were people you wouldn't want — but it was in a kind of secluded — not many apartments — it's a neighborhood that's just — and my sister's little boy goes to the same school as — "

"Grace," said Harry, "am I an old enough customer here to ask for a drink?" (142–43)

"Dinner" (1928) is a far cry from "Who Dealt?": not only do the two "peaches," Miss Bell and Miss Coakley, not know anything and not reveal anything, but neither narrates the story. Lardner uses a Jamesian third-person narrator who tries to maintain an ascetic detachment from the conversation at dinner but cannot help siding with Harry Barton, the good-looking thirty-three-year-old bachelor that Grace Halpern invites to dinner to make up an even number of men and women, and Harry and the narrator both politely despair at the women's conversation. On the face of it, the story is a fairly sardonic attack on women's speech, which it portrays as empty and irrational and agrammatical: Miss Coakley never completes a sentence, and Miss Bell rambles on associationally, listening only to Others in her own head, never to the others sitting around her.[11]

But look more closely at Miss Coakley's discourse: "Mr. Barton, I was just telling Mr. Walters about — I don't know whether you'd be interested or not — maybe you don't — but still everybody I've told, they think — it's probably — ". What is missing here, clearly, is "content," "substance," "matter," the semantic payload that language is supposed, in the West, meekly to convey — supposed to do so, specifically, by men, in a patriarchal tradition that privileges meanings over words, structures over speech, spirit over body, reason over emotion, transcendent truth over human emotional interconnectedness. Spoken words and the somatic responses that guide them in specific social situations are fleshly, worldly, evanescent, and therefore normatively feminine; abstract meanings and the semantic fields that ground them in ideal structure are spiritual, transcendental, permanent, and therefore normatively masculine. Women blabber on about nothing; men sit silently, thinking great thoughts. Miss Coakley never *gets to the point*; Harry Barton makes polite noises, but mainly sits alone with his boredom and despair, and finally (with the distinct sense all Lardner drinkers have of giving in to temptation) fills the hole left by her lack of verbal substance with a highball.

This use of alcohol as a surrogate for conversational meaning already suggests that more is at stake in the story than sheer woman-bashing. In fact, if Miss Coakley's stammering discourse is a caricature, it is one largely in the etymological sense of being emotionally "charged," loaded: there is a force preventing her from completing her sentences, an inner force or "charge," and Lardner feels it, and lets it speak (or charge) him, too. If Harry, the polite sexist male who drinks rather than spill his semantic payload into the dirt of verbal expression, is spoken by Lardner's Other-as-majority, Miss Coakley is spoken by his Other-as-minority: by a minoritarian voice full of timid appeal, full specifically of a fear of being interrupted by those in the social majority (men, adults, probably parents). Miss Coakley "stammers," never completes a sentence, because she is constantly being interrupted by the Other-as-majority, which tells her that she has nothing to say, that no one is going to be interested in anything that comes out of her mouth, that even if people seem to be listening, they are just being polite and hiding their boredom. Since, despite her timidity, she does open her mouth and let her stammering speech pour out, it is a safe guess that she was systematically interrupted in her childhood by a talkative parent who urged her to join the conversation, *and* by a taciturn parent who silenced her with a disapproving look: a double-binding dual parent-voice (mother/father) who told her, as the voice of the Other-as-majority in her head keeps on telling her, to talk and not to talk, to speak and not to say anything, to start sentences and not complete them, to think of herself as a great talker and a terrible bore.

This is being written by the politely taciturn Lardner, of course, and being written, no doubt, in order to ridicule women, to express a resignedly "normal" masculine desperation with the way they talk. There is, in other words, a sexist impulse in the story. On the other hand, the feminine voice is coming from *somewhere*. It might be reasonable, I suppose, to attribute Miss Coakley's voice to Lardner's "good ear," to his ability to listen attentively, and leave it at that. He heard some woman talking that way at a dinner party he was drinking at, and reproduced her speech in his story. Harry starts drinking out of understandable frustration: period. This is how the writing of fiction is usually mystified. The writer has some mysterious knack, some talent or genius — Lardner's "ear" — which he or she just sort of uses, mysteriously, and poof: a story. A poem. A novel. Any attempt to probe deeper is "dime-store psychologizing" (Yardley 87).[12]

Lardner's biographers agree, however, that he inherited his "ear" from his mother, and while they do not explore the dynamics of that inheritance, it seems reasonable to suggest that it was at least as much social as it was genetic: that, in addition to the perfect-pitch chromosome he inherited from her (if that is what it was), he learned to listen attentively to people's voices and mimic them in his speech and writing by listening attentively to the "ebullient" Lena Lardner. She was, after all, a great talker who delighted in mimicry; to please her, her clownish youngest son would naturally work to hone his ear to the pitches and timbres of other people's voices, and to get his mouth to reproduce those pitches and timbres.

But recall also that Lena Lardner was an exacting because easily distracted judge of humor, a woman who frantically loved to be amused, and would turn from one amusement to the next (also, from one guest or child to the next) in search of just the right tone. All her children, apparently, worked hard to amuse her, please her, humor her — to get her attention and with it, perhaps, her love — and little Ringgold, the baby of the family, was almost certainly both indulged and interrupted: encouraged to be funny and cute, but also cut off numerous times in the middle of a spiel. It happens in every boisterous family, and the Lardners seems to have been more boisterous than most. What I am working toward is a sense that the author of "Dinner" felt his way to the blockage behind Miss Coakley's stammering discourse through his own childhood memories of being simultaneously urged to perform verbally and interrupted by his mother (who was herself no doubt interrupted, or at least assaulted, by the disapproving looks of her husband and sons): that, in the attempt to achieve a credible caricature of women's speech, he tapped a voice in his own head and charged his caricature with real minoritarian power. Lardner was a timid man who masked his timidity in "normal" masculine taciturnity, modeled on his father; but the timid little boy's clownish attempts to please his mother with the sharpness of his ear still found expression in his columns and stories, spoken by minoritarian Others. Miss Coakley, we might speculate, is spoken by Lardner's (m)Other-as-child: she speaks at once as the child in him, timid, nervous about piping up at the dinner table (the youngest in a big family), getting tongue-tied, stumbling over his words; as his father (Henry-as-Harry), sternly disapproving but despairingly withdrawn, unable to contribute to the hilarity or to silence it, vacillating between hapless gestures of authoritarian control and helpless isolation; and likewise as his mother, nervously and erratically vivacious, bossy, demanding, unpredictably supportive or indifferent, unable to concentrate on any one subject or any one child for more than a few moments at a time, constantly changing subjects or directions in midsentence. She packs all of Lena Lardner's verbal volatility and all of Henry Lardner's oppressive silence into every vivacious but stoppered sentence; she embodies little Ring's emotional timidity and desire to please, his fear of losing his parents' love if he is too quiet or too loud, too much like his father or too much like his mother. She neither dominates the conversation with her larger-than-life personality, as Lena did, nor retires into taciturn silence (fortified with highballs), as Henry (and "Harry") did. She just—stammers.[13]

Because she talks, in fact, however stammeringly, she has an important advantage over her creator, or for that matter, over her neighbor at dinner, who keeps his wish that she might complete a sentence to himself, and fortifies the inward fullness of that wish with booze. It is possible, for example, to imagine someone actually expressing that wish to her in a safe, reassuring context, getting her alone for a moment and saying: "Wait, please slow down for a second. I love you. You are my sister, my daughter, my lover, my companion, my wife. I want to listen to you. I want to hear what you have to say. If you don't want to talk, that's all right, too." It is possible to imagine a sympathetic and caring and strong-minded listener channeling her stammering therapeutically, helping her to stammer (free-associate) her way into self-knowledge, maybe over a course of years, maybe through intense anger, fear, guilt, need, all the emotional "substance" that her Other-as-majority coaches her to unsay.[14] Lardner's "normal" masculine (defensively unfeminine or anti-feminine) taciturnity all but precluded any such turn in his life. It is difficult to imagine anyone cracking his shell long enough to engage the hurt little boy inside him, to comfort that little boy, make him feel loved and wanted. One of the most pathetic scenes in the biographical literature about Lardner is from the last year of his life: Lardner sitting alone, his head in his hands, weeping. "Whether it was *lacrimae rerum* or only sheer exhaustion that broke him down it is impossible to know," Elder comments; "he always lived close to tears" (377). This is terribly moving—terribly, because it is too late. Lardner is terminally ill, close to death. Elder's powerfully insightful remark that Lardner had always lived close to tears suggests both that the tears were there, close to the surface, ready to be accessed, if only someone had known how—and that they were only *close*, that Lardner kept his shell hard so that they could never surface.[15]

They only surfaced, perhaps, in his stories, in displaced form—displaced both into the voices of other people (and of an alienated persona, the increasingly oppressive wise boob) and into somatic responses other than tears: a hostile frustration in "Horseshoes" (1914) and "Women"

(1925), a kind of frantic exhilaration-desperation in "I Can't Breathe" (1926), a defensive breeziness in "Zone of Quiet" (1925), a martyred resignation in "Old Folks' Christmas" (1929; from the parents' point of view) or "Bob's Birthday" (1933; from the child's point of view), and, perhaps most strikingly of all, a somatic associationism in the nonsense plays, a descent into the swirling feel of words. In some ways these plays from the midtwenties were anticipated by experimental writing in the columns over the previous decade. In 1915, for example, he did a parody of Gertrude Stein's *Tender Buttons*, which had just appeared the previous year, called "Cubist Baseball":

> A SELDOM
>
> A White Sox base hit, a base hit with a man on third base is a seldom. Is strange to. Is a curiosity. Is sincerely fainting to fans. Why not once in a while? Or why? The time to make a base hit a White Sox base hit is too late or later. The whole thing is unconscious. (quoted by Yardley 175)

This is still pretty primitive, too obviously saying, "I wish the White Sox would get a base hit once in a while," compared to the nonsense plays of the twenties. Some of these — "The Tridget of Greva," for example, in 1922 — were actually performed, while others appeared in various literary magazines and Lardner's own collections (*What Of It?* from 1925 has three). One of the best, "I. Gaspiri (The Upholsterers)," was first performed at the annual dinner of the Authors' League and then published by Ernest Hemingway in the *Chicago Literary Times* in February 1924, with an unsigned introduction by Hemingway praising it as an example of what Maxwell Geismar in *The Ring Lardner Reader* dubs "native dada" (xxix): "what profound admiration we have for Americans who really do know French and how tired we get of others who pretend to and how very much better dadas the American dadas, who do not know they are dadas . . . are than the French and the Roumanians who know it so well" (quoted by Yardley 270). It is a "drama in three acts," but the second act has been "deleted by the censor," and the third act consists entirely of stage directions and a single line, "Well, my man, how goes it?" (47). Let me quote Act I in full:

> ACT I
>
> (*A public street in a bathroom. A man named Tupper has evidently just taken a bath. A man named Brindle is now taking a bath. A man named Newburn comes out of the faucet which has been left running. He exits through the exhaust. Two strangers to each other meet on the bath mat.*)

FIRST STRANGER

Where was you born?

SECOND STRANGER

Out of wedlock.

FIRST STRANGER

That's a mighty pretty country around there.

SECOND STRANGER

Are you married?

FIRST STRANGER

I don't know. There's a woman living with me, but I can't place her.

(*Three outsiders named Klein go across the stage three times. They think they are in a public library. A woman's cough is heard off-stage left.*)

A NEW CHARACTER

Who is that cough?

TWO MOORS

That is my cousin. She died a little while ago in a haphazard way.

A GREEK

And what a woman she was!

(*The curtain is lowered for seven days to denote the lapse of a week.*)

(45–46)

I have been arguing that the emotionally blocked Lardner displaced all his healthiest, most life-enhancing impulses (feelings, reactions, experiences) onto fictional others, spoke them through Other voices; what the nonsense plays do is turn this displacement into a structural principle. Their guiding force is an associationism that works by dissociation, a series of somatic or autonomic or "automatic" linkages that proceed by an unconscious severing of conscious ties between collocational entities, cuts made stammeringly by Lardner's Others in the ideological flow of language. In many of the plays these cuts seem defensive, self-protective—Lardner's way of *not* making connections with the Others that speak him, through the sheer inundative force of non sequiturs; in fact, Lardner's biographers seem inclined to reduce them all to this sort of defensive flooding.[16] At its best, however, Lardner's nonsense cuts down to the speaking of the Other; the cuts are made both in and by the speaking of the Other. "I. Gaspiri" in particular is charged or loaded with the cutting voice or force of the (m)Other-as-child, who is both "in" and "out of wedlock," both locked into a wedded state and locked out of it, and who finds that simultaneous interiority/exteriority at once "a mighty pretty country" and a state of confusion ("There's a woman living with me, but I can't place her"). The dead cousin's cough invokes both the five-years-dead mother ("And what a woman she was!") and the living somaticized mother ("Who is that cough?") — the dead (m)Other-as-cough, you might say, who lives on in Lardner's body like a nervous tic, prompting him to speak (to "cough it up") and displacing his self-disclosure as coughing. The displacement of ideologically "normal" familial relations (being born out of wedlock, not being able to "place" the woman you're living with) is repeated in the speaking of two "strangers to each other," as Ring and Ellis certainly were — and as all "normal" married couples are, indeed, all "normal" *people*.[17] Remaining strangers protects the ideological idealizations that guarantee normality, and "normal" rational discourse helps people remain strangers by precluding unexpected cuts in the flows: we don't really understand each other or get along too well, but that's just the way we are, and at least we have each other. What more can you expect from marriage (or life)? This stranger-discourse is then compounded in the sudden shift to "A NEW CHARACTER," "TWO MOORS," and "A GREEK," who speak of a "haphazard" (manner of) death. The speaking of these cartoon characters is just as haphazard as the cousin's dying, which is just as haphazard as the unplaceable woman's living; but this does not mean it is random, meaningless. On the contrary, it is at once "happy" and "hazardous," at once fundamental to one's "hap" or luck or lot and unpredictably and unavoidably dangerous. The speaking of strangers, the living with and dying of (un-/dis-)placeable women — all this is haphazard in the sense of being both incomprehensible and inescapable, both frighteningly alien and oppressively familiar.

In a word, it is haphazard in the sense of being Other. Lardner's achievement as a minor(itarian) writer is the writing of this haphazard Other, the accessing of a hazardous hap in his own dialogized body: a somatic nexus that terrified him so much that he expended massive amounts of emotional energy to keep it down, keep it locked up (in or out), yet that also fascinated him, and almost certainly vitalized him, so powerfully that he threw open the jail-cell doors in his writing, let it out, let it flow, let it sweep away (for heady moments) his masculine asceses.

III

WHO READ?

5

Lardner's Dual Audience

. . . appeals to two types of mind that are at opposite extremes
. . . read with delight by people who talk in the very way that he
writes, and by highly educated people who find relief and amusement in a lack of education in others . . .

GRAHAM, *The Bookman's Manual*

. . . wrote originally for people who do not read books . . .

MATTHEWS, "Lardner, Shakespeare and Chekhov"

. . . that a newspaper humorist, a comic-strip designer, a baseball
writer, should rise to the heights of art and do it without turning a
cold shoulder to the *Saturday Evening Post* public . . .

NEVINS, "The American Moron"

. . . recognized by both *hoi polloi* and intelligentsia as one of our
best writers of short fiction . . .

TIVERTON, "Ring Lardner Writes A Story"

. . . stories convey simultaneously two different impressions, one
for the *Saturday Evening Post* reader and one for the civilized
reader . . .

FADIMAN, "Ring Lardner and the Triangle of Hate"

. . . gave him a sense of existing in the literary world as well as
with the public . . . an increasingly solid reputation on top and below . . .

FITZGERALD, "Ring"

. . . developed from a popular humorist into a genuine artist whose
best work bore the stamp of genius . . .

WHEELER, "Unforgettable Ring Lardner"

. . . a striking example of the writer as both popular entertainer and
genuine artist . . . almost as well known to the average American as
Babe Ruth . . . recognized by writers and critics as a craftsman and
satirist of rare talent . . .

HOLMES, "Ring Lardner: Reluctant Artist"

Lardner wrote for two audiences. It is, as the above excerpts suggest, one of the refrains of Lardner criticism. He was popular and he was recognized by the critics as a great artist. He had the best of both worlds. As Dana Tiverton elaborates in an interview piece published nine months before Lardner's death, "he has two distinct audiences — "

> the sporting crowd who have long followed his stories of ivory-headed baseball players and fighters and who laugh at his innocent-faced grotes-queries, and the pack of intelligentsia, who, of late years, have come to see that behind this man's foolishments there is poignant feeling and a sense of realistic art. The same crowd "discovered" Charles Chaplin long after the "great unwashed" had placed the stamp of approval on his shuffle and his pies. (9)

This, in a culture dedicated to doubly bound ideals of egalitarianism and excellence, democracy and genius, spells success: pleasing both the masses and the elite, or as Fitzgerald says, both the bottom and the top — being at once popular and great. Only a few of our writers have achieved that American measure of success: Fitzgerald himself, Twain, Emerson, a handful of others. Placing Lardner in this company is high praise indeed.

So, at any rate, runs the standard critical line. Lardner is a great American writer *because* he pleased both the hoi polloi and the intelligentsia. Never mind that the intelligentsia have always treated him with condescension, as a potentially great but finally (and sadly) minor writer who never attained the heights to which his talent seemed to point. Never mind that Lardner criticism was quite literally nonexistent from his death to the 1956 publication of Donald Elder's biography, and since then has by and large been a desultory, dispirited affair. Never mind that Lardner stopped pleasing the hoi polloi (people, in Matthews's tentative characterization from 1929, who don't read books) when he died and stopped producing humorous columns for the daily newspapers. Never mind that we do not know, and have no way of discovering, what it meant for him to please the hoi polloi — whether it was, as Tiverton assumed, a matter of "laughing at his innocent-faced grotesqueries" or something else altogether. Never mind all this. Lardner pleased two audiences. He was a great American writer.

In this chapter I do intend to "mind" these things — to worry them, perhaps excessively. I want to explore the complexities of reader response to Lardner's writing across the "hoi polloi/intelligentsia" divide in its cultural context — and, more particularly, as partially formative of that context. What was (and is) at stake in a reading of Ring Lardner? What convergence of textual and social factors made it possible for Lardner in his heyday, writing for John Wheeler's Bell Syndicate, to reach a potential weekly audience of eight million newspaper readers? What did reading Lardner's "Weekly Letter" do to those readers, and how did having those readers shape his writing (and our understanding of his writing)? What difference did (and does) it make whether one read(s) a Lardner column in a newspaper the day it appears, in microform seven decades later, in a collection of Lardner pieces, or as excerpted in the Elder or Yardley biography—or whether one read(s) a Lardner short story in the *Saturday Evening Post* or his definitive short-story collection *Round Up*? What kind of professional critic has Lardner's writing attracted, and what kind of Lardner have these critics constructed? What kind of America has Lardner been lionized and neglected in, and what has the lionization and neglect of Lardner done to (or for) American culture?

In order to explore these questions here in chapter 5, I propose to resurrect the five-step schematization of the double bind I developed in chapter 1, using it specifically to construct an image not so much of Lardner's readers or even of his readers' Lardner image as of the ideological use to which the Other-as-culture has put the writer-reader dialogues between Lardner and his dual audience. By the Other-as-culture I mean something like what is colloquially called "society," society as an abstraction for collective activity, as in "Society imposes certain norms on its members and expects them to conform their lives to those norms."[1] The problem with this usage is that is begs the crucial question of how this happens, how a many-headed abstraction like "society" can *do* things to individual human beings. What *is* society's power over us, and how is it wielded? The classic liberal explanation of society's power revolves, like the game of bridge, around a social contract and its attendant conventions, implying that each one of us has personally signed an agreement to behave along certain commonly accepted guidelines. This is obviously not the case; but how else might society shape and direct our behavior?

In the context of my expansion of Lacan, the notion of the Other-as-culture suggests that "society" has its most tangible existence in the ideosomatic programming of each individual, in the somatic *concretization* (not abstraction) that each of us feels in our bodily sense of what is right and what is wrong, what the "good citizen" does and does not do, and so on. The Other-as-parent participates in this programming, of course, and in many specific contexts (especially in patriotic bourgeois families) the Other-as-parent can speak as the culture, and the Other-as-culture speaks in and through the voices of parents. Parents socialize their children, condition children's bodies (somatic responses) to guide them to socially acceptable behavior and to stymie any impulses they might have to asocial or antisocial behavior, and in "normal" families (native-born bourgeois WASP parents) this parental conditioning forms the bedrock of the Other-as-culture. Obviously, in immigrant families, especially from non-Western cultures, the Other-as-culture will be less normatively convergent with the Other-as-parent, as will in fact be the case, more complexly and problematically, in "minority" families (a fortiori minoritarian families, determinedly "deviant" families), families excluded from the "normal" cultural majority (ethnic and racial minorities, gay and lesbian households, alternative communities, etc.). But even in "normal" child rearing, the Other-as-parent will always be exceeded by the Other-as-culture, channeled as the latter typically is not only through parents but also through schoolteachers teaching "civic duties" or "citizenship" (the Other-as-responsibility), through ministers and Sunday school teachers teaching Christian "ethics" or "morality" (the Other-as-conscience), through friends and relatives and neighbors imparting incidental lessons in "being a good friend" or "neighborliness" or "helping out" (the Other-as-decency). All these voices join in the internalized (somatized) chorus of the Other-as-culture.

In the United States, of course, the Other-as-culture is definitively bourgeois (in the broadest sense of that word: "modern" or postmedieval, liberal, capitalist) in both its historical origins and its social program; my description in the previous paragraph of the "typical" channeling of the Other-as-culture is not, in other words, universal, but oriented specifically to "normal" American citizens, individuals socialized (especially in the twentieth century) as "good" citizens of the United States. But the ideosomatic structure of the Other-as-culture is highly stratified: it buries beneath its most public strata the sedimentation of previous cultural loci as well, less visible but no less powerful for having been superseded in cultural history. Most notably in the bourgeois West the dominant liberal Other-as-culture is undergirded with powerful and still active layers of medieval European territorialism (my home is my castle and I will shoot anyone who invades it; my wife and my children belong to me and they will do what I tell them to do) and totalitarianism (rigidly hierarchical legalism, blind adherence to moral principles taught in childhood).[2] As a result, in some historical periods and/or geographical regions and/or social classes, genders, and races, the Other-as-culture may speak individuals with submerged antibourgeois voices: the "normality" in various social contexts of violence directed by whites at blacks, for example, or by fundamentalists at pro-choice people, or by men at women, reflects the survival within bourgeois society of a territorial/medieval Other-as-culture. The Other-as-culture is a collective but individually internalized construct, so that it is possible for different individuals, shaped by different social voices, to be spoken by different Others-as-culture, and to argue over the "true" spirit of American democracy or freedom. Is freedom, for example, the right to run your family or your business without government interference (conservative deregulation policies, resistance to the liberal conception of corporal punishment as child abuse), or is it the right to decide what will be done to or with your body (liberal legislation permitting abortion and forbidding date rape)? Structurally these definitions are congruent, but conservative and liberal Others-as-culture have polarized political debate around them. In periods of social transformation (like ours) there is a proliferation of Others-as-culture, and the result is inevitably widespread social disorientation—no one is quite sure which Other-as-culture is speaking him or her at any given moment, and both carefully monitored pluralism and desperate fundamentalism abound. In periods of revolution there is an attempt to displace Others-as-culture perceived by the revolutionary cadre as outmoded and replace them with a new one, but Others are not so easily displaced, and all too often the new social order is spoken by the old Other-as-culture, making social change largely cosmetic.

Others-as-culture always proliferate, perhaps; it may be sheer apocalyptic mythopoeia that convinces us that we live in a time of greater social disorientation than previous generations. In fact, if the bourgeois era has been notably a time of fragmentation and factionality, it has also—and the paradox is only superficial—been a time of intensely concerted and unprecedentedly effective social control. The runaway success of the bourgeois Other-as-culture has largely been a by-product of that Other's skill at replacing external authority with itself, with its own internal channels of control. Medieval society was deeply divided, with the military territorialism of the nobility on one side and the theocratic totalitarianism of the Church on the other—a clash between the ideologies, to put it aphoristically, of might-makes-right and right-makes-might.[3] The bourgeois Other-as-culture has successfully transcended this division by privatizing both ideologies and subsuming them into its own brand of eirenic inclusivism: we all belong, we are all part of the socius, the demos, the people, and all will be sweetness and light as long as we agree (unconsciously first, consciously second if at all) to put aside our differences and conform to shared social norms. The bourgeois Other-as-culture has dominated by speaking us as *united*. This is the secret of its success: Democrats or Republicans, liberals or conservatives, freethinkers or fundamentalists, we are all Americans. We are all in the same boat and pulling on the same oar.[4]

In actual practice the bourgeois ideology of inclusivism, of incorporat-

ing ever larger segments of the population into the normatively "classless" middle class,[5] has required enormous expenditures of political
energy by the Other-as-culture—which is to say, by every included individual, every member of the democratic polls whose task as a member is
to conform to collective norms and to urge and pressure others to conform as well. Literacy campaigns, universal suffrage campaigns, just-
say-no campaigns, civil rights movements, English Only movements,
programs instituted by the Other-as-capital to transform independent
artisans into wage earners (midnineteenth century) and thrifty producers
into spendthrift consumers (early to midtwentieth century)—what is all
this but an immense effort by the bourgeois Other-as-culture to herd
every last soul on this continent into the "classless" middle class? This
esemplastic effort, this drive toward inclusivist conformity and consensus, is the characteristic impetus of the bourgeois Other-as-culture: that
which distinguishes it from the territorial and totalitarian Others-as-
culture of the European Middle Ages, for example, both of which vacil-
lated between a tolerant indifference toward and the rigid enforcement
of hierarchically exclusive social categories. *Everyone shall belong*, is
the bourgeois imperative, and that imperative has been insinuated most
effectively into the ideosomatic programming governing all "normal"
social behavior since at least the eighteenth century.

The greatest failure in this massive collective project, the one overwhelming wrench in the bourgeois works—and the one that begins to
direct these rather general remarks toward Ring Lardner—was the
nineteenth-century proletarianization of the artisan class.[6] The Other-
as-culture's idea, we may speculate, was to "protect" artisans from the
vicissitudes of self-employment by bringing them under the umbrella of
capital: capitalists would invest workers' labor in production and pay
them dividends in the form both of wages and of job security. Workers
would be happy in their financial security and eager to assimilate their
life-styles to that of the cultured middle class. For better or worse, that
is more or less what the Other-as-culture has managed to do in the
twentieth century, most successfully perhaps (although, in terms of the
stratified survival of superseded Others-as-culture, much more complexly) in Asian cultures like Japan and Korea. But when that project
was first attempted in the nineteenth century it failed miserably, no
doubt owing to the survival of a medieval Other-as-culture within the
ideosomatic structure of capitalism. Rather than striving to assimilate
workers into the middle class with decent wages, reasonable working
hours, safe and pleasant working conditions, varied work tasks, job
security, adequate health care, and a democratic voice in management,
capitalists systematically dehumanized workers in order to maximize

profits. This behavior was more reminiscent of the territorial lords of the Middle Ages than of an enlightened modern bourgeoisie, and the ruling class paid for its failure in the decades around the turn of the century through general strikes and social conflicts bordering alternately on anarchy and revolution.

The new task posed for the ruling class in this period, therefore, was to usher into the bourgeoisie not an independent but upwardly mobile artisan class but rather a disaffected and disenfranchised proletariat. Much of the resulting social change was labor-political, involving new liberal legislation and ideological pressures placed on factory owners to "rehumanize" their workers: pressures to accept labor unions and their right to influence the factory owner's seignorial control of his privately owned domain, and later, pressures to make voluntary concessions to labor (voluntary insofar as they were coerced not by labor activists but by the Other-as-culture).[7] Significantly, however, a good deal of this "welfare capitalism" was culture-political as well, in the liberal sense of "culture": new concerns for universal literacy and the assimilation of proletarian speech patterns to norms of bourgeois written language (the war on "ain't," for example); the English Only movement (the attempt to eradicate ethnic differences through the systematic application of pressure on workers who spoke foreign languages and/or spoke English with an accent); the public library movement and the endless debates over what books should be made available to proletarian book borrowers who used libraries because they could not afford to buy their own books; and the outcry against story papers and dime novels that *were* cheap enough for workers to buy, and the attempt to "educate" the proletariat by upgrading its reading habits.[8]

Effective as this project was, it had one glaring defect: it required the application of external pressures on recalcitrant social groups. It required that managers, teachers, and librarians impose unwelcome rules on workers, children, and book borrowers, and that they use monetary, physical, or emotional force (economic sanctions, corporal punishment, humiliation) to drive their lessons home. It had the effect, as the wielding of external authority invariably does, of facilitating the articulation of resistance. It made it possible (though that possibility was not always actualized) for workers and their children to become aware of the intense pressures being brought to bear on them, for them to name those pressures for what they were—an intrusion from an alien social sphere, waving a stick that was all too familiar from the past and a carrot that did not look particularly attractive—and, in response, for them to dig in their heels.[9]

Far more effective, probably in large part because it was never conceived as a movement or a campaign, was the American literary tradition

of vernacular humor, which in the midnineteenth century began to cod-
ify, as it were, proletarian speech—to transform it into "literature." This
is clearly, as Merritt Moseley has shown, the tradition Lardner most
consistently and successfully mined in his own dialectal writings: the
tradition of "Josh Billings" (Henry Wheeler Shaw, 1818–85), "Petroleum
V. Nasby" (David Ross Locke, 1833–88), "Artemus Ward" (Charles Far-
rar Browne, 1834–67), "Mark Twain" (Samuel Langhorne Clemens, 1835–
1910), and, closer to home, Lardner's humorist predecessors on the
Chicago newspapers, George Ade (1866–1944) and Finley Peter Dunne
(1867–1936).[10] Moseley comments:

> Because these comedians write for newspapers, or at least for magazines,
> the typical production is short and frequently ephemeral. In fact, it is usually
> nonfiction, taking the form of the essay, the letter (especially a newspaper
> dispatch), the fable, or collection of *sententiae*—but usually some form of
> the essay. The language is in dialect, or some distorted variety of American
> English. And the writer tends to use a persona, who mishandles the lan-
> guage, but frequently exposes the author's real opinions. (45)

Moseley is mainly interested in the verbal techniques of this humor,
and traces at some length the "deviations" from "normal" or "standard"
American English used by these writers—which is itself, as I will show,
the "normal" or "standard" or majoritarian critical approach to minoritarian writing. He is also interested primarily in the writers themselves
rather than the social contexts in which they wrote and were read, and
so lists the typical features of this tradition in terms of what the writers
did: wrote for newspapers and magazines, wrote essays or letters, wrote
in dialect, used a persona. This is a useful list, but I want to come at it
from the other direction: what cultural factors motivated the use and
popularity of these features?

What is it, for example, about the ephemerality of newspapers and
magazines that makes them appropriate vehicles for dialogue between
the proletarian reader and the writer chosen by the Other-as-culture to
address that reader? We saw T. S. Matthews suggesting in 1929 that this
reader is one who doesn't read books—one who reads, by implication,
the newspapers and magazines in which Lardner, like almost all the
vernacular humorists, was first published. As Michael Denning has
shown in his recent study of dime novels and their working-class readers,
this characterization is not strictly accurate: such readers did read dime
novels, and avidly.[11] But Denning also shows that dime novels and the
story papers they evolved from were as ephemeral as newspapers, and
reading one was "like reading a newspaper with a plot" (91).

In this context one might also say that the serial novel was one attempt to push the book back into the ephemerality of the newspaper, or even further, into the radical ephemerality of what Leslie Shepard calls "street literature" ("the cheap ballad-sheets, pamphlets, and other ephemera of the masses" [13]). The humorous columns and letters of the vernacular humorists were clearly an older form of writing than serial novels, more disposable, more topical and less plotted, more patently tied to a street tradition in literature.[12] Serial novels were typically reprinted in book form soon after completion of the serial, and were sold *as* books to the same class of readers who had read the serial; the newspaper pieces of the vernacular humorists were typically only collected in book form much later, often at the behest of a more "sophisticated" middle-class audience who wished to impart cultural permanence to the literary productions they enjoyed.

This drive toward permanence, toward the construction of a stable cultural object for bourgeois consumption, has a good deal to do with the proletarian preference for ephemeral writing (which proletarian readers would prefer not to call "literature"). The characteristic literary artifact for the culturally literate bourgeoisie in this period (from the mid-nineteenth century to the 1920s) is the leather-bound edition of a literary classic — an *Odyssey* or an *Aeneid* in English translation — which has been provided with a normative cultural permanence not only by expensive bookbinding techniques but by an educational system that has programmed bourgeois minds with a stable ideosomatic structure called the "great books."[13] Possession of these books in both the material and the intellectual sense, as both physical objects and as "immortal works of art" (as both economic and ideological commodities), is one of the telltale signs of membership in the bourgeois polis: the possessor of such books is literate, educated, cultured, hence worthy of inclusion in the great bourgeois movement. Thus the appearance in the teens and twenties of new commercial channels for the dissemination of middle-class books: Collier's publishes Charles William Eliot's fifty-volume *Harvard Classics* (the "five-foot shelf of books") in 1909–10; John Erskine introduces the first course in the "Great Books of the Western World" at Columbia College in 1918, and this curricular concept quickly becomes the cornerstone of the liberal arts; DeWitt Wallace and Lila Acheson found the *Reader's Digest* in 1922, and Harry Scherman founds the Book-of-the-Month Club in 1926, both (though in different ways) giving middle-class readers easier access to "important" books.[14]

By contrast, the characteristic literary artifact for the proletariat in the same period is one or another form of disposable paper: the newspaper, the magazine (often a weekly story paper, like the *Saturday Evening Post* at its birth in 1821[15]), the paperbound dime novel. It is literally "trash lit," literature meant to be read and thrown in the trash.[16] Because the leather-bound classic, with the "reading map" attached to it by the Other-as-culture and somatized by the ideal conformist middle-class reader, was the majoritarian norm of the period (and remains so to our day), it is easy to conceive "trash lit" as somehow failing to rise to the normative level — as unable to escape what Leslie Fielder calls the literary ghetto.[17] From a minoritarian viewpoint, it is just the reverse: the real prison is the middle-class literary norm, from which the well-trained bourgeois reader cannot escape and in which the proletarian reader does not want to be incarcerated. Reading and trashing ephemeral literary productions is at least potentially a form of nomadic literacy, a way of participating in literary culture without being ideally conformed to *bourgeois* literary culture, and to the esemplastic norms that culture enacts and enforces.

Potentially — not necessarily in reality. The vernacular humor tradition was minoritarian in impulse and outward form, but it nevertheless frequently, and subtly, and very effectively, served majoritarian purposes. Where campaigns against trash lit have by definition been authoritarian, attempting to impose alien cultural norms on a proletarian readership from without, weaning readers from the trashy writing they prefer and putting them on a more "solid" diet of "good literature," vernacular humor has been what we might call "lectoritarian," approaching proletarian readers from inside their own heads, inside their own vernacular speech.[18] This lectoritarian approach motivates the other three features in Moseley's list, the essay or letter form and the use of dialect and a persona: all three offer proletarian readers idealized projections of the self, proletarian personas or masks who write letters and tracts and other familiar texts in familiar linguistic forms. Because these selves are so constructed as to be easy for the proletarian reader to identify with, they are much more effectively internalized than such normative middle-class figures as teachers and librarians, novelists and poets — or, to put it the other way, they are much less effectively resisted. They get inside the proletarian reader's skin and *become* the reader — or coach that reader to (re)define him- or herself in terms of them.

What is thus internalized is, of course, from a middle-class viewpoint, still deviant: the vernacular humorist's persona distorts standard American English, or as Moseley says, "mishandles the language," sneers at (at best scrambles) venerated cultural artifacts, revels in a kind of idealized ignorance, and generally thumbs his nose at majoritarian culture. But the very fact of that deviance also serves to bridge the cultural gap between the disenfranchised proletariat and the bourgeois "franchise," the inclusivist destination toward which the Other-as-culture is pushing the excluded classes. The idealized ignorance of the vernacular persona subjectifies the proletarian reader *as* deviant, *as* ignorant and proud of it, and in getting him or her to laugh at this idealized self nudges the reader a few steps closer to a transitional middle ground between the proletariat and the "classless" middle class, between peripherality and centrality, between ephemerality and permanence.[19]

Nor is that laughter necessarily a channel of ridicule, of satire, as so many of Lardner's elitist critics (Mencken, Seldes, Geismar) have insisted. To say that the vernacular humorist coaches the proletarian reader to laugh at an idealized subjectivity, or to subjectify a laughable self, is not necessarily to say that the reader is being taught to despise him- or herself. I have argued that self-loathing in Lardner is always mixed up with a powerful dose of sympathy, with a sense that the laughable self is desperately needy and acts largely, and poignantly, out of that need — and the same is true, mutatis mutandis, of all the vernacular humorists. They coach readers to subjectify profoundly sympathetic selves, in both the English sense of feeling sympathy and the European sense of drawing it. If these selves were not sympathetic, in fact, they would not be attractive to readers and the magic would not work: there would be no identification and thus no subjectification of the self as deviant.

The impact of American vernacular humor on the late-nineteenth-century and early-twentieth-century proletariat might be compared, in fact, to advertising, the quintessential channel of bourgeois social conditioning, which also begins to emerge as a potent social force in the early twentieth century.[20] The successful television commercial, for example, does not tell the viewer what to do. It does not stand above or outside the viewer's social world and hand out advice on the best way to improve his or her life. It goes into that life and speaks the viewer from the inside, from inside his or her own head, own speech, own life experience. It subjectifies that experience in Althusser's double sense of fleshing out an articulated subjectivity where before there was confusion, and of subjecting that articulation to a desirable behavior pattern — buying the company's product, believing in the company's name, becoming a regular customer. To drink Coke or Miller beer is no longer then merely to consume a beverage; it is to participate in a life-style, to have the Coke experience (the "real thing") or to live in Miller time. The commercial gives definition to an inchoate existence, and the definition includes, structurally, buying the advertised product.[21]

In the same way the vernacular humorists make proletarian readers laugh at themselves, easily, affectionately, and in so doing flesh out a world where it is acceptable to be "ignorant," "semiliterate," and generally resistant to bourgeois culture. They *define* proletarian life for their readers, give it literary form and give them literary existence, a structured verbal subjectivity. There is no attempt to force readers into an alien cultural grid; the subjectivity created for them feels familiar, feels right, and the very rightness of the fit is a large part of what makes them laugh. It is the laughter of recognition, the laughter of the mirror-stage infant recognizing its reflection and feeling securely (though divisively) ordered by it. The effect of vernacular humor is to enable proletarian readers to "be themselves"—for the first time. It creates selves for them to be, and the selves seem uncannily to fit.

Again, this is not a conspiracy theory. Just as, a moment ago, I stressed that this writing did not necessarily teach proletarian readers to despise themselves, so now let me stress that it was not a concerted effort (let alone a cynical plot) to subject them to a cultural stereotype, to reduce them to stick-figure caricatures. It was, I believe, a sincere attempt to bring proletarian speech into literary existence, give it literary form.

But it was also, I believe further, spoken by the Other-as-culture—which is neither a group of conspirators nor a disembodied conspiratorial impulse. It was another project designed—not by the writers themselves, not even recognized as such by the writers themselves, but by a bourgeois Other-as-culture that needed to remedy the proletarianization of the artisan class—to bring workers into the idealized classlessness of the middle class. Where literacy and library campaigns had attempted to achieve this same result by reshaping them in the cultural image of the bourgeoisie, however, vernacular humor worked to define the working class, to articulate it, to give it its own form and resolution, to subjectify it "as is," and then simply *append* it to the bottom of the middle class. It was not necessary, the Other-as-culture realized in and through the work of these writers, to force the proletariat into cultural conformity with existing bourgeois behavior; it was enough simply to give them cultural definition and include them in the "classless" polis of liberal ideology, where they would share certain common features with the bourgeoisie (literacy, the desire to improve their financial and social standing, a qualified feeling of belonging) but would retain their hostility to "culture" and the whole array of "bosses," management from industry to education.

I am talking, of course, of the creation of a new lower middle class in the early decades of this century, which in actual fact involved the inclusion of a large sector of the working class in an expanded middle-class base. It is a brilliant conception: let us stop polarizing management and labor, the middle class and the working class, and simply *call* the proletariat part of the bourgeoisie, a lower but nevertheless included part. Pay them decent wages and stimulate and guide the spending of those wages on consumer goods, so that they increasingly begin to live a middle-class life-style; upgrade their job titles (earth-moving contractor, sanitation engineer) so that they can hold up their heads in middle-class society; introduce training programs for various lower-middle-class "professions" into the curricula of high schools, junior colleges, and universities, and pass legislation requiring a certain level of vocational training (but call it "education") for employment or business licensing.

For this co-optation to be successful, of course, the proletariat had to be called part of the middle class from the inside, from inside every worker's head. It would not be sufficient merely to declare, in the press or in a legislative resolution of some sort, that henceforward the working class will no longer be called the working class but will be referred to as the lower middle class. Every worker must rather be subjectified as middle-class, must hear the voice of his or her own subjectivity calling him or her into the classless middle.

And this, I am suggesting, is an important function of the vernacular humor tradition—along with sports, movies, comic strips, jazz, and other plebeian entertainments. (By the post-World War II period the list would include television, rock music, and glossy soft-core pornography like *Playboy* alongside the older entertainments and their modern variants, such as Monday Night Football, stand-up comedy, and animated cartoons for adults like *The Simpsons*.) Or rather—since this depiction of the use of these entertainments by the Other-as-culture makes it sound like a one-way process, by which an esemplastic art form is generated in order to mold readers into the desired social shape—this subjectification of the working class as lower middle class is a function of the dialogue or dialectic between vernacular humorist and lower-middle-class readers, between Lardner and the hoi polloi. I am imagining a kind of Bakhtinian transformation of Michel Foucault, a dialogization of Foucault's arguments in "The Discourse on Language" and "What Is an Author?" to the effect that "institutions" (what I would call, roughly, the Other-as-culture) dominate and distribute the production of discourse:

> Inclination speaks out: "I don't want to have to enter this risky world of discourse; I want nothing to do with it insofar as it is decisive and final; I would like to feel it all around me, calm and transparent, profound, infinitely open, with others responding to my expectations, and truth emerging, one by one. All I want is to allow myself to be borne along, within it, and by it, a happy wreck." Institutions reply: "But you have nothing to

fear from launching out; we're here to show you discourse is within the
established order of things, that we've waited a long time for its arrival,
that a place has been set aside for it—a place which both honours and
disarms it; and if it should happen to have a certain power, then it is we,
and we alone, who give it that power." ("Discourse" 215-16)

But what is that "power"? It is, for Foucault, the power to include or
exclude, to allow or to prohibit, to fuse or divide; but include or exclude
what? People, clearly—"subjects," individuals subject(ifi)ed by hegemonic discourse—but Foucault does not explore that subject(ificat)ion
in his discourse. He treats it as simply the ground on and toward which
discourse is hegemonically directed, the target hit by the aimed arrow of
discourse, that which, by being hit, demonstrates the effect of institutional guidance on the archer's performance. The closest he comes in
"The Discourse on Language" to a dialectical or dialogical understanding
of the writer-reader or speaker-listener interaction is his discussion of
the speech of the mad:

> It is curious to note that for centuries, in Europe, the words of a madman
> were either totally ignored or else were taken as words of truth. They
> either fell into a void—rejected the moment they were proffered—or else
> men deciphered in them a naive or cunning reason, rationality more ra-
> tional than that of a rational man. At all events, whether excluded or
> secretly invested with reason, the madman's speech did not strictly exist. It
> was through his words that one recognized the madness of the madman;
> but they were certainly the medium within which this division became
> active; they were neither heard nor remembered. No doctor before the end
> of the eighteenth century had ever thought of listening to the content—
> how it was said and why—of these words; and yet it was these which
> signalled the difference between reason and madness. Whatever a madman
> said, it was taken for mere noise. (217)[22]

It is instructive to note Foucault's syntactic evasions of the interpreting
subject: he/she/it appears in the succession of passive constructions
("were either totally ignored or else were taken," "were neither heard nor
remembered"), in the depersonalized "one" ("that one recognized the
madness"), in the masculinized/genericized "men" ("men deciphered in
them"), and in the negated "doctor" ("no doctor . . . had ever thought").
Implicit in this passage, but only implicit, is a channeling of "institutional" discursive power through subject(ifi)ed interpreters as well as
utterers: the division between mad and sane discourse is activated (imposed on mad speakers) by interpreters, by "men" or "doctors" who did
or did not construct mad speech as language. The implication, sub-

merged in Foucault's discourse, is that interpreters (readers and listeners) are not merely the depersonalized backdrop for the institutional control of discourse but active subjects constituted as active and as subjects in dialogical interaction with utterers (writers and speakers), who in turn are active subjects constituted as active and as subjects in dialogical interaction with interpreters.

Foucault hints more strongly in this direction in his next paragraph, where the interpreters of mad discourse become "we," our "selves" as listeners to our own "madness":

> Of course people are going to say all that is over and done with, or that it is in the process of being finished with, today; that the madman's words are no longer on the other side of this division; that they are no longer null and void, that, on the contrary, they alert us to the need to look for a sense behind them, for the attempt at, or the ruins of some *"oeuvre"*; we have even come to notice these words of madmen in our own speech, in those tiny pauses when we forget what we are talking about. But all this is no proof that the old division is not just as active as before; we have only to think of the systems by which we decipher this speech; we have only to think of the network of institutions established to permit doctors and psychoanalysts to listen to the mad and, at the same time, enabling the mad to come to speak, or, in desperation, to withhold their meagre words; we have only to bear all this in mind to suspect that the old division is just as active as ever, even if it is proceeding along different lines and, via new institutions, producing rather different effects. Even when the role of the doctor consists of lending an ear to this finally liberated speech, this procedure still takes place in the context of a hiatus between listener and speaker. For he is listening to speech invested with desire, crediting itself — for its greater exultation or for its greater anguish — with terrible powers. If we truly require silence to cure monsters, then it must be an attentive silence, and it is in this that the division lingers. (217)

I have quoted this passage at length because it points so strongly not only to the methodological problem I am raising, but to the cultural locus I am exploring: in a very real sense the voicing of the proletariat in the work of the vernacular humorists *is* the voicing of the mad, the silenced, those who are excluded from bourgeois society (as defined in and by rational discourse) on the grounds that they cannot speak so as to be heard, and are not-heard so as to be excluded. In the history of the proletariat, the utterer-interpreter dialectic that Foucault adumbrates in "The Discourse on Language" was once the Other-as-culture's channel of exclusion, the dialogical ground on which the proletariat was not-heard, not-voiced, and not-included; in "vernacular humor" (which is, dialectically understood, neither funny writing nor the reader's laughter but the "humorous" dialogical interchange), that dialectic becomes the Other-as-culture's channel of inclusion, the dialogical ground on which the proletariat becomes heard/voiced and included. And just as Foucault notes the survival, in our new attention to the content and the contours of mad discourse, of the old hegemonic divisions, so too does the voicing of the proletariat in vernacular humor still contain within it reverberations of exclusion: the voicing of the proletariat allows us to determine just how different or deviant they are, how distorted their speech is, how ungrammatical their writing is, how ignorant and semiliterate they remain.

The ideological congruence between the mad in Foucault's discourse and the proletariat in mine might in fact be underscored by paraphrase: "we have even come to notice these words of *workers* in our own speech, in those tiny pauses when we forget what we are talking about," when proletarian "ignorance" or "semiliteracy" strikes us from within our own middle-class discourse; when the idealized control of our verbal representation of an object that constitutes us as rational middle-class speakers deserts us, for a moment, and leaves us stranded in a blank world devoid of representable objects or significant words; when grammar, punctuation, and spelling—tools of bourgeois verbal reason-building—desert us and leave us stranded in unhearable verbal incoherence.

Now, just as the rise of psychoanalysis voiced the mad, so too, after the work of the vernacular humorists (in columns, stories, comic strips, movies, television shows, stand-up comedy), the voice of the proletariat is no longer silenced, no longer not-heard. But insofar as it is heard, that voice is no longer proletarian. In the nineteenth century, for a middle-class speaker to hear the silenced voice (or the voiced silence) of the proletariat in his or her own speech was to experience a momentary return of the repressed. But it does not follow from this that the vernacular humor tradition constituted a release of repression. Throughout the history of the bourgeoisie, to be proletarian or otherwise subbourgeois and yet be heard, be voiced, has been by definition to become bourgeois. Before what we might call the "esemphonic" assimilation of the proletariat to the middle class in our own century, there was only one means to this end: to learn your master's voice, to accommodate your voice to the speech of the cultured middle classes—Samuel Johnson, for example. This is still a viable alternative (witness Harold Bloom), but the bourgeois annexation of the working class in the form of a lower middle class opened up the possibility of being heard in your "own" voice, which is, of course, not really your own at all, but a prole version of your master's voice, the Other-as-culture's collective impersonation of the working class. The principle remains the same—you can be heard if you speak in a recognized or "received" voice—only now there is a slightly wider variety of received voices.

In the midst of this change, however, the old association of the proletariat (as of the mad) with silence survives. The stratified sedimentation of the Other-as-culture means, among other things, that no hegemonic formation is ever lost—it is simply buried under a new layer of cultural norms which conceal but do not deactivate it. In Foucault's gnomic words, "if we truly require silence to cure monsters, then it must be an attentive silence." The dual implication is both that the silencing of the mad and the proletariat survives even their apparent voicing (in the "attentive" forms of psychoanalysis and vernacular humor), and that the monsters of the Other-as-plebe, the Other-as-madness, the Other-as-anarchy are never really cured, only repressed, and may surface in the midst of our esemphonic self-silencing when we least expect it.[23]

The interior dialogue in which we hear disturbing gaps in our own speech suggests a number of fruitful pathways past the authoritarian construction of an "author" who first generates discourse (by imitating other people's speech, for example) and then disseminates it to vague "readers." Most obviously—though complexly—it suggests Bakhtin's thesis that all speech is internally dialogized, that there is no external verbal object to imitate, only pre- and constantly redialogized encounters in which another's speech to me is internalized and subtly transformed in(to) my speech to myself, which in turn is internalized and transformed again in(to) my speech to another. Thus the stammerings of baseball players' and other plebeian speakers' dialogues with Lardner are transformed into Lardner's dialogues with proletarian readers, remaining charged, throughout the series of dialogical transformations, with both distance and intimacy. Foucault calls the distance the "hiatus between listener and speaker," which in Lardner's dialogues with proletarian speakers and readers is typically actualized in the form of submerged class distinctions; it is built into the dialogues in various shades of ironic detachment, condescension, and ridicule, all of which leads some elitist readers to believe that Lardner is doing satire. The intimacy is the connection between dialogists, the interchange between dialogical equals in which each becomes the other, each internalizes the other's words *as self*, so that, for example, Lardner becomes the proletarian speaker and the reader becomes the upper-middle-class writer, and the dialogues fairly seethe with conflicted sympathy, with an uneasily poignant and mournful fellow feeling.

This dialogical channeling of what I have been calling the esemphonic assimilation of the working class to the middle class suggests the importance not of isolating for study either Lardner as author or the hoi polloi as readers, but rather of studying the two as dialogically intertwined. In some sense, in fact, this is what many of Lardner's critics have perforce done in their attempts to flesh out a sense of his proletarian readership: in the absence of hard evidence of proletarian reading, of who was reading Lardner and why and how, these critics have projected their own dialogues with Lardner outward onto an imagined proletarian readership, have constructed a writer-reader dialogue between Lardner and the "masses" or the "wide audience." These imaginary dialogues typically resonate out of the critic's own political unconscious, as elitist critics have imagined Lardner sneering at or at best condescending to his proletarian readers, who in turn are too dense to realize that they are themselves the targets of his attack; and populist critics have imagined those readers appreciating Lardner's artistic worth long before the intellectual critics jumped on the bandwagon.

And it seems to me that, given the absence of empirical research into Lardner's actual contemporary proletarian readers—research on the order of Janice Radway's or Elizabeth Long's study of the readers of romances—there is not much more that we can do than this sort of dialogical projection.[24] The little more that we can do is dual; the first part has been my concern in this chapter so far, and the second will be my concern in the next few pages, and in an extended sense in the rest of the chapter. We can both (1) ground the projections we make in as detailed a social context as we can, and (2) bring the unconscious resonances of these projections to complex conscious articulation.

I understand the first task, to encapsulate my argument so far, in terms of the Other-as-culture's esemphonic assimilation of the late-nineteenth-century American proletariat into the bottom of the early-twentieth-century American bourgeoisie through dialogical encounters between Lardner (and other vernacular humorists like him) and his (and their) readers. The second task is to construct a sense of what the Other-as-culture said to and through these dialogists: what the Other-as-culture led proletarian readers to read in(to) Lardner, what impact the Other-as-culture directed Lardner's work to have on these readers. My approach to this latter task, in accordance with the "deterministic" or "actantial" thrust of my odd-numbered chapters in this book—my attempt to explore the ways in which Lardner's work and its reception have been prestructured by hegemonic forces—is Foucauldian, with the Bakhtinian or dialogical adjustments discussed above. I will be concerned with the "institution's" or the Other-as-culture's structuring not only of the production of discourse, but of its production *and* consumption in Other-directed dialogical interchange.

As I mentioned earlier in the chapter, the specific form I propose to give to the Other-as-culture's direction is the double bind, which I intend to untangle twice, once with each of Lardner's audiences: first with his proletarian readers, then again with his "literate," "articulate," "intellectual" bourgeois readers, the authors of published criticism on him. Clearly, each of these dialogues is itself (at least) dual, since it can be inhabited on either Lardner's or his reader's side: we can imagine the Other-as-culture's commands to Lardner, for example, detailing how he is to address his reader, or its commands to the reader, detailing how he or she is to construe Lardner. (It is also multiple, since Lardner had potentially millions of proletarian readers and fifty or sixty published critics, and a double bind could be articulated for each of those dialogues.) I propose to reduce this potential multiplicity to a mere two dialogues, inhabiting the reader's side of the dialogues (since I have already considered Lardner's side at some length in part II) and specifically two reader roles in succession, projecting the Other-as-culture's commands that coach first "the" proletarian reader, then "the" professional critic, to read Lardner in a certain way.

I conceive the double bind with and through which the Other-as-culture speaks the proletarian reader in terms of a conflicted call simultaneously to proletarian self-acceptance *and* to bourgeois self-improvement. Be proletarian; become bourgeois. Stay as you are and like yourself the way you are; be ashamed of your ignorance and semiliteracy and educate yourself, cultivate your intelligence, increase your word power (as that lower-middle-class magazine *Reader's Digest* urges, on the correct assumption that word power is the key to social power). In dialogue with Lardner, I imagine the reader being coached by the Other-as-culture to construct this conflict in terms of identification with and admiration for Lardner, the simultaneous pressure toward equality and inferiority that facilitates incorporation into the middle class without opening all doors to social advancement:

(1) Identify with Lardner.

(a) Feel that Lardner is your social equal: your neighbor, your best friend. Feel that he *is* you, or that he could have been you, or you him. Feel that he understands you; that you and he see eye to eye.

(b) Feel that he is his narrative persona, that he stands behind the persona, "vouches" for it, and that his persona is the verbal ground on which you and he meet (and become one). Feel confirmed as a person by this meeting.

(c) Laugh at his jokes; never suspect that he is laughing at you. Laugh with him. Take his humor for affectionate banter between equals. Let this banter make you feel like one of the gang.

(d) Take Lardner's success as a writer of your kind of writing to be an imprimatur of *your* social success, an indication that your speech has been granted social acceptance. If newspapers pay Lardner all that money to write the way you talk, the way you talk must have a social mandate.

(e) See his success as something anyone could achieve—you too, if you put your mind to it. It's simply a matter of writing down the way you talk. That Lardner is the successful writer and you are the anonymous reader is sheer luck, just the way things happened. They could have gone the other way.

(2) Admire Lardner.

(a) Look up to him as a "name," one of the greats, someone who made it big. See him as superior to you.

(b) Take strength from his superiority. To the extent that you have any worth at all, it lies in the fact that he cares and writes about you. Take pleasure even in his ridicule of you and your friends (see Holmes, "Lardner" 38).

(c) Admire and envy his skill with words. Wish you could write the way he does, and get paid as much money as he does for writing that way. Dream of doing what he does, and know that your dream is impossible (and that the impossibility is right). Try to remember the funny things he writes in the paper so you can repeat them to your friends, but garble them whenever you attempt a rendition.

(d) Do not write about him. Do not even consider the possibility of writing about him. Tell yourself that you don't know how to "write" (i.e., write well and effectively about something), and wouldn't have anything to say even if you did.

(e) Submerge yourself in Lardner, in the laughter he provokes in you. Feel filled by him—temporarily, while you read him. Wonder at your emptiness when you are not reading him.

(3) Internalize the commands in both (1) and (2).

(a) Understand without being told that what is at stake is more than your enjoyment of a weekly column or a short story; it is your validation as a human being. If you can conceive yourself as simultaneously Lardner's equal and his inferior, you will be a good citizen and a good person.

(b) Feel his equality as a pressure for you to do better, improve yourself, live up to his example, and his superiority as resignation to never being able to rise above your present station. Feel his equality as superiority, and his superiority as your inferiority.

(c) Allow Lardner's condescension to you to make your current self seem worthwhile, funny, expansive, worth writing about. Feel that there is no need to change it or to rise above it. Your equality with Lardner proves your equality with everyone else.

(d) Allow Lardner's superiority to you to make you feel superior to yourself (see Geismar, *Lardner* 21). By identifying with him you raise yourself above your (present but now discarded) self. Reading him, you are already better than you were, are, or ever will be.

(e) Allow your superiority (as Lardner) to yourself to prove your superiority to everyone else (see Fadiman 316, Spatz 105). Because you're better than everyone else, you are at least as good as you think (hope, dream) you are.

(f) As you rise in your own estimation, feel increasingly uneasy about your identification with Lardner's "ignorant" and "semiliterate" speakers. Tell yourself that Lardner's writing is really very childish, after all, and that you have better things to do than waste your time reading it.

(4) Repress all this, and resent anyone who reminds you of it.

(a) Believe that you are Lardner's equal and anyone's equal. This is the land of equality. Resent anyone who makes you feel inferior (including Lardner).

(b) Believe that Lardner is a great American, a cultural hero, a star whose brilliance makes you feel dull and secure. Resent anyone who suggests that Lardner is a man like anyone else.

(c) Resent anyone who suggests that there might be a conflict between identifying with and admiring Lardner: between egalitarianism and exceptionalism, between democracy and hero worship, between your sense of equality with and inferiority to Lardner.

(5) Idealize the culture that gives the command: "Forbear resenting injuries so much as you think they deserve" (Franklin).

(a) Feel proud to be an American, to live in a country where a writer like Lardner can become rich and famous writing the way you talk, and where you are free to read and enjoy his writing.

(b) Feel the infinite opportunities offered you (and people like you) through the agency of Lardner's success and stories (his success story and his successful stories). Feel pride in the potential superiority implied by these opportunities, and repress both the actual inferiority enforced by the fact that they are only opportunities, not realities, and the potential anger awareness of this discrepancy might generate.

(c) Believe that no one "gives" you a command. This is a free country. You are a free man or woman. You *want* to do all these things. You *decide* to do them out of the fullness of your personal autonomy.

(d) Forbear resenting anyone who suggests that you might be the victim of social programming or manipulation. Scoff at such arrant nonsense. Rest easy in your scoffing. Don't show your anger. Don't bloody the person's nose.

What is interesting about this formulation of the Other-as-culture's command to the proletarian reader in dialogue with Lardner is that it is partly spoken through the intelligentsia who are also reading him — that what we find ourselves dealing with is not, in other words, two distinct audiences, "two types of mind that are at opposite extremes" (508), as Bessie Graham wrote in *The Bookman's Manual* of 1928, but two intertwined social dialogues. The very fact that, as Graham went on to say, Lardner is "read with delight by people who talk in the very way that he writes, and by highly educated people who find relief and amusement in a lack of education in others" (508), suggests that the two audiences are both politically and emotionally intertwined: the "relief" and the "amusement" that the educated find in the uneducated not only parallel but in some sense perpetrate the "relief" and the "amusement" that the uneducated are to find in themselves. To be relieved and amused by the proletariat is to feel unangered and unintimidated by them — it is to feel that they are harmless enough to be amusing, which is a great relief to the educated, the cultured ruling class — and this is precisely the lower-middle-class self-conception that the Other-as-culture wants to instill in proletarian readers.

This dialogical intermeshing of readers and writers across class and other social barriers has the effect of replicating the duality of Lardner's audience all up and down the social scale, transforming the intellectual/ semiliterate hierarchy into a proliferating series of doubly bound hierarchies. Thus in the first major period of Lardner criticism, from 1922 to 1934, the dual audience is ideologically folded into intellectual readings in the form of a *polemos* between elitist-intellectual and populist-intellectual, each of which takes an upper and a lower form: the elitist-intellectual critique is torn between readings of Lardner as superior satirist and as failed artist, the populist-intellectual between condescending and compassionate readings. In the second period, from 1956 to the present, there is a carryover of the elitist-populist distinction, but now it is increasingly displaced by a scientific-intellectual vs. moralist-intellectual opposition, each of which again operates in a tension between upper and lower: the scientific-intellectual between detached sociopsychoanalytical readings and classifications of mode and character, and the moralist-intellectual between readings of Lardner as morally admirable because superior to his morally reprehensible characters and as morally reprehensible because indistinguishable from those characters.

In all these dialogues the Other-as-culture utilizes Lardner as a counter or marker for social status, as a measure of the reader's standing in society.[25] The difference between any two audiences is complementary and relational rather than polar: the "upper" reader (the critic in relation to the proletarian reader, the elitist or scientific intellectual in relation to the populist or moralist intellectual) sees Lardner as an equal but feels inclined to regard him as an inferior, whereas the "lower" reader (proletarian, populist, moralist) sees Lardner as superior but dreams of equality.

In particular, Lardner's address to the proletarian reader arouses the elitist or scientific critic's suspicions: is this satire or slumming? Is Lardner ridiculing the speech of the lower orders, or is he identifying with it (and thus with them)? In traditional terms, we might phrase this interpretive decision as one between Lardner as peer and Lardner as class traitor; but the binary purity of that traditional frame doesn't really work with American vernacular humor, or even, perhaps, with American culture in general. The American Other-as-culture is simultaneously dedicated to the disturbing liberal ideal of equality (sameness, leveling of social hierarchies) and the reassuring political fact of inequality (difference, hierarchies of wealth, status, and power), and balances the two by coloring both stable class distinctions and unstable class transformations with ideologically plastic liberal ideals. Thus the fact of class differentiation in a supposedly classless society is glossed over through an unconscious attentiveness to or Other-directed awareness of pluralism (different but equal) and tolerance for difference, while the fact of upward mobility, giving the lower orders access to cultural goods once available only to the ruling class, is glossed over through an attentiveness to or awareness of egalitarianism (equal rights, equal opportunities) and inclusivism. When it becomes necessary for social stability to incorporate the working class into the bottom of the middle class, therefore, the Other-as-culture works at once to speak the proletarian as inferior but equal (and hence as happy but firmly in their place), and to speak the ruling class as equal but superior (and hence as still in control but tolerant of potentially threatening change).

This two-pronged assault on social unrest makes it exceedingly difficult for American literary critics to cling to any clearly defined social-critical stance. It means that any feeling of superiority, equality, or inferiority is "inherently" (ideologically) suspect, because the Other-as-culture always whispers the excluded complement of any stance the critic cares to adopt. Lardner's elitist critics in the twenties and thirties, for example, would like him to be a Fitzgerald, a Hemingway, a Sherwood Anderson, but he's not; he cares too little about "literature," about literary majority, and about majoritarian characters to be assimilated to that caste. Barring that, they would like him to be a hack, easily dismissable, but he's not; he has too good an ear, and influenced too many of the period's major writers, to be ignored. So they see him as a satirist, a writer whose virulent attacks on the people whose voices he records raises him above them, places him on an equal footing with his elitist critics (Mencken, Fadiman, Seldes); but satire is a narrow mode, based, as Fadiman says, on the rather repetitive venting of sheer animosity, and in any case not all Lardner's writing fits the satiric rubric (what do you do with the nonsense plays, or sentimental pieces like "There Are Smiles"?). Or they see him as a *potentially* great writer, a writer of hidden genius that he is wasting on inferior subjects and literary forms but might one day learn to exploit (Wilson, Fitzgerald, Hemingway); but no matter how you pushed him he absolutely refused to try his hand at the "right" sort of literature (a "big" novel).

His populist critics from the same period, on the other hand, would like to see him as great *because* he is popular, *because* he is forging a new vernacular humor out of the speech of the people; but either they can't quite reconcile his ephemeral, topical popularity with lasting greatness and so liken him to Shakespeare and Chekhov (Matthews), or they can't quite reconcile the notion of his lasting greatness with his popularity and so liken him to a good baseball player so possessed by the play action that he is completely devoid of self-awareness (Woolf, Van Doren, Tiverton).

One populist critic, Robert Littell, is so conscious of his inner divisions on this issue that he writes his review of *The Love Nest and Other Stories* in dialogue, with one voice ("R.L.," presumably signaling the authorial voice but leaving an interesting ambiguity as to *which* author is meant) mouthing the elitist critical platitudes, while another, "S.S.V." for "STILL SMALL VOICE," launches a powerful lower-middle-class polemic against the entire project of criticism: "Now have you said, are you ever likely to say, anything about Lardner which will be the whole truth about him, and not also part of the truth about something else?" (149). "R.L." says no, and realizes that is would now be fraudulent for him to write about Lardner at all; "S.S.V." says that this is all he wanted, to keep

"R.L." from writing, and leaves, whereupon "R.L.," calling his interlocutor "our misguided friend," finishes up in a carefully unparodic (and therefore even more subtly parodic?) one-paragraph review of the book. In the course of deciding not to write about Lardner, Littell does write about Lardner; in the course of ejecting as "misguided" the still small voice of his Other-as-plebe, he writes the usually silenced voice of the "inarticulate" proletarian reader (at least the one in his own head) into populist Lardner criticism.

In each of these camps there is also a constant jostling for position, a shifting attempt to "place" Lardner in relation not only to his popular audience but also to critics of the opposite camp; suggestive examples of this jostling from Lardner's own lifetime might be T. S. Matthews in 1929, speaking for the populist camp, and F. Scott Fitzgerald writing to Maxwell Perkins on May 1, 1925, speaking for the elitist camp:

> Ring Lardner has at last been accepted by the critics, but more as a curiosity than anything else — in much the same way that jaded hostesses, a few years ago, used to import professional boxers after dinner to entertain their guests. It always becomes fashionable, among civilized people at a certain point of decadence, to admire the low, the vulgar and the criminal; and, though there may be other qualities which Ring Lardner's stories best exemplify [as Matthews will in fact insist], these subjects are present in his work, and they form the principal reason, I think, why he has become almost a fad with the intelligentsia. (Matthews 35)

> The boob critics have taken him up and always take a poke at the "intelligentsia" who patronize him. But the "intelligentsia" — Seldes & Mencken discovered him (after the people) while the boob critics let *The Big Town* and *Gullible's Travels* come out in dead silence. (Fitzgerald, in Kuehl and Bryer 104)[26]

Both Matthews and Fitzgerald agree that Lardner is essentially (as Matthews would say), or was originally (as Fitzgerald would say), a popular writer who is belatedly taken up by the intellectuals and touted, often condescendingly, as a potentially great writer. The difference in their critical perspectives revolves around the relative status they assign elitist and populist critics: for Fitzgerald, elitist critics not only beat populist critics to the draw, but also discovered in Lardner something that the "people" never saw, his literary greatness; for Matthews, populist critics voice the popular mandate that, he claims, every great writer has invariably had, and must have, to be great. In large part this is an argument over what constitutes literary greatness: a reified universality of theme, characterization, and style, as the elitist critics insist, or an empirical universality of popular appeal, as the populist critics insist.

Just as the bourgeois/proletarian split among Lardner's readers is purified or transcended in the elitist/populist split among his critics during his lifetime, so also is the elitist/populist split purified or transcended among his professional critics after 1956 in a scientist/moralist split and a whole series of proliferating upper/lower tensions within it. Some of the earlier polemics flare up after 1956, most notably in various review essays on Elder's biography, especially John Berryman's powerful elitist dismissal of Lardner in 1956, and in Kenneth S. Lynn's Fadimaniac review of *The Ring Lardner Reader* — edited by the equally Fadimaniac Maxwell Geismar — in 1963. By and large, however, by 1960 a new tonal professionalism had set in: with Howard W. Webb, Jr.'s, two excellent articles from that year and Norris W. Yates's sensitive chapter on Lardner in 1964, Lardner criticism was firmly established in a new mode that continues to our day.

This new "mode" is of course mixed; but it is a mixture of depoliticized and argumentatively sanitized critical moves that has come to constitute post-World War II critical discourse. Critical scientism, for example, reifies political battles as textual structure or abstract logical categories, so that arguments over Lardner's relative position in social-cum-literary hierarchies fade into more scholarly (detached, dispassionate, disinterested) debates over whether Lardner was primarily a satirist or a humorist, and which stories should be classified under which rubric (Hasley, Holmes, Moseley), or over whether his greatest strength as a short-story writer lay in his depiction of the vacuity of middle-class life or the grotesqueries of baseball and other sports (Schwartz, Patrick, Yates, Smith, Spatz, Yardley), or over the classification of Lardner's characters' deviations from a monolithically reified "grammar" (Webb ["Development"], Yates, Moseley, Bordewyk). Even among these critical "scientists," determinedly calm in their detached superiority to the moralists, there is a tension between an upper echelon who integrate classifications into complex social, psychological, and historical analyses (Webb, Patrick, Yates, Smith, Spatz, Yardley, Holmes, Moseley) and a lower echelon who just classify (Hasley, Bordewyk) or do plot summaries (Hart). And even the most determinedly scientistic of them feel the pull toward moralism: Yates, for example, in 1964 cannot quite hide his nostalgia for "the old-time Christmas atmosphere of love, cheer, and family solidarity" (187) and notes that, "although exposition ['scientism'] rather than evaluation ['moralism'] is the main task of this volume, one cannot help suggesting that Lardner too often shared the values and interests of his basic character type" (166).

(Similarly, I should note, in my "scientistic" classification of Lardner critics into various proliferating splits or tensions, I am just barely concealing both my reifications and my moral disapproval of such reifications under the ideological argument that these splits are driven by the Other-as-culture. It is "normal" for the professional critic to classify, so I classify: this is the bottom line. My insistence in this parenthesis that the Other-as-culture speaks me as "normal" professional critic by getting me to classify is my desperate and secondary attempt to defuse and redirect some of the esemphonic power of that cultural Other to normatize me, to make me do the normal thing. To repoliticize and rehistoricize a critical practice that has been "purified" of politics and history and established as normal in the abstract, in the null context, is — I hope — to deprive it of some of its power to prescribe what I write.)

Critical moralism in this period reads uncannily like a professionalization or institutional voicing of the lower-middle-class reader, or what Fitzgerald called the boob critic. Elizabeth Evans, in fact, tries to combine the scientistic and moralistic approaches, classifying Lardner's characters into players, cheats, spoilsports with a pointedly moralizing tone: Lardner satirizes characters who "demean" themselves by cheating or otherwise breaking the rules that bind and order sports, but Lardner himself is "above such immature and common behavior" (88), and his ability to keep the reader removed from that behavior makes his writing morally admirable. These moralistic critics again replicate the upper-lower rift, so that where Evans considers Lardner morally upright, Allen F. Stein in 1971 invokes the same criteria to find the opposite: like Jack Keefe, he says, Lardner doesn't take "baseball or any baseball 'code' very seriously" (29); in "Horseshoes" "there is no real sense . . . that justice has been done, and the World Series, in which so many people expect to see a test of skill and character under pressure, is depicted as a kind of comical fraud" (31). There is a social code, a set of rules, that brings order to human existence and a reassuring sense of meaning and security to the moralistic critic; Lardner adheres to that code himself but satirizes characters who break it and lauds characters who learn to live up to that code (Ingram, Evans, DeMuth), or fails to adhere to it and hence fails as an artist (Stein).[27]

Critical moralism is typically concealed in this period through an idealization of the "the reader" as a universalized spokesperson for the moralizing critic. Thus, as I began to show early in chapter 1, it is ostensibly not Donald Elder or Walton Patrick or Jonathan Yardley who is foisting his masculine contempt for women on Tom's wife in "Who Dealt?," but "the reader," the lectoritarian norm, who feels severe discomfort as she lays bare their private life and destroys their marriage. Similarly, it is

not Elizabeth Evans who is foisting her moral judgments on that narrator but the "bridge buff," who upholds high standards for correct play
and shudders as this inept player fails to pay adequate attention to the
other players' bids. It is not Forrest L. Ingram who praises Tom Finch
for his macho defense of his wife's honor in *The Big Town*, who describes Tom as an "upright man" (116) who "undergoes a minor moral
decay during his trip to the east" (117), but "the reader," whose "respect"
for Tom is either won or lost. It is extremely important for these critics
that "the reader" respect an author and his characters, and respect is
won through adherence to a conservative moral code that usually in-
volves never lying, cheating, drinking, breaking the rules, showing disre-
spect for social authorities, or otherwise "demeaning" oneself. A demystified shorthand for all this would be to say that "the reader" who
demands adherence to this code is the lower-middle-class Other-as-
culture, who speaks the critic as moralist and the moralist as critic in
order to defend the integrity of that social group against a "fall" into
either upper-class decadence (sophisticated flouting of the rules) or
lower-class degradation (ignorance of good manners).[28]

Now it may seem as if, the further down the social scale I have de-
scended from the upper-middle-class elitist critics of the twenties to the
lower- or middle-middle-class moralist critics of the seventies and eight-
ies, the more obtrusive or overwhelming the Other-as-culture's dictation
to professional readers in dialogue with Lardner has become—as if critics have less discursive "autonomy" on lower rungs of the ladder, as if
the lower-middle-class intellectuals are more insistently "spoken" by the
Other-as-culture than the upper crust.[29] This is not the case, nor was it
my intention to make that sort of case; but I do recognize the seeming.
The patent fact that the further down the social scale I moved, the
greater emphasis I began to place on the Other-as-culture is no doubt
largely due to the way I am myself spoken by my Other-as-culture—
most particularly in the form of my Other-as-parent. As I entered the
realm of critical scientism, for example, I began to feel and to resist
pressure from my engineer Other-as-father; as I entered the realm of
critical moralism, I began to feel and to resist pressure from my conservative Other-as-(grand)mother. Since I have learned (from an elitist-
intellectual Other-as-culture) to resist those pressures largely by articulating the operation of the Other-as-culture, it does seem as if people like
me are freer of Other-speech than people like my parents.

The very fact that there is a "normal" way to resist parental moralism,
of course—through intellectualism—makes it clear that my supposed
freedom from Other-speech is largely illusory. Any behavior that is rec-

ognized by some segment of society as normal is unquestionably spoken by the Other-as-culture — and, however suspiciously it is viewed by the hegemonic majority of society, the intellectual attempt to understand what others take for granted certainly qualifies for that sort of normality.

More than that, the liberal Other-as-culture does foster the illusion that people who conform easily and comfortably to bourgeois ideological norms without harping on the morality or immorality of others' behavior — that is, members of the upper middle class — are freer, more autonomous, than the insecure lower middle class that must escalate shaky ideological vigilance by imposing rigid rules on peers. It does seem "natural" or "normal," therefore, that elitist intellectuals from the twenties like H. L. Mencken, Edmund Wilson, and Gilbert Seldes should be more autonomous, freer of the speaking of the Other-as-culture, than moralist critics from the postwar period like Allen F. Stein, Forrest L. Ingram, and Elizabeth Evans.

This naturalness is an illusion — a carefully controlled fiction of the Other-as-culture. None of these critics is any freer, any more autonomous, any less effectively controlled by his or her Other-as-culture, than any other. To illustrate the speaking of all Lardner critics by the Other-as-culture, therefore, and to begin to sum up my analysis of Lardner criticism, let me formulate the doubly bound commands by which the Other-as-culture shapes critics' dialogues with Lardner:

(1) Praise Lardner for his popularity and populism.

(a) Defend his popularity by reference to other great writers who began popular and then were "discovered" by the critics. Feel uneasy with highbrow attempts to elevate him to major status. Defend his proletarian readers for their prescience is recognizing his greatness.

(b) Praise him for his sensitivity to, his accuracy in representing, "real" speech — the speech of the "people," the *demos*, the true constituency (however despised) of American democracy. Analyze his linguistic representations as a series of deviations from "standard" English. Don't identify "standard" English as normatized upper-middle-class speech.

(c) Praise him for his topicality. Insist that "topical writing . . . is just the kind of writing which nine out of every ten writers who are worth their salt are engaged in producing" (Matthews 35).

(d) Praise him for financial success; quote Dr. Johnson on the only sensible reason for writing (Yardley, epigraph). Don't identify Dr. Johnson as a working-class upstart who assimilated his writing style (but never his behavior) to the upper middle class.

(e) See yourself as giving the inarticulate readers who love Lardner a voice, and thus as replicating Lardner's fictional achievement in criticism. See yourself (and Lardner) as expanding the verbal base of proletarian resistance to bourgeois conformism. Develop theories of Lardner's (and by implication your own) Other-as-minority that will justify your claim to vocal-ideological identity or solidarity with the proletariat.

(2) Condescend to Lardner's popularity.

(a) Assume that you are superior to both Lardner and the hoi polloi. You can recognize and appreciate great literature: Lardner couldn't write it (and didn't read enough of it), the hoi polloi couldn't read it. See him as a minor writer of primarily historical significance, as a reflection of social mores and popular tastes of the twenties.

(b) Attribute his popularity to his sensationalist pandering to the lower orders' lust for behind-the-scenes revelations: "Lardner's stories convey a perpetual effect of going behind an appearance — perpetual, and cheap, because the appearance is not one that could have taken in an experienced man for five minutes: the revelation is to boobs" (Berryman 421).

(c) Explain his failure to rise above popular writing: the lure of easy money (Wilson), the regressive influence of baseball (Fitzgerald), the shortcomings of the short-story form and his reluctance to write a "big" novel (Wilson, Fitzgerald), his prudery (Hemingway), his "habit of silence" (Fitzgerald, Berryman), his failure to read anything weightier than the sports page (Berryman), his lack of invention or imagination (Berryman), his mother-locked repression (Robinson), his misguided attraction to the musical stage.

(3) Internalize the command to do both (1) and (2). Repress the conflict between them. Damn him with faint praise, praise him with mild condemnations.

(a) See him at once as superior to his popular audience and equal to his professional audience (because he, like you, could *write*), and equal to his popular audience and inferior to his professional audience (because he, unlike you, wrote dialect, knew nothing, and remained uncritically subject to his narrow little fears and prejudices).

(b) Portray him as more moral than either his characters or his professional readers, and view this moralism as at once a liability and his greatest strength (Evans, DeMuth); portray him as having the same moral failings as some of his characters and thus as an artistic failure (Lynn, Stein), and as having the same moral strengths as other characters and thus as an artistic success (Ingram).

(c) Find ways of praising him for his fear of the highbrows (Anderson), his lack of imaginative variety (Van Doren), his lack of artistic awareness (Woolf), his use of a lowbrow mask to hide his highbrow proclivities (Schwartz), his fading journalistic brilliance (Pritchett). Praise him for the professors' neglect of him (Mencken). Praise him for his misanthropy: call him a born hater who by some fluke (his secret affinity with his targets [Lynn], or his targets' "public masochism" [Holmes 38]) retained his popularity among the readers he despised. Laud his emotional limitations, his narrowness of scope, by saying that, "except Swift, no writer has gone farther on hatred alone" (Fadiman 315).

(d) Place your condemnation of his artistic failures in the context of your great personal love and admiration for him: speak of his kindness (Fitzgerald), your indebtedness to him (Hemingway), your childhood love of his baseball stories (Robinson).

(e) Keep your praise and condemnation compartmentalized, while pretending that you're writing about a single author. For example, divide your discussion of Lardner into alternating chapters that show how trapped he was by his doubly binding ideological programming and how he mapped out in the speech of his characters a liberation from that programming.

(f) Do not allow yourself to be tarred by the brush of his minor status. Call him a potential major writer who never quite realized his potential, or retheorize minority as a liberating becoming-minoritarian.

(g) See your failure to reconcile (1) and (2) into a single coherent reading as Lardner's fault.

(4) Repress the commands in (1), (2), and (3). Despise anyone who reminds you of them.

(a) Think of your Lardner criticism as essentially descriptive, representational in a neutral, dispassionate, detached scientific sense. It is "about" Lardner and shaped by the contours of his writing.

(b) Think of your work as emotionally, socially, ideologically unmotivated. You have no reason to believe that you need a reason to study Lardner. He is a writer, you are a critic — critics study writers. Not much work has been done on Lardner, which means that (i) the work needs doing, thus justifying your effort, and (ii) the work should be relatively easy to do, and you should be able to get a quick article or book out of it. Beyond such pragmatic concerns (which you should only give passing private attention to and never mention publicly), do not explore why you chose him rather than other writers to study.

(c) Describe both Lardner and your own work as apolitical. Note Lardner's conservatism, but downplay it in the light of his apolitical nature. He was conservative by "habit," not by "ideology." Do not think of your work as conservative or liberal. These are simply irrelevant descriptors for scholarly work.

(d) Believe that you have no theoretical, methodological, or interpretive (let alone ideological) ax to grind. Think of literary theory as just so much hot air anyway, and dangerous to boot; think of literary criticism as something any sensitive reader who has been exposed to a lot of good literature can do.

(e) Repress awareness of critical desire, will, intentionality, subjectivity (and a fortiori the ways in which those things are directed by collective forces) by reference to "the reader." Assume that all right-thinking readers will be like you anyway, that your experience is universal (can humans be so different?).

(f) Never let it occur to you that your work as a teacher and critic might serve some social function, that you might be "training" students ideologically or transmitting ideology to your readers. Think of colleagues who suggest such things as single-minded dogmatists with a chip on their shoulder who have no right or reason to be in academia — certainly not in an English department.

(5) Idealize the command-giver.

(a) Do not think of the command-giver as the ruling class, or as the voice of the ruling class in your head. Think of yourself as directed, guided, shaped (if at all) by "literature," "art," "culture," "truth."

(b) To the extent that you are given commands by "literature," think of popular writing as a force opposed to "literature" or "art." Associate that counterforce with the "masses" or the "general public" — with the "illiterate" and "uneducated." Think of yourself as discerning existing distinctions between great literature and ephemeral trash, shining the clear light of aesthetic insight through the muddied waters of mass culture and helping "literature" emerge from those waters triumphant. Think of yourself as discovering the gems of "true art" or "genuine literary expression" in the mud of Lardner's ephemeral writing.

(c) To the extent that you are given commands by "truth," think of historical and biographical fact as both logically and methodologically prior to mere cultural concerns like the triumph of literature. Face the facts of Lardner's minority, alcoholism, sexism, and critical neglect with equanimity. Record them neutrally.

(d) Feel the commands but think about them little, talk about them less. Think about them, if at all, as institutional practices (but don't use that phrase for them) — as the way things are done.

I am painfully aware, as I start to bring this chapter to a close, of just how much I am leaving unsaid, unexplored, unanalyzed. My tentative formulation of the double binds with which the Other-as-culture speaks readers of Lardner is still more heuristic than analytic: more a first probe into the ideological shaping of dialogical reading than a solidly researched and argued piece of scholarship. This whole book, in fact, is methodologically provisional in this sense, aimed more at opening up an entire series of new critical and theoretical perspectives than at solving, once and for all, the focal issues of Lardner criticism.

One issue I do want to explore in a bit more detail before I conclude this chapter, however, is the one raised in (4f) above: the question of the social or ideological function of Lardner criticism. Since I devoted quite a few pages to the social function of the proletarian reading of Lardner — subjectifying proletarian readers as members of the lower middle class — it may seem again as if published criticism of Lardner serves no social function at all, that it serves only truth. Obviously, I believe that it does have a social function — but what? To answer this I want to take a look at the one critical debate that has been waged over a Lardner story, "Haircut."

The debate is opened in 1973 by Charles E. May, who takes issue with the traditional reading offered by Brooks and Warren in *Understanding Fiction* (1959) and Walton Patrick in 1963, according to which Jim Kendall "richly deserves his fate" (Patrick 106).[30] This reading subtextually sets the story up as a morality play in which evil is punished "almost" by accident, "as if" by the hand of God, through the agency of a kind of holy fool who is exonerated by the small town's authorities both for his "folly" — his half-wittedness, the fact that he cannot be held morally responsible for his action before the law — and for his "holiness" — the true underlying morality of his deed. The moralizing reader thus comes away from the story with his or her sense of justice renewed or restored; Doc and Julie triumph in their love, the evil prankster is duly punished for his attempted rape of Julie, and Paul and Whitey, the story's two half-wits, are seen as mere vehicles: Paul of justice, Whitey of telling (Paul makes sure evil is punished; Whitey makes sure the narratee and the reader know what it was).

May challenges this moralistic reading by noting that it "ignores the act in the story which is more evil than Jim's jokes; that is, Jim's 'accidental death'" (no page). Murder, May says, even the murder of a sick, warped person, is not to be condoned — and the entire town conspires in both the murder and its coverup. Furthermore, Whitey's task as narrator is to get the reader too to conspire in the coverup, to bring the reader into the same "obtuse moral sense" of the small town, to get the reader "to approve of the extreme penalty for Jim as his just deserts for his practical jokes." The story is ultimately, May argues, Lardner's savage satire on the reader's complicity in an immoral act: "The barber says at the end that 'Jim was a sucker to leave a new beginner have his gun. . . .' But the biggest sucker of all is the reader who, by allowing himself to be taken in by Lardner's control of the story and thus feel so morally superior to the barber, becomes an accomplice to the most evil act of all."

This is clearly still a moralistic reading, simply one at a higher level of interpretive sophistication: where Brooks and Warren and Patrick align Lardner and the reader with the "just" people in town in order to reaffirm everyone's faith in humanity, May pays closer attention to the gaps and contradictions and uneasinesses in Whitey's narration and aligns Lardner *against* the reader and the now *un*just people in town. May still assumes that the story must have a moral, a lesson or message clarifying our imperfect human perceptions or applications of a universalized morality. Jim's practical jokes are cruel, and cruelty is immoral; but murder is far crueler, indeed the cruelest and hence the most immoral act of all. May's reading has the effect of shaking up our moral complacency, our willingness to place on events or stories whatever interpretation is most conducive to our immediate peace of mind. But it does not challenge critical moralism; it merely complicates it. It steals from us the reassuring sense that there is a moral agency (God, or at the very least Lardner) who will see to it that justice is done and our peace of mind restored. It leaves us with the rather barren belief that murder is always wrong but that there is nothing in the universe, or even necessarily in society, to enforce that categorical imperative. In undermining the conservative faith in a providential morality, it also broaches the naked political fact of power, which all too often clashes with morality — and all too often wins.

May's reading went unchallenged for over a decade, and when it was challenged, by Sarah Gilead in 1985, it was really only complicated, not undone.[31] Gilead comes to "Haircut" out of Foucault, and in her title ("Lardner's Discourses of Power") and first paragraph promises a Foucauldian engagement with the naked political fact of (discursive) power that May had implicitly invoked twelve years before. In her reading of

"Haircut" Gilead extends May's critique of the hypocritical town and reader to Lardner himself—the one person May had exempted from censure. Lardner, she asserts, "both condones Jim's murder and covertly attacks the reader for condoning it. The author, like the readers, separates himself by an insuperable moral gulf from Jim's vicious jokes; indirectly defends Jim by ultimately portraying him as a victim of greater violence than even he had been capable of; and, finally, identifies with Jim by himself taking on the role of trickster" (333). Gilead clearly assumes that if a reader sees something in a text it must be there, and the author must therefore have put it there; thus in her second sentence of the passage just quoted she accuses Lardner of setting up first the traditional reading ("insuperable moral gulf"), then May's reading ("victim of greater violence"), then her own ("role of trickster"). Her conclusion: "The author is thus guilty at the very least of radical incoherence as an authoritative presence 'behind' the text" (333). Indeed, since Jim is killed for the "ruthless exposure of weakness," Lardner's sentence for a similar ruthlessness must be death as well, so that "a kind of authorial suicide takes place—the morally reliable authorial *persona* we believed present somewhere in or near the story's satire is himself 'murdered' by the story's ambiguity of purpose" (333).

The Foucauldian impetus of Gilead's reading seems to be that the "radical incoherence" of Lardner's story undoes the bourgeois illusion of authorial intention, of an autonomous subject who creates the story out of the fullness of his creative freedom in order to send a message or inculcate a lesson or paint a picture or whatever. Clearly, however, Gilead still clings to that illusion in her own reading: she accuses Lardner of incoherence, claims that he condemns himself to death, melodramatizes his Foucauldian transcendence as "suicide." The Lardner at whom these accusations are directed is no institutionally generated author function, but a responsible moral agent. The anger that the traditional readers felt toward Jim, which May redirected toward the town and the complicitous reader, Gilead redirects toward Lardner himself, who abdicates the role of "the morally reliable authorial *persona*" and leaves us "'shorn,' bereft of moral lessons and certainties" (333). Gilead's reading too remains a moral one: she knocks one more prop out from under the reassuring moral reading offered by Brooks and Warren and Patrick, the last remaining one, the notion that there is *any* moral agency in the world; but she mourns that loss and seeks someone to blame for it, someone to be "guilty" of destroying it.

Implicit in Gilead's reading, of course—and this may in fact be closer to her plan for the article than I am giving her credit for—is the Foucaul-

dian vision of a deterministic universe in which "authors" are empty
spaces filled in by institutional projections, mechanistic vacuities which
do not intend anything and therefore cannot be held responsible or
found guilty for the moral certainties or uncertainties readers find in
their texts. Gilead cannot quite bring herself to accept this vision with
Foucault's aplomb (or coldness, if you prefer): she holds fast to the last
remaining vestiges of a moral vision. But I note this tonal resistance to
Foucault in Gilead not to attack or ridicule her, but rather to build
into her reading a second view of the story, an implicitly invoked but
argumentatively unrealized view. If we take the two poles of Gilead's
interpretation (one tonally explicit, the other implicit in her references to
Foucault) to be separate readings, I suggest, we can generate a useful
cline of critical responses: first, the traditional reading, in which Jim
Kendall is evil and everyone else is good, and evil is punished; second,
May's reading, in which Lardner is good and everyone else is evil, and
evil is only punished implicitly, in the submerged accusations of Lardner's satire; third, Gilead's residually moral reading, in which Lardner is
as evil as everyone else, indeed his evil ("radical incoherence") makes it
ultimately impossible to distinguish good from evil, and that's bad; and
fourth, Gilead's Foucauldian reading, in which there is no good or evil,
no moral authority at all, and that's just the way things are.

This is a gross ("scientistic") simplification of the readings, of course,
perhaps even a caricature; but it points up the direction they are heading
in and suggests what the next step might be: to flesh out a fuller Foucauldian reading, one amplifying Foucault through a Bakhtinian dialogue
and an articulated Lacanian Other, one such as I have been setting up
throughout this chapter. The obvious next step beyond Gilead's Foucauldian reading, it seems to me, would be to argue that the Other-as-culture
wields Lardner's *and* the critic's combined authority to provide each of
their audiences with a satisfying and ultimately paralyzing "message."

To Lardner's and the Lardner critic's lower-middle-class audience, for
example, the Other-as-culture offers a morality tale that warns against
Jim's brutish behavior: the behavior of the uneducated, unemployed
hick, the poor white trash, the kind of person the Other-as-culture is
trying to "civilize" or "cultivate," to educate into the middle class or,
barring that, to weed out. The message to this audience is clear: shape
up or die. Act more like Doc Stairs or Julie Gregg, or you will not enter
polite society. You will be "accidentally" gunned down.

To their middle-class audience, the Other-as-culture offers another
kind of morality tale, one that warns not against proletarian bad manners but against simple-minded lower-middle-class morality based on the

mystification of revenge. Here the message is more "civilized," more liberal: it encourages a tolerance for and openness to moral ambiguities, for situations in which there is no simple right or wrong, and therefore no simple solution. Here May channels a mediatory liberalism, a liberal tolerance for moral complexity but not for murder (the liberal ideology of pacifism, nonviolence), while Gilead (as residual moralist) channels a more extreme intellectual liberalism, a liberal resignation to the political fact of murder (or rather, to the power structures that justify murder) but not to the destruction of all moral coherence. As Foucauldian Gilead channels the most extreme form of intellectual liberalism of all, an existentialist liberalism that has resigned itself to the utter absence of coherence, rationality, meaning: that has learned to live without the fictive comforts of morality.

A wide variety of social functions can be postulated for this series of "messages," but they all seem to me to converge in some form of quietism, in the sense that there is nothing the subject need or can do: either there is nothing that needs doing because everything is okay (God's in his heaven and all's right with the world), or there is nothing that can be done because there is no source of moral authority to make one act better or worse than another (all's one and one's all, so what the hell). In a political context they all specifically encourage passivity, passive "good citizenship," acceptance of the status quo, contentment of one sort or another with the way things are (including fatalism, resignation, and self-protective blindness). All these messages from the Other-as-culture to Lardner's readers keep citizens from articulating and channeling resistance to the "way things are," keep them from building support groups, consciousness-raising groups, action cooperatives, lobbies, oppositional political parties, revolutionary cells. This, it seems to me, is the overwhelmingly conservative social function of Lardner criticism in particular and literary criticism in general: to spread satisfaction with the status quo.[32]

What bothers me about analyses like this, however—the one I have just done of Lardner's dual audience—is that it is ultimately not all that different from the passivizing criticism I have been analyzing. There are, I think, important differences between my approach in this chapter and more traditional readings: by undermining the illusion of naturalness of a belief structure and demystifying the social functions to which it is aimed, ideological analysis does clear the ground for resistance to that belief structure. The problem is that it only clears the ground; it does not (necessarily) offer suggestions toward a restructuring. Ideological analysis too is finally all too conducive to quietism, because it enables the reader to stare the horrors of ideological manipulation square in the face with still no clue as to what might be done. If ideology is so all-pervasive, if the Other-as-culture manipulates even our attempts to resist it, what is there *to* be done? How can we fight it? Isn't it too strong, too well protected, for us to fight?

This is why I have insisted throughout the book on a dialectical pairing of ideological analyses of the problem in odd-numbered chapters with emancipatory programs, provisional escape maps out of the problem in even-numbered chapters. Ideological analysis is the essential first step: one must know what one is fighting. But then one must take the second step — break out.

6

Reading Beyond the Ending

In all the readings of "Haircut" explored so far, Jim Kendall was sick, nasty, twisted. He deserved to be destroyed, put down like a dog. But if he was sick, so was the town that destroyed him: they were so neurotically obsessed with order, propriety, doing the right thing, that they committed legal murder. But if the town was sick, so was the reader who approved of the murder, and the writer who set the reader up to approve of it, and the *Liberty* editor who agreed to publish it in his magazine, and the society that condones such writing and reading and publishing . . .

Where does this chain stop? Can it be stopped? Should it be stopped? Is there a natural or obvious or inherent stopping place, or must it be wrested to an artificial halt? Is the desire to stop a chain like that, to plug the hole out of which meaning and hope are leaking, a fearful, self-protective, escapist desire, or a sign of ethical courage?

As usual, the bourgeois Other-as-culture has given us a choice. Either we can believe, along with millions of "normal" good citizens, that there really is no problem at all, that the stopping place is natural and obvious, that it is just plain common sense, that it stands to reason, that "everyone knows" where the stopping place is (viz., the town did the right thing); or we can play the opposite but equally "normal" intellectual game of epistemological brinksmanship. Either we blindly believe whatever we are taught or we compete to see who can believe the least of what we are taught. And whichever route we take — this is the ideological common ground that renders both these opposite behaviors "normal" — we resign ourselves to the impossibility and/or the undesirability of changing the status quo.

Fortunately, this "normal" choice is not "made," not accepted as the only choice to be made, by all recent academics. The academy today harbors insistently oppositional forces, groups spoken powerfully by oppositional Others, the Other-as-minority, the Other-as-prole, the (m)Other-as-child, that struggle to unmake this prescribed choice, to make Other choices: black critics, gay and lesbian critics, Marxist critics, feminist and masculist critics, many of them pushing at the politically paralyzing choice between "normal" intellectual complacency and "normal" intellectual despair. The Other-as-culture musters all its authoritarian voices (the Other-as-patrician, the (m)Other-as-father, the Other-as-majority) to deter these oppositional forces, to render these critics harmless, both from without and from within: plucking at the norm-anxiety strings in editors and external evaluators so that radically oppositional books and articles do not get published, and whispering to the writers themselves that the only way to get published, to get heard, to get taken seriously, is to be tamely oppositional. Depersonalize your voice, tone down your polemics, retreat to a high level of abstraction. Analyze a static external reality without attempting to change the reader's behavior in that reality. Make your case against ideological norms in the discourse prescribed by those norms. Above all, don't be dogmatic. Dogmatism — which is to say, believing in something strongly enough to fight for it — is the kiss of death for "normal" intellectuals, for whom skepticism is all. To doubt is smart; to believe is stupid. To argue against something is smart; to argue for something (except for disbelief, skepticism, doubt) is stupid.

These remarks are by way of leading up to some stupid remarks that I want to make in this concluding chapter — some methodological suggestions (and their pedagogical corollaries) that to normal intellectuals will sound obviously or intuitively or patently (which is to say, normatively) stupid. In some sense, in fact, all the aggressive smartness in this book, all the complicated inversions of the obvious, all the incorporations of difficult French theorists (Lacan, Kristeva, Deleuze and Guattari, Foucault) — all this has at least partly been a way of winning some small credibility for a methodological and pedagogical project that to the majority of intellectuals (indeed, majoritarian intellectuals) should seem very stupid indeed.

I refer to the project of reading beyond the ending, a project I have in fact broached twice before in this argument, in connection with "Who Dealt?" (the possible therapeutic effect of revelation on Tom after the ending) and "Dinner" (the possible therapeutic effect on Miss Coakley of a caring, sensitive, and dedicated listener). Put this baldly, it certainly does sound inane. It sounds like the people Northrop Frye talks about in *Anatomy of Criticism* who send checks to suffering heroines on radio programs (76), identifying so strongly with a fictional character that they blur the distinction between fiction and reality, so that the character begins to seem real, alive, extratextual.

To compound the inanity before I begin to reanimate it, consider "Haircut" once more. Jim Kendall is sick; how then shall we cure him? He is dead, you say, past all healing. But how do we know he is dead? We have only Whitey's word for it, and Whitey is an unreliable narrator who never even saw Jim dead and would probably not give us the straight story about it if he had.[1] Whitey took Doc Stair's word for it, and in our intellectual sophistication we suspect Doc Stair's reliability also. May's and Blythe and Sweet's readings are predicated on the assumption that Doc Stair has something to conceal, that in pronouncing the death accidental he is covering up his own complicity in the shooting ("the Doc had told him [Paul] that anybody that would do a thing like that [try to rape Julie] ought not to be let live" [32]). As Blythe and Sweet also point out (452), Doc Stair knows that Paul is "gettin' better, that they was times when he was as bright and sensible as anybody else" (27): to give a "half-wit" the motive and means and justification for murder with the full knowledge that his "witty" or sane half is perfectly capable of carrying out a plan is to be an accessory to homicide.

If Doc is lying about Jim's *accidental* death, therefore, might he not also be lying about Jim's accidental *death*? What if Jim is still alive — wounded, say, locked up in a deserted boat house? What if Doc Stair arrived to find Jim "critically" but not fatally wounded (by his half-wit critic) and found himself in a moral dilemma: mend him and let him loose, perhaps to succeed next time where he failed (in raping Julie), or kill him and save Julie and the entire town much grief? What if, unable to bring himself to do either, Doc Stair pronounced him dead and buried a John Doe, and stashed Jim away somewhere?

Then Jim Kendall is not past healing. Then, let me say inanely once more, we can still cure him, rescue him both from his own and the town's violence and restore him to health.

What makes this scenario sound stupid is, in fact — to pull rank on those readers who might be tempted to concur in calling my project inane — a naive objectivist epistemology that sees Jim Kendall or any literary character as absolutely and inescapably outside our own bodies, as an external verbal object with some yet-to-be-specified formal stability. If his objective stability is maintained representationally — if he has a referent in the real world, if "Haircut" is a news report or history and people named Doc Stair and Julie Gregg and Paul Dickson and Whitey might be (or have been) found living in some real town together, uneasily recalling Jim Kendall — that stability places certain normative constraints on the kinds of claims we can make. We can talk about Doc's and Paul's and Whitey's moral or legal complicity in Jim's death; we can talk about whether Jim is really dead; if we establish that he is in fact alive, we can bring his kidnappers to justice and place him in psychiatric care in hopes of curing his sociopathic tendencies. This scenario's underlying beliefs in justice and psychiatric cures might be called naive, but only on ideological grounds — which is to say, from this objectivist perspective, on subjective or fictional or artificial or illusory grounds (individuals can doubt the "normatized" efficacy of justice and psychiatry). Objectively it is clear that people can be put on trial and either acquitted or sentenced; objectively it is clear that people can be sent to a psychiatrist and declared either sane or insane.

What we cannot do in a "representational" or "real-life" case like the above is discuss the symbolic meaning or authorial intention of the story. If "Haircut" refers to a true story, then in the normative secularity of modern bourgeois objectivism it has no author and therefore can have no intended symbolic or other meaning. It just happened. It would be categorically naive, would sound medieval, fundamentalist, stupid, to read a meaning into it. The world is no longer God's morality play, with humans as both players and audience. Human events are an epistemological dead end.

If, on the other hand, Jim Kendall's formal stability as a verbal object is fictional, textual, if he has no referent in the real world, we are again constrained in the kind of claims we can make, but in reverse: we can discuss symbolic meaning and authorial intention, but we cannot discuss the possibility of actually putting the conspirators on trial for murder or of curing the sociopath. They have no existence in the real world, which is where such things happen. In Ryle's term, talk of meaning in a true story or of justice and a cure in a made-up story is a category mistake.

But both mistakes depend, clearly, on the reification of categories, ideologically "normal" objectivist categories. Talk of meaning in a true story was not a category mistake in the Middle Ages, because the ruling Other-as-culture spoke human reality as God's morality play. What has rendered such talk naive is an ideological shift, the secularization of medieval theology through bourgeois science and other demystifying discourses. God was once an all-pervasive objective force who could at once write and direct a morality play with humans as players and enter the human audience in the form of the Holy Spirit and control their response. Now he has become a privatized subjective fiction which some unsophisticated people rather pathetically and pointlessly invoke in an attempt to gain some control over their environment. The belief that this fiction has any power over either minds or matter has become a category mistake.

Now I'm not going to invoke the medieval God to make my case; my point is only that the ideological norms that make my case seem silly are historically grounded in the secularization of medieval theology, in the speaking of a bourgeois Other-as-objectivist. In this Other's desire to discredit the medieval God, who was an ideological front for the medieval Other-as-theocrat, it spoke the split between subject and object, between self and other, and denied the possibility of transpersonal communion: the simultaneous speaking of God in heaven and in the Christian's head, for example. In this sense my articulation of Lacan's Other throughout this book is what Kenneth Burke would call a "God-term," a conception that is logologically related to the medieval God, or to the medieval ideological norm that power (whether thematized as divine or political) is at once individual and collective, at once centrally formulated and disseminated and inside the individual's head. The Other, as I have fleshed it out, is a simultaneously politicized and psychologized avatar of God: a social force rather than a cosmic one, but a force nevertheless which, like the medieval God, operates both inside and outside individual heads and spans the ideological distance between.

It is a conception that is heavily indebted, in fact, to Deleuze and Guattari's radical reinterpretation in *Anti-Oedipus* of Freud's *Civilization and Its Discontents*:

> Psychic repression distinguishes itself from social repression by the unconscious nature of the operation and by its result ("even the inhibition of revolt has become unconscious"), a distinction that expresses clearly the difference in nature between the two repressions. But a real independence cannot be concluded from this. Psychic repression is such that social repression becomes desired; it induces a consequent desire, a faked image of its object, on which it bestows the appearance of independence. Strictly speaking psychic repression is a means in the service of social repression. What it bears on is also the object of social repression: desiring-production. But it in fact implies an original double operation: the repressive social formation delegates its power to an agent of psychic repression, and correlatively the repressed desire is as though masked by the faked displaced image to which the repression gives rise. Psychic repression is delegated by the social formation, while the desiring-formation is disfigured, displaced by psychic repression. (119).

The only qualm I have about this passage concerns the claim that social repression is not unconscious. Social repression must be unconscious, it seems to me, if it is to work. Social repression is staged in and by the Other-as-culture, a collectivized unconscious force that speaks society by speaking every individual psyche in it. Especially in bourgeois society the speaking of the ostensibly autonomous subject by a collective force must remain unconscious and radically mystified. Deleuze and Guattari are probably referring, in fact, to the overt and therefore "conscious" (legal, socially articulated) repression of criminals, the insane, and other undesirables through various forms of incarceration; but as they themselves hint, this does not mean that the very legality or social articulation of this repression is not steeped in the political unconscious. Conscious repression is itself unconsciously repressed in and through the rhetoric of justice and cure: incarceration in this rhetoric is *not* repression, *not* an attempt to remove criminals and the insane from conscious perception; it is punishment for a crime ("justice"), or it is a hospital stay to be treated for mental illness ("cure").

These remarks have an obvious bearing on "Haircut." Whether Jim Kendall has been murdered or, in my reading beyond the ending, merely kidnapped and held prisoner somewhere outside of town, he is the victim of the town's social repression, just as the town had been the victim of his psychic repression. He is incarcerated in the town's unconscious, whether in death or in some form of unofficial prison, "repressed" both for and as vicious pranks: both for committing them and as the imperfectly externalized embodiment of those pranks in the repressive murderers/jailers. Jim's pranks are the return of the social repressed, at once inside and outside good citizens' bodies — far enough outside to make him an excellent sacrificial victim, but still far enough inside to generate in those bodies a disturbing anxiety that makes the ritual sacrifice more than empty repetition. The murder or incarceration of Jim Kendall is the good citizens' attempt to eject Jim's sociopathic violence from their own unruly bodies, to restore social rule or order to their bodies through cathartic violence — and it is motivated by the survival in their bodies of the unruliness or disorder that he represents.[2]

It is instructive to note the ideological congruence between this sacrificial externalization and the bourgeois Other-as-culture's categorical objectivism: both constitute a repressive attempt to purify the subject by emptying its undesirable elements out into the object, which can then be manipulated externally in the rituals of either sacrifice or science. The repressive normativeness of this congruence in the bourgeois era renders the notion of the ideological continuity between subject and object — between psyche and society, scapegoater and scapegoat, and the real reader and a fictional character like Jim Kendall — deviant and therefore profoundly disturbing. It has the effect of undoing, or at the very least of threatening, repression. Hence the importance of ridiculing it as na-ive, stupid, inane. Laugh at it and it can't hurt you.

Hence also, in our retellings of "Haircut" (including Whitey's), the importance of rendering Jim Kendall entirely other, alien, a separate person whose vicious pranksterism is his alone, some freaky personality disturbance, some genetic defect or chemical imbalance, something "wrong" with him. This "normal" conception, spoken by the objectivist bourgeois Other-as-culture, allows us to see Jim as a problem to be solved by one of several procedures, all of them involving the radical alienation of Jim from ourselves, both *in* the story (incarceration in jail or hospital or deserted cabin, an official death penalty or "accidental death") and *as* the story (incarceration in fictional or textual status). Jim can't touch us, then. He can't pull one of his infamous pranks on us, can't speak us from within by impersonating someone we respect. He is other, different, apart. We know who he is. We know that he is no more. We have jailed or killed him. He is dead, defunct, defused.

Allowing Jim's pranksterism to leak across the ideological boundaries between self and other, subject and object, inside and outside, undoes this self-protective construct. Jim then becomes the impersonator or impersonation of his society's taboo humor and violence, of Whitey's and Doc Stair's and Paul Dickson's and our own repressed pranksterism. "One trick Jim had," Whitey tells us, "was the knack of changin' his voice. He could make you think he was a girl talkin' and he could mimic any man's voice" (29–30). He can "be" anyone he wants, because he can "voice" anyone he wants: can speak with any man's or woman's voice.

Thus when he sees a sign out a train window, "Henry Smith, Dry Goods," he sends Henry Smith an anonymous postcard saying, as Whitey recalls, "'Ask your wife about that book agent that spent the afternoon last week' or 'Ask your Missus who kept her from gettin' lonesome the last time you was in Carterville.' And he'd sign the card, 'A Friend'" (25). The anonymous "friend" is no one and everyone; it is God the Father and God the Holy Ghost; it is the societal norm against adultery and it is Henry Smith's own suspicion, which is to say, it is the "normal" masculine suspicion with which Henry Smith has been spoken as "husband." It is Jim "mimicking any man's voice." It is Jim "being" or "voicing" any man, or everyman.

When Jim tries and fails to rape Julie Gregg, again, he is acting out the doubly bound behavioral norm with which the patriarchal Other-as-culture speaks men in relation to women: desire them and don't desire them; dominate them and be dominated by them; take what you want from them and never get what you want from them; believe that they want to have sex with you and do not want to have sex with you; and so on. In this sense, attempted and repulsed rape is "normal" in patriarchal society. It is normal *as* attempted (as date rape, as sexual harassment, as the programmed masculine impulse to be sexually aggressive, to "go as far as she'll let you") and also *as* repulsed.[3] It is the masculine counterpart to, and requires for its "normal" completion, the behavioral norm that speaks women as enticing but inaccessible, as arousing and deflecting sexual desire, as sexy but antisex. This entire scenario is programmed into patriarchal male-female relations by the Other-as-culture. In "Haircut," in fact, we might say that "Jim" and "Julie" are merely characterized markers for generic (ideologically prescribed) male and female figures: "the man" or "Jim" *must* try, and "the woman" or "Julie" *must* resist.

Like the other characters in the story, Jim is what Deleuze and Guattari call a "faked image," a displaced image of our own repressed desire that we project outward both into "society," the world of living others, and into the "text," the world of fictional otherness. The idea attendant on this image is that Jim Kendall wants it, not us. As Deleuze and Guattari say, "the repressed desire is as though masked by the faked displaced image to which the repression gives rise" (119): because Jim wants to rape Julie, "we" (Lardner's male readers) don't want to rape the women in our lives. The desire is "other," alienated, split off from us, incarcerated in another man's body and in the text, which enables us to believe that it is not in us.

But my ruminations on the normativeness of the double bind which Jim acts out in relation to Julie suggest some refinements in Deleuze and Guattari's rather rough sketch of the displacement of repressed desire into a faked image. What they call "social repression" and I am calling the Other-as-culture induces both the production and the repression of that desire *as "normal"*: it is "normal" for a man or a "Jim" to want to rape a woman or a "Julie," and it is "normal" for him to repress that desire. It is also "normal" for society to punish a man who fails adequately to repress the socially produced desire to rape a woman, and for that punishment to act as a "faked image" of repression. Moreover, it is "normal" for the faked image of the punished rapist to be doubly bound: for a rape trial to constitute the rapist as official defendant and the rape victim as unofficial defendant (for the man to be officially accused of raping the woman but acquitted, the woman unofficially accused of provoking the assault and "convicted"); and for the most effective faked image to be extralegal, generated by the boyfriend/husband (or his proxy), who takes the rape to be an attack not on the woman but on him, on his female property and thus on his autonomy and untouchability as a man. Thus the legal system, spoken by the bourgeois Other-as-culture as "impartial" and "objective," maintains a faked image of those repressive qualities while continuing to produce and protect the "normal" desire to rape. And the extralegal tradition of vengeance, spoken by the medieval Other-as-culture as "chivalrous" and "honorable," maintains a faked image of the "normal" desire *not* to rape, while continuing to produce and protect the "normal" patriarchal principle that rape is an acceptable male practice (only) when practiced on female possessions (wives, girlfriends, the spoils of war).

In this light it should be clear why I believe it essential to read beyond the ending and discover Jim alive and redeemable. As long as Jim is repressively other—not-alive, not-real, and not-me—he remains a figure for, and ideological instrument of, our own incarceration in doubly bound faked images of repressed desire. As long as our conviction that Jim is the would-be rapist allows us to believe that "we" (male readers) are not, we not only are would-be rapists but also have no recourse against that repressed desire. To recognize ourselves in Jim, therefore, and Jim in ourselves, is to unmask ourselves, to remove the faked image that helps us reenact social repression in our own bodies, and thus to confront the naked fact of our programmed desire: rape and do not rape. To confront that desire is in turn to attend to the double bind with which the patriarchal Other-as-culture speaks us, to listen to it attentively, to trace its contours in our bodies, and to explore ways by which we might free ourselves of it.

Given this preparatory skirmishing (this exploratory regress from the literary faked image to the desire it helped conceal), reading beyond the ending becomes a technique for fighting back, for generating a new faked image with which to oppose social repression. The patriarchal Other-as-culture used the conservative vernacular humorist Ring Lardner to create Jim Kendall, and used the vicious prankster Jim Kendall to keep us at once tied to and blind to the ideosomatics of desire and its repression, transgression and punishment, and so on. Having opened our eyes to that ideosomatic cluster, we can begin to untie and unblind ourselves by creating a different Kim Kendall beyond Lardner's ending, a Jim who is not other but us, not a mere fiction but a faked image of ourselves, and not dead but alive. Identifying with Jim enables us first to articulate and resist repression, then to recognize and analyze desire; seeing him as not dead enables us to envision change, improvement, hope for the future—for *our* future. If he is not dead and buried but merely kidnapped and imprisoned, held hostage by the agents of social repression, then he can be rescued, liberated — and by extension we can, too. And if he can be liberated from his captors, who wanted us to believe he was dead, then perhaps he (and we) can be liberated from the ideological double bind that pushed him toward vicious and violent pranks in the first place, from the agent of psychic repression that constituted him as a sociopath and caused him to be killed or incarcerated.

This is, if you like, literary criticism as counterespionage: if Jim Kendall as faked image is the agent of social repression, we "turn" him, reconstitute him as the agent of our own social liberation. We read beyond the ending of the Other-as-culture's scenario and impose a new scenario, with a new and open ending, an "unending," in order to undo the old ending's designs on us: Jim Kendall is rescued from Doc Stair and cured of his patriarchal programming and discovers, for example, that he is gay, that he loves Whitey (this especially for the gay reader); he and Whitey leave town together, leave behind the scene of their repression by and as straights and set out on the road of shared self-discovery. Or he discovers how similar he is to the other working men and women in town, especially the other unemployed, and becomes a social activist — this for the Marxist reader. Or he starts listening to his wife, starts attending to the needs and the fears she is voicing in her bitter diatribes against him, and gradually, dialogically, they begin to discover that they are not so different after all, that their differences (and the conflicts built upon them) go deep but are not the rock bottom of their being, that beneath the many layers of mutual hostility there is a hurt fellow feeling which eventually ripens into love — this for the straight liberal masculist like me.

In each scenario projected beyond the ending, the "reader" (each *real* reader) summons out of his or her emancipatory needs a "faked image" of Jim which enables him or her to fight ideological incarceration and struggle toward liberation, struggle out onto the road of ideological regeneration. This image both is and is not the emancipatory reader him- or herself: it is the reader insofar as it is an image of the reader's own incarceration and liberation, but it is not the reader insofar as it is "faked," a mere identificatory vehicle, a tool the reader uses and then discards. And it is important that the reader beyond the ending recognize the duality of this faked image of him- or herself: recognize that it is somatically contiguous with his or her self, that its dramatic fortunes can have an immense impact on his or her own construction of the world, and that it is therefore essential to take the reshaping of that image seriously; but recognize also that it is only an image, only a homunculus that can be molded until its shape is useful and discarded when it has exhausted its usefulness.

You may have noticed that in my list of possible readings beyond the ending of "Haircut," I did not imagine a feminist reading — this despite the patent fact that my emancipatory revisionism both here and throughout the book has been heavily shaped by feminist theory and critical practice. From a feminist standpoint, of course, the problem with "Haircut" (as with most blatantly sexist fictions) is that the only women who appear in it, Julie Gregg and Jim's wife, are virtually uncharacterized stereotypes who never actually do, say, or become anything. An emancipatory male reader can *read* beyond the ending, read Lardner against the grain and construct out of the several repressed masculine faked images new counterrepressive images for self-transformation; an emancipatory female reader would have to *write* beyond the ending, start the story from scratch with an entirely new focus on the public and private lives of Julie Gregg and Mrs. Kendall.

I am alluding, here, to Rachel Blau DuPlessis's feminist argument in *Writing Beyond the Ending* — a title I am obviously adapting to my own post- or transfeminist purposes. DuPlessis is interested (to quote her subtitle) in "Narrative Strategies of Twentieth-Century Women Writers" who have, she argues convincingly, begun to write "beyond" the traditional endings of feminine fiction, or romance:

> In nineteenth-century fiction dealing with women, authors went to a good deal of trouble and even some awkwardness to see to it that *Bildung* and romance could not coexist and be integrated for the heroine at the resolution, although works combining these two discourses in their main part (the narrative middle) are among the most important fictions of our tradition. This contradiction between love and quest in plots dealing with women as a narrated group, acutely visible in nineteenth-century fiction, has, in my view, one main mode of resolution: an ending in which one part of that contradiction, usually quest or *Bildung*, is set aside or repressed, whether by marriage or by death. It is the project of twentieth-century women writers to solve the contradiction between love and quest and to replace the alternate endings in marriage and death that are their cultural legacy from nineteenth-century life and letters by offering a different set of choices. They invent a complex of narrative acts with psychosocial meanings, which will be studied here as "writing beyond the ending." (3-4)

The "ending" here is not, for DuPlessis or the twentieth-century authors of whom she writes, primarily the ending of an actual story (though historically it has often been that), but the ending of what we might call the "virtual" story whispered to the woman writer by the patriarchal Other-as-culture. It is, to put it in the terms I have employing, a doubly bound narrative resolution imposed on women writers "inwardly" by the cultural Other-as-plotter: kill her and let her live; let her live outwardly by marrying her off to the patriarchal hero, but kill her inwardly; let her live inwardly, in the reader's self-stifling imagination, by killing her outwardly. Make her an emblem of death in life (a faked image of self-mortification as the key to minimal social survival) and/or of life in death (a faked image of idealized transcendent womanhood as the only salvation for a woman punished for her rebellion with death).

What DuPlessis is arguing, then, is that, while nineteenth-century women writers largely gave in to this voice and either married off or killed their questing heroines, twentieth-century women writers began to resist it, twist it, and gradually undo and reconstitute it. Kate Chopin, approaching the end of *The Awakening*, cannot silence the voice in her head whispering *kill her, kill her, kill her*, and so Edna Pontellier drowns herself; Marge Piercy, approaching the end of *Woman on the Edge of Time*, is strong enough to fight that voice and keep Connie Ramos alive, and to instill in her reader a sense both of outrage at her continuing incarceration and of new hope for the future. Alice Walker doesn't even have to approach the ending of *The Color Purple* to begin reconstituting her narrative along emancipatory lines.[4]

My revision of DuPlessis's conception of *writing* beyond the ending arises out of a reader-response answer to a troublesome question: what is the emancipatory critic to do, then, with authors who don't write beyond the ending? What does one do with Chopin's Edna Pontellier? With Edith Wharton's Lily Bart? Get angry at the culture for not allowing these women to move toward fulfillment without being destroyed — or at their creators for not resisting the collectivized inner voices calling for failure, humiliation, death? Repress one's anger and assimilate one's voice to the calm whispering of the bourgeois Other-as-objectivist — that is, become an academic literary critic who describes and does not polemicize? What is the feminist critic to do with blatantly sexist male authors like Lardner? Ignore them? Rage at them? Analyze their sexism calmly, dispassionately, descriptively?

Reading beyond the ending is the critical next step, when writing beyond the ending fails. To put it succinctly: if the author cannot write beyond the ending, the emancipatory critic must. Or, to unpack that a little: if a given author has failed to (convince a given reader that she or he has) read beyond the ending whispered by the Other-as-culture, and so has reproduced that ending on the page, the critic must read backward from the ending on the page to the ending in the author's (Other's) collectivized head and read (and then write) beyond it.

Reading beyond the ending might be thematized, in fact, as a kind of transgressive amalgam of DuPlessis's writing beyond the ending, which subjectifies the writer as transgressor, and David Bleich's and Norman Holland's theories of reader response, which subjectify the reader as transgressor. The writer is supposed to be spoken by the Other-as-cultural-tradition, the reader by the Other-as-cultural-text; both are given "voice" in the culture, as obedient members of what Stanley Fish calls the interpretive community, only insofar as they allow themselves to be molded by this speaking — which is to say, only insofar as they consent to becoming channels of officially approved Other-speak. Fish's authoritarian theory of reader response is manifestly an attempt to reassure his conservative detractors about the political dangers of critical relativism: it is all right, he is saying in *Is There a Text in This Class?* and *Doing What Comes Naturally*, to cut interpretation adrift from objective meaning, because interpretive communities will always shape readers' responses in hegemonic ways:

> Abrams, for example, wonders how, in the absence of a normative system of stable meanings, two people could ever agree on the interpretation of a work or even of a sentence, but the difficulty is only a difficulty if the two (or more) people are thought of as isolated individuals whose agreement must be compelled by something external to them. (There is something of the police state in Abrams's vision, complete with posted rules and boundaries, watchdogs to enforce them, procedures for identifying their violators as criminals.) But if the understandings of the people in question are informed by the same notions of what counts as a fact, of what is central, peripheral, and worthy of being noticed — in short, by the same interpretive principles — then agreement between them will be assured, and its source will not be a text that enforces its own perception but a way of perceiving that results in the emergence to those who share it (or those whom it shares) of the same text. (*Is* 377)

We no longer need a police state with informers to rat on dissidents and deviants, in Fish's vision of the modern bourgeois polity, because *everyone* has been "in-formed," formed inwardly in the image of authority. Because the "democratic" Other-as-culture gives inwardly controlled conformity the outward form of freedom, we no longer need the external constraints that belatedly medieval authorities like M. H. Abrams and E. D. Hirsch demand: we can trust in the efficacy of our own social programming to control readers for us.[5]

In this political context, the attempts made (especially in the seventies) by David Bleich and Norman Holland and others to elicit and validate divergent and therefore deviant "personal" reader responses to literary texts are embryonically subversive. They are a channel through which actual readings flow into public articulation without first being subjectified as at once "free" and "correct" by the Other-as-culture, or by what Fish calls the authority of interpretive communities. As Fish says, "In a classroom whose authority figures include David Bleich and Norman Holland, a student might very well relate a text to her memories of a favorite aunt" (*Is* 343) — an interpretive strategy that, as Fish makes clear earlier on that same page, would normally be ruled out of court by the interpretive community as a whole. By creating a space within the literary-critical community in which it is acceptable to explore unconformed idiosyncratic readings, readings based on what Holland calls individual "identity themes," Bleich and Holland move one step beyond Fish's liberal/authoritarian trust in the in-formed reader to a liberal/lectoritarian trust in the (relatively) uninformed reader — the reader who is, certainly, shaped or spoken or informed by the Other-as-culture, but who has not yet successfully learned to silence all competing voices when he or she speaks or writes in public. This new trust enables the reader to undergo a process of liberal self-(in)formation, subjectification as self-discovery: instead of learning how his or her professor reads a text, the student is encouraged to learn how he or she reads it.

This is an unquestionably valuable process. Note, however, that it remains an analytical rather than a therapeutic process, able to bring unconscious material to consciousness but unable to transform it, and that it remains a largely private rather than social process, able to uncover "identity themes" but unable to connect those private identities up with the social conditioning forces that structure and maintain them.

One of the most productive convergences of emancipatory (specifically feminist) and reader-response criticism and theory in recent years has been *Gender and Reading*, edited by Elizabeth A. Flynn and Patrocinio P. Schweickart. As Schweickart says bluntly in her excellent piece, "reader-response criticism needs feminist criticism" (36)[6]; but also, apparently, feminist criticism needs reader-response criticism, at least the kind of ideologically aware and emancipatorily oriented reader-response criticism that she attempts to construct[7]:

> Feminist critics of male texts, from Kate Millett to Judith Fetterley, have worked under the sign of the "Resisting Reader." Their goal is to disrupt

the process of immasculation by exposing it to consciousness, by disclosing the androcentricity of what has customarily passed for the universal. However, feminist criticism written under the aegis of the resisting reader leaves certain questions unanswered, questions that are becoming ripe for feminist analysis: Where does the text gets its power to draw us into its designs? Why do some (not all) demonstrably sexist texts remain appealing even after they have been subjected to thorough feminist critique? The usual answer — that the power of male texts is the power of the false consciousness into which women as well as men have been socialized — oversimplifies the problem and prevents us from comprehending both the force of literature and the complexity of our responses to it. (42)

Schweickart's solution to the problem is very close to what I call reading beyond the ending: drawing on Fredric Jameson's notion that "the effectively ideological is also at the same time necessarily utopian" (Jameson 286, Schweickart 42) and Jameson's dialectic between negative and positive hermeneutics, Schweickart argues for a feminist approach to (some) sexist male texts that recognizes the ideological prisons that constitute them and, through them, their readers, and at the same time seeks to rework the unconscious utopian impulse in them in liberatory ways. "*Certain* (not all) male texts," she says, "merit a dual hermeneutic: a negative hermeneutic that discloses their complicity with patriarchal ideology, and a positive hermeneutic that recuperates the utopian moment — the authentic kernel — from which they draw a significant portion of their emotional power" (43–44).[8]

This is, more or less, the dialectic I have built into the seesaw structure of my book: a negative hermeneutic in odd-numbered chapters, a positive hermeneutic in even-numbered chapters. In Jameson's terms, this has meant a pendulum swing between ideology and utopia: between a close analytical look at ideological formations and the extent to which Lardner and his characters are trapped in them in the first chapter of each part, and a utopian or anticipatory or hopeful look at textual and biographical moments that might be expanded into an emancipatory future in the second.

To schematize: the negative hermeneutic thematizes a text as "ideology," as a prison of the past from which there is no escape; the positive hermeneutic thematizes a text as "utopia," as a paradise of the future toward which the reader is encouraged to quest. The ideological prison is real, actual, and hence the more depressing and daunting, the more convincingly it is mapped out; the utopian paradise is ideal, virtual, and thus the more easily dismissed as a wish-fulfillment fantasy, the more

passionately it is educed. In fact, of course, it is the exclusion of the
utopian impulse that renders ideology a prison, and the exclusion of the
ideological impulse that renders utopia a mere fantasy: for there to be
hope beyond ideological analysis and substance to utopian dreams, ideology and utopia must be dialectically intertwined.

Schweickart illustrates that dialectic in a one-page feminist reading of
Lawrence's *Women in Love*, a sexist novel that continues to appeal to
her, through the "trick of role reversal":

> If we reverse the roles of Birkin and Ursula, the ideological components
> (or at least the most egregious of these, e.g., the analogy between women
> and horses) stand out as absurdities. Now, if we delete these absurd com-
> ponents while keeping the roles reversed, we have left the story of a woman
> struggling to combine her passionate desire for love and for other human
> bonds. This residual story is not far from one we would welcome as ex-
> pressive of a feminist sensibility. Interestingly enough, it also intimates a
> novel Lawrence might have written, namely, the proper sequel to *The
> Rainbow*. (45)

Here the negative hermeneutic identifies the sexism of Lawrence's portrait of Ursula, and is superseded by the positive hermeneutic, which
initiates the role reversal that appropriates for Ursula the positive (proto-
feminist) characteristics Lawrence assigns restrictively to Birkin; then the
negative hermeneutic takes over and identifies the "absurd components,"
which are in turn "deleted" by the positive hermeneutic on its way to the
construction of a "residual" feminist story. Schweickart does not exfoli-
ate the full complexity of her reading, but does enough of it to show
that her dialectical exploration of that complexity itself increasingly becomes a kind of prison from which she wistfully longs for escape:

> The identification with Birkin is emotionally effective because, stripped of
> its patriarchal trappings, Birkin's struggle and his utopian vision conform
> to my own. To the extent that I perform this feminist rereading *uncon-
> sciously*, I am captivated by the text. The stronger my desire for autono-
> mous selfhood and for love, the stronger my identification with Birkin,
> and the more intense the experience of bifurcation characteristic of the
> process of immasculation. (43)

Given the fact that the ideological deck is stacked against change, against
escape, it is not surprising that even explicitly emancipatory critical programs like Schweickart's should experience the positive/negative herme-
neutical dialectic as a "bifurcation" conducive to captivity. My dialectic
in this book too, however dedicated I am to the positive hermeneutic,

will probably come off sounding like a carceral structure, a "captivating" analysis of the double bind that brooks no opposition and therefore tolerates no change.

It is no accident, for example, that in my "negative" or ideological analysis of Lardner criticism in chapter 5, I had to resort to elaborate schemas in order to cover the field — not even a large field, compared with, say, Fitzgerald criticism — while in my "positive" or utopian approach to Lardner criticism here I am forced to rely almost entirely on my own interpretations. Fortunately, however, not entirely: early in my work on Lardner I showed a rough draft of my utopian reading beyond the ending of "Who Dealt?" (actually, the hundred manuscript pages of part I) to my colleague Ellen Gardiner, who responded by writing her own equally utopian but explicitly feminist reading beyond the ending of the story, " 'Engendered in Melancholy': Ring Lardner's 'Who Dealt?' " Through my readings of her drafts and her readings of my drafts, our respective positive hermeneutics were progressively dialogized, infused not only with the dialectical pushes and pulls of traditional readings of the story, but also with the collaborative crossovers of our own interchange, with me helping Ellen to formulate a feminist reading that corroborated and undermined my masculist reading, while Ellen helped me to formulate a masculist reading that corroborated and undermined her feminist reading.

It became clear to me in this process that, however sympathetic my reading of "Who Dealt?" in part I was to the female narrator and to the feminist literary criticism that has worked to recover the silenced voices of female speakers in literature, it was still focused on Tom Cannon, Lardner's fictional persona in the story; this was so even in chapter 2, where I was ostensibly working, like many feminist critics, to voice the female dummy. Even there I was more concerned with the two focal males, Tom and Ring, and with the narrator's female voice as the speaking of their (m)Other-as-child. I make no apologies for this; it seems to me that for a male critic reading a male writer, the only alternatives to this kind of attention to male voices are (1) speaking as a woman, (2) speaking as a man but for women, and (3) ignoring gender and speaking for all "mankind." I find none of these alternatives viable, and have offered in place of a "feminist" (1 or 2) or a "humanist" (3) reading a masculist reading that seeks to articulate and undo patriarchal masculine programming.

Appropriate as I feel this critical approach to be for a profeminist male critic, however, it obviously paints only part of the picture. The narrator of "Who Dealt?" *is* a woman, and a female/feminist reading of her voicing in the story must generate a radically different set of critical concerns. In fact, part of the reason I feel so unapologetic for my masculist reading is that, as a result of our ongoing dialogue on the story, my reading stands alongside Ellen Gardiner's as the masculist half of a dialogical entity that is masculist/feminist in its totality. Where I identified with Tom and constructed a positive hermeneutic that set up the story's narrator as his best chance at masculist transformation, Gardiner identifies strongly with the narrator and buttresses what she calls the narrator's "hurt monologue" with feminist and psychoanalytical theory in order, as I read her essay, to clear a vocal space for female transformation — out of melancholy, out of a repressive marriage, into a new and healthier construction of self.

In conversation, however — audiotaped (August 28, 1991), transcribed, and slightly edited — Gardiner shied away from this formulation of her intentions in the piece:

GARDINER: One of the things I wanted to talk about was that, whereas you see your reading of the story as therapeutic, I never considered mine that way.

ROBINSON: What was it then?

GARDINER: I guess it was an attempt to somehow objectify the whole experience — even as I'm arguing that one of the problems in criticism is the need to distance and objectify and take yourself out of the criticism.

ROBINSON: But isn't that process of objectifying your own complicity in a problem — isn't that therapeutic? I mean, that's the whole point of Freudian psychoanalysis, to name your illness.

GARDINER: Yeah, I guess so — except that we have a tendency to see ourselves as being better readers than the rest of the world, or to privilege ourselves as the only ones in a classroom who can read properly. And I think that the move to say "look at how I've healed myself" can be read as that same type of move, to elevate ourselves in some way as a critic by saying, "having accepted therapy, I'm one step ahead of you."

ROBINSON: I can see where it might come across that way . . .

GARDINER: In the back of my mind is M. H. Abrams's criticism of Carlyle as a proto-Freudian critic — that focusing on the self elevates the self to the exclusion of the community, leads to a peculiar sort of self-absorption — an individualism that is at once the American way but also, of course, antidemocratic, and therefore anti-American . . .

ROBINSON: Hm. For me, I guess, therapy is a breaking down of defensive ego structures, a phasing out of the aggressively individualistic self. Ego is the disease for which we seek a cure.

GARDINER: Does that mean, then, that you strive to be an egoless reader, someone who's totally subsumed into the text?

ROBINSON: I don't know. That's an interesting idea. The possibility of becoming an egoless reader intrigues me, but I'm not sure I'd necessarily associate it with being totally subsumed into the text.

GARDINER: I guess what bothers me about some reader-response people is that I don't think the reader should be the most important figure—that the text shouldn't just be an object—the same way the narrator in "Who Dealt?" becomes an object when Helen, Arthur, and Tom refuse to speak to her—refuse to treat her as though she had any substance. When we keep reminding ourselves that the story and its characters aren't real, we distance ourselves from them, make it easier to repress the anxieties and insecurities that an active participation in the story, and the situation described in the story, brings to the surface. I want to believe that I become a character in the story when I read it, which means I have to be aware of my emotional responses. I don't think I have to become less human as a professional reader in the way that serious bridge players learn to become less human—Sheinwold says someplace that "the better the player, the less human he must act" [445]. Sheinwold thinks any emotion in a bridge game is histrionics; he says, "Bridge is a game of skill and judgment, not a contest of histrionics" [445], and we've been taught to think the same about criticism. If we "forget" that we're supposed to stay "outside the story" and start responding emotionally to it, as critics we become like the misbehaving "dummy" narrator.

ROBINSON: I agree, though a Marxist critic might object that paying attention to your emotional response to a story or whatever does "elevate the self to the exclusion of the community." The only way to guarantee the surrender of ego to the community is to dehumanize yourself, to make yourself completely dispassionate, emotionless, mechanistic—

GARDINER: Scientific.

ROBINSON: Right. I'd say just the opposite. I think the only way to surrender ego is through passionate identification with others.

GARDINER: You mean, for example, by becoming a character in the story you're reading.

ROBINSON: I guess so. It sounds a little naive when you put it that way, but I guess that's what I mean. Breaking down the idealized barriers between self and other, reader and text.

GARDINER: It does sound naive, and I—I suppose that's why I've always been hesitant to come forward and admit to reading literature this way. But for example, one of the things that was so interesting to me about the Lardner story in the first place, even reading your chapters first—at least I think it must have struck me first, because it's the thing that's stayed with me for a long time—is your reading of the narrator as someone who must be plump. I guess that was the signal for me, in some respect, because a woman of lower-middle-class origins is plump—and that's me! All these other things, too: my brother's name is Tom, and he's a sportswriter . . . when we were kids, because we were all chubby—I remembered this a couple of months ago when I was thinking about all the connections to the story—when kids made fun of us they'd call us "Lardner"—

ROBINSON: "Lard"—because you were lardy.

GARDINER: And especially my brother, my brother was "Tom Lardner."

ROBINSON: Amazing! So you had all kinds of personal connections with this story that my reading just sort of actualized or catalyzed in you.

GARDINER: Yeah, and that's what made it necessary to go and read the story.

ROBINSON: Yeah, and in some sense you were objectifying your response; you were naming your response in the sense of externalizing it. Instead of allowing it to lie inchoate and unconscious, you actualized what Freud says, "Where id was, there ego shall be"—you turned id into ego, in some sense.

GARDINER: Yeah, because it was a gut reaction—and then I obsessed the whole weekend over it.

ROBINSON: I remember that.

GARDINER: I went to the library, *immediately* went to the library and tracked down the story, and I kept saying to myself, "look what he missed, look what he missed."

ROBINSON: Wasn't that process therapeutic for you in any way? You've said that the process of writing about "Who Dealt?" helped you find a voice or a new authority for your voice in critical writing—that objectification of your personal response to Lardner has been therapeutic, right?

GARDINER: Well, I guess so.

ROBINSON: In some sense, you've begun to undo your repression as a critic.

GARDINER: Yeah, I think that's true, I mean, because part of my anxiety has always been that my relationship to books and reading, the reason I got into this business in the first place, is that I've always had such an emotional response to texts. One of my professors one time told me, "You have such a romantic relationship with texts," and I've always felt a little guilty about being so emotionally attached to what I'm reading about, so it's always made it very difficult to do academic writing. My writing has always been—sort of "evangelistic," I guess.

ROBINSON: Have you tried to paper over your love for literature with some quasi-masculine intellectualism?

GARDINER: Yeah, sure, basically thinking, well, maybe it is possible to have a science of literary criticism where I can be totally objective about the text that I'm reading. Maybe even the real reason I went into literary criticism is that—I was a medical technologist first, right, which was a very scientific thing, and I remember one of my professors in grad school talking about the science of literary criticism, and because I wanted so badly for him to respect me as a critic I kept saying, "Well, yeah, it's sort of like medical technology," the whole time denying the fact that the reason I got out of medical technology in the first place was that—

ROBINSON: It was too mechanistic.

GARDINER: Yeah.

ROBINSON: And that chasm between those who love literature and those who analyze literature, which is partly a gender thing, and a power thing, is replicated in our relation with our students. They become English majors because they love literature, and we train them to analyze literature. And something of the same thing is going on in "Who Dealt?"

GARDINER: Yeah, between the narrator and Tom, but also, maybe, between the story and the critics, you know, who want to analyze everything in it down to these short little plot summaries. One of the things that was really interesting to me about the Lardner criticism was—it suddenly occurred to me as I was reading through some of our earlier drafts, I looked at your piles and you had a hundred pages, and here I've got this paper that is still relatively underdeveloped but it's thirty-three pages long, and there are lots of things I had to leave out and things I need to add to it. I was just rereading the Guthrie stuff this morning and realizing that I give just a couple of sentences about all this detail, and there's so much to unpack in there. But then looking at the other criticism on the story, what, it's like a page and a half, some of it—

ROBINSON: Yeah, a paragraph.

GARDINER: But it's so angry, on the other hand—you have to be fairly angry to call someone "rattle-brained," "dreary," "insensitive," a "gurgler"—and suddenly it struck me that there's a lot of repression going on in that criticism. Basically the readers of the story before we get to it, and I'm not trying to be pompous about this, but they seem to be reading the narrator's monologue in exactly the same way that Helen and Tom and Arthur do. Tom keeps giving her these terrible looks, so he's obviously very angry and disturbed about the whole thing. My feeling was that what we're describing in our analysis, or at least what I'm describing in my analysis, is a cultural melancholia—

ROBINSON: Yeah, what I call our double bindedness.

GARDINER: Right. And the reason that certain literature doesn't get read or doesn't get considered "beautiful" is that it doesn't allow the critic to repress the economic, emotional, psychological—

ROBINSON: Generally ideological—

GARDINER: It doesn't allow them to repress that.

ROBINSON: Yeah, that's good. It's too great an assault on their repression, so they have to work too hard to maintain the smooth surface of their repression in their criticism, and they fail. I mean, Lardner criticism is full of failures to maintain that repressive smooth surface. Lardner was very repressed himself, of course, and probably would have agreed with his critics on the importance of keeping things hidden away; but there was something in him that refused to be repressed.

GARDINER: Yeah, but that's what causes the anger, too, that you don't want to hear that maybe—I don't know why someone wouldn't want to hear, say, that there was something seriously wrong with the Cannons' marriage.

ROBINSON: Yeah, all the critics in the fifties and sixties want to think of the marriage as perfect until the narrator ruins it.

GARDINER: They basically admit that the marriage is incompatible, but they think, what a horrible thing to do, to end a bad marriage — it's just amazing!

ROBINSON: And the repression that is still operating in the critics as readers is what compresses their response. They all give this one paragraph — it's like if you said any more about it you might have to deal with your own repression. My first experience with the story was teaching it to sophomores in an Introduction to Lit class: this thing was anthologized and I taught it several semesters in a row, and every time I taught it, it frustrated me. There was so much there and it was so complex and all intertwined that I just couldn't deal with it. I couldn't reduce it to some nice, tidy formula that they could learn. It just kept bothering me and bothering me, and that was the germ of the idea to write the book — actually, that combined with my reading of Lacan's Schema L and bridge metaphor for that. You have this tiny little story and you try to say something about it, and it constantly threatens your barriers.

GARDINER: Yeah, it did threaten my barriers — remember I told you how embarrassing it was when you first read my essay and said that you thought my reading was generated by my own insecurity, my melancholy in the academy,[9] but that's what made it so useful for me. In fact, it's that assault on our barriers and the way we embrace that assault that makes me think we've been developing a new theory of reading, a new critical approach to texts. It seems to me that this reading process we've been doing isn't exactly like reader response, nor is it exactly like historical materialism, and I don't know if it's exactly like anything else.

ROBINSON: I think it's probably closest to reader response, but it's reader response as transformed by feminists and Marxists and people like them who want to see this as leading someplace rather than just sort of uncovering a response.

GARDINER: Yeah, that's what I mean, because Bleich has always been dissatisfying to me, mostly because, okay, he talks about getting students to see that their responses to texts are subjective and to a certain extent shaped by their experience in the world, but then he doesn't ask them to critique that at all.

ROBINSON: Yeah, it doesn't go anywhere. Like with Holland — Holland just looks for the identity theme and that's it.

GARDINER: Right, it basically allows students to say, or me to say, "Well, gee, I feel this way because I had an aunt that played bridge," and leave it at that.

ROBINSON: And your brother's name is Tom and all that.

GARDINER: Yeah, and isn't that neat! But I think that if critics have any purpose at all, it isn't just to ask the students to understand how the forces shape them, but to critique the forces that shape them and to ask them to move beyond them.

ROBINSON: Which is a therapeutic process, I think. Maybe you just don't like the word.

GARDINER: Part of what worries me a little bit about my own position on what should happen with students is that it means that there is still something wrong with their experience that needs to be healed.

ROBINSON: I guess I do assume that, and I also assume that there is something wrong with *me* that needs to be healed, because my basic assumption is that society is sick, and it's programmed us in sick ways. The whole thing about the double bind in my book is saying, "Look what our society is doing to us, look at how it's screwing us up, what are we going to do about it?" And that's why I like to look for texts that won't let me rest easy in the double bind — texts that make me painfully conscious of how doubly bound I am.

GARDINER: Yeah, and we do that in different ways —

ROBINSON: Because we're different people.

GARDINER: Right. In your reading what you're basically trying to do is understand the relationship between you and your mother; in my reading it's more important for me to understand my position as someone who has always considered herself lower-class and a female, and insecure about that, about my place.

ROBINSON: And silenced by both of those.

GARDINER: Yes. It's — I guess it's that allowing yourself to critique or examine your own ideological position generates a much richer reading, a much more complete or full reading.

ROBINSON: Dialogically complete, because the whole idea of objective interpretation, in Hirsch's term, where the critic represses subjectivity in order to allow the text to speak in its fullness — *that* has usually been idealized as the fullest kind of interpretation. But in fact what that's doing is aiding and abetting the critic's repressions, and so maintaining the critic's blindness to his or her own constructions.

GARDINER: I don't want to fall in the same trap, you know, of one-upmanship, but part of me really believes that [laughs] since we've done these readings of the story, there is *nothing left to say*.

ROBINSON: Except that one of the things that happens when you conceive criticism as a dialogical relationship between the reader and the text — and for me a therapeutic one, so that the dialogue continues beyond the ending of the text — one of the things that happens is that every dialogue is different, so that the fullness of my dialogue with Lardner is different from the fullness of your dialogue with Lardner.

GARDINER: Yeah, no, that's true.

ROBINSON: And so I would imagine that there would be lots of things to say, because there are lots of readers who could read that fully in a dialogical sense, and every one would be different in some significant way. It's only when you refuse to make that dialogical link between the reader and the text that you are able to reduce an interpretation to the one correct reading.

GARDINER: The problem is that the academy feels that there really are correct readings, or at least better readings. Like the first time I sent this article out and got back the response, "Well, I know it's trendy to insert personal detail," or comments like "But why doesn't so-and-so use the Lardner criticism?" It's like you can't ever say what you want to say unless you've got five books under your belt, so basically what I have to do as a critic is temper my criticism, repress myself. I make people uncomfortable by asking them to look at their own biases and prejudices in terms of the lower class and in terms of women.

ROBINSON: So do I.

GARDINER: But you have those four or five books.

ROBINSON: That helps, and I have that male voice of authority —

GARDINER: Yeah, so you're *there* —

ROBINSON: But still I'm pushing the criticism into areas that are very unsettling to a lot of academics, so I have to have that balance between the negative hermeneutic and the positive hermeneutic that Jameson talks about. My positive hermeneutic is embarrassing, it's therapeutic, it's emotional, it's talking about love and living a better, richer, more abundant life, so I have to balance that with lots of aggressive smartness.

GARDINER: You know, part of me is putting the story of my life in there just to defy authority, but it also made me able to see that even in the stuff I've been working on before, on the eighteenth century, where I've tried to say that women are repressed, women's language is suppressed, it's much more complicated than that. I can't write any more criticism that treats any kind of group as a monolithic, monologic subject. I can't just say this is what it's like for women. I have to say that for this particular class of women in this particular area of the population, it's sort of like this, and there were men of the lower class who were . . . Reading practices aren't a monologic thing.

ROBINSON: Ultimately what you're saying is, "This is what it's like for me." And by articulating and objectifying your response as thoroughly as possible, you are modeling one kind of response for other readers; and that's what I'm doing too, of course. That's what a critic ought to do, I think.

I began this chapter saying some stupid things; let me end it by saying some other stupid things, in the hope that an ending that embarrasses me a little will bring me into the vicinity of what the Other-as-culture teaches me to repress. I want to tick off some implications of reading beyond the ending for critical reading and writing and for such "trivial" things as hiring, giving and responding to conference papers, and the like, and then to expand a little on the pedagogical implications of all this, especially in a time when the counterhegemonic tendencies within academe are increasingly threatened by the hegemonic Right.

1. Every critical reading begins not in the head, in the intellect, in the analytical selectivity of the cerebral cortex — but in the body, in the emotions, in the autonomic responses of the limbic system. We like a book or a poem, or we dislike it. It gets under our skin or it repels us. It gives us a funny feeling, or it intrigues us, or it leaves us cold. This somatic response to a text is experientially primary in all literary criticism, and we ignore it at our peril. To ignore it successfully — look at it squarely and then calmly sacrifice it to scientism — is to disembody literary criticism, to leave only an empty formal husk. To ignore it unsuccessfully — repress it quickly, furtively, uneasily, and convince yourself that it's really gone — is to devote all your intellectual effort to the systematic reification of likes and dislikes as the objective qualities of the text (or the author, or the cultural background, or whatever). But paying close attention to somatic response — what Wimsatt and Beardsley called "affective criticism" — requires that we develop a vocabulary for talking about it. In the antisomatic Western philosophical tradition, we have (and need) words for analyzing thoughts only, not gut feelings. Intellectuals analyze the products of the intellect; nonintellectuals are "dumb" in both senses of the word. Because they know nothing, and what they know is only about feelings, they can say no more than "I don't know nothing about art, but I know what I like." We need a carefully explored middle ground between (perhaps encompassing and mutually transforming) disembodied intellect and emotive stupidity. The distinction I made in chapter 2 between ideosomatic response (spoken by the Other-as-culture) and idiosomatic response (spoken by a personalized rebellious anarchic Other) is a start, but only that. My analysis of the various Others that speak us *in* our bodies, in and through our somatic responses to events, remains sketchy at best. How do our bodies know what to do, what somatized "voices" speak them, how can we tell them apart, what can we do to change or redirect the myelinated synaptic paths down which the messages run?

2. The Western self-other dualism must go, along with all the private-public baggage that accompanies it. I've drawn on the theories of Bakhtin, Lacan, and Deleuze and Guattari to combat it, but it's not enough. The notion that we are spoken in our individual, private, personal bodies by various collectivized Others is a start, but it is ideologically so deviant that it seems counterintuitive and therefore merely clever, overingenious in an admirably (or dangerously) foolhardy French sort of way. Certainly it is going to be a nondistributed middle for many readers: overly

psychologistic for Marxists, overly sociologistic for liberals. We need to explore the hegemonic control of intuitions, the way in which deviant ideas are laughed out of court before they can be tested in ideological practice. And we need to take emotional risks, wander into realms of knowing that embarrass us, make us uneasy, threaten our carefully guarded peace of mind—and cling to what we find there, despite the ideologically prescribed ridicule it provokes. Collective resistance to ridicule is the only effective weapon against ideosomatic normativeness.

3. Emancipatory reading beyond the ending offers a powerful challenge to objectivist specialization. You do not need to be a Miltonist to read beyond the ending of *Paradise Lost* in transformative, therapeutic ways; indeed, the whole idea of a Miltonist, or a Shakespearean, or a Jamesian, or a Faulknerian, should be called into question. Devoting your professional life to the study of one author is only valuable if the ultimate goal of literary criticism is the amassing of value-free knowledge about objectified texts. This is not a call for a return to eighteenth-century amateurism, but an insistence that we reexamine professionalism: that we reconsider the goals of literary criticism, and in that context recognize alternative models of "competence." There is already a kind of new generalism afoot, presaged by major twentieth-century figures like Kenneth Burke and Raymond Williams—critics attempting large cultural syntheses (or just eclecticisms) in a concern not for the objective contours of specific literary texts but for the future of our civilization. An overriding concern for emancipation will direct the critic to different secondary materials than the traditional emphasis on "coverage": instead of reading everything that has been written on an author and a smattering of books and articles on the historical background, for example, an emancipatory critic may well ignore the criticism and read the biographies and apparently unrelated works in psychology and sociology and political philosophy. Ellen Gardiner, for example, read Lardner not through Lardner criticism or Lardner biographies or historical studies of the twenties, but through psychoanalytical studies of melancholia and femininity (and my drafts of this book); her area of specialization is in the eighteenth century. I read the criticism and the biographies and the letters and the historical background; but compared with the best of Lardner's earlier critics (Yates, for example), my knowledge of the twenties is paltry. Should Gardiner and I be banned from Lardner criticism until we "know" more—or should the parameters of Lardner criticism, or the criticism of any author, be reexamined?

4. Emancipatory reading beyond the ending will also challenge objectivist rules of evidence. Despite the New Critics (and nearly everyone

since), it is still ideologically normal to tie evidence for a critical reading restrictively to authorial intention: if the author cannot be imagined as having intended his or her text to be read as the critic suggests, the reading is not grounded in the "evidence" (textual and/or biographical), and cannot be taken seriously. (Hence, for example, the assumption that the narrator of "Who Dealt?" *is* a blabbermouthed, birdbrained woman, period, because Lardner most likely intended the story that way.) Even when the evidentiary link to authorial intention is cut, as in many structuralist and poststructuralist readings, a reified "text" (however "abysmed") still sets the normal bounds of interpretive evidence. Reading beyond the ending, for example, is extratextual, therefore ungrounded in the evidence, therefore unserious. Wherever endings are spoken by a conformist Other-as-culture (and they usually are), restricting what is acceptable to what is "in the text" will be a profoundly conservative move. To challenge the text of the Other-as-culture's speaking, we must challenge the specific texts (through which) the Other-as-culture speaks.

5. Objectivist publishing practices continue to block emancipatory writing: editors, external evaluators, editorial boards, and copy editors have all been trained to defend established norms of academic decorum, and collectively constitute a system of checks and balances that effectively damps out personal idiosyncrasies, both in authorial and in editorial behavior. We need to examine and challenge the assumptions on which this system is based and the practices by which it proceeds, and begin to construct alternative models for the acquisition and editing of academic manuscripts for publication. What alternative models exist — those used by many feminist presses and journals, say — should be studied and publicized. In the meantime we should inundate university presses and trade publishing houses with innovative manuscripts that are driven by a personal voice and emancipatory political vision, risking (and withstanding) rejection after rejection in the hope that sheer exposure to alternative writing will begin to wear down editorial staffs' resolve.

6. In a hiring situation, everything else being equal, which job candidate should be ranked first: the smartest or the most collegial? Different departments will make this decision in different ways with different candidates; but the very fact that collegiality is regularly taken into consideration in university-level hiring in the United States (unlike in most other countries) is a sign that we recognize the importance of personal qualities like friendliness and flexibility in our colleagues, and do not like to hire even very smart people who lack those qualities. We tend to think of these personal qualities as important for getting along with the appointee and then give it no further thought; but I suggest that a more significant

issue is at stake. Think of it this way: if one candidate is friendly in a highly ritualized way, paying compliments to members of the opposite sex, effusively admiring intellectual points an interviewer makes in asking a question, laughing pompously and insincerely, will that candidate be more or less attractive than one who cares less about the impression he or she is making, is more relaxed, more casual, is willing to say, "Heck, I don't know," or to smile politely and refuse to do battle with a pugnacious interviewer, or to take a potentially unpopular intellectual stand (a comp and rhetoric candidate openly showing little interest in literature, for example)? If we offer the job to the former candidate, my sense is that our commitment to collegiality is a sham, and what we are really looking for is smart people, period—people who *know* things and can manipulate them brilliantly. If we offer the job to the latter candidate, it seems at least likely that we implicitly conceive of our faculty as a kind of unofficial support group, a group of people who help each other to grow emotionally and politically as well as intellectually, and that we are recruiting not only scholars and teachers but productive participants in that group.

7. Is there a significant difference between "reading" a paper and "talking" a paper? Is it just scholarly convention that one writes a conference paper and then reads it (that's what everybody else does), or is there more to it than that? If you find papers that are read boring and want to break away from that convention, do you then memorize your paper? If you don't memorize your paper, do you use copious notes, so that you won't leave out anything really important? Behind the normativeness of reading papers lies an entire web of objectivist assumptions: there is a body of material that needs to be conveyed to the audience; it should be conveyed in as clear, precise, and comprehensive a manner as possible; it should be conveyed so as to convince the audience that you not only know what you are talking about, but radiate intellectual brilliance. Never mind that no one can really listen to a brilliant paper read aloud (much less a boring one), especially if it is read badly and fast (ten pages and only fifteen minutes!); never mind that reading a paper written before the session restricts interaction among speakers in the session, and thus the mutual exploration of common concerns. Never mind all that—just do it, and think of it as the way things are done, or as a practical necessity. Talking a conference paper beyond the ending requires of cowardly academics the courage to speak without knowing in advance, clearly and precisely and comprehensively, what is going to come out of their mouths—which is to say, it requires a willingness to risk sounding stupid. It also requires a commitment to open-ended

interaction as a channel of *group* intellection (and emotion), a commitment to the dynamics of unplanned group heuristics rather than the static reified products of individual brilliance—which is to say, it requires a willingness to enter the flow of a conversation, even an artificial conversation like a series of four talks given before an audience, and emerge at some unexpected place, transformed. We recognize the importance of this willingness when we say that you don't go to a conference for the papers, you go for the professional contacts: a clumsy and defensively cynical vocationalization of open-ended conversation with colleagues over drinks, which seems so pleasant as to be without redeeming substance. But why not assert the significance of open-ended group interaction not only at conference parties and cash bars, but in the sessions as well? What stops us is not just the fear of sounding stupid; that fear, that terror of embarrassment, is a tool wielded by the esemphonic Other-as-culture to keep us all doing the static, closed, tedious, deadening, accepted thing.

8. If to read beyond the ending is to read more (or less) than what the author put "into" a text, to teach beyond the ending is to teach more or less than an object called "literature." Endemic to our current situation in the "teaching of literature," as we call it, is a lopsided tension between *lecturing* on the text and its backgrounds and *discussing* the text and its backgrounds with students. The tension is lopsided because it leans so heavily toward lecturing: even in "open discussion" with students, the professor's reading is "normally" the correct one (ideologically prescribed as normal), and students are made perfectly aware of this by the near-absolute impossibility of bringing the professor around to their position. Many professors regularly tell their students that any interpretation is correct if it is convincingly enough argued and evidenced; but since the professor is the one who has to be convinced, in practice this almost invariably means that only the professor's "correct" reading will ever be convincingly enough argued and evidenced. Indeed, so insistently is our teaching spoken by the objectivist Other-as-culture that when we do allow students to develop interpretations freely, out of their own somatic responses to a text, and "fail" to impose a normatized reading on it at the end, it seems both to us and to our students that we have not "taught." No "teaching" has taken place.

This suggests the need for a new understanding of teaching. Emancipatory reading beyond the ending will transform the traditional classroom from a hierarchical institution for the inculcation of normatized knowledge into a personalized, radicalizing support group, in which convergent readings help discussants explore the speaking of the Other-as-culture, divergent readings help them explore the speaking of various Others-as-escape-artist, and all discussion helps them liberate themselves, individually and collectively, from the ideological structures that oppress them most.

In the National Association of Scholars' eyes, of course, we are already doing that far too effectively: the reactionary NAS sees the oppositional forces I have been discussing not as oppositional but as hegemonic or esemphonic in the sense of having "seized control" over academic discourse both in and out of the classroom in order to displace or unspeak "normal" religious, patriotic, and family values. This misconception is based on the mystification of (and by) Other-speech that characterizes the Right: people for these unconscious Lockeans are not complexly Other-spoken beings but eternal blank slates that can be written on anew, almost at will—and thus utterly transformed, for good or ill—by every external voice that happens along. Whenever an oppositional voice is given a hearing in the academy, therefore, its hearers (hapless students, the endangered children of paternalistic parents) are automatically perverted or contaminated. Hence the importance for the NAS of silencing these voices (through lawsuits, smear campaigns, and the like) and replacing them with "normal" voices that will confirm and consolidate students' (above all, their parents') hegemonic values.[10]

The NAS/PC debate over hegemonic/counterhegemonic control of the classroom seems to me to have gotten completely out of hand—to have become impossibly polarized, exacerbated into the mutual repulsion of conflicting paranoid fantasies, by an inability to come to terms with the complex pulls and pushes of Other-speech. Let me begin to move toward (perhaps beyond) an ending to this book, then, by suggesting some benefits that might accrue in the current political/pedagogical scene from my explorations of the Other.

For the NAS, for example, the "oppositional" scenario imagined by "politically correct" instructors is a paranoid fantasy, because these instructors have total control over their students; they are not oppositional at all, but comfortably (and dangerously) ensconced in the seat of power. For these instructors, on the other hand, the NAS scenario is a paranoid fantasy because their students are still almost immutably shaped by the esemphonic voices of their parents, teachers, religious leaders, politicians, advertisers, peers, and the like; the NAS is not a romantic underdog fighting for justice, but an arm of sociopolitical hegemony extended to smash any isolated pockets of rebellion. For the NAS, "PC," or politically correct, academics have all the discursive power, and they use it to pervert their students; for counterhegemonic instructors, the NAS and the hegemonic forces they represent have all the discursive power and use it to maintain a perverted system.

Clearly, as long as the political battle between these two forces is waged on this polarized ground, no dialogue can take place. A dialogical mediation can only begin to be constructed once we realize that no social force is absolute—that neither the instructors who resist social hegemony nor the hegemonic students who resist their instructors can reshape or reject the other at will. The psychosocial Others that speak us are far too conflicted for that, both in and among themselves. The Other-as-culture is resisted from within by the very counterhegemonic voices that it systematically represses, for example, and its resistance is keyed to its repression, so that the more carefully the Other-as-culture silences various Others-as-anarchy, the more insistently those voices will disrupt the hegemonic flow. The good, decent, obedient, well-behaved child at the dinner table or in Sunday school or in civics class or in front of the television set will be spoken "negatively" by all the idiosomatic voices her or his hegemonic parents or teachers or advertisers/programmers subliminally instruct her or him to deny; as those negated rebellious voices accumulate, so too will the authoritarian impulses to deny them, forget them, ignore them, banish them; and as the child internalizes new protections against those voices, she or he will ingest more vocal rebelliousness along with them. This rebelliousness will one day incline the child "dangerously" to agree with counterhegemonic professors— and will simultaneously escalate her or his resistance to those professors.

At the same time, of course, any attempt to articulate and affirm counterhegemonic, idiosomatic voices, any concerted effort to elicit the speaking of the Other-as-minority that unspeaks the majoritarian Other-as-culture, will itself be powerfully spoken by the Other-as-majoritarian-culture. There is no "pure" rebellion, no "perfect" escape from the carceral speaking of the hegemonic Other. Hence the famous failure of revolutions: their tendency to replicate the authoritarian regimes they overthrow, with only a few institutional, thematic, or personnel changes.

Hence also—and this is where the NAS reactionaries have a point— the tendency of many oppositional academics to "authorize" their insurrections against the speaking of the Other-as-culture by replicating its authoritarianism: refusing to teach hegemonic texts (the Bible, "Eurocentric" classics, works by white middle-class males), enforcing political correctness and punishing deviations from PC norms (ridiculing or silencing students who use discriminatory terms in class, failing students who refuse to assimilate their beliefs and behaviors to "democratic" and "egalitarian" values).[11] As the Other-as-culture never fails to whisper, the only really effective way to articulate and expand resistance against it is to adopt its methods. A pretheoretical and unsystematic "intuitive" or "exploratory" articulation of resistance to hegemonic authority is spineless, nonconfrontational, and therefore ineffectual—a mealy-mouthed form of "liberalism." Antisexist, antiracist, anticlassist, anti-ageist, anti-Eurocentric insights must not be left to languish at the level of "insight," on the breaking edge of understanding; they must be theorized, systematized, and above all institutionalized at the pedagogical, curricular, and if possible bureaucratic levels.

The critical problem from the Other-as-culture's point of view is that these insights are brought forth out of the black hole of repression in the name of freedom, equality, and mutual respect, profoundly dangerous impulses for the democratic Other-as-culture because they invoke the repressed reality concealed behind its own libertarian rhetoric. Here is the scary thing for the NAS: "PC-man" (the Right's cartoon antihero, designed to satirize the Left) is politically correct *in the Other-as-culture's own terms*. Sexism is an atavistic (medieval, primitive) assault on the freedom and equality and dignity of individual women, who are protected under the Constitution and every hegemonic ideal that it represents. Racism is an atavistic assault on the freedom and equality and dignity of (in the United States) individual Afro-Americans, Hispanics, Asian Americans, Jews, Native Americans, and so on. The democratic Other-as-culture's fear, voiced and politicized by the NAS and other reactionary groups, is that its principles might actually be put into transformative and therapeutic practice, thus undermining social stability and bringing about the possibility of real healing in the minds and bodies of the chronically (because normatively) ill.

Lest this nightmarish perversion ("substantiation") of its empty rhetoric become a reality, therefore, the Other-as-culture whispers its instructions into the ears of those who struggle toward healing: *if your students don't want health, tie them down and inject them with it*. If they despise freedom and long for rigid authoritarianism, bring all your professional authority to bear to compel them to be free and to respect the freedom of others. If they ridicule the idea of equality and long for the reassurance of hierarchical differences, make sure they know who's giving the grades in the class and what will happen to their grades if they don't behave in an egalitarian fashion. If they sneer at the notion of respecting other people's dignity, ridicule them into submission. Thus the Other-as-culture protects itself against real change, real innovation, real transformation.

This sounds like a caricature, and perhaps to some degree it is. Certainly not every PC classroom is authoritarian, hierarchical, humiliating. But the Other-as-culture does infect our attempts at transformation-from-within with a massive amount of authoritarianism, and in so doing leaves us wide open to NAS reactionaries crying "PC!" Personally, for example, I like to think of my caricature as more typical of some of my colleagues than of myself; then I notice how angry I get at some of my students who cling smugly, superciliously to their sexism and racism, to their belief that middle-of-the-road American Protestantism (for instance) is the only true religion and everybody else is going to hell, and how hard I work to transform my anger into a hammer subtle enough and powerful enough to smash through those students' defenses and *force* them to see the truth — *my* truth, which (of course) is no dogmatic belief system but a universal human desire for openness, understanding, and mutual respect (yeah, sure). I congratulate myself for being more tolerant of diversity (including the diversity represented by conservative students) than some of my colleagues; but then I observe a TA's classroom where students can say all kinds of vile reactionary things without the slightest protest from the instructor, and I feel anxiety and anger creeping toward articulation (in the form of an observation report recommending greater ideological vigilance).

So what do we do? What (to begin tying these strings back together) does it mean to teach beyond the ending? One of the things it means, I would suggest, is a flexible and constantly shifting *pedagogical* dialectic between what Fredric Jameson calls positive and negative hermeneutics. This is close to the distinction I draw in an article on Henry James between euphemism or "speaking well" and dysphemism or "speaking ill," but I want to disjoin the two distinctions just slightly, to keep them from locking into absolute synonymity. Dysphemism in that article became a channel of speaking ill of a person or a group, for example by assaulting a text or a belief structure which that person or group holds dear. And while Jameson's negative hermeneutic might well be construed as necessarily involving some such assault, I would argue that the very dialectical interchange between positive and negative hermeneutics must infect even the most negative assault on a belief structure with a positive attitude toward the person who holds it — just as, conversely, that interchange must infect even the most positive attitude toward a person or a group or a text or a belief structure with a negative suspicion that everything cannot be quite as hunky-dory as it seems.

In other words, I believe that an effective pedagogical dialectic between positive and negative hermeneutics must be fundamentally "euphemistic" in the etymological sense I elaborated in that article—must proceed out of respect for other people and take place in an atmosphere of mutual and self-esteem:

> There is no sense here that the teacher-critic is clearing away (or "boiling down") euphemistic subterfuges and discovering unmediated realities; rather that the euphemistic process is advancing, gaining ground, getting an increasingly solid purchase on reality without necessarily becoming less euphemistic. After all, no matter what terrible things we discover about ourselves we continue to have a need to talk about them in palatable ways, to "speak well" of ourselves—to avoid the sudden pendulum swing that would construe our discoveries dysphemistically, as "bad talk," or in terms of self-hatred. To a certain kind of self-styled straight-talker, this sounds like coddling yourself and others, wrapping yourself up in the wool of self-deception, protecting yourself from ugly truths—for this sort of thinker everything that is not boldly and crudely dysphemistic is timid self-delusion. Typically, however, this sort of thinker has a hidden euphemistic term that permits the transformation of dysphemistic discourse into self-praise ("I am more ruthlessly honest and self-searching than anyone else; I can stand more unpleasant truths about myself than anyone"). ("James" 421)

In the literature classroom, as I say, this euphemistic principle means teaching more (and less) than "literature," more and less than the objectified literary text. It also means doing both more and less than teaching. It means, to risk inanity once again, teaching "life," exploring the complexities of psychosocial existence in the crossovers between text and reader, reader and author, author and historical context, historical context and reader; and it means letting this exploration take place in a dehierarchized and therefore constantly destructured classroom. To the extent that the institution imposes certain hierarchical structures on the university instructor, in the form of grades and mandatory final exams, say, some accommodations to hierarchy will have to be made; but those accommodations can be made openly and collectively, with the group demystifying the institutional structures that traditionally protect the instructor's authority.[12] Anything not specified by the institution then goes up for grabs: the selection and interpretation of texts; the power to decide who speaks and who is silent; who speaks with authority and who resists that authority; who is right and who is wrong; and who is politically correct and who is politically incorrect.

And of course, say the pundits, chaos ensues. But it doesn't—partly because students trained to deference are bound to go on granting the instructor some residual authority; partly because any instructor with the nerve to break so determinedly with tradition is bound to earn and keep a certain amount of student respect; and partly because, like all adults, students have gone through an extensive period of social conditioning that prepares them for fairly complex group interactions. The Other-as-culture, in other words, will help an alternative classroom succeed. Putting it in these terms helps us see that a large portion of our students' social conditioning is in passive submission to authority, and that this unconscious impulse will have to be raised to consciousness and with any luck unlearned in the first few weeks of class. It is difficult for many students, trained as most of us are in passive submission, to take responsibility for a class they take, to stand up for an eccentric interpretation, or to complain about an authoritarian practice—especially since they have no guarantee that the instructor won't suddenly turn on them and fail them for insubordination (it happens).

But the success of an alternative classroom is not entirely the Other-as-culture's doing. Part of it can be attributed, I would suggest, to the Other-as-culture's repression of egalitarian impulses in children: systematically trained to compete, to dominate or submit, to win or lose, and to repress all tabooed sympathy for a victorious or defeated peer, a child growing to adulthood will have internalized such sympathy in negated form and will be able, in an atmosphere conducive to trust, increasingly to access and activate it. It may come out in the guise of ridicule at first, since that is the Other-as-parent's finest repressive tool—as more or less affectionate banter, say, or as cynically witty quips that "liven up" a discussion—but as most students relax into an accepting, caring atmosphere (and as the cynics and the anarchists realize that their quips aren't getting the expected authoritarian response but are being largely ignored or smiled upon indulgently), this too passes and the sympathy or "with-feeling" that the individualistic Other-as-culture represses will begin to flow. Gradually, freed from fear, students will begin to take risks—first with the instructor's anger, then (and this is hardest of all) with other students' ridicule.

What does this mean in practice? It means providing plenty of opportunities for students to voice their opinions, of course, through frequent journal writes or informal essays and student presentations, even turning the whole class (to the extent that anyone actually "leads" it or "leads off") over to a succession of student presenters; but it also means creating a classroom atmosphere in which there are no right or wrong answers. And I am suggesting that the best way to do this is to allow the ending of the text under discussion to become the beginning of discussion beyond the text. As long as the text is the focus of classroom discussion, there are right and wrong answers, and someone (guess who) will have to adjudicate among them. Once this class, students and teacher together, moves beyond the ending of the text to each reader's individual and collective responses to the text, then there can be no right or wrong answers. Then there are just answers (and answers, and more answers).

In a classroom discussion of "Haircut," for example, note the difference between a question like "Who killed Jim Kendall?" and one like "What do you think, did Jim Kendall really die?" The first has an answer, or a gradated series of answers, depending on your frame of reference ("Paul Dickson," "the town in the form of Doc, Whitey, and Paul," "Lardner," "the reader," etc.); the second invites open-ended speculation that can fruitfully turn back on the speculators. Note further the difference between a response to such speculation like "Yes, right, very good" and one like "Hm, interesting, why do you say that?" The first response solves the problem and thus ends discussion: anyone who had a divergent answer quickly begins conforming his or her thinking to the answer valorized as correct. The second response opens the discussion up to a new level of collective and individual self-exploration, an inquiry into our conscious and unconscious motivations for reading in certain ways.

And it seems to me that if we cannot move our classroom discussions onto that level, into that self-exploratory mode, then what we are doing is precisely as useless as the anticritical Other-as-culture wants it to be. Individual and collective self-exploration without right answers, without a predetermined direction, is the dangerous ground the Other-as-culture desperately wants us to avoid, and will coach us to avoid, for instance, by guiding us to a new authoritarian articulation of the perversities of "normal" or hegemonic culture. Whether we are telling our students to believe what is morally "right" (i.e., normative, hegemonic), or what is politically "correct" (i.e., radically and therefore dangerously democratic), or what is objectively "true" (i.e., safely depoliticized), as long as we are *telling* them, the social stability that is the Other-as-culture's primary concern remains secure. If we are facilitating open-ended self-exploration, anything can happen.

One way of putting this is that we should move beyond esemphonic to "asymphonic" teaching: instead of working to conform our students' voices to our own, or to a norm based on our group's conception of correctness, we should open our own and our students' ears to Other voices, divergent, deviant, discordant voices, voices that are asymphonic in their playful disregard for the conductor's signal ("syn") that brings each instrument ("phone") into idealized conformity with all others. These asymphonic voices are in our own heads, if we would but listen;

they are in our own speech, even when we are trying to sound most authoritative (and our students hear them); and they are in our students' heads and speech—that is, in fact, one of the things that traditionally irritates teachers about their students, that they are unable or unwilling to repress asymphonic voices. If we can relax that irritation, relax that Other-driven need to enforce conformity, we can increasingly allow our classrooms to be permeated by asymphonic dialogues, interchanges in which speakers are in fact interchanged, in which each speaker becomes all others by being spoken by their Others—and something truly democratic, and potentially healing, can begin to occur.

Suppose, for example, I am teaching "Who Dealt?" and some women in the class begin to articulate a reading of the story like Ellen Gardiner's, arguing that the narrator knows (perhaps unconsciously) exactly what she is doing, that *she* springs the trap on Tom (and in some sense on Lardner), and that the story enacts a movement toward divorce and feminist healing. What do I do? Tell them they're wrong? Insist with a big guffaw that the narrator is a booby, an idiot, a blabbermouthed birdbrain? Obviously not—although this may not be obvious in every literature classroom. Demand that they substantiate it with evidence from the text? They might be able to do it, and then what would I do? Shoot down their argumentation? Since they are probably just working it out as they go along, working it out by talking it out, they will most likely not be able to muster all the relevant passages and construe them in academically persuasive ways; so do I write their interpretation off until such time as they are prepared to convince me? Ah, power: the power to impose forensic tests on people, to require them to jump through hoops before you will consent (in your judicial wisdom) to take them seriously. Shall I smile, nod appreciatively, praise them for their innovative reading, and then move on? Nice try—that would effectively defuse (at least for the moment) any empowerment they might have been feeling, but is that what I want to do? The implication of a quick smile and a change of subject is that they have a right to their interpretation, but the rest of us don't have to listen to it. It's private, personal, and therefore doesn't (and *shouldn't*) impinge on the group. They are welcome to work on it on their own time, perhaps for their paper (but will they dare, if I won't even let them talk about it in class?). Should I adopt a feminist point of view and point out the interpretive implications they are missing? Kind of takes the fun out of it for them, doesn't it—not to mention the empowerment. And where do I get that feminist point of view anyway? How do I, a man, validate it? What, finally, do I *do*?

The question is predicated on the assumption that as the teacher I

always have to *do something* — namely, teach. What if the something I
chose to do were a "nothing" — or rather, a responsive listening that is
only a nothing for a culture obsessed with goal-oriented activity? Would
it be so terrible for me to sit quietly (but attentively, responsively) while
three or four or five students talked among themselves? Would that
undermine my authority in the classroom? Would I feel I was earning
my paycheck?

One step beyond sitting quietly and attentively and listening, obviously, is to facilitate other students' entry into the same discussion:
"Sharon, isn't that a little like what you were just saying about Mrs.
Guthrie?" Now the three or four or five students who have been domi-
nating the conversation have to stop, listen, adjust their thinking to a
new point of view, perhaps regroup and start over, but not at the beginning — at a different point, perhaps a different conceptual level.

But I might, finally, dive into the conversational fray myself — how?
Can I find anything in the experiential range of my total response to the
story or the discussion so far that allows me to connect up with what
these students are saying? Something personal, political, an event, a
memory, a newspaper article, a story, a joke? Can I get the students to
step back from their interpretation (not too soon, not too fast, but at
some point) and explore their motivations for developing it? Can I (and
here we begin to move into the ideological sphere) encourage them to
explore the commonality between this interpretation and the last one
they tried in class, and between their interpretations of Lardner and their
responses to, say, their fathers, mothers, sisters, brothers, boyfriends,
girlfriends, husbands, wives, daughters, sons? Imagine Tom as your
father; how do you respond to his ridicule? Do you see other fathers
doing this? Other men? Do you do it yourself? When? Can you identify
with the Tom that his wife sees, or that his wife as seen by Ellen Gardiner
sees? What happens as you ease into that self-image? What anxieties
begin to surface? What connections might there be between those anxieties and Tom's (and men's) behavior?

As we begin to collectivize our responses, to compare individual responses with larger social patterns of response, any number of things
may happen. Some students (or the instructor) may have a ready-made
answer derived from feminism, or Marxism, or conservatism, or some
other ism: "Tom Cannon is a repressed male whose awkward silence
conceals his true hatred for his wife." "Tom's wife is a typical birdbrain
woman, all talk, no substance." Other students will resist this movement
toward the collective, toward larger patterns: "Oh, come on, it's just a
story, you make it sound like the Bible, or something." Pontification,

ridicule: mirror-image defenses against the frightening thought that everything *I* say, everything *I* do, has meaning, is connected, ties in with bigger pictures in complex and unsettling ways. Ridicule here is a way of sticking your fingers in your ears and loudly humming the national anthem: please don't make me *think*! The feminist who calls Tom a repressed male is right, in a trivial, abstract, and thus ultimately defensive sense; the conservative who calls Tom's wife a typical birdbrain woman is right also, in an equally trivial and defensive sense. Like many men in patriarchal society, Tom has been trained (we can speculate) to repress his emotions; like many women in patriarchal society, Tom's wife has been trained to act stupid.

And so I could, at this point, give a minilecture on social programming and the way we are coached not to see it (and to ridicule those who would force us to see it); or, given my complication of the feminist attack on Tom in part I and Ellen Gardiner's complication of the macho attack on Tom's wife, I could give a minilecture on all the subtleties these pontificating students are missing. But what does a minilecture achieve? It shuts the students up; it reminds them that I am in charge and they should really be listening to me more submissively; it "shows" them how much smarter I am than they, and how far they will have to go before they can pretend to know as much and interpret literary texts as well as I do. If I am insecure enough in my professorial role, maybe that is precisely what I will do.

More interesting, as Ellen Gardiner suggested in conversation, and ultimately more useful, is to question why it is important for these students to react as they do: what drives the feminist to pigeonhole Tom and, through Tom, other (real) men, and what drives the conservative to pigeonhole Tom's wife and, through her, other (real) women, in this dysphemistic way—and what drives the "Oh, come on" student to ridicule the class discussion? Are these innocent responses, purely personal, individual, spur-of-the-moment gut reactions—or are they themselves collectively programmed defenses?

Here the literature classroom begins to shift toward group therapy, and the instructor with a Ph.D. in English and no training in counseling must walk carefully: it is relatively easy to push a student too far too fast, and with terrifying suddenness, down the precipitous slope into traumatic psychic material, ultimately into the hospital. Certainly literature instructors should not see themselves as group therapists and attempt to "cure" their students. But it is possible—and, I am suggesting, desirable—to instigate potentially therapeutic processes in students, to nudge them toward (and provide them with a few rudimentary tools for) idiosomatic and ideosomatic self-exploration, without risking psychic breakdown.

I'm talking, after all, about consciousness-raising, or what John Rowan calls *un*consciousness-raising (33); I may even, at some level, be talking about the old-fashioned "moral imperative" of the teacher, the requirement that he or she help students grow personally so as to lead happier, healthier, more integrated and productive lives. This is not, in other words, anything new, anything radically innovative — except, of course, insofar as we highly professionalized literature teachers have gotten away from it and, I think, need to get back.

But not *straight* back — not back to Mr. Chips, not to some nostalgic pedagogical ideal glorified by the NAS. The sexism, classism, racism, ageism, and other addictive fixations of our society are terrible, pernicious diseases that cannot be blithely allowed to spread, least of all by retreating into some preideological cloud-cuckooland of the political Right. The much-ridiculed conceptual density of recent critical theories is invaluable, too (if not always, for undergraduates, in its most jargonistic form) in exploring the incredible complexity of the double binds in which our culture imprisons us. I am not, in other words, calling for a return to the little red schoolhouse — only for a detoxification of embarrassing, old-fashioned notions like helping students to grow.

For isn't that, finally, the true end of all so-called politically correct or emancipatory teaching, and the true crime of which the NAS and other right-wing organizations accuse us: that we would teach our students to grow up, mature, leave behind the fear-driven passivity and xenophobia imposed on them by their parents and other agents of the Other-as-culture, and begin to explore and enjoy the rich diversity of life? The real question, it seems to me, is not whether we oppositional or emancipatory teachers want to help our students grow, develop intellectually and emotionally, live richer, more abundant lives, but what is the most effective way to work toward that goal. And if anything is redolent of the little red schoolhouse, it seems to me, it is the authoritarianism, the coercive pedagogical practices, of much PC teaching: ramming "freedom" down the throats of recalcitrant conservative students. That is not only doing our students no good; it is doing us no good with our right-wing detractors, who seize on our authoritarianism and exclusionism and accuse us of curbing their children's freedom.

And maybe we are; maybe we are too afraid of being wrong (after all, doesn't the Other-as-culture keep whispering to us that we are?) to slacken the reins of control. Maybe, in fact, what we need is to "grow up" (struggle toward emancipation) ourselves: to discover the sources of our coercive pedagogies in our own carefully programmed fears, in the double binds that frustrate us sometimes to the point of tears or violence, and to *let go*. If we relax even a little, stop trying so hard to know everything and control everything, we might even learn from our students — or from the ongoing dialogues we have with our students in class. If literature, and our discussions of literature beyond the ending of any given text, can't help us do that, then what *good* is it?

Conclusion

In the spring of 1933 Ring Lardner was hospitalized for tuberculosis at Doctors Hospital in New York. Ellis Lardner took a hotel apartment on East 86th Street near Madison Avenue and visited her husband daily. His oldest son John was working for the *Herald Tribune*, and was living at the Hotel Peter Stuyvesant at 86th Street and Central Park West. He worked sixty-hour weeks but had Mondays off, and at noon every Monday he would walk to his mother's apartment, eat a late breakfast with her, then take a cab with her over to see his father.

This story is told by Richard Tobin, Lardner's nephew (Anne's son), who was rooming with John and, like him, working for the *Herald Tribune*. Writing for the *Saturday Review of Books* in 1964, thirty years after the events he recounts, Tobin tells the story of one visit he made to his uncle's bedside with his aunt and cousin. Around Lardner's forty-eighth birthday, in March of the last year of his life, the entourage arrive at his room to find Sherwood Anderson just leaving, and Tobin engages his uncle in conversation about writers from small towns and from big cities. Lardner wonders why he ever left Niles, Michigan, and his son John blurts out, "Because you had something to say." "This was the longest sentence from John in months," Tobin remarks wryly, "and it startled me."

"I guess it wouldn't have been so great at that," Ring said. "Small towns are fine to grow up in and a writer finds out a lot of things in small towns he can't learn anywhere else. But it wouldn't be the same as you got older in a small town."

"I like New York," I said, having just come from the same small Michigan town.

"Well," said Lardner, "Dickens didn't have any trouble learning to write and the town he lived in wasn't exactly an open field."

"I think Dickens was sentimental," I said pompously. Lardner looked

up sharply but said nothing. I went on at length that Dickens was a sentimental fool.

"Well," said Ring after a bit, trying not to hurt me, "Dickens isn't read
any more and it's a shame. He could write about people and make you
want to put your arm around them."

"He was awfully sloppy," I persisted.

Lardner took a Turkish cigarette and lighted it with his trembling hands.
He did not look at John or me for a while. He coughed hard and punched
out the cigarette expertly.

"How can you write if you can't cry?" said Ring Lardner. (6)

It is in this period that Lardner is occasionally found sitting alone,
sobbing into his hands: he knows, perhaps, finally, whereof he speaks.
And if Lardner the writer has been no more a weeper than a laugher,
if he has built his professional reputation on iron(ic) self-control and
self-protection, perhaps what he is finally realizing here is that it has all
been a sham, a mummery—not the reputation, but the reserve; not the
writing, but the way he conceived the writing. This sickbed plea for
sentimentality implies that the most supportive response to the narrator
of "Who Dealt?," for example—the best way to "put your arm around
her," as Lardner says Dickens makes you want to do to his characters—
is not to sneer at her but to congratulate her, to pat her on the back for
her success at taking the first step toward regaining her life. It implies
that the best response to Miss Coakley in "Dinner" is to stop her, look
her in the eyes, and say, "Go ahead, I'm listening. Take all the time you
want. Use any words you want, leave all the gaps you want; I'll figure
out the rest. I want to hear what you have to say."

This is an embarrassing scene, at Lardner's sickbed and at the sentimental side of his characters. It is a scene that embarrasses many men in
real life, programmed as we are for autonomy, self-sufficiency, emotional isolation; but in critical discourse it is somehow *absolutely* embarrassing, sappy, corny, inane. It is beyond the pale, beneath contempt;
voicing it here, in my conclusion, taints my entire argument, tarnishes it
with the brush of the cheapest sentimentalism.

And I admit it—with a good deal of inner resistance. I do not come to
sentimentalism easily or comfortably. I ache to be intellectually imperi-
ous, dismissive, sardonic. But consider this: to the extent that we deny,
suppress moments like this, sentimental moments, moments of caring,
sharing, supporting, we lock ourselves into the ideologically normal masculine cage in which Lardner languished and perished, and which he
himself began to question in the last year of his life. The protective
carapaces of academic discourse are qualitatively no different from the

walls behind which Lardner hid from those who loved him: they are spoken by a conservative Other-as-father who wants everything to stay *exactly as is*, and knows that rigid antisentimental self-protection is the best possible guard against flux. If you can't cry, laugh, or console, you can write; but you can't change. Lardner learned this—maybe. Maybe it's time critical writers, you and I, learned it as well.

APPENDIX A

Ring Lardner, "Who Dealt?"

You know, this is the first time Tom and I have been with real friends since we were married. I suppose you'll think it's funny for me to call you *my* friends when we've never met before, but Tom has talked about you so much and how much he thought of you and how crazy he was to see you and everything—well, it's just as if I'd known you all my life, like he has.

We've got our little crowd out here, play bridge and dance with them; but of course we've only been there three months, at least I have, and people you've known that length of time, well, it isn't like knowing people all your life, like you and Tom. How often I've heard Tom say he'd give any amount of money to be with Arthur and Helen, and how bored he was out there with just poor little me and his new friends!

Arthur and Helen, Arthur and Helen—he talks about you so much that it's a wonder I'm not jealous; especially of you, Helen. You must have been his real pal when you were kids.

Nearly all his kid books, they have your name in front—to Thomas Cannon from Helen Bird Strong. This is a wonderful treat for him to see you! And a treat for me, too. Just think, I've at last met the wonderful Helen and Arthur! You must forgive me calling you by your first names; that's how I always think of you and I simply can't say Mr. and Mrs. Gratz.

No, thank you, Arthur; no more. Two is my limit and I've already exceeded it, with two cocktails before dinner and now this. But it's a special occasion, meeting Tom's best friends. I bet Tom wishes he could celebrate too, don't you, dear? Of course he could if he wanted to, but when he once makes up his mind to a thing, there's nothing in the world can shake him. He's got the strongest will power of any person I ever saw.

I do think it's wonderful, him staying on the wagon this long, a man that used to—well, you know as well as I do; probably a whole lot

better, because you were with him so much in the old days, and all I
know is just what he's told me. He told me about once in Pittsburgh —
All right, Tommie; I won't say another word. But it's all over now, thank
heavens! Not a drop since we've been married; three whole months! And
he says it's forever, don't you, dear? Though I don't mind a person
drinking if they do it in moderation. But you know Tom! He goes the
limit in everything he does. Like he used to in athletics —

All right, dear; I won't make you blush. I know how you hate the
limelight. It's terrible, though, not to be able to boast about your own
husband; everything he does or ever has done seems so wonderful. But
is that only because we've been married such a short time? Do you feel
the same way about Arthur, Helen? You do? And you married him four
years ago, isn't that right? And you eloped, didn't you? You see I know
all about you.

Oh, are you waiting for me? Do we cut for partners? Why can't we
play families? I don't feel so bad if I do something dumb when it's Tom
I'm playing with. He never scolds, though he does give me some terrible
looks. But not very often lately; I don't make the silly mistakes I used
to. I'm pretty good now, aren't I, Tom? You better say so, because if
I'm not, it's your fault. You know Tom had to teach me the game. I
never played at all till we were engaged. Imagine! And I guess I was
pretty awful at first, but Tom was a dear, so patient! I know he thought
I would never learn, but I fooled you, didn't I, Tommie?

No, indeed, I'd rather play than do almost anything. But you'll sing
for us, won't you, Helen? I mean after a while. Tom has raved to me
about your voice and I'm dying to hear it.

What are we playing for? Yes, a penny's perfectly all right. Out there
we generally play for half a cent a piece, a penny a family. But a penny
apiece is all right. I guess we can afford it now, can't we, dear? Tom
hasn't told you about his raise. He was — All right, Tommie; I'll shut
up. I know you hate to be talked about, but your wife can't help being
just a teeny bit proud of you. And I think your best friends are interested
in your affairs, aren't you, folks?

But Tom is the most secretive person I ever knew. I believe he even
keeps things from me! Not very many, though. I can usually tell when
he's hiding something and I keep after him till he confesses. He often
says I should have been a lawyer or a detective, the way I can worm
things out of people. Don't you, Tom?

For instance, I never would have known about his experience with
those horrid football people at Yale if I hadn't just made him tell me.

Didn't you know about that? No, Tom, I'm going to tell Arthur even if you hate me for it. I know you'd be interested, Arthur, not only because you're Tom's friend, but on account of you being such a famous athlete yourself. Let me see, how was it, Tom? You must help me out. Well, if I don't get it right, you correct me.

Well, Tom's friends at Yale had heard what a wonderful football player he was in high school so they made him try for a place on the Yale nine. Tom had always played half-back. You have to be a fast runner to be a half-back and Tom could run awfully fast. He can yet. When we were engaged we used to run races and the prize was— All right, Tommie, I won't give away our secrets. Anyway, he can beat me to pieces.

Well, he wanted to play half-back at Yale and he was getting along fine and the other men on the team said he would be a wonder and then one day they were having their practice and Tex Jones, no Ted Jones— he's the main coach— he scolded Tom for having the signal wrong and Tom proved that Jones was wrong and he was right and Jones never forgave him. He made Tom quit playing half-back and put him tackle or end or some place like that where you can't do anything and being a fast runner doesn't count. So Tom saw that Jones had it in for him and he quit. Wasn't that it, Tom? Well, anyway, it was something.

Oh, are you waiting for me? I'm sorry. What did you bid, Helen? And you, Tom? You doubled her? And Arthur passed? Well, let's see. I wish I could remember what that means. I know that sometimes when he doubles he means one thing and sometimes another. But I always forget which is which. Let me see; it was two spades that he doubled, wasn't it? That means I'm to leave him in, I'm pretty sure. Well, I'll pass. Oh, I'm sorry, Tommie! I knew I'd get it wrong. Please forgive me. But maybe we'll set them anyway. Whose lead?

I'll stop talking now and keep my mind on the game. You needn't look that way, Tommie. I *can* stop talking if I try. It's kind of hard to concentrate through, when you're, well, excited. It's not only meeting you people, but I always get excited traveling. I was just terrible on our honeymoon, but then I guess a honeymoon's enough to make anybody nervous. I'll never forget when we went into the hotel in Chicago— All right, Tommie, I won't. But I can tell about meeting the Bakers.

They're a couple about our age that I've known all my life. They were the last people in the world I wanted to see, but we ran into them on State Street and they insisted on us coming to their hotel for dinner and before dinner they took us to their room and Ken—that's Mr. Baker—

Ken made some cocktails, though I didn't want any and Tom was on the wagon. He said a honeymoon was a fine time to be on the wagon! Ken said.

"Don't tempt him, Ken," I said. "Tom isn't a drinker like you and Gertie and the rest of us. When he starts, he can't stop." Gertie is Mrs. Baker.

So Ken said why should he stop and I said there was good reason why he should because he had promised me he would and he told me the day we were married that if I ever saw him take another drink I would know that —

What did you make? Two odd? Well, thank heavens that isn't a game! Oh, that does make a game, doesn't it? Because Tom doubled and I left him in. Isn't that wicked? Oh, dearie, please forgive me and I'll promise to pay attention from now on! What do I do with these? Oh, yes, I make them for Arthur.

I was telling you about the Bakers. Finally Ken saw he couldn't make Tom take a drink, so he gave up in disgust. But imagine meeting them on our honeymoon, when we didn't want to see anybody! I don't suppose anybody does unless they're already tired of each other, and we certainly weren't, were we, Tommie? And aren't yet, are we, dear? And never will be. But I guess I better speak for myself.

There! I'm talking again. But you see it's the first time we've been with anybody we really cared about; I mean, you're Tom's best friends and it's so nice to get a chance to talk to somebody who's known him a long time. Out there the people we run around with are almost strangers and they don't talk about anything but themselves and how much money their husbands make. You never can talk to them about things that are worth while, like books. I'm wild about books, but I honestly don't believe half the women we know out there can read. Or at least they don't. If you mention some really worth while novel like, say, "Black Oxen," they think you're trying to put on the Ritz.

You said a non-trump, didn't you, Tom? And Arthur passed. Let me see; I wish I knew what to do. I haven't any five-card — it's terrible! Just a minute. I wish somebody could — I know I ought to take — but — well, I'll pass. Oh, Tom, this is the worst you ever saw, but I don't know what I could have done.

I do hold the most terrible cards! I certainly believe in the saying, "Unlucky at cards, lucky in love." Whoever made it up must have been thinking of me. I hate to lay them down, dear. I know you'll say I ought to have done something. Well, there they are! Let's see your hand, Helen. Oh, Tom, she's — but I mustn't tell, must I? Anyway, I'm dummy.

That's one comfort. I can't make a mistake when I'm dummy. I believe Tom overbids lots of times so I'll be dummy and can't do anything ridiculous. But at that I'm much better than I used to be, aren't I, dear?

Helen, do you mind telling me where you got that gown? Crandall and Nelson's? I've heard of them, but I heard they were terribly expensive. Of course a person can't expect to get a gown like that without paying for it. I've got to get some things while I'm here and I suppose that's where I better go, if their things aren't too horribly dear. I haven't had a thing new since I was married and I've worn this so much I'm sick of it.

Tom's always after me to buy clothes, but I can't seem to get used to spending somebody else's money, though it was dad's money I spent before I did Tom's, but that's different, don't you think so? And of course at first we didn't have very much to spend, did we, dear? But now that we've had our raise— All right, Tommie, I won't say another word.

Oh, did you know they tried to get Tom to run for mayor? Tom is making faces at me to shut up, but I don't see any harm in telling it to his friends. They know we're not the kind that brag, Tommie. I do think it was quite a tribute; he'd only lived there a little over a year. It came up one night when the Guthries were at our house, playing bridge. Mr. Guthrie—that's A. L. Guthrie—he's one of the big lumbermen out there. He owns—just what does he own, Tom? Oh, I'm sorry. Anyway, he's got millions. Well, at least thousands.

He and his wife were at our house playing bridge. She's the queerest woman! If you just saw her, you'd think she was a janitor or something; she wears the most hideous clothes. Why, that night she had on a— honestly you'd have sworn it was a maternity gown, and for no reason. And the first time I met her—well, I just can't describe it. And she's a graduate of Bryn Mawr and one of the oldest families in Philadelphia. You'd never believe it!

She and her husband are terribly funny in a bridge game. He doesn't think there ought to be any conventions; he says a person might just as well tell each other what they've got. So he won't pay any attention to what-do-you-call-'em, informatory, doubles and so forth. And she plays all the conventions, so you can imagine how they get along. Fight! Not really fight, you know, but argue. That is, he does. It's horribly embarrassing to whoever is playing with them. Honestly, if Tom ever spoke to me like Mr. Guthrie does to his wife, well—aren't they terrible, Tom? Oh, I'm sorry.

She was the first woman in Portland that called on me and I thought it was awfully nice of her, though when I saw her at the door I would have sworn she was a book agent or maybe a cook looking for work. She had on a—well, I can't describe it. But it was sweet of her to call, she being one of the real people there and me—well, that was before Tom was made a vice-president. What? Oh, I never dreamed he hadn't written you about that!

But Mrs. Guthrie acted just like it was a great honor for her to meet me, and I like people to act that way even when I know it's all apple sauce. Isn't that a funny expression, "apple sauce"? Some man said it in a vaudeville show in Portland the Monday night before we left. He was a comedian—Jack Brooks or Ned Frawley or something. It means— well, I don't know how to describe it. But we had a terrible time after the first few minutes. She is the silentest person I ever knew and I'm kind of bashful myself with strangers. What are you grinning about, Tommie? I am, too, bashful when I don't know people. Not exactly bashful, maybe, but, well, bashful.

It was one of the most embarrassing things I ever went through. Neither of us could say a word and I could hardly help from laughing at what she had on. But after you get to know her you don't mind her clothes, though it's a terrible temptation all the time not to tell her how much nicer— And her hair! But she plays a dandy game of bridge, lots better than her husband. You know he won't play conventions. He says it's just like telling you what's in each other's hand. And they have awful arguments in a game. That is, he does. She's nice and quiet and it's a kind of mystery how they ever fell in love. Though there's a saying or a proverb or something, isn't there, about like not liking like? Or is it just the other way?

But I was going to tell you about them wanting Tom to be mayor. Oh, Tom, only two down? Why, I think you did splendidly! I gave you a miserable hand and Helen had—what didn't you have, Helen? You had the ace, king of clubs. No, Tom had the queen. Or was it spades? And you had the ace of hearts. No, Tom had that. No, he didn't. What *did* you have, Tom? I don't exactly see what you bid on. Of course I was terrible, but—what's the difference anyway.

What was I saying? Oh, yes, about Mr. and Mrs. Guthrie. It's funny for a couple like that to get married when they are so different in every way. I never saw two people with such different tastes. For instance, Mr. Guthrie is keen about motoring and Mrs. Guthrie just hates it. She simply suffers all the time she's in a car. He likes a good time, dancing, golfing, fishing, shows, thinks like that. She isn't interested in anything but church work and bridge work.

"Bridge work." I meant bridge, not bridge work. That's funny, isn't it? And yet they get along awfully well; that is when they're not playing cards or doing something else together. But it does seem queer that they picked each other out. Still, I guess hardly any husband and wife agree on anything.

You take Tom and me, though, and you'd think we were made for each other. It seems like we feel just the same about everything. That is, almost everything. The things we don't agree on are little things that don't matter. Like music. Tom is wild about jazz and blues and dance music. He adores Irving Berlin and Gershwin and Jack Kearns. He's always after those kind of things on the radio and I just want serious, classical things like "Humoresque" and "Indian Love Lyrics." And then there's shows. Tom is crazy over Ed Wynn and I can't see anything in him. Just the way he laughs at his own jokes is enough to spoil him for me. If I'm going to spend time and money on a theater I want to see something worth while — "The Fool" or "Lightnin'."

And things to eat. Tom insists, or that is he did insist, on a great big breakfast — fruit, cereal, eggs, toast, and coffee. All I want is a little fruit and dry toast and coffee. I think it's a great deal better for a person. So that's one habit I broke Tom of, was big breakfasts. And another thing he did when we were first married was to take off his shoes as soon as he got home from the office and put on bedroom slippers. I believe a person ought not to get sloppy just because they're married.

But the worst of all was pajamas! What's the difference, Tommie? Helen and Arthur don't mind. And I think it's kind of funny, you being so old-fashioned. I mean Tom had always worn a nightgown till I made him give it up. And it was a struggle, believe me! I had to threaten to leave him if he didn't buy pajamas. He certainly hated it. And now he's mad at me for telling, aren't you, Tommie? I just couldn't help it. I think it's so funny in this day and age. I hope Arthur doesn't wear them; nightgowns, I mean. You don't, do you, Arthur? I knew you didn't.

Oh, are you waiting for me? What did you say, Arthur? Two diamonds? Let's see what that means. When Tom makes an original bid of two it means he hasn't got the tops. I wonder — but of course you couldn't have the — heavens! What am I saying! I guess I better just keep still and pass.

But what was I going to tell you? Something about — oh, did I tell you about Tom being an author? I had no idea he was talented that way till after we were married and I was unpacking his old papers and things and came across a poem he'd written, the saddest, mushiest poem! Of course it was a long time ago he wrote it; it was dated four years ago, long before he met me, so it didn't make me very jealous, though it was about some other girl. You didn't know I found it, did you, Tommie?

But that wasn't what I refer to. He's written a story, too, and he's sent it to four different magazines and they all sent it back. I tell him though, that that doesn't mean anything. When you see some of the things the magazines do print, why, it's an honor to have them *not* like yours. The only thing is that Tom worked so hard over it and sat up nights writing and rewriting, it's a kind of a disappointment to have them turn it down.

It's a story about two men and a girl and they were all brought up together and one of the men was awfully popular and well off and good-looking and a great athlete — a man like Arthur. There, Arthur! How is that for a T.L.? The other man was just an ordinary man with not much money, but the girl seemed to like him better and she promised to wait for him. Then this man worked hard and got money enough to see him through Yale.

The other man, the well-off one, went to Princeton and made a big hit as an athlete and everything and he was through college long before his friend because his friend had to earn the money first. And the well-off man kept after the girl to marry him. He didn't know she had promised the other one. Anyway she got tired waiting for the man she was engaged to and eloped with the other one. And the story ends up by the man she threw down welcoming the couple when they came home and pretending everything was all right, though his heart was broken.

What are you blushing about, Tommie? It's nothing to be ashamed of. I thought it was very well written and if the editors had any sense they'd have taken it.

Still, I don't believe the real editors see half the stories that are sent to them. In fact I know they don't. You've either got to have a name or pull to get your things published. Or else pay the magazines to publish them. Of course if you are Robert Chambers or Irving R. Cobb, they will print whatever you write whether it's good or bad. But you haven't got a chance if you are an unknown like Tom. They just keep your story long enough so you will think they are considering it and then they send it back with a form letter saying it's not available for their magazine and they don't even tell why.

You remember, Tom, that Mr. Hastings we met at the Hammonds'. He's a writer and knows all about it. He was telling me of an experience he had with one of the magazines; I forget which one, but it was one of the big ones. He wrote a story and sent it to them and they sent it back and said they couldn't use it.

Well, some time after that Mr. Hastings was in a hotel in Chicago and a bell-boy went around the lobby paging Mr. — I forget the name, but it was the name of the editor of this magazine that had sent back the story, Runkle, or Byers, or some such name. So the man, whatever his name was, he was really there and answered the page and afterwards Mr. Hastings went up to him and introduced himself and told the man about sending a story to his magazine and the man said he didn't remember anything about it. And he was the editor! Of course he'd never seen it. No wonder Tom's story keeps coming back!

He says he's through sending it and just the other day he was going to tear it up, but I made him keep it because we may meet somebody some time who knows the inside ropes and can get a hearing with some big editor. I'm sure it's just a question of pull. Some of the things that get into the magazines sound like they had been written by the editor's friends or relatives or somebody whom they didn't want to hurt their feelings. And Tom really can write!

I wish I could remember that poem of his I found. I memorized it once, but — wait! I believe I can still say it! Hush, Tommie! What hurt will it do anybody? Let me see; it goes:

> "I thought the sweetness of her song
> Would ever, ever more belong
> To me; I thought (O thought divine!)
> My bird was really mine!

> "But promises are made, it seems,
> Just to be broken. All my dreams
> Fade out and leave me crushed, alone.
> My bird, alas, has flown!"

Isn't that pretty. He wrote it four years ago. Why, Helen, you revoked! And, Tom, do you know that's Scotch you're drinking? You said — *Why, Tom!*

APPENDIX B

"Engendered in Melancholy":[1] Ring Lardner's "Who Dealt?"

Ellen Gardiner

I

In Ring Lardner's "Who Dealt?," two couples, Arthur and Helen Gratz and Tom Cannon and his unnamed wife, the narrator of the story, meet for dinner and a game of bridge. During this bridge game the young newly married narrator spoils the evening in part by not playing very well, but primarily by talking a lot. During the course of the game, the narrator recites among other things the story of her courtship with Tom, but most important, she reveals an important secret which results in Tom, an abstaining alcoholic, taking a drink and Helen failing to follow trump — in bridge terminology, revoking. The secret the narrator reveals, seemingly without realizing that she is doing so, is that Tom was jilted by Helen some four years previously and has probably never gotten over her.

Traditionally, professional readers of this story have identified with Tom and the Gratzes. Their reaction has been, in fact, remarkably similar to that of this intratextual audience — either entirely unspoken like Arthur's (and that of other less experienced "amateur readers" of the narrator's story) or violently negative like Tom's and Helen's. In the few published evaluations of the story, for example, Donald Elder reads the narrator as "dreary," "insensible," and "rattlebrained," Walton R. Patrick calls her "stupid," and Jonathan Yardley characterizes her as a "mindless gurgler." Even women critics seem rather put out by the narrator as a character: Elizabeth Evans in particular is annoyed by her inability to play bridge properly.

More important, though, both the general lack of critical response and the brevity of these few critical remarks on Lardner's work raise an important issue. Does certain literature not get taught in the academy because it provokes extreme discomfort, and thereby emotional repression and linguistic suppression? Has the story revealed secrets about marital relationships that provoke anxiety and repression in its extratextual readers? Even those willing to talk about this particular story typically ignore virtually every important detail of the narrator's story. Does repression in fact provoke these hostile and abbreviated critical hiccups?

As critics, our own particular position in culture in terms of class, race, and gender influences our reading of literature — what we choose to read and how we choose to read it. Certainly we all recognize the impact of class, race, and gender on language production, both its transmission and reception. We have begun to study more fully the ways in which these three criteria affect authors' emotional and imaginative representation of the world and their audiences' reception of those representations. Nonetheless, within the professional arena of academic literary production, there are those powerful discursive norms that train us to present our readings as "true" or "valid" and thus tacitly cause us still to repress the impact of our own class, race, and gender on what and how we read — so that we might be seen as "neutral," or "objective." Ironically, this attempt to repress our emotional response may also lead us to ignore or overlook the details of the story that provoke that response. It might even lead us to refuse to engage a piece of literature altogether.

Certainly the vehemence of the criticism directed against the narrator of "Who Dealt?" suggests hostility on the part of the few readers willing to talk about the story; indeed, the scarcity of evidence to support their views suggests that, like Tom and the Gratzes, these critics (and perhaps many other readers as well) may want certain things about the ways in which men and women relate to one another in society kept secret, and that their anger is in direct proportion to their anxieties at the narrator's revelations. Ideologically speaking, any sign of unhealthiness in the institutions of marriage or the family means there is trouble elsewhere as well — in our businesses, in our churches, in our schools — in American society as a whole. To maintain our sense of cultural order and stability, we must sometimes ignore signs of trouble in institutions like marriage and the family — signs, for example, that people sometimes hate each other in marriage, that a father or mother or both sometimes really hate the children. Or that sometimes we ourselves don't like who we married. To admit trouble is to admit failure, which is to admit our society is not perfect. To maintain the status quo, we learn to repress painful feelings like resentment, grief, and anger.

Likewise, to accord the narrator of "Who Dealt?" any level of acumen would be to admit that she transmits something worth knowing to us about the American family, which is to say, that it is, for the most part, a dysfunctional institution. In order to acknowledge the ways in which we might identify with the narrator's story, we would also have to deal with the emotions such an acknowledgment undoubtedly would stir up. Hence because, on an emotional and psychological level, it's as risky for us as it is for Tom and the Gratzes to admit that she reveals problematic truths about marriage and relationships, unwittingly the narrator becomes the scapegoat, the enemy, the Other to both the characters in the story and to the readers of the text.

In *The Resisting Reader* Fetterley asserts that "the first act of the feminist critic must be to become a resisting rather than an assenting reader and, by this refusal to assent, to begin the process of exorcizing the male mind that has been implanted in us" (xxii). In my view, it is not simply a matter of exorcizing *a male mind*, it is exorcizing the mind of a particular class and profession that has been implanted in me—the mind of the traditional male and/or female academic literary critic. It is ideologically "masculine," perhaps, in that it is coldly and unfeelingly rational, objective, and neutral—but in fact both men and women, especially well-established (i.e., published) men and women, give their assent to this hegemonic academic mind-set. It is the mind-set that argues that one cannot give a "valid" interpretation of a text if one allows personal experience to spill out onto the page. In order to resist "the 'objective' academic mind," I believe I must confront the ways in which my gender, race, and class shape my reading of this story, despite the fact that it makes me uncomfortable to do so. To suppress those influences that cause me discomfort would lead, I believe, to a less than full interpretation of Lardner's story. To be a resisting reader is first to refuse to suppress an account of the ways in which my own experience allows me to begin to interpret the narrator sympathetically.

Douglas Robinson begins something like this in this book. Deploying Lacanian psychoanalytic theory, he reads the narrator as most often spoken by "the Other-as-child"—subversive, unruly and revelatory, she voices the secrets Tom struggles to repress. She becomes Tom's therapist, a liberating agent who paves the way for Tom's psychical healing. Robinson's avowed purpose is to become an emancipatory critic, to recognize himself in the character of Tom in order to confront those ways in which the patriarchal Other-as-culture speaks us. Such a confrontation, he argues, allows us to explore better the ways we might escape the more damaging effects of social repression that result in neuroses and obsessions.

Since Robinson reads the narrator as "Tom's Other," however, he cannot take into account her subjectivity as a fictional character; as an instrument of Tom's (and not her own) healing in his reading, she remains powerless and anonymous. I write this essay, therefore, to engage Robinson in a dialogue that examines Lardner's portrayal of what I will call a cultural melancholia, from the perspective of the woman who, because she tells the story, is its true subject.[2]

II

As a woman literary critic reading Lardner's story (and Robinson's analysis of it), I found myself identifying with a narrator thrust into a new social situation where she must perform well socially in the company of people whom her husband admires greatly. This social performance also requires that she excel at playing a rather complicated game that she has only been playing for a short time. Rather than feeling the anxiety and embarrassment that Tom, Helen, and Arthur feel, therefore, I felt the anxiety and insecurity of the inexperienced bridge player whose self-esteem is already low as a result of her gender and position in culture. The narrator reflects back to me some of the insecurities and anxieties I have suffered as a woman of lower-middle-class origins: my experiences as a child taught me that both my gender and my class would prohibit me from succeeding in the type of social situation in which the narrator of "Who Dealt?" finds herself.

When I was young I played a lot of cards with my family, but one game my parents could not and would not teach me to play was bridge. Playing cards was a way to socialize and have fun with friends and family. Bridge, my mother would say, was an exception because if you played you were not supposed to talk. Players needed to concentrate wholly on their cards, especially because there was usually money at stake. "Your aunts know how to play, though," my father would say a little wistfully, perhaps a little enviously; "they tried to teach your mother and me to play one time, but it was too complicated." My father is a fanatical card player and one of the most competitive people I know; he was once told by a professional card player of sorts, for instance, that he was the best cribbage player this man had ever seen. Yet he never tried to play bridge again after the first time; he believed that it was a game for people in the upper and educated classes. My aunts, you see, were not only much more comfortably middle-class than he, but they both had Master's degrees from Pembroke (now part of Brown University). Neither of my parents had more than a high school education.

My sympathy for this character first arose, then, from my sense that the narrator is a lower-middle-class woman trying to be middle-class and social in a situation designed to prohibit her from succeeding either socially or at the game she is playing. To be socially accepted in this type of middle-class ritual, one must play bridge correctly; to play bridge successfully one must be antisocial: "The language of bridge is limited to exactly fifteen words. . . . That is all" (Sheinwold 444). Furthermore, she has been placed in a position of having to socialize with a couple who in his estimation, as her husband has constantly reminded her, have more "class" than she in every way imaginable and who are infinitely superior to her. Add to that the fact that he is in love with one half of the couple and you have a situation which probably provokes in her more than a little anxiety. From my point of view, there's little wonder she neither plays well nor socializes well. In fact, it seems quite likely that the bridge game itself helps to unleash the narrator's torrent of revelations.

III

I want to argue that, shortly after their wedding, the narrator discovers that her husband loves another woman. Tom has written (and she has read) a poem and a story about his love for Helen that reveal to her that their marriage is an illusion; but, as I will show, she suppresses that knowledge until this bridge party. Both spouses, I believe, suffer from a neurosis that arises from the failure of each to achieve or sustain a love relationship: melancholia. Tom's neurosis grows out of his failure to detach completely from the lost object of his love; the narrator's arises from her inability to establish a real relationship to her husband. Lardner's story in fact illustrates the problematic nature of early-twentieth-century culture's socialization of men and women to heterosexual relationships in terms of both class and gender. In the process he shows how one woman resolves the problem of a marriage in which she and her husband are destroying each other.

Sigmund Freud first theorized in "Mourning and Melancholia" that melancholy, like grief, derives from the loss of a love object. For the grieving individual, however, this loss is usually "real," that is, a loved one has died. Hence, because the love object no longer exists materially, the griever can eventually and successfully withdraw from his or her attachment. For the melancholiac, the loss of the love object is of a more ideal nature, as in the case of an individual who discovers a partner's infidelity. Freud suggests that the continued material existence of the love object inhibits the melancholiac's ability to withdraw from the relationship, or even admit to him or herself that he or she has in fact suffered a loss: "melancholia is in some way . . . an unconscious loss of a love object, in contradistinction to mourning, in which there is nothing unconscious about the loss" (Freud, "Mourning" 127). Helen has jilted Tom four years prior to the bridge game, resulting for Tom in the type of idealized loss of a love object that Freud described. Unable to withdraw completely from this relationship, he turns the anger and hurt he feels on himself: "the sufferers usually succeed in the end in taking revenge, by the circuitous path of self-punishment, on the original objects and in tormenting them by means of the illness, having developed the latter so as to avoid the necessity of openly expressing their hostility against the loved ones" (132–33).

Prior to his meeting the narrator, Tom's form of self-punishment seems to have been his alcoholism; at least that is what the narrator suggests as she recounts to Helen and Arthur, "I do think it's wonderful, him staying on the wagon this long, a man that used to — well, you know as well as I do; probably a whole lot better, because you were with him so much in the old days. . . . He told me about it once in Pittsburgh — All right, Tommie; I won't say another word" (228).[3]

The narrator's account of her courtship and marriage implies that her own appearance on the scene leads the abstinent Tom to displace his anger from himself onto her, a more obvious symbol of the woman who spurned him. As the story opens, she points to what I take to be the first signifier of his revenge, Tom's constant disparagement of his life with her in Portland: "How often I've heard Tom say he'd give any amount of money to be with Arthur and Helen, and how bored he was out there with just poor little me and his new friends" (227). In his diminishment of her through unfavorable comparisons with Helen and Arthur, Tom projects onto her the anger he feels about his own sense of inferiority.

IV

Tom's sense of inferiority seems tied to his economic position in culture. When, during the course of the game, the narrator retells Tom's thinly disguised autobiographical account of his courtship with Helen, we discover that the main character has lost his love because he was not rich enough (a version of the Jay Gatsby–Daisy Buchanan story which Lardner had read in page proof before he wrote "Who Dealt?"):

> It's a story about two men and a girl and they were all brought up together and one of the men was awfully popular and well-off. . . . The other man, the well-off one . . . was through college long before his friend because his friend had to earn the money first. And the well-off man kept after the girl to marry him. He didn't know she had promised the other one. Anyway she got tired of waiting for the man she was engaged to and eloped with the other one. (234)

Tom's story represents Helen's decision to marry Arthur rather than him as one rooted in economics. Because he cannot get through school fast enough, and because he cannot demonstrate his superiority over Arthur financially with the kind of high-paying job that comes with an Ivy League degree, Tom suffers a consequent loss of self-esteem. Four years later Tom's fictionalized account of the events ends with the other man inviting the couple over and pretending everything is all right, even though his heart is still broken. In order to prove everything is all right in this kind of situation, a character would have to prove not only that his heart has mended, but that he has achieved the financial stability which eluded him previously. That is why Tom and his wife are visiting Helen and Arthur. We can speculate that, three months previous to this card game, Tom has decided that he cannot wait too long to prove to Helen that everything is all right—he has already waited almost four years. (Is it a coincidence? He may not have been able to finish a college degree in time, but by God give him four years and he can get promoted to vice-president and find a replacement for her.) Unfortunately, as a man suffering from melancholy, filled with self-loathing, his sense of class inferiority may have played a part in his choice of a marriage partner. He marries the narrator, a woman of lower-middle-class origins, for at least three reasons: because he feels he can do no better; so he can appear, at least, to be superior to *someone*; and to get back at Helen.

Tom's unhappy relationships with women result in part from his socialization as a man in American culture. Many American men are trained as children to seek success competitively, to see that love and approval are dependent upon their ability to succeed in the public world. Their socialization, argues Nancy Chodorow, produces both anxiety and dread of female sexuality because of their need to win women's (ultimately their mother's) approval while also needing to deny and devalue women in order to maintain their masculine identity. Tom behaves like the men Chodorow describes; his desire for Helen engulfs him and swallows him whole. He attempts to win her approval, but his inability to succeed in the material world reveals to him his own inadequacy—makes him question his own masculinity. In the race to prove who is the better breadwinner, the superior man who therefore is most worthy of winning Helen as lover and wife, Arthur "beats Tom to pieces" by getting both his degree and a higher paying job first. Tom's inability to succeed in the material world as well as Arthur reveals to him his own inadequacy— makes Tom question his own masculinity. When Helen chooses Arthur, she strips Tom of any control that he might have had as a partner in this relationship and also implies to Tom that he is the lesser man. To prove his virility and his worthiness as a man and to regain control of the women in his relationships, Tom therefore constructs a courtship with the narrator in which he controls female sexuality by making it an object to be won or lost at *his* will.

The narrator suggests to the reader that she has always had to compete for signs of love and affection from Tom: "Tom could run awfully fast. He can yet. When we were engaged we used to run races and the prize was— All right, Tommie, I won't give away our secrets. Anyway, he can beat me to pieces" (229). Cynthia Cockburn has argued that in patriarchal, capitalist cultures, "[b]oys are conditioned from childhood in numberless ways to be more physically effective than girls" (87), and that their training, which builds superior muscles and strength, is one important source of women's subordination. Tom alternately glorifies and adores Helen (as his spoken and written words reveal) and hates her for jilting him, for not giving herself to him alone. Hence, physically, he proves that he has the speed as an athlete that he lacked as a scholar and breadwinner. The narrator's abrupt "All right, Tommie, I won't give away our secrets" implies that the prize for winning the race may have been sex. Therefore the prize he names also provides him with numerous opportunities to prove to the narrator (and Helen, too, if she were only here) that he performs well sexually—he is a virile stud who can have any woman he wants. Tom's need to prove to himself that he is not a lesser man than Arthur, at least physically or sexually, and that he is both better than and worthy of Helen, too, for that matter, means that he must challenge his fiancée to races he cannot lose. The narrator must compete for some show of his love for her by proving that, like all women (and particularly the unfaithful Helen who gave herself as trophy to Arthur), she is his inferior.

Despite his desire to show Helen that he does not need her or desire her any longer, Tom has also ensured that the narrator can never really take Helen's place. In my portrait of Tom as a melancholiac, he marries a woman wholly unlike Helen because he still loves Helen and has not been able to detach himself successfully from her. He has not lost his desire for either Helen or her life. Tom wants Helen and Arthur's life, not his own. This characterization seems to be borne out when we examine Tom's reactions to his wife's disclosures about his life. She tells Arthur and Helen that he's recently gotten a raise, is now a vice-president, and has been asked by leading members of the Portland community to run for office. Apparently he has achieved a certain social status as a respected member of his community: "Oh, did you know they tried to get Tom to run for mayor?" Nonetheless, he seems not to want Helen and Arthur to know: "Tom is making faces at me to shut up, but I don't see any harm in telling it to his friends" (231). To hold office is to identify oneself with a particular region or city, to declare openly one's allegiance to one's environment. It is to say "I want to live here." Tom wants to distance himself from anything that reminds him of his class inferiority. Winning the race for mayor of a podunk town (in relation to the city in which Helen and Arthur live) is like winning foot-races with his wife. The prize offered still pales in comparison to the prizes he might have won if he had Helen. Again, Tom has made it clear to his wife his contempt for life in Portland ("How often I've heard . . . how bored he was out there with just poor little me and his new friends" [227]). He doesn't invite Helen and Arthur over to his house, as his fictional character does the woman who betrayed him in the story he writes. To be like Helen and Arthur, to really belong to their class, he must go to them: "he'd give any amount of money to be with Arthur and Helen."

Finally, his discomfiture at his wife's hinting at their "secret" may be because he does not want Helen to imagine him sleeping with another woman, particularly this woman. He may well hope that, if Helen imagines him in bed with anyone, it is with herself, his first, his one and only true love.

In a further show both of his own self-destructiveness and his desire to punish women, Tom has set up his wife to discover the truth. Unlike many critics of this story, Tom knows his wife has formidable investigative skills: "he often says I should have been a lawyer or a detective, the way I can worm things out of people." The only thing he needs to do is act as if there is something to hide, because, as the narrator tells us, "I can usually tell when he's hiding something and I keep after him till he confesses" (228). Tom has already begun to confess to the narrator that there is something that hovers above their heads, waiting to destroy their marriage: "he told me the day we were married that if I ever saw him take another drink I would know that—" (230). The narrator cuts herself off, leaving Helen, Arthur, and the readers of this story wondering, "You would know what?" Given what happens at the end of the story (Tom takes a drink when she divulges his heartbreak over the jilting), the answer must be "I would know that Tom had not been able to get over his love for another woman." The question is, did Tom complete the sentence for her on his wedding day? If he did, the narrator already knows she has been set up. She is competing with an absent woman from his past.

V

Her narration suggests she does know. More evidence to indicate that her husband does not love her appears shortly after their wedding, when like a supersleuth she looks through his papers and comes "across a poem he'd written, the saddest, mushiest poem! Of course it was a long time ago when he wrote it; it was dated four years ago" (233). The poem is about a bird; looking through Tom's things, she sees numerous books with the name Helen Bird Strong written in them. He continually talks about Helen: "he talks about you so much that it's a wonder I'm not jealous; especially of you, Helen" (227).

Perhaps that is one reason why she tells the story of her races with her husband, to announce to Helen that even by losing those races, she has won Tom. Her prize, whether she won or lost the race, was Tom's "love." Like her request to "play families" in the game, this anecdote is a reminder to Helen (and Tom?) that Tom married her because he considered her a prize worth winning. And if she tells the story enough times, she might be able to convince herself that it's true, that she did win Tom's love, that the race was not another means by which he could convince her to believe herself to be "poor little me."

Saturday nights were "Time with Dad" nights when we were little. Besides having us put on a talent show for him each week, he trained the six of us to wrestle. My arch-rival in these matches was my brother Tommy. He wanted desperately to beat me, but because he was younger than I, he did not have the physical strength or size. When we began spending more time with my aunts on Saturdays, these weekly wrestling matches stopped for a while. One day, though, when I was eleven and Tommy was ten, my father decided that, for old times' sake, we should wrestle for the championship. My sisters refused—they had never liked competitive sports. But my athletic ability in sports had always been a means of getting approval from my father, so I agreed to the match in order to maintain my title as most athletic in the family. The only problem was that Tommy was now bigger than me. I managed to win, but just barely. Afterward, I broke out in a cold sweat and it took an enormous act of will not to faint. As I sat on the stairs afterward, with my head between my knees, praying that no one in my family would see me in my moment of weakness, I knew I would never again be able to win.

During her courtship, she may not have realized that she was competing against a woman from Tom's past. After she finds her husband's writing, though, the narrator knows whom she is actually running against. The discovery of the poem and his story both reveal to her that, like her footraces with her husband, she has lost before she even got to the starting line. These written documents reveal to her that her relationship with her husband has been nothing but a figment of her imagination, the root cause of her melancholy. John Bowlby has recently argued that melancholy is not so much a result of individual psychical weakness as it is a response to cultural repression. Moreover, his research documents that the type of melancholy the narrator experiences, a failure to attach rather than, as in Tom's case, a failure to detach, is in fact more prevalent in women owing to their different socialization in culture.[4]

Adult life in an industrial society like the United States does not always provide women with ways of nurturing their ties to others, or with the means of sustaining a rich, ongoing inner object world. In fact, the narrator's life in Portland apparently inhibits her ability to establish a rich social life.[5] Having no other family, the narrator has given over her life to her marriage, and within that marriage Tom has helped to cut her off from healthy connections outside of it. That is to say, for the narrator her unhappiness is not simply a matter of failing to attach to Tom; she is generally starved for relationships: "You know, this is the first time Tom and I have been with real friends since we were married. I suppose you'll think it's funny for me to call you *my* friends when we've never met before, but Tom has talked about you so much and how much he thought of you and how crazy he was to see you and everything" (227). Tom constantly denigrates the people they live among and makes clear that they are not worthy of his regard. She understands that Helen and Arthur are the only people Tom feels are worthy of his and her affections. In her melancholic condition, she has lost her sense of self, her subjectivity. (Interestingly, Lardner emphasizes her lack of subjectivity by making her the only character in the story who is not given a name.) So this narrator chooses only those friends that Tom might choose, increasing her own sense of isolation in the marriage: "But you see it's the first time we've been with anybody we really cared about; I mean, you're Tom's best friends and it's so nice to get a chance to talk to somebody who's known him a long time. Out there the people we run around with are almost strangers and they don't talk about anything but themselves and how much money their husbands make" (230).

Chodorow argues that culture's representations of romantic love and marriage further exacerbate the problems the narrator confronts in her marriage. Society teaches women that good wives look up to their husbands. They must repress their disappointment and resentment if their marital relations are lacking.[6] In Chodorow's discussion of the problems facing middle-class white America, she asserts that if a married couple's relationship suffers from a "fundamental incompatibility," it is often the woman who must accept the blame, believe herself to be the "dreary, insensible, rattlebrained girl" that Elder and others are all too willing to label her. Because society asks women to swallow their unhappiness, to take the blame for the failure of relationships, to devalue themselves, melancholia is in actuality the "normal" state of being for many American middle-class women. By the time she is an adult, many women are already socialized to low self-esteem, and they have also already been trained to blame themselves, to believe themselves the inadequate partner in a relationship with a man.

Initially, the narrator appears to be a typical American middle-class housewife of the 1920s produced by the culture Chodorow describes, carrying out her role as the idealizing wife. Throughout the story she praises Tom for his many accomplishments, "everything he does or ever has done seems so wonderful" (228), and claims to enjoy her role as wife and caretaker. As her lonely plaints reveal, nevertheless, her daily life is not centrally involved with other people. She has little possibility of establishing relationships in or out of marriage. For most women in the same position, children would "normally" fill the holes created by a general lack of affective relationships. Having been married a mere three months, the narrator has no children. To fulfill the role she has been socialized to adopt, therefore, the narrator turns Tom into her child. She often calls him by a diminutive nickname, "Tommie," and she very maternally "cures" him of what she perceives to be bad habits:

> Tom insists, or that is he did insist, on a great big breakfast—fruit, cereal, eggs, toast, and coffee. All I want is a little fruit and dry toast and coffee. I think it's a great deal better for a person. So that's one habit I broke Tom of, was big breakfasts. And another thing he did when we were first

married was to take off his shoes as soon as he got home from the office and put on bedroom slippers. I believe a person ought not to get sloppy just because they're married. (233)

Early in her marriage she still has the desire to ignore her husband's failings, but her suppressed disappointment and resentment turn inward, undercutting her marriage and leading her to avenge herself on her husband — subtly here, and "normally," through her mothering of him. She takes away things that he enjoys, making his life even more boring than he claims it already is (You want boring? I'll give you boring). Like Tom, she punishes herself by giving him more reason to insult her even as she exacts her revenge by denying him that which would give him pleasure. More important, she degrades Tom by calling into question his masculinity. As she regales the Gratzes with the habits she has cured Tom of, she exclaims: "But the worst of all was pajamas! What's the difference, Tommie? Helen and Arthur don't mind. And I think it's kind of funny, you being so old-fashioned. I mean Tom had always worn a nightgown till I made him give it up. And it was a struggle, believe me! I had to threaten to leave him if he didn't buy pajamas" (233). The narrator's story calls to mind a mother describing how she broke her son of carrying a security blanket around; similarly, the narrator threatens Tom with separation anxiety, a particularly apt punishment for a man who already suffers from that ailment owing to his lost love object. Second, she calls his bedwear a nightgown, rather than by its more masculine appellation, nightshirt. Real men don't wear nightgowns: "I hope Arthur doesn't wear them; nightgowns, I mean. You don't, do you, Arthur? I knew you didn't" (233). She trivializes Tom's attachments and convinces herself that she can break them easily enough if she wishes. In this anecdote a resisting reader senses her underlying hostility and suspects that while Lardner may have meant her "mindless outburst," as Yardley puts it, to be read as stupidity, he has made it possible for us to read it as motivated by her anger and her need to confront her husband with what she knows.

At Tom's apparent discomfort at her disclosures, she promises, "All right, Tommie; I'll shut up. I know you hate to be talked about, but your wife can't help being just a teeny bit proud of you" (228). She doesn't "shut up," however, and one begins to sense that her inability to quiet herself is a form of revenge upon a husband who wants her to be "dummy" both in and outside the game they are playing. Tom provokes her monologue, it seems to me, by having set her up to fail in a competitive situation one too many times.

VI

Despite her attempts to repress from her consciousness her knowledge of Tom's love for another woman, the bridge game, as it metaphorically represents to the narrator the problematic nature of her marriage, catalyzes her disturbing monologue and forces all parties to face the truth. The bridge game becomes the catalyst because it is here that she physically confronts for the first time the woman with whom she competes for her husband's affection. Furthermore, she must literally compete with her in a game she has had little experience playing. To top it all off, as hostess of the game Helen has decided that they will not play families, they will play partners. "Do we cut for partners? Why can't we play families? I don't feel so bad if I do something dumb when it's Tom I'm playing with. He never scolds, though he does give me some terrible looks" (228). Not only does this remind her of the fact that, if given the chance, her husband would not choose her as his partner, but now Helen seems to be suggesting that she would like Tom as a partner, rather than Arthur. While Helen and Arthur apparently accede to her request to play families, again the narrator has to demean herself to get Tom as her partner. She simply cannot win for losing. Thus, in the face of her own overwhelming anxiety, anger, and hostility, she erupts with the torrent of words that will set her free at last.

Research has demonstrated that in Western culture girls and boys are socialized to play games differently. For example, Jean Piaget found that when playing games, boys stuck to the rules no matter what. On the other hand, little girls would end a game in order to avoid arguments. They sought to preserve relationships of the players. Researchers have found, furthermore, that girls' games tend to reinforce nurturant skills, expressions of personal feelings, and cooperation rather than competition. Girls' and boys' different socialization toward games mirrors their different socialization to gender identification and relationships (Gilligan et al. 264).

Whenever I asked my aunts if they knew how to play bridge, they would respond vaguely, "Yes, sometimes, but we only play for fun," intimating that to play for fun was not to play correctly. Upon further questioning, they admitted that they rarely played because most people who played bridge seriously got mad at those people who played only for fun, and they told the story of the rich old retired oil company executive who, while being very gracious to them, made obvious his frustration and exasperation at their failure to care whether they won or lost.

To please her husband, Lardner's narrator has tried to learn to play bridge in the spirit of cooperation, as a means of expressing her love for her husband, to further develop their affective ties. Having to play by a man's rules, having to be competitive when she wants to play in order to be social, makes the narrator nervous. Tom's behavior heightens her anxiety even further: "He never scolds, though he does give me some terrible looks" (228). Whenever they play, Tom manages to communicate to her, albeit silently, his opinion of her playing. "I believe Tom overbids lots of times so I'll be dummy and can't do anything ridiculous" (231).[7] In the same way that he inhibits her ability to develop affective ties outside their relationship in everyday life, he marginalizes her from the game, and reduces the possibility of her successful interaction with other players, particularly himself.

During the course of the game, Lardner's narrator objectifies herself when she speaks, and appears to feel sorry for Tom for being stuck with someone like herself. She peppers her monologue with self-denigrating remarks. For instance, she constantly intimates that she lacks the intelligence necessary to play the game: "I don't feel so bad if I do something dumb when it's Tom I'm playing with." Furthermore, she seems to be sabotaging her own play, being both afraid to make mistakes and intent on making them: "I wish I could remember what that means. I know that sometimes when he doubles he means one thing and sometimes another. But I always forget which is which. Let me see; it was two spades that he doubled, wasn't it? That means I'm to leave him in, I'm pretty sure. Well, I'll pass. Oh, I'm sorry, Tommie! I knew I'd get it wrong. Please forgive me" (229).

One might say, in fact, that the critics who have called the narrator "dreary," "insensible," "rattlebrained," or a "mindless gurgler" have for the most part used her self-denigrations as evidence to support their readings. But if she is so mindless and insensible, how has Tom managed to be so successful? In the American corporate system, "behind every successful man is a woman." Being a good wife, homemaker, and social hostess helps the husband climb up the ladder of success. Since marrying the narrator, Tom has been promoted to vice-president and asked to run for mayor. If she is truly stupid, why do Tom's boss and fellow citizens trust his judgment? Why do these past critics feel sorry for him for choosing her, rather than, say, sneering at his stupidity for marrying such a lamebrain? The obvious answer is that, at the time Lardner wrote this story, he meant for his readers to laugh and sneer at his narrator; for him, then, those critics whose reading I resist here actually did get it right. But I want to argue that it's ideologically normal for uneducated women of lower-middle-class origins to be told they are not as smart as they should be, to internalize that judgment, and then to live down to it.

My father and my grandfather often roll their eyes when my grand-mother speaks; my grandfather, Tom, often in fact calls her a "banana head." My grandmother plays the part, laughs at herself, tells me how she could never be like me. Yet years ago, after her first husband left her a widow with a four-month-old child, she learned a trade and eventually bought and ran her own thriving business. My mother now complains, "I don't know why a woman who ran her own business for so many years, and who used to go out by herself all the time, can't even go to the bathroom by herself anymore." For perhaps the same reasons that the narrator constantly makes mistakes and then berates herself, my grandmother has internalized the comments of her male relatives and gradually suppressed her natural intelligence, independence, and self-sufficiency in her second marriage. She has come to believe those comments herself.

To resist the negative responses of past readers to the narrator, I am arguing that the narrator's monologue does not reveal her insensibility, but her psychological malaise. Melancholia takes various clinical forms, but one of the most obvious symptoms is a fall in self-esteem. The narrator, like most melancholiacs, abases herself in front of others because she has a need to represent herself to others as worthless: "One could almost say that the . . . trait of insistent talking about [her]self predominates in the melancholiac" (Freud, "Mourning," 129).

VII

Bridge is the game of the rich and upwardly mobile classes: "In the fashionable world, knowledge of at least the mechanics of . . . bridge is deemed a social necessity, and proficiency at the game is a social asset" (Goren 114). Playing bridge is an important middle- and upper-class ritual, and the central role it plays in Lardner's story helps to show that the melancholia which plagues the narrator is a matter not only of her gender, but of her class as well. Elizabeth Evans's lack of sympathy for the narrator has more to do with class issues than a failure to empathize with a fellow woman. She simply cannot understand how a middle-class woman could not know how to play bridge properly: "Ideally the bridge player keeps track of all fifty-two cards. . . . [Tom's] wife has botched every hand" (87). What she (along with other critics, for that matter) misses is that the narrator is not the only one who does not play properly in this story. As she talks, the narrator discusses the Guthries, a couple with whom she and Tom play bridge back home in Portland.

The Guthries' marriage is a mirror image of the Cannons', and it suffers from similar problems. Mr. Guthrie is a lumberman, probably a self-made man who started out chopping wood and eventually came to own his own company—a successful blue-collar worker, a man who lives by his own rules. Part of the Guthries' incompatibility arises because they apparently come from different classes; like the narrator, Mr. Guthrie has married into a class above his own: Mrs. Guthrie is a well-educated woman from old money. Because they are from different classes, they also have different tastes: "I never saw two people with such different tastes. For instance, Mr. Guthrie is keen about motoring and Mrs. Guthrie just hates it. She simply suffers all the time she's in a car. He likes a good time, dancing, golfing, fishing, shows, things like that. She isn't interested in anything but church work and bridge work" (232). Mr. Guthrie seems to be the typical middle-class outdoorsman. But his wife is a blue blood, of the American aristocracy, so to speak, trained to behave properly, demurely. One imagines him marrying Mrs. Guthrie after getting his money in order to gain the respectability of her class. This is, after all, the American way. It's what might have happened to Jay Gatsby if he had won Daisy Buchanan. Life always threatens to give you what you wish for.

Like the narrator, Mr. Guthrie does not play properly, but while the narrator insists that she is too dumb to do so, he obstinately and vociferously refuses to play by the conventions of bridge. For one thing, he chafes at playing by the more cooperative rules of bridge. Like Tom, he is a man who doesn't like to lay his cards on the table, but unlike Tom, he is very vocal about it: "he says a person might just as well tell each other what they've got. So he won't pay any attention to what-do-you-call-'em, informatory, doubles and so forth." The competitive Mr. Guthrie's wife "plays all the conventions, so you can imagine how they get along" (231). In other words, Mrs. Guthrie is quite willing to pass signals that will give her husband an idea of what she holds, in a spirit of cooperation with her partner. As a member of the upper middle class, Mrs. Guthrie always behaves properly, follows all the rules which mandate that she cooperate with her partner in a bridge game even if she does not get along with him outside the game. Both her class breeding and her education as a woman have trained her to sit silently as he rages at her for not being more secretive. Tom too obeys the same antisocial rule of bridge that prohibits "human" social interaction; he sits silently, giving terrible looks, as his wife suffers from the same inability from which Mr. Guthrie suffers: an inability to adopt the social conventions of the class to which she has risen. Mr. Guthrie can refuse to adopt the social conventions of the upper classes, nevertheless, because he has the economic stability to do so. He can express his anger and resentment at his wife freely. In the twenties, however, women like the narrator depend upon their male relatives for financial support: "Tom's always after me to buy clothes, but I can't seem to get used to spending somebody else's money, though it was dad's money I spent before I did Tom's, but that's different, don't you think so? And of course at first we didn't have much to spend, did we, dear?" (231). If the narrator feels any resentment or anger toward Tom, she must repress it. As with Mrs. Guthrie, part of the narrator's acceptance, without quarrel, of verbal and/or nonverbal emotional abuse from her mate comes from her training as a woman. The narrator's inferior economic status gives her a more compelling reason to accept and then internalize abuse than Mrs. Guthrie has; she cannot afford to lose her husband's financial support.

Mrs. Guthrie, like the narrator, has no children, though she wears clothes that seem to express a desire for pregnancy. Her desire to perform her maternal function drives her to seek activities that will allow her to adopt a caretaker role. Thus her philanthropic community work becomes an important activity. Joining clubs and playing bridge constitute another important social occupation for women of this class. In middle-class culture women need to perform well socially, to cultivate their ability to ingratiate their husbands into the more important social clubs and organizations, to help them compete at the office. The better able a wife is to entertain her husband's contacts and employers, the better able he is to move up both socially and professionally in the corporation. For the upper class a couple's position in the social circuit is maintained through active involvement in the social world and clubs of that class. In order to maintain her status, to see and be seen, Mrs. Guthrie must do as the fashionable do—she must play bridge. Playing bridge for Mrs. Guthrie can thus be considered work; as the narrator inadvertently notes: "She isn't interested in anything but church work and bridge work" (232).

For the narrator her Freudian slip, "bridge work," connotes other things. Getting Tom to tell her anything is like pulling teeth for the narrator; his secrets open holes in their marriage that need filling. Playing bridge is the narrator's attempt to build bridges to other people, a way of establishing connection to Tom and others. The narrator plays bridge in order to make connections, but these connections are as false as the teeth in bridgework. After all, the bridge game mirrors her relationship to her husband Tom; they are only *playing* at being a family.

Finally, when she contracted to marry Tom in order to rise as a woman within the American social class system, she began her apprenticeship as a bridge player ("I never played at all till we were engaged" [228]). And it is "bridge work" because, despite her protests that she would rather play bridge than anything else, it is not an enjoyable activity for her—it is laborious. Research indicates that in women's stories about themselves, problems in relationships compromise their ability to work (Gilligan et al. 254). The problems and tensions in the relationships among all the bridge players, including herself, compromise the narrator's ability to play bridge properly, or rather, to perform her "bridge work." Bridge is not a game for the narrator but a rather difficult test that her husband has set her up to fail.

One of the reasons the narrator's monologue is so disturbing both to her fellow players and to the readers of this story is that bridge etiquette requires that players sit quietly: "It is the most natural thing in the world for people to act like human beings—even in a bridge game. The better the player, the less human he must act" (Sheinwold 445). Her chattering would only be ideologically "normal" if she were playing in an all-women game: "Table conversation in general varies with the players and the game. As a mere man, I wouldn't dream of saying how much conversation is proper in a ladies' afternoon game" (Sheinwold 443). Throughout the story the narrator promises to "shut up," at one point sounding very much like an alcoholic or other addict: "I can stop if I want to." Also like an alcoholic, she fails to contain her incessant need to talk. The narrator's inability to stop herself, despite her repeated promises to do so, indicates that she has entered the manic phase of melancholia, "when a man finds himself in a position to throw off at one blow some heavy burden, some false position he had long endured. . . . All such situations are characterized by high spirits, by the signs of discharge of joyful emotion, and by increased readiness to all kinds of action, just like mania, and in complete contrast to the dejection and inhibition of melancholia" (Freud, "Mourning" 135). This description seems to match with the narrator's own description of her emotional state: "I *can* stop talking if I try. It's kind of hard to concentrate though, when you're, well, excited" (229).

VIII

In my resistant reading of "Who Dealt?," the narrator talks uncontrollably because she needs to cure herself. She protests that she has come to the Gratzes in the spirit of cooperation, to meet Helen, to sustain her marriage. From the outset of the story, however, from the time that she fails to follow both the game and the social conventions of bridge, she implicitly admits to an opposite desire: she wants to break from this marriage. Her dialogue becomes a different sort of labor, a "working through" the causes of her melancholy. Her words will be the instruments of her healing; she initiates her own "talking cure." Like many analysands, she suspects that her analyst "knows" what troubles her, suspects that he or she can interpret her words, give her the answer to the question she poses. The narrator uses Tom, Helen, and Arthur as her analysts — unconscious though all four may be of the roles they take on in this game of language — "for there is no Word without a reply, even if it meets no more than silence" (Lacan, *Speech* 9). During the course of this bridge game, then, she will get Tom to reveal once and for all the secret that he tries to hide from Helen. She will make it impossible for him to accomplish his desire to "pretend everything [is] all right." Lardner has his character ramble, moving from one anecdote to the next. In psychoanalytic terms, what she has achieved is discourse that embodies the "free association" of a "talking cure." As Lacan argues, "the unconscious is structured like a language"; it is the discourse which "through the mouth of the analyst, calls for the reopening of the shutter," the return of the repressed. Moving back and forth through time, the narrator reconstructs her history — her courtship, her wedding night — all the traumatic events that will force her "analysts" to reveal back to her the answer to the question she poses for them: "Does Tom still love Helen?"

She begins by testing Helen's devotion to Arthur, and by hinting to them that she does so for a reason. First she boasts about Tom, noting that "everything he does or ever has done seems so wonderful. But is that only because we've been married such a short time? Do you feel the same way about Arthur, Helen? You do? And you married him four years ago, isn't that right? And you eloped, didn't you? You see I know all about you" (228). The narrator here sounds very much like a private detective or a lawyer interrogating the suspect. First she plants the seed that feelings for spouses change over a period of time. A wife begins to recognize the ways in which everything a husband does is not so wonderful any longer. Does Helen still think Arthur is as wonderful as when she married him? What she does subtly, perhaps unconsciously, is to ask Helen if the honeymoon is over. How much of a conscious adversary is Helen, anyway? She "knows all about" them, knows the triangle in which the three of them were involved, knows what kind of shock to Tom's system it was when Helen suddenly ran off with Arthur four years ago.

Given Tom's testimony with regard to her investigative skills, her inter-
rogation is an indication that, on some level of consciousness, the narrator understands that Tom and perhaps Helen are trying to hide something, and she needs to "worm" it out of them. Tom, Helen, and Arthur
become the filters, the refractors of her discourse. Throughout the story
her "analysts," particularly Tom, reply to her words through facial expressions. Their nonverbal cues help to propel her through her dialogue,
even as she promises to keep quiet in response to their disapproving
glances.

Her recitation of Tom's fictional account of his failed love affair
moves her ever nearer to the truth she seeks. Certainly the reader of
Lardner's story knows for certain at this point that Tom has not gotten
over Helen. Here, the narrator describes for Arthur and Helen one of
the central characters in Tom's story: "It's a story about two men and a
girl and they were all brought up together and one of the men was
awfully popular and well off and good-looking and a great athlete — a
man like Arthur. There, Arthur! How is that for a T.L.? [True likeness? — Robinson's guess, and I agree]" (234).

I suspect most strongly that the narrator knows about Tom and Helen,
however, when she recites the poem near the end of the story in the most
climactic moment of her revenge. What screams knowledge, it seems to
me, is her sudden attention to detail. It's most curious that the narrator,
unable until this moment to correctly follow what is happening in the
game, is suddenly astute enough, immediately following her recitation
of the poem, to recognize that Helen has failed to follow trump. In my
vision of the narrator's monologue as her "talking cure," however, it
illustrates a certain phenomena that often occurs in the analyst-
analysand relationship. In this last stage of the game, the narrator exhib-
its "negative transference," a kind of transference in which the analysand
feels she has "to keep her eye" on her analyst. I argue that the narrator is
the one to discover that Helen has revoked because she has been "keeping
her eye" on Tom and Helen, watching for the "reply" that will "reopen
the shutter" into her unconsious: "Why, Helen, you revoked! And, Tom,
do you know that's Scotch you're drinking? You said — *Why, Tom!*"
(235)!

IX

Past critics have produced obvious interpretations of Lardner's story
through superfluous plot summary. In reading "Who Dealt?" through

the lens of my own experience, I have produced an interpretation that on the surface also seems incredibly obvious — and the most common response to earlier drafts of this essay has been, "yes, yes, that's obvious" — except for the fact that such an obvious reading has never been articulated.

One of the possible arguments is that all this obviousness is Lardner's, that "Who Dealt?" is simple, up-front, easy to grasp — and that such "obvious" stories are aesthetically bereft. "Why are you reading Lardner?" I was once asked. After all, the implication was, our literary canon is made up of texts whose language, style, and themes are much more complex than Lardner's or those of minor writers like him. "Obvious" stories are boring, not worthy of our attention.

The distinction between interesting and boring texts reminds me, though, of Roland Barthes's definition of a text of bliss: "the text that imposes a state of loss, the test that discomforts (perhaps to the point of a certain boredom), unsettles the reader's historical, cultural, psychological assumptions, the consistency of his tastes, values, memories, brings to a crisis his relation with language" (Barthes 14). It's possible that there is some literature, like "Who Dealt?," which makes us as critics squirm with anxiety and look for ways to avoid having to read that literature. In the story Tom, when he's not drinking, looks for ways to dull, blot out, or ignore the pain he still feels because of his loss. The only other way he can avoid confronting the unhappiness in his life, without taking a drink, is to refuse to participate in it, to denigrate it and dismiss it as boring ("How often I've heard Tom say . . . how bored he was out there with just poor little me and his new friends"). Like Tom's boredom with his role of husband and breadwinner in Portland, our critical "boredom" with certain literature may be our psyches' way of protecting us against the return of the repressed, our hostility and dissatisfaction with our lives and human relationships. To avoid confronting the issues which might cause us pain as readers of texts, we refuse to participate in the story, refuse to engage the text in any significant way.

In the same way that Tom plays the narrator and Helen against each other, for example, we say that "obviously" Lardner's story about love and marriage in America is less beautiful than F. Scott Fitzgerald's. Part of the beauty of Fitzgerald's text is that there is an ideal True Love held up for admiration; we can sigh and say, "Ah, if only Jay and Daisy had married; he really loved her." On the other hand, the problem with Lardner's rewriting of that plot is that he makes it obvious that Daisy and Gatsby probably would have ended up like the Guthries, unhappy and angry because their class and gender differences made them incom-

patible. To avoid believing that such a love may be unrealistic and unten-
able in our culture, to avoid the pain and anger such a realization might
bring, we can skim and describe the most obvious surfaces of "Who
Dealt?" and, like Tom, distance ourselves from it as text, make sure we
don't read between the lines. After all, hearing the obvious story of his
courtship and the obvious poem about his inability to stop loving Helen
drove Tom to drink and Helen to misplay. We would not want *our*
emotions to interfere in *our* ability to play the game of literary criticism
properly.

"Who Dealt?" forced me to misplay as well—albeit a very different
game. Revealing all my family secrets is outside the vocabulary of criticism, to be sure, though it is a "trend," I've been told, in feminist criticism. ("As a mere critic," one might argue, "I wouldn't dream of saying
how much conversation is proper in a ladies' . . . game.") But facing
those memories and feelings from my own experience forced me to confront and change my assumptions about the ways in which gender and
class influence not only the production of texts, but their reproduction
through acts of literary criticism. As a resistant reader, I had to be
willing to throw off the burden of the voice in me of the academic critic
who says, "There is certain literature not worth reading. There are certain characters whom we must decry in our readings, pretending all the
while to be 'neutral' and 'objective,' but without considering our own
vested interests and emotions that produce our violent responses to literature or its characters."

I realize, of course, that I am now in as much danger of having my
text labeled "insensible" as the narrator was when she disclosed the intimate details of her relationship with her husband.

X

As past critics have pointed out, the narrator's disclosures quite possibly
result in the end of her marriage. In supplying my own standard by
which I measure this narrator, I do not watch her, as others suggest I
must, "tie the rope around [her] neck with [her] own words" (Patrick
114–15)—rather, I see her slip free of the noose. With her monologue
she has "at one blow" (Freud, "Mourning" 135) thrown off the heavy
burden, the false position of wife that she has endured for the past three
months. With Tom's drink she has confirmed that he still loves Helen,
and that explicit knowledge may make it possible for her to break free
from this destructive relationship.[8] Tom's love for Helen is purely a

romantic love, and for this reason it may be harder for him to ever recover from his melancholia. Reading the narrator's monologue as her attempt, albeit a violent one, to initiate the breakup of a bad relationship, allows us to be hopeful at the end of the story rather than depressed by it. For at least one member of this incompatible relationship may now have a chance to pick up the pieces and start anew.

Notes

Introduction

1. "Masculist" is my coinage for men working in the profeminist men's movement to liberate themselves from patriarchal programming and become "new men." Masculism is the exact morphological equivalent of feminism and should, it seems to me, be used in the same positive sense, to denote an emancipatory movement. The only term currently derived from "masculine" is "masculinist," an essentialist term invariably used derogatorily to equate the "essence" of masculinity with patriarchal oppression. The only positive term used for profeminist men is "male feminist," a marked extension of a universalized ideal which stands in the same morphological relation to "feminist" as "woman" or "wife-man" does to "man," and usually connotes male self-hatred.

2. These two emancipatory disclosures are not in fact as different as I may be suggesting. Feminism and masculism converge in their perception of the individual as engendered into an oppressive and humanly destructive ideological system, and in their insistence that individuals work collectively to articulate and dismantle that system; they diverge only in their concern for the liberation of a particular gender. Feminists work to liberate women, masculists work to liberate men. In that concern for their/our own gender, feminists and masculists also have an impact on the opposite gender — femininity and masculinity are always relationally defined, and any shift or change in one will invariably cause reverberations in the other. The men's movement, most notably, arose in response to feminist challenges, both in the form of specific articulations of patriarchy and in the form of women's refusal to conform to patriarchal expectations. On the negative side, the men's movement arose also in response to many feminists' (ideologically "normal") tendency to blame individual men for the operation of patriarchal ideology; as a result, that movement has sometimes taken the (ideologically "normal") form of blaming women, especially the mother. This is the battle of the sexes which patriarchy uses to thwart male-female solidarity in the battle against ideological "normality."

For good introductions to the men's movement, see Jack Nichols's *Men's*

261

Liberation, Herb Goldberg's *The New Male*, and John Rowan's *The Horned God*; for collections of readings in men's studies and men's liberation, see Michael Kaufman, ed., *Beyond Patriarchy*, and Harry Brod, ed., *The Making of Masculinities*.

Chapter 1

1. Ernest Hemingway in 1934 likes only two stories: "Some Like Them Cold" and "The Golden Honeymoon" (158B). John Berryman in 1956 agrees, but adds "Haircut" and "I Can't Breathe" (421–22). Charles S. Holmes in 1976 is more catholic, excluding only "I Can't Breathe" from Berryman's list and including "My Roomy," "Alibi Ike," "A Caddy's Diary," "Zone of Quiet," "The Love Nest" (but he finds "Champion," along with "A Day with Conrad Green," "artistically Inferior" [39]), *You Know Me Al*, *Gullible's Travels*, and *The Big Town* (38–39).

2. Six years later, in fact, in 1985, Sarah Gilead would publish a Foucauldian analysis of "Haircut," "Zone of Quiet," and "The Maysville Minstrel" that is much more sophisticated theoretically than Evans's book, but no less normatively masculine in its reader response: "But the neurotic obsessiveness with which she carries out her aggression [Gilead writes of Nurse Lyons in "Zone of Quiet"] is literally—not only symbolically—murderous. She has no interest or energy left for reaching a minimal professional competence" (334). Despite Nurse Lyons's unprofessional neglect of her male patient, the patient survives, which Gilead attributes to "his being a good reader of her verbal and personality traits. He maintains the 'Zone of Quiet' which she repeatedly violates, mollifying her by playing the role her compulsive identity-theme has assigned to him, that of attentive listener" (334). I shall return to this story in chapter 3, in connection with Lardner's problematic relations with his mother (and to Gilead in chapter 5, in connection with "Haircut"); at this point it is worth noting that Gilead makes no attempt to explore Nurse Lyons's motivations, but simply condemns her for murderous unprofessionalism, nor does she explore the ideological construction of the male listener's "zone of quiet," but simply commends him for "reading" her well.

3. Note also Forrest L. Ingram: "There are some laughs for the reader, but Tom's wife's fun dooms her to a wasteland marriage" (120–21).

4. Note in this context also Forrest L. Ingram's insistence in 1975 that Tom Finch, the narrator of *The Big Town* (1921), "wins the reader's respect in the first story" (115) by beating up a man who has made "improper advances" to his wife. Who is this "reader"? It is Ingram, obviously, but who else? The medieval chivalrous ideal of defending your wife's honor with physical violence is still around, but it is no longer normative among middle-class males. Even in 1922, in chapter 5 of *Babbitt*, Sinclair Lewis was satirizing the notion that Paul Riesling should beat up a man who didn't let Zilla cut in front of him in the box office line at the movies, and it is just as likely that Lardner (who never beat anyone up in his life) wants his reader to be appalled at Tom's knee-jerk machismo.

5. Elder, you will recall, says that "Tom has gone on the wagon at her request," a claim for which there is no textual evidence at all; in fact, on the first page of the story the narrator says: "I do think it's wonderful, him staying on the wagon this long, a man that used to—well, you know as well as I do; probably a whole lot better, because you were with him so much in the old days, and all I know is just what he's told me" (227–28). Although the suggestion cannot be literally true (because Tom has only been on the wagon three months, since the day they got married—presumably she saw him drinking before their wedding), this suggests that she knows about his alcoholism only from stories he has told her about the "old days" with Arthur and Helen. The phrase "all I know is just what he's told me" is of course a crucial one in the story, and I will be returning to it.

6. Here is Yardley's paragraph on Lardner's drinking:

> Ring held his liquor exceedingly well; it brought him out, relaxed him, and made conversation easier for him. He started drinking because he liked the taste of beer and liquor, and he liked what alcohol did for him, and for some time he was able to keep his consumption under control. He did, however, establish fairly early a pattern in which a period of very heavy drinking would alternate with a period of abstinence, and when he entered the hard-drinking business of sports writing, the periods of abstinence grew less frequent. (58)

7. The "captain of my soul" line is from William Ernest Henley's "Invictus," of course, and, as Bateson tells us in a footnote, it is a phrase that Alcoholics Anonymous uses in derision of the alcoholic who thinks he can control his urge to drink. Kenneth Burke's reading of the poem in "A Dramatistic View of the Origin of Language" in terms of Henley's repression of the "negative" (masculine fear of emotion, need, vulnerability, loss, failure) is germane, too:

> One need not be in the literary business long to detect a considerable amount of whistling in the dark here. We don't know the facts of the case, but we shouldn't be surprised to learn that, about this time, the poet had been scaring himself intensely. In any case, the poem is obviously infused with the genius of the moralistic negative. Pressing upon it are implied Commandments of this sort:
>
> > Thou shalt not be conquered;
> > Thou shalt not wince nor cry aloud;
> > Thou shalt not bow thy head, even be it bloody;
> > Thou shalt not fear;
> > Though thou art burdened with threats,
> >   thou shalt not fail to say:
> > It mattereth not.
>
> Whereupon, we note how the exaltation in the words *master* [of my fate] and *captain* [of my soul] derives from their sylistic [*sic*] transcending of this hortatory negativity by two positive-seeming propositions. The zest is in the fact that, behind the word *master* there lurks, "Thou shalt not be enslaved," and behind the word *captain* there lurks, "Thou shalt not fail in self-guidance." (444–45)

I would add to Burke's analysis only the proviso that Henley needn't have been "scaring himself intensely" around the time he wrote the poem; the negated fears

Burke articulates may have been self-imposed, but they are "self-imposed" on men specifically in the culture, by the accepted ideological norms for masculine self-definition.

8. The phenomenon of "male feminism" from John Stuart Mill to the essays collected in Jardine and Smith's *Men in Feminism* (1987) is a case in point: feminist critiques of patriarchal masculinity, no matter how painful to men, have a deep ideological resonance with our training in mother-guilt, and have won male allies right from the start (as early as the seventeenth century, as Michael Kimmel has shown).

9. I am drawing heavily here on Alice Miller's revisionary reading of Freud in *Thou Shalt Not Be Aware* and *For Your Own Good*.

10. Jonathan Yardley and Ring Lardner, Jr., both stress the significance of the friendship between Lardner and Fitzgerald. Lardner gave *The Great Gatsby* a close reading in manuscript around the time he was writing "Who Dealt?," and probably provided Fitzgerald with the information that Arnold Rothstein (Meyer Wolfsheim in the novel), friend of Herbert Swopes (the Lardners' next-door neighbor, who gave what Lardner described as "an almost continuous house-party" [Ring Jr., *Lardners* 163]), fixed the 1919 World Series. Fitzgerald in turn had a catalytic impact on the publication and structure of an entire series of Lardner collections.

11. The similarity of the names Tom Buchanan (Fitzgerald's Arthur Gratz, the man who married Daisy) and Tom Cannon (Lardner's Jay Gatsby, the man who didn't marry Helen) is of course suggestive, especially since both *The Great Gatsby* and "Who Dealt?" were written in Great Neck in 1925. ("Who Dealt?" appeared in *Cosmopolitan* in January 1926.) The symmetry would have been complete, had Lardner named his unnamed narrator Myrtle.

12. A convention in its ordinary sense is, of course, a kind of socially validated or institutionalized repetition compulsion, a repeated action or regularity of action that society compels its members to repeat. In bridge, as in speech, it is specifically a repeated regularity that enables communication through the abstract signs of words (language) or bids (bridge). But it is also a defensive structure, a defense against idiosyncratic or innovative communication through the anxious ritualization of communication, its restriction or reduction to certain patterns or channels. As I hope to show in chapter 2, Lardner's narrator is not so much "unlucky at cards, lucky in love" (230), as she says, as she is bad at conventions, good at innovation. She remembers everything Tom has ever told or shown her, but in no particular order; she remembers details, not patterns. And since the conventional patterns Tom tries to teach her (overtly in bridge, covertly in marriage) are specifically defensive or protective patterns, patterns designed to maintain or perpetuate his repressive ascesis, her scatterbrained narration constitutes a potent (and ultimately successful) threat to his defenses.

13. In French the *nom du père*, Lacan's term for the Symbolic Father, also sounds like and, Lacan claims, is grounded in the *non du père*, the father's negative command, the "thou shalt not" that constitutes the child as son by denying or negating his inclination toward the "undifferentiated" mother, and thus initiates him into the Symbolic (differentiated) realm of language.

14. This reciprocal engenderment model incorporates, but I believe brings a larger social perspective to bear on, the "mother domination" theory of masculinity developed in the late nineteenth and early twentieth century (in order to engineer a remasculinization of liberal society) and recuperated by some early members of the profeminist men's movement in the seventies (in order to defend against blanket feminist associations of masculinity with oppressive patriarchy). Joseph H. Pleck summarizes the argument:

> The male child, the argument goes, perceives his mother and his predominantly female elementary school teachers as dominating and controlling. These relationships *do* in reality contain elements of domination and control, probably exacerbated by the restriction of women's opportunities to exercise power in most other areas. As a result, men feel a lifelong psychological need to free themselves from or prevent their domination by women. The argument is, in effect, that men oppress women as adults because they experienced women as oppressing them as children.
>
> According to this analysis, the process operates in a vicious circle. In each generation, adult men restrict women from having power in almost all domains of social life except child-rearing. As a result, male children feel powerless and dominated, grow up needing to restrict women's power, and thus the cycle repeats itself. It follows from this analysis that the way to break the vicious circle is to make it possible for women to exercise power outside of parenting and parent-like roles and to get men to do their half share of parenting. (Pleck & Pleck 419)

Pleck admits that this model has some basis in fact, but "has been quite overworked. This theory holds women themselves, rather than men, ultimately responsible for the oppression of women — in William Ryan's phrase, 'blaming the victim' of oppression for her own oppression" (Pleck 420).

While agreeing with Pleck that the theory has often been "overworked" in the sense of being used defensively by men who feel emotionally threatened by feminist charges of sexism and oppression, I find his reading overcautious. There is no reason, for example, to equate the vicious circle of patriarchal engenderment with "blaming the victim." If it is a vicious circle prescribed by patriarchal ideology, then no one is to blame, neither the mother nor the son (and, in feminist critiques, neither the father nor the daughter). The reciprocally self-reproducing engenderment system is to blame. It programs all of us to perpetuate the oppressive system. The model has been used by defensive men, but it is not an inherently defensive model.

Indeed, my sense is that Pleck's own overcautiousness is itself the flip side of defensiveness, a way of bending over backward so as not to offend feminists, not to seem to be accusing women of anything, *not* blaming the mother — an injunction that, as I will soon suggest, is likewise part of our patriarchal programming, part of the patriarchal double bind. Men's accusations of women (the mothers did this to us!) and of ourselves (we did this to ourselves!) are complementary ideological/emotional/somatic straitjackets that we must learn to take off. I think my model can help to explain how this happens — we are taught by our fathers to blame our mothers, and by our mothers to blame ourselves (and our fathers) — and also (see especially chapter 2, when I add the Other-as-child to the equation), to show us how to remove the straitjacket.

15. This conception of patriarchal gender programming relies heavily upon the "masculist" psychological work of Herb Goldberg, Samuel Osherson, Paul Olsen, and Guy Corneau.

16. See also my analysis of *Lear* in "Dear Harold" (243–44).

Chapter 2

1. One of the techniques Lardner uses in this story to refract marital dynamics through bridge play is to have his narrator comment on the bridge behavior of a couple the Cannons have gotten to know in Portland, the Guthries:

> She and her husband are terribly funny in a bridge game. He doesn't think there ought to be any conventions; he says a person might just as well tell each other what they've got. So he won't pay any attention to what-do-you-call-'em, imformatory, doubles and so forth. And she plays all the conventions, so you can imagine how they get along. Fight! Not really fight, you know, but argue. That is, he does. It's horribly embarrassing to whoever is playing with them. Honestly, if Tom ever spoke to me like Mr. Guthrie does to his wife, well—aren't they terrible, Tom? Oh, I'm sorry!
>
> . . . But she plays a dandy game of bridge, lots better than her husband. You know he won't play conventions. He says it's just like telling you what's in each other's hand. And they have awful arguments in a game. That is, he does. She's nice and quiet and it's kind of a mystery how they ever fell in love. Though there's a saying or a proverb of something, isn't there, about like not liking like? Or is it just the other way?
>
> . . . And yet they get along awfully well; that is, when they're not playing cards or doing something else together. But it does seem queer that they picked each other out. Still, I guess hardly any husband and wife agree on anything.
>
> You take Tom and me, though, and you'd think we were made for each other. It seems like we feel just the same about everything. That is, almost everything. The things we don't agree on are little things that don't matter. Like music. (231–33)

And shows, and things to eat, and things to wear—the list goes on and on, with the narrator preferring lower-middlebrow things and Tom preferring upper-middlebrow things, and the whole list showing that the Guthries act as a foil for the Cannons, and the Cannons for all "normal" married couples, who hardly ever "agree on anything."

2. Note that Lacan speaks not of the "need" but of the "desire" of the mother (e.g., 200); I have assimilated Lacan's terms to my own of the end of chapter 1.

3. Here I am relying on and responding to part 2 of Voloshinov's *Marxism and the Philosophy of Language*.

4. I am drawing here on my discussion of reflective vision in Emerson (cf. Lacan's paternal ego-ideal, reflected in the inwardly alienated ego) and refractive vision in Poe (cf. Lacan's objectified other, refracted through the specular image of the mirror stage) in *American Apocalypses* (117–22).

5. I don't have space to develop my reading of Lacan in detail here, but these remarks do suggest that the theories of the mirror stage and of the name of the

father (the Imaginary and the Symbolic) are somehow incompatible with Schema L, which sees the subject as subject not to the inert structures of the specular image and the phallic signifier but to the animating play of the Other. To the extent that we are subjected to specular images and phallic signifiers and the rest of the Freudian thing that Lacan transforms through Saussure, they are repressive ideals imposed on us by the Other in its normative function, its function as ideological or ideosomatic voice of the (maternal/paternal) culture. Lacan tries to map those ideals onto Schema L in Schema R, but Schema R strikes me as an abysmal failure. To the extent that it works at all, it works in a given fantasmic projection provided us by the Other as "normal" patriarchal programmer; but to systematize that fantasy as a map of the psyche is to ignore (agree to repress) the *play* of the signifying Others.

6. For the little girl, of course, it is just reversed: her thesis is the Other-as-mother, her antithesis is the Other-as-father, and the Other-as-culture guides her to the construction of her own femininity as the new thesis.

This seems to me to be what Freud was trying to get at in his theory of the Oedipus complex, except that his insistence that it is the child's *fantasy* that engineers this gender construct forces him to posit a biological mechanism that prompts the same fantasy in succeeding generations, which is little more than a way of saying "God does it" or "I don't know how it happens." The theory of the Other as ideosomatic programming allows me to discard most of the useless junk Freud cluttered up his theory with — penis envy, castration fear, horror at the mother's genitals — and to extend his notion of the repetition compulsion to a dynastic conception of ideosomatically transmitted "tradition," the continuity of patriarchal programming from generation to generation (which I adapt from Alice Miller). It also provides a convincing explanation for the "normal" construction of femininity, which neither Freud nor Lacan ever did.

7. This seems to me to be the substance of Deleuze and Guattari's attack on Freud and Lacan in *Anti-Oedipus*, especially in "The Disjunctive Synthesis of Recording" (75ff.): in their terms, Freud and Lacan assume the role of Other-as-Oedipus in order to oedipalize their patients. In some respects, especially in their diagnosis of Western patriarchy (which they call Oedipus), my approach is very close to Deleuze and Guattari's: "In short," they say, *"the 'double bind' is none other than the whole of Oedipus.* It is in this sense that Oedipus should be presented as a series, or an oscillation between two poles: the neurotic identification, and the internalization that is said to be normative. On either side is Oedipus, the double impasse" (80). In others, especially in their idealization of the schizo as the anti-Oedipal hero, I swerve from them. I will be returning to Deleuze and Guattari in chapters 4 and 6.

8. The stream-of-thought theory, developed in *The Principles of Psychology* (1890), precedes Freud's mechanistic structuralism of the psyche both historically (by a decade) and, I would claim, experientially — or rather, Freud's psychology seems intuitively sound until you begin to read James, and the Other-as-child that is speaking James begins to convince you that Freud's theory is the speaking of the Other-as-parent, and that James's theory is experientially prior.

Chapter 3

1. "It isn't often that I care," Lardner writes to Rascoe, "what the boys and girls say about me in print, (Author's note: That's a dirty lie!) but honestly, Burton, that stuff you wrote under date of October 2, well, you must have got the information from Willie Stevens [an unreliable witness in a celebrated murder case of the day]." Lardner continues with the passage Yardley quotes:

> The first "busher" story was never sent back by the Post; it was accepted promptly by Mr. Lorimer himself. I didn't show it to Hugh Fullerton or Charlie Van Loan first; I sent it to Mr. Lorimer at the Post's office, not to his residence; I didn't write "Personal" on the envelope in even one place; I didn't write any preliminary, special delivery, warning letter to Mr. Lorimer; no sub-editor ever asked me to correct the spelling and grammar, and I never sent any sub-editor or anyone else a bundle of letters I had received from ball players. Otherwise— (Caruthers, *Letters* 222)

2. There are significant parallels here between the young manhood of Ring Lardner and the young manhood Frank Lentricchia portrays for Wallace Stevens in *Ariel and the Police*: neither wants to be portrayed as a writer, Stevens explicitly because he associates writing with poetry and poetry with femininity (writing is not manly), and Lardner implicitly because he associates writing with his mother's charming but feminine avocation (writing is not real work). Both men write poetry in their spare time (Lardner's was light doggerel verse, mainly sent to friends in letters). But there are also important divergences. Stevens takes a job in an insurance company, becomes a businessman; Lardner writes for a living almost from the start, first as a sports reporter, later as a fiction writer and columnist. Both men are in patriarchal terms manly at work, "ladylike" after hours; but where Stevens maintains a rigid wall between masculine insurance-as-work and feminine writing-as-play, Lardner allows a relatively free interchange between the two, incorporating even his doggerel verse into his journalism and fiction. Also, where Stevens confines both his "manly" vocation and his "ladylike" avocation within the upper middle class (insurance and "serious" poetry), Lardner plays freely across the entire range of the middle class, writing in a variety of voices about (and as) people at a variety of social levels. Both Stevens and Lardner lived an upper-middle-class family life, but where Stevens pampered himself with comfort and rare collectibles, Lardner remained an ascetic who renounced comfort and amassed comfortable things "only" for his family.

Let me add also that Lentricchia's section on Stevens's young manhood is my focal methodological model for this chapter, and that reading Lentricchia's reading when it first appeared in *Critical Inquiry* was one of my formative experiences for this entire book.

3. The ideas that seemed to serve him best from beginning to end were typically autobiographical: for newspaper columns, taken frankly from his home life (his wife's shopping habits, his vacations, his children) and, more surreptitiously, for stories, from his emotional predilections and heavily refracted per-

sonal experiences. Nor did Lardner's imagination always keep these genres distinct: at the interface between the "autobiographical" and the "fictional" pieces collected by Matthew J. Bruccoli and Richard Layman in *Some Champions*, for example, is the dark autobiographical story "Insomnia" (first published in 1931, two years before his death), a midnight meditation on the difficulty he has sleeping and his need to write a story. Bruccoli and Layman class it as "autobiographical" (91–98), but it could equally well be classed as fiction; indeed, the editors themselves describe it in their introduction as "a stream-of-consciousness sketch" (xiv). The piece does end up telling a story, self-consciously fictionalizing a true story he has heard from a friend — either "wasting" a good story idea on an autobiographical sketch or "faking" an autobiographical sketch in order to set up a metafictional experiment, depending on how you look at it. Revealingly, the story he tells, about an altruistic drunk who sacrificed his happiness and his life to leave his estranged wife financially sound, reeks of Lardner's own wishful self-projection.

4. Henry Lardner died in 1914, Lena Lardner in 1918.

5. Another story from *Round Up* that inculcates a similar moral is "Rhythm," about a popular composer named Harry Hart who cheerfully steals all his tunes and makes a good living as an unpretentious musical craftsman (precisely what Lardner aspired to do but never quite could), but who lets critical raves go to his head and starts writing "serious" classical music that no one likes. He loses his girlfriend and his money and finally has to face up to the fact that his real talent is for stealing tunes and twisting them a little to make them sound original; like Job, he then promptly gets his girlfriend and his money back and the story ends happily. It is significant, as I shall argue in chapter 4, that both "The Maysville Minstrel" and "Rhythm" are written in the third person: they are moral stories, stories written by the Other-as-parent to enforce Lardner's own moral norms (which he playfully describes as "immoral" in "Rhythm" [347] — immoral for culture worshippers but not for Lardner), and the third person is Lardner's preferred narrative voice for that purpose.

6. I refer to the letter Lardner wrote to Ellis's father on February 5, 1910, in thick conservative strokes clearly intended to signal his solidness to Mr. Abbott. He was working at the time as editor of the St. Louis *Sporting News* (a baseball weekly), but was unhappy (his boss, Charley Spink, was a quarrelsome tightwad); a few months after landing the job, he was already looking around for a new position. He was offered and accepted a job running the front office for the Louisville ball club, but Ellis wrote back that her father "thinks a 'sporting man' is a 'sporting man' and can't change his spots — and that his daughters are delicate and rare things that must not come in contact with that 'damned sporting crowd.' He is in fact quite strenuously opposed to the Louisville idea" (quoted in Yardley 112). Here is part of Lardner's reply to Mr. Abbott:

> She told me you were opposed to the Louisville idea and I quite understand your opposition. I myself am opposed to some features of it. However, it is a much different thing, in respect to my relation to the ball players, from my former job with the Tribune. Then it was up to me to mingle with them so that I might know what was

going on. In the Louisville proposition, it will be to my interest and the interest of the owner, to keep away from everyone but the manager, who, in this case, is one of the most decent men I ever met. You can depend on it, Ellis won't ever have to see a ball player or a ball game. She can go to a game when she wants to, but I'm just as much opposed to her being "mixed up" in it as you are.

Strangely, Lardner reneged on his promise to go to Louisville, apparently out of a desire to please Mr. Abbott — but only to take a job as baseball editor of the Boston *American.*

A note on my citations from Lardner's letters. There is no complete edition of them; Clifford Caruthers has brought out two separate "selected letters" volumes, *Ring Around Max: The Correspondence of Ring Lardner and Max Perkins* (1973) and *Letters from Ring* (1979). In addition, Lardner's biographers Donald Elder, Jonathan Yardley, and Ring Lardner, Jr., quote extensively from the correspondence. Whenever a letter I cite is available in print in one of the above works, I will give the published source (citing *Letters* whenever possible — the Caruthers volume that is most germane to my argument — and one or more of Lardner's biographers when they print a letter Caruthers omits). Wherever I give a date but no source, as at the start of this note, my reference is to a previously unpublished letter in the Ring Lardner Papers at the Newberry Library in Chicago.

7. I found reading the letters to Ellis an oppressive experience, in fact — one compounded by the careful control imposed on the reading process by the staff of the Newberry Library, who, like Lardner, impose their rigid rules (one file at a time, no ink) on readers with unflagging friendliness and tact. It is as difficult to imagine reading the actual letters in, say, someone's bustling kitchen, with food spilling, people squeezing past, a beer in your hand, as it is to imagine Lardner writing freely, openly, honestly to Ellis. Fortunately, thanks to Caruthers's edition, quite a few of the interesting letters to Ellis *can* be read in a bustling kitchen, if the reader prefers; but strangely, in retrospect the tight Newberry ship seems the more appropriate place to submerge yourself in the strait world of Lardner's "love."

8. A similar exchange at a deeper and more threatening level ensued in February 1910, when Ellis (always the more emotionally courageous of the two) took the bull by the horns and wrote to Ring about the falsity of their relationship:

But, honestly Ring, you know there is something the matter with us. I wouldn't have the courage to say it at all but I know that you know it, too. You know that neither of us feels very much at ease when we are together and I know that I always have a feeling of restraint. I never can say any thing I want to or be the least bit natural. I dont know whether it is because you dont really love me or because I dont love you. Sometimes I think it is one and sometimes the other. You spoke of that evening in the 'piano-room'. Do you know its queer but I was thinking just then that perhaps I didnt love you after all and I was trying to make up my mind. And yet with my head on your shoulder and your arms around me I was perfectly sure the next minute that I did. But listen, dear, I'll never marry you until I am absolutely sure. I have wanted to say all this before but couldnt, and it is awfully hard to say it now but I just cant go on this way. If you will only tell me the real truth, if you really do care for me enough to want me forever and ever—it is a long time you know and I am a foolish thing. (*Letters* 50–51)

What Ellis doesn't realize, and indeed is not supposed to realize, is that this feeling of "unnaturalness" is perfectly (that is, ideologically) natural. (See Chodorow, *The Reproduction of Mothering*, especially ch. 12.) What is unnatural is merely her awareness of the unnaturalness. She is supposed to bask in the false certainty that she feels when her head is on his shoulder and his arm is around her and repress her sense of unnaturalness until the wedding; then to prolong the repression by transferring her false certainty onto her children, and to defer her desire to act on her uncertainty (by leaving him, say) for the children's sake. In Lardner's February 27 reply, all the death imagery resurfaces, this time in the form of an ostensibly suicidal self-sentencing that conceals his actual accusation that Ellis has sentenced him to death:

I have been thinking about the letter and you for two hours and wondering how to answer. I feel as if I were writing my own death sentence and that's not a pleasant task. I feel as if you were slipping away from me. I don't know how to prevent it and I don't think I ought to try. You ought to know just what I believe and feel about both of us and I'm going to try to tell you. In the first place, there is no doubt at all in my mind about my love for you. You have all of it—to keep and keep forever. I'm simply sick when I'm away from you and I have no real interest in anything but you. You are just everything to me. Please don't think this is an appeal for sympathy—I'm just trying to let you know the truth. When you consider my "circumstances," the fact that I told you I wanted you may seem strange proof of love, but I offer it in evidence anyway. I would be less worthy than I am now if I had told you without meaning it and had asked you to share a lot anything but enviable if I hadn't cared so much that I couldn't help it. I don't believe I made that very clear, but I hope you'll understand it. What I think is the "matter with us" is just this—I don't honestly believe you care as much about me as you sometimes think you do—and you don't know all the time whether you do or not. And in that connection, I have another truth—I think it's a truth—in my mind that it's just impossible to tell you, because you wouldn't understand it, and wouldn't believe it if you did. You can't know how it hurts me to look at these things squarely and to come to the summing up. If I were a "good catch" instead of a bad muff, I could talk differently. As it is, I can say just this—if you don't *know* that you love me, you don't love me enough. I'm not fishing. Ever since that night at Anne's I have felt that it was only a question of time before hell would follow heaven. I believe people get out of life just what they earn. I have not earned such happiness as life with you would be. I don't deserve you. I don't think you want to be bound to me now, and I know you don't want to say so, so I am saying it for you. You are to consider yourself free unless you are *sure* and until you are sure. And if, as I think, you realize it was a mistake and that you never can care, please tell me so. And never reproach yourself for anything, dear. There is no one to blame except me. And you have given me a taste of more happiness than I ever thought of. I'm not trying to pose as a martyr. This all seems, natural, as if it couldn't have happened any other way. (*Letters* 51–52)

The absence of defensive cuteness makes Lardner's tone sound painfully honest here, and certainly I prefer this to most of the other letters; but of course the impression of honesty is the product of masterful tonal control. Lardner says all the right things in precisely the right tone, and has precisely the right effect on Ellis, who replies: "Cant the judge reconsider the death sentence and make it a life sentence or make the punishment just to take me back and keep me forever. I do know now, dear" (*Letters* 53). Ostensibly self-abnegating, Lardner's letter is in fact emotionally manipulative in the extreme: by carefully escalating Ellis's uncertainty into rejection and claiming that the rejection is well deserved, he makes Ellis feel heartless (what feeling woman could reject such a loving, giving, unselfish man!). "And if, as I think, you realize it was a mistake and that you never can care, please tell me so." Of course it isn't a mistake, it is an uncertainty which she wants to *deal* with openly, honestly. Lardner retreats from her call for open discussion into the shell of sentimental self-sacrificing rhetoric, specifically into the rhetoric of either-or: if you realize that you can *never* care. This is not the issue (she has already told him that she cares for him *sometimes*). The issue is what that caring consists of, what their relationship really is, what they really feel for each other. That is something Lardner cannot talk about. "And never reproach yourself for anything, dear" — this is brilliant. This is the double-binding voice of the (m)Other in Ring: reproach yourself, but don't admit your self-reproaches to yourself; blame me, but blame yourself for blaming me; cope with self-division by repressing it, repressing all blame of yourself and of me, and willing yourself to "love" me, to conform to the controlled social image of "love."

Coincidentally (but tellingly), the night before he received Ellis's letter, Lardner had talked Cub right fielder Frank Schulte into going on the wagon with him; after he had written his beautifully crafted (and crafty) reply, he talked Schulte into going *off* the wagon with him, and they binged for two days until Ellis wrote again rescinding the death sentence and promising herself to him forever and ever, whereupon Lardner got the pliant Schulte to join him on the wagon again (Ring Jr., *Lardners* 51).

9. Some samples: in a letter to Ellis after he proposed and before she accepted, he adds "some special inducements" to his proposal of marriage:

1. If you tire of my companionship, I will leave home and stay away until you recall me.

2. If you don't want to hear me talk, I'll remain absolutely silent for days at a time.

3. If you cease to care for me as you do now, I will leave the premises, not to return until the old fire is kindled anew. (July 29, 1909; *Letters* 41)

These promises (or threats) sound strikingly like something the narrator of "Who Dealt?" might have said to Tom (especially after the ending of the story). In 1910 Lardner writes:

By rights I should be glad I'm away because the less you see of me the more you will like me. (March 11, 1910)

I want to write [to you, Ellis] whenever I have time and the only thing that keeps me from doing so oftener is the fear that you will be tired of hearing from me. (March 12, 1910)

I'm not a pessimist, honey. That's the first time anyone ever accused me of being one. I guess the trouble is that I have spells when it seems unbelievable that you should care for me. I'll try not to have them any more, but you must help me. (April 11, 1910)

You haven't told me you loved me for a long while. And you haven't told me about your flirtation. (July 13, 1910)

Three days after this last letter, on July 16, prompted by a coy letter from Ellis relating a wonderful day she spent with one Captain Willhite, he writes her a "lecture on flirtation" which Ellis must have thrown away, for it does not survive; the next day, on July 17, he apologizes for the lecture and promises not to do it again:

I'm very much afraid I wrote you a crazy letter yesterday. Also I'm afraid that one like it or almost as bad will disillusion you some time and then you'll wonder how you ever stood for me at all. Please forget the crazier parts of that one and I'll try not to be guilty again. I guess it's just the thought of some one else's having the luck to be with you that drives me temporarily insane. I ought to have more sense and to realize that my luck in having you care for me is much better than anyone else can boast of.

10. As he later says in the same letter: "So you see, Miss Abbott, you mustn't jilt me now, for I never could face my family if I lost you. There are three things that could prevent the June 28th event [their wedding] — 1. You might stop caring for me. 2. You might die. 3. I might die. I'll promise faithfully not to, if you'll promise not to let the other two happen" (*Letters* 89).

11. Here is Ring Jr. again:

One of the main effects on the individual of addictive drinking such as Ring's is a loss of self-respect. The addict knows that he should stop, he feels shame and guilt over the fact that he is unable to, and remorse over what he is doing to other people and himself. These feelings lead to episodes of depression under both drinking and nondrinking conditions. His image of himself deteriorates, sometimes even provoking suicidal impulses. At all stages the process is a cumulative and self-sustaining one: the more intense the depression, the greater the craving to relieve it with alcohol; the stronger the self-destructive drive, the less inhibitory the subject's realization that he is indeed destroying himself.

That is the usual cycle. Imposed upon it in Ring's case were a strong religious background, personal moral standards that were always more rigid than those of his contemporaries, and a highly idealized concept of love and marital bliss. The guilt in him must have been oppressive in the extreme. In a time when alcoholism was regarded as a character weakness rather than a disease, when the conventional image of the alcoholic was the town drunk like Huck Finn's father or the Bowery bum, the effect on the addict's self-esteem was catastrophic. One of the clearest benefits Alcoholics Anonymous brings to the neophyte member is the discovery that so many of his peers have been hooked in the same way he has, unsuccessfully fought the same cravings and suffered the same grim effects. The solitary struggler like Ring doesn't have the example and comradeship of those who have won the battle. (*Lardners* 194–95)

I would add only two remarks: first, no alcoholic has ever won the battle; second, Lardner's guilt was probably equaled in oppressiveness by the massive effort of emotional self-control that kept him from feeling the full force of the guilt.

12. It is emphatically *not* matriarchy, despite maternal dominance: the values passed on by this sort of couple to their children and projected outward into society are still strictly patriarchal, assigning all public authority to the father and all private or moral authority to the mother. For a provocative reading of Harriet Beecher Stowe's *Uncle Tom's Cabin* along similar lines (though it does equate Stowe's patriarchal maternalism with matriarchy), see ch. 6 of David Leverenz's *Manhood and the American Renaissance*.

13. For a good discussion of the conflicting role pressures on Victorian men and women, see Charles E. Rosenberg, "Sexuality, Class and Role in 19th-Century America."

14. "My grandmother," Ring Jr. writes, "was a remarkable woman with an outgoing personality and a far greater influence on my father than her husband, a quiet man who was forty-five when Ring, their last child, was born. She was intensely religious but in an affirmative, optimistic way that celebrated life by trying to get as much fun as possible out of it" (*Lardners* 10). This is a close paraphrase of Elder, his primary source for the portrait. Yardley gives us a slightly less idealized portrait, pointing out that the three youngest Lardner children "lived in what amounted to a compound" (49) and carefully constructing a rather more ludicrous image of Lena than either Elder or Ring Jr.; but he too quickly backpedals when the portrait seems to be turning too negative:

> It would be easy, in fact, to make fun of Lena Lardner, for at first glance she was one of those female eccentrics of whom each small town is expected to have one. Her energies were ferocious, her charities were both infinite and unpredictable, and her indifference to social convention was complete. It is tempting to dress her up in lorgnette and floppy hat, grant her the presidency of the Wednesday Literary Club, and leave it at that. Except for the evidence indicating that, her occasional peculiarities to the contrary, she was a person of formidable and beneficial influence on all her children—considerably more than their genial but quiet father, who remained much in her shadow. (48)

That her influence on her children was formidable is undeniable; in what ways, aside from Elder's and Yardley's knee-jerk patriarchal need to praise all mothers, was it beneficial? For that matter, in what ways, apart from these critics' knee-jerk patriarchal need to praise all fathers, was Henry's quietness "genial"? There is an overwhelming need to construct an ideal family for Lardner that shines out of all these accounts, a defensive need that insistently denies the unpleasant sides of family life, casting only a light (but "harmless") sprinkling of ridicule on the "eccentric" mother. Lardner, not to put too fine a point on it, was a neurotically reticent, self-despising, rigidly conservative alcoholic who wrote a lot of columns and short stories but never liked a single one of them, and who killed himself with drinking and other destructive behavior at the young age of forty-eight, and even as he was dying refused to let anyone take care of him. Most of this can be traced back to the "formidable" influence not only of his mother, but of his mother and father's symbiotic relationship, she overwhelmingly verbal, he overwhelmingly silent. I think his mother did have some beneficial influences on him, but, almost certainly owing to the disapproving or silencing influence of his father, they are in areas that Lardner either denied or despised in himself, like his humor; further, his denial/despising of them can also be traced right back to Mom and Dad.

There is only one critic to date who has resisted Elder's idealization of Lardner's childhood: John Berryman, in his 1956 review-essay on Elder's biography. He does describe Lardner, paraphrasing Elder, as "the precocious, petted ninth of nine children born into a cultured family of long-established wealth" (417), but then goes on to refer sardonically to Lardner's mother, "whose rather wild, deeply religious personality appears to have been eight feet high" (417). Since the thrust of Berryman's essay is to cut Elder's Lardner down to size, this magnification of Lena's personality is more satirical than analytical, and very much in keeping with patriarchal (and, I would guess, Henry Lardner's) defenses against the mother. Berryman wants to ridicule the Victorian *haut bourgeois* childhood and the woman who presided over it, and so portrays her as a kind of towering giantess: perceptive, but in little more than a cutting way.

What is lacking in these accounts, and what I have tried to provide, is an understanding of the ways in which Henry and Lena and Ring Lardner were the victims of a patriarchal Other-as-parent that spoke them in mutually defining and mutually destructive ways, and then coached them (and us) to idealize that speaking as idyllic.

15. Hence, I assume, Lardner's "habit of silence," as Fitzgerald put it in his obituary essay in *The New Republic*: "He had agreed with himself to speak only a small portion of his mind" (254); "He refused to 'tell all' because in a crucial period of his life he had formed the habit of not doing it — and this he had elevated gradually into a standard of taste. It never satisfied him by a damn sight" (255). Fitzgerald's speculation that had Lardner been able to write down "a larger proportion of what was in his mind and heart . . . it would have saved him longer for us" (255) suggests Alice Miller's claims: Lardner was killed, in this reading, by a kind of emotional implosion, the turning inward of nearly everything that wanted to get out.

16. He was born with a deformed left foot which was surgically repaired in infancy, but he had to wear a metal brace on his foot until he was eleven, and, as Elder says, "he limped slightly and clanked when he ran" (16). Elder, who also grew up in Niles, interviewed townspeople who had known Lardner and was told that he was never self-conscious about his leg brace. He concludes his paragraph on Lardner's handicap on a classic upbeat note: "it is probable that he played harder at ball than he would normally have done to keep up with other children" (16). The rugged American boy's steel is tested and tempered

in the fire of hardship. It is at least possible that his outward lack of self-consciousness was the result not of carefree indifference but of determined image management, and that his handicap added to his sense, as the baby of the family, that he had to work extra hard to prove his worth to the rest of the family (and the world).

17. One of the most sensitive readings of Lardner's personality, published by his friend Sherwood Anderson in 1922, takes a similar tack:

> I said that I thought I knew what was the matter with Mr. Ring Lardner. He comes from out in my country, from just such another town as the one in which I spent my own boyhood, and I remember certain shy lads of my own town who always made it a point to consort only with the town toughs — and for a reason. There was in them something extremely sensitive that did not want to be hurt. Even to mention the fact that there was in them a real love of life, a quick sharp stinging hunger for beauty, would have sent a blush of shame to their cheeks. They were intent upon covering up, concealing from everyone, at any cost, the shy hungry children they were carrying about within themselves. (172)

18. Elder is aware of this also:

> Ring felt some misgivings about the dangers of excessive feminine influence on men, loyal as he was to his mother, his sisters, his wife, and his women friends. It is reflected in the plight of the husbands in his stories: almost all of them are henpecked, resigned, and submissive to their assertive wives. Ring himself was not in the least submissive, but he recognized the perils of matriarchal authority. He had a rather significant admiration for a novel of 1916, *In Cotton Wool* by W. B. Maxwell, the story of a man who is smothered with love by his mother, sisters, and wife, who shield him from experience until he is left without any will or character of his own. (154)

Elder's willingness to live with the obvious contradictions in his portrait of Lardner — the loyal admirer of the women in his life who is determined to restrict their dangerous power, the product of an idyllic childhood watched over by a strong woman who is determined not to repeat with his own sons the same mistakes his mother made — is a testimonial to the soothing, reassuring mystifications of the Other-as-parent.

19. Lardner's rejection of his own "pampered" childhood as overly feminized is not an isolated case; indeed, the tendency for men born to strong, assertive mothers in the late nineteenth century to impose various antifeminine regimes on themselves and their sons in the first decades of the twentieth century seems to have been quite widespread. Social historians have shown that the resurgent cult of masculinity in the first half of this century — the creation of the Boy Scouts in 1908, the emergence of bodybuilding as a sport, the virility cult surrounding Teddy Roosevelt, the rise of an aggressively masculine form of Christianity (associated with Bruce Barton's *The Man Nobody Knows* and the ex-pug preacher Billy Sunday), and so on — was tied by its proponents to the "emasculizing" effect of dominant mothers. Robert C. Bannister has shown in a series of case histories of prominent proponents of the virility cult that a significant number of them were raised by strong, assertive mothers with deeply religious

backgrounds — Victorian upper-middle-class women powerfully reminiscent of Lena Lardner. David Graham Phillips (1867–1911), for example, a muckraking journalist and novelist, deplored his own softness and passivity, which he blamed on his overbearing mother, and defended against them through obsessive work; surprisingly, however, he also campaigned for women's rights and urged women to become stronger, more independent, more like "men," as he put it — but in a deeper, transferential sense he doubtless wanted them to become more like his own (m)Other. Other men of the period, like Teddy Roosevelt and the journalist and novelist William Allen White, more successfully repressed such ambivalence about strong women, and argued openly for a return to demure, passive womanhood. For further discussion, see Rupert Wilkinson's *American Tough* and the essays in part 3 of Pleck and Pleck, *The American Man*, especially Hantover on the Boy Scouts, Dubbert on Progressivism, and Filene on World War I.

It is instructive to note that James Thurber, nine years Lardner's junior and in many ways his most illustrious successor as popular American humorist, was born to parents very similar to Lena and Henry Lardner: "The domestic society in which Thurber grew up," Charles S. Holmes writes in his book on Thurber, "was strongly matriarchal, and in contrast to the strong-minded females who dominated his recollections of youth, the figure of his father is passive and indistinct" (7). Holmes continues:

His mother was a lively unconventional person, a natural clown and inveterate practical joker. . . . Deprived of a larger audience [in the theater], Mamie Fisher delighted in entertaining friends and even strangers with impromptu comic performances. "Mamie would grab up a shawl . . . a string of beads and begin to dramatize. She thought up all her own scripts, and with nothing to help her but her own keen wit and her own wild imagination, she would emote," recalls a family friend. . . . Not everyone shared this admiration for Mame Thurber's talents. She was, like her son, a non-stop talker and show-off, and some of the neighbors found her trying. One old Columbus resident observed that she was "sadly afflicted with logomania." "I've known a lot of talkative women in my day," he went on, "but none to hold a candle as a compulsive talker from whom you would run." . . . Thurber's mother was high-strung and erratic, and when the burdens of domestic responsibility became too much for her, the boys were sent off to stay with Aunt Margery Albright. (7–9)

One significant difference between Thurber and Lardner: where Lardner had only his mother and a nanny, Thurber had a strong-willed mother and grandmother and eleven maternal aunts. Whether it was this proliferation of mother figures in Thurber's childhood (allowing him the emotional space to identify with his mother without fear?) or some other factor that pushed him in a different direction as an adult, we don't know; but Thurber retained his mother's gift of witty chatter, precisely that which Lardner most carefully suppressed. Still, Thurber brought to his writing the same ("normally" masculine) idealized fear or fearful idealization of strong women that Lardner brought to his.

20. John, James, and David wrote straight journalism for newspapers and magazines of the order of the *New York Times*, *Newsweek*, and the *Herald Tribune*; Ring Jr. wrote screenplays and fiction (and of course the memoir of

his family that I have been citing throughout). Among his screenplay credits are George Stevens's *Woman of the Year* (1942; he and Michael Kanin won an Oscar for this screenplay about a sports reporter played by Spencer Tracy—and based on his father?); Fritz Lang's *Cloak and Dagger* (1946); Norman Jewison's *The Cincinnati Kid* (1965; in collaboration with Terry Southern); and *M*A*S*H* (1972; this won him his second Oscar). In 1947 he refused to cooperate with the House Un-American Activities Committee and was blacklisted (for more than a decade) and sentenced to a year in prison; he continued to do pseudonymous scripts for movies and television programs while blacklisted, and published his first novel, *The Ecstasy of Owen Muir* (1954), under his own name. His second novel, *All for Love*, was published the year he turned seventy, in 1985.

21. See Yardley for a good discussion of Lardner's influence on Hemingway and, more cursorily, on writers like James T. Farrell, Sherwood Anderson, Nathanael West, John O'Hara, and James Thurber (181–82), and on Damon Runyon (200). Yardley quotes a Lardner imitation written by Hemingway in high school (entitled "Ring Lardner Returns"); a letter of Hemingway's to his sister Marcelline, who was editor of the school paper the *Trapeze*; and the paper's faculty supervisor to the effect that "I was always having to fight criticism by the superintendent that Ernie was writing like Ring Lardner—and consequently a lost soul!" (181).

22. One such act of loyalty, surely, was what Fitzgerald in his *New Republic* obituary called Lardner's "odd little crusade in the *New Yorker* against porno-graphic songs" (254), and what Hemingway called "those pitiful dying radio censorship pieces that he wrote in the New Yorker" (158D). In the last years of his life Lardner contracted to write a *New Yorker* column on radio called "Over the Waves," and after a number of pieces on mispronunciations and inane song lyrics, he launched a campaign against immorality—an early harbinger of the Parents' Music Resource Center. Lardner, a political and social conservative who had identified with umpires and managers in his baseball reporting days, now identified with the radio censors and suggested that they were lying down on the job. Here is a representative passage from a November 19, 1932, column entitled "Lyricists Strike Pay Dirt":

> This department has been laughed at for prudishness, but has not been laughed out of it. This department has reached a stage where it almost doesn't mind a song whose only faults are inanity, terrible rhyming, and glaring infractions of simple grammatical rules. Unfortunately, the "lyricists," the singers, and the whimperers are not satisfied with that comparatively harmless kind. They are polluting the once-pure air of Golly's great out-of-doors with a gas barrage of the most suggestive songs ever conceived, published, and plugged in one year. . . . I don't like indecency in song or story, and sex appeal makes me madder than anything except fruit salad. (252–53)

Lardner singled out for particular censure such song titles as "Take Me In Your Arms," "And So to Bed," and "Let's Put Out the Lights and Go To Bed" (the last word of this last title was changed to "Sleep" in response to Lardner's attack, but even then Lardner pronounced it a borderline case), and such lyrics as "And now, come take me, my very soul is yours, / As you desire me, I come to you."

Other offensive song titles that display the intensity of his obsession even more clearly were "You're Telling Me," "Please," and "Ain'tcha Kinda Sorry Now?"; he also protested against the humming and whistling of a refrain in a song called "Paradise," because the previous verse made it clear that the humming and whistling hinted at a sex act.

"The oddest thing about [these columns]," Ring Lardner, Jr., writes, "when you look at the lyrics he was trying to have banished from the airwaves, is that they aren't pornographic at all, even by majority standards of the time. The objectionable feature in every one of them is the same: the countenancing of intimate physical love between persons not licensed by church or state to enjoy such pleasures" (*Lardners* 63). But even this may be overstated. The objectionable feature in the offending songs was probably that they generated anxiety signals in Lardner, whether he could identify the source or the cause of those signals in a given instance or not. His body screamed at him to do something about them: get up and leave the room, as he says in a July 30, 1932, piece entitled "Allie Bobs Oop Again," but beyond that, and more important, get them off the air. Do whatever it takes to protect sensitive ears (and the bodies that respond to aural input) from such smut. Like most conservative campaigners against smut, Lardner imagined those tender ears as adolescent (we must protect the purity of our youth); but my guess is that the ears he was most (if unconsciously) worried about were already fourteen years in the grave: his mother's. The eccentric, supposedly rebellious Lena Lardner would suffer no whiff of sexual or sacrilegious innuendo, and she passed her anxiety about purity in these matters on to her children, who in turn passed them on to theirs. (Ring Jr. recalls having his allowance confiscated for a month for telling a joke at the dinner table about Joshua going from Jericho to Jerusalem on his ass [*Lardners* 63].) The voice of the (m)Other-as-parent whispers to the ailing, dying Lardner, sitting in his hospital room listening to the radio, worrying about his family's financial welfare after his death, trying to think up a topic for his next "Over the Waves" column; it mobilizes him, spurs him into action, charges his aching flesh with purpose, drives him to the typewriter: "Somewhere else in the book there must be a rule against songs that are suggestive or songs that are immoral" (quoted by Elder, 354).

There must be a rule: this is the conservative response to the prompting of the Other-as-parent, the determined reduction of the doubly bound inner cacophony to an authoritarian univocity, and it is the response most typical of Lardner in his "own" voice, in the voice with which he fronted the world. There must be a rule: he believed this, and his body confirmed it.

Chapter 4

1. See my "No Less a Man . . . ," ch. 9.

2. These are, of course, problematic examples, as is Deleuze and Guattari's equation of Joyce's *Ulysses* with majority. Given that Leopold Bloom is and remains a lower-middle-class Jew in an Irish-Catholic society, he might be read

either as a "minor" character who is peripherialized by Dublin society but "majoritized" by Joyce's stream-of-consciousness technique and by proximity to the majoritarian Stephen Dedalus; or (as I would prefer) as the "becoming-minoritarian" of Joyce's literary project, the minority character who opposes and undermines his majoritarian (Dedalian) pretensions—as Benjy and Jason and perhaps Dilsey as well did Faulkner's Quentinian majoritarianism in *The Sound and The Fury*, or, in a later era, as Slothrop did Pynchon's Bliceronian majoritarianism in *Gravity's Rainbow*. Significantly, the Bloomian and Slothropian impulses in Joyce's and Pynchon's novels are steeped in minoritarian popular culture, and the Jason chapter in Faulkner's novel has been read as a postmodern moment in a high-modern fiction. In this connection, see also Deleuze and Guattari's book on Kafka.

3. This is a problematic I want to return to in part III, but obviously it cannot be ignored here, especially since my task in this chapter is to write a minoritarian critique of Lardner in order to set him up as a minor(itarian) writer: by naturalizing my criticism as "fact" (and relegating self-reflexive discussions of critical constructivism to another place, to what in this chapter is an argumentative periphery), I place Lardner in a static literary field and thus undermine my own argument.

4. It is telling, of course, that Fitzgerald's narrator is a majoritarian moralist who tells us early on in the novel that Gatsby "represented everything for which I have an unaffected scorn" (2), and that, after Gatsby's death, "I wanted the world to be in uniform and at a sort of moral attention forever; I wanted no more riotous excursions with privileged glimpses into the human heart" (2). Nick is able to overcome his moralizing distaste for Gatsby by modeling him on the visionary heroes of medieval romances, an earlier majoritarian discourse that (in Gatsby's case alone) temporarily supersedes his Victorian Midwestern middle-class majoritarianism.

5. Note also the names of these teams: the Yankees invoke the Puritan spirit, cold, haughty, almost otherworldly in their Spartan reserve and spiritual superiority; the Dodgers invoke the tricksterism of the urban lower class, Dickens's Artful Dodger, dodging the law, dodging parental authority.

6. As I write this, my three-year-old daughter Anna comes up to me and says, in syntax reminiscent of Jack Keefe: "Daddy, of the banana of the top of it was all full of yucky things because I don't like it because I can't eat it because I threw it in the garbage, so I don't like it." "Because" is a kind of accumulative explanatory conjunction for her: its repetition does not so much signify a causal chain as mark a series of attempts to explain why she has done what she's done. The series of "of's" that opens the explanation is new to me, but it seems to have a similar function: she is trying to say "the top of the banana" and knows that she has to glue the parts together with "of," but approaches the relationship iconically rather than hierarchically, working up the banana in her hand to the brown part at the top that she doesn't like, and liberally applying "of's" in hopes of sticking one into the right slot.

This seems to me an interesting parallel to Jack Keefe's epistolary narration because it shows, I think, just how powerfully lodged in language our selves are, our rational adult mastery of our world, our instrumental control of self and other. Anna is faced with a dual dilemma: how to separate the bad part of her banana from the good part, throw away the bad part, and eat the good part (how to control her environment, in the form of food); and how to justify throwing the whole banana away to Daddy (how to control her self-presentation before an adult authority, to validate her self-image as big enough to handle things like this on her own). Anna's stammering syntax not only reveals the ways in which the world still baffles and thwarts her; it suggests as well that our own more controlled syntax (and how controlled is it?) is really only a way of covering up the ways in which the world still baffles and thwarts us as well.

7. For Bakhtin's discussion of carnivalesque laughter, see *Rabelais and His World*, where he explores laughter's power to liberate the subject "from the oppression of such gloomy categories as 'eternal,' 'immovable,' 'absolute,' 'unchangeable'" into "the gay and free laughing aspect of the world, with its unfinished and open character, with the joy of change and renewal" (83). Kristeva, coming out of Lacan and Derrida, is not nearly so sanguine about this laughing liberation as Bakhtin — the "joy of change and renewal" is always complexly wrapped up with gloomy oppression — but, coming out of Bakhtin, she is also strikingly more liberatory than her deconstructive mentors.

8. Note that these character roles (Gatsby as romantic hero, Daisy as seductress) are majoritarian, not "true" — or "true" only insofar as the majoritarian ideology that motivates them mystifies them as such. They do not, in other words, constitute my reading of the novel, but rather my caricature of Fitzgerald's majoritarian plot — a caricature that is heavily influenced by Judith Fetterley's *The Resisting Reader*.

9. An example: the majoritarian linguistic philosopher John Searle wants to convince us that language is rule-governed, and to prove his point alludes to baseball.

> An analogy: I know that in baseball after hitting the ball fair, the batter runs in the direction of first base, and not in the direction, say, of third base or the left field grand stand. Now what sort of knowledge is this? On what is it based? How is it possible? Notice that it is a general claim and not confined to this or that instance of baserunning behavior. I have never done or even seen a study of baserunner behavior, and I have never looked the matter up in a book. Furthermore, I know that if the book, even if it were a rule book, said anything to the contrary it would be mistaken or describing a different game or some such. My knowledge is based on knowing how to play baseball, which is *inter alia* having internalized a set of rules. I wish to suggest that my knowledge of linguistic characterizations is of a similar kind. (14)

But notice how Searle's use of the baseball analogy tips his hand, sends his majoritarian theory of linguistic rule-governedness racing. Baseball is a created game. It was invented at a specific place and time by a specific individual (by Abner Doubleday in Cooperstown, N.Y., in the summer of 1839, as the usual story has it), in a relatively coherent form, with specified rules that are codified in rule books. The rules can be changed, but only by elaborate legal proceedings (committees, proposals, votes, etc.). If language rules are analogous with baseball rules, language too must have been invented in a coherent, rule-governed form at a specific place and time by a specific individual (Adam?), and changed in formal ways, one rule at a time, by grammarians and other linguists, the "commissioners" of language.

The patent absurdity of this scenario undermines not only Searle's "scientific" theory of speech acts, but, by minoritarian infection, his conception of baseball (and the constitutive rules governing all games) as well. Even in organized baseball the operation (and especially the changing) of rules is not nearly as simple as Searle wants to make it out to be. Ring Lardner was never reconciled to the introduction of the so-called "rabbit" ball in 1920, for example, and to his dying day felt that baseball was no longer baseball—it was too easy to get a home run with the new ball. The introduction of the designated hitter rule in the American League in 1973 had a similar effect on those of us who grew up with baseball before the rule, and on most National League fans after the rule: every time the DH comes up to bat, our "knowledge of baseball" (our somatized knowledge of the way the game is played, independently of rule books) tells us that this is flat-out *wrong*. As Searle says, "I know that if the book, even if it were a rule book, said something to the contrary it would be mistaken or describing a different game or some such." This suggests that Searle's linguistic philosophy simply institutionalizes somatized nostalgia: baseball and language are "rule-governed" in the sense that we cling to what *feels right*, and what feels right is the way the game was played (or words were used) in our childhoods. For most people majoritarian rules are grounded in an emptying out of minor animal fears, the "elevation"-cum-transcendentalization of those deeply personal fears to the abstract level of the majoritarian Nobody.

Even more important, pick-up baseball games constantly flow around and through the rules, are incessantly reconstituting the rules to adjust to varying playing circumstances. You only have ten people, so you play rotation. You have only nine people, so you play rotation with right field closed. You only have three people, so you hit fungoes or play pickle. You only have a softball, and you have to decide whether to pitch overhand or underhand, fast or slow; whether to allow leading off and stealing. You don't have enough people for an umpire, so you decide to let the batter call his or her own balls and strikes—and then argue over individual pitches. A small child is batting, so the pitcher moves up to about ten feet in front of the batter and keeps pitching (never mind balls and strikes) until the child gets a hit; nobody tries very hard to throw the base runner out; without agreeing to do so in advance, everyone involved in the play may even stage a little drama called "bad fielding," fumbling the ball, throwing and catching badly. You're not playing on a regular baseball diamond, so you have to decide on where to locate the bases and the pitcher's mound (and you argue or decline to argue over what to use for bases, and whether someone moved one), and on how to tell when someone has run too far off the base path and should be declared out. The batter hits a grounder into someone's beer cup, and you argue over whether he or she should get a free base or new pitch, or whether the unconscionable spilling of beer constitutes an instant out.

This minoritarian feel for baseball seems closer to how language actually gets used than the majoritarian fantasy that Searle spins out. The striking thing is that the minoritarian impulse of baseball itself introduces this centrifugal moment into his majoritarianism, infects his robotic ideal first with the needs and fears of real bodies and then with fluid and socially and situationally contingent rules—sends the majoritarian theory of language racing.

10. For a useful discussion of American popular culture in these terms, see George Lipsitz, *Time Passages*.

11. And of course, whenever the critics comment on this story, they second Lardner's overt sexism: Patrick refers to the "two shallow-minded females" and calls the story Lardner's "most caustic indictment of the brainless tongue-wagger" (105); Bordewyk notes that, "far from impressing the bachelor with their social charms, the two women alienate him with their mindless chatter" (55).

12. Here is Yardley:

> This silence of Ring's is a mystery, doubly so since he was not shy or silent as a child. Its sources can be guessed at, but only that. His shyness and aristocratic aloofness have already been mentioned. In the summer of 1908, pure insecurity may have had something to do with it; for years his "real and only ambition was to associate with big league ball players," and now he was doing that—so he may in some degree simply have been awed into silence. Yet dime-store psychologizing of this sort is far less fruitful than what appears to be the simple truth: he was laconic, a listener rather than a talker. (87)

The absurd suggestion that Lardner may have been "awed into silence" by big-league baseball players is indeed dime-store psychologizing, of course: not only does Yardley ignore Lardner's maturation into ideologically prescribed manhood through the invocation of the taciturn Other-as-father to silence the ebullient Other-as-mother, but the "awed into silence" explanation is utterly at odds with the evidence. *Nothing* suggests that Lardner may have felt awe toward the major-league ballplayers he was traveling with—or that the son of Lena Lardner ever felt awe toward anyone, including Presidents of the United States and world-famous entertainers. Timidity, self-deprecation, even self-loathing, combined with a mixed dose of sardonic superiority, yes. Awe, no.

Ironically enough, Yardley offers the "awed into silence" explanation only in order to rule out psychological interpretations and repeat Lardner's own repressive ascesis by reducing biographical commentary to a "simple truth: he was laconic, a listener rather than a talker." That's just the way he was. This is the equivalent of saying that Lardner drank because he enjoyed the way it made him feel: it perpetuates a psychological defense rather than exploring the roots of behavior.

13. Much the same could be said about the stories about talkative women I mentioned in chapter 3. What we might call the manic "manizing" (the female equivalent of womanizing) of Nurse Lyons in "Zone of Quiet" and the diarist of

"I Can't Breathe" similarly reflects their desperate attempts at once to land a husband (the normative sign of feminine success and self-worth in patriarchal society), to conceal or rationalize or explain away their failures in this endeavor, and to pretend to the world that, succeed or fail, they don't really care.

14. There is, in fact, a similar turn in "Travelogue" (1926): "But after all [this third-person narrator shows us things through shy Mildred's consciousness], she *was* dumb and Hazel's erudition made her seem all the dumber. No wonder their new acquaintance had scarcely looked at her since luncheon" (308-9). The few times Mildred tries to join in the conversation, Dan and Hazel stare at her for a moment and then move on; but by the end of the story, Dan has become interested in Mildred (or perhaps has been interested in her all along, and has been putting up with Hazel's chatter in order to be around Mildred), and the story concludes with Dan trying to bring Mildred out, listen to her, get her to talk.

The difference between this scenario and the one I am imagining with Miss Coakley is that Dan is attracted to Mildred precisely because she is shy and demure—"ladylike," an ideologically "normal" woman—so that, in trying to get her to open up, he is really looking for more shy, quiet comments, no potentially transformative deluge of free association. Early on she has pleased him by agreeing that girls are less adventurous than boys (305), and at the end she pleases him again by fussing over his recent ordeal of having a tooth pulled, both nurturing his hurt (mothering him) and admiring his bravery ("daughtering" him) (315). There is no opening up here, no therapeutic shift—only a traditional boy-meets-girl story.

15. For a similar reading, see Howard W. Webb, Jr., "The Meaning of Ring Lardner's Fiction." Webb argues persuasively that the overriding theme of Lardner's fiction is "the comedy, the pain, the terror of being incommunicado" (435), and closes his essay with a plea:

> Finally, we should dismiss the charges of misanthropy which have long been lodged against Lardner. His creations, even those he loathed, were the product of his sympathetic understanding of the catastrophe that befalls anyone who is cut off from communication with his fellows. We should, at last, allow Ring Lardner to communicate with us. (445)

It is instructive to note the professionalization of this reading twenty-two years later, in Gordon Bordewyk's classification of Lardner's "four types of communication failures that contribute to alienation" (51). Bordewyk seems unaware of the ways in which his typological approach to Lardner itself contributes to alienation by ignoring Lardner's pleas to be heard.

16. Yardley is typical:

> Ring wrote many other nonsense plays in the years to come, the best of them being "Cora, or Fun at a Spa" and "Taxidea Americana," but "I Gaspiri" is eminently representative—which is to say that it is a dazzling collection of verbal and visual nonsequiturs, all of them wildly comical. The plays do not submit to rational analysis for the simple reason that they are antirational. Though they were often seized upon

as Dada or surrealism, they were not consciously written to conform to any literary movement or passing fancy. They were simply the direct products of Ring's invention, the final summations of all the nonsense he had seen in the world around him. (272)

Lardner "sees" nonsense "in the world around him" and sums it up. They are "not consciously written" to be dadas or anything else; "they were simply the direct products of Ring's invention." Period.

Maxwell Geismar's reading of "Clemo Uti — 'The Water Lilies'" in *Ring Lardner and the Portrait of Folly* is more attentive to the psychological and philosophical implications of a line like "What of it? We're twins, ain't we" (though I disagree with his reading: "this Lardnerian answer is better than searching vainly for supernatural solutions to our dilemmas or blaming our parents for our own faulty behavior" [85]), but even he backs away: "Can you really explain the nonsense humor of 'I. Gaspiri'? As soon as you try to explain it, it stops being funny" (88). This has always seemed a peculiar claim to me. It assumes that humor must always be based on ignorance, and that the funniness of ignorance-based humor is somehow sacred, that we must somehow protect whatever makes us laugh from our own demystifications. I agree with Freud that laughter is always steeped in repression and fear, and with Bakhtin that laughter can liberate us from repression and fear, from both the internal censor and external power:

> It unveils the material bodily principle in its true meaning. Laughter opened men's eyes on that which is new, on the future. This is why it not only permitted the expression of an antifeudal, popular truth; it helped to uncover this truth and to give it an internal form. And this form was achieved and defended during thousands of years in its very depths and its popular-festive images. Laughter showed the world anew in its gayest and most sober aspects. Its external privileges are intimately linked with interior forces; they are a recognition of the rights of those forces. This is why laughter could never become an instrument to oppress and blind the people. It always remains a free weapon in their hands. (Bakhtin, *Rabelais* 94)

17. Another such displacement appears in the list of characters: "FFENA — *their daughter, later their wife*" (45), which recalls the line Ring Lardner, Jr., cites as an example of his father's delight in unconscious humor: "I treat every woman like they was my sister, till I find out different" (see p. 107). The sister/different shift and the daughter/wife shift both compound the number confusions (woman/they and an unspecified "their"), suspending both "every woman" and "Ffena" in a limbo of deterritorialized kinship relations and identity.

Chapter 5

1. More technical terms that cover roughly the same ground as the Other-as-culture are "ideology" as used by twentieth-century Marxist theorists, Gramsci's concept of "hegemony," and (perhaps closest to my term) Fredric Jameson's term "political unconscious," a powerful socioideological demystification of Jung's "collective unconscious." The traditional abstractions for what I am calling the

Other-as-culture would include the ancient philosophical agents Truth, the Good, the Right, the Law, and so on.

All these, like the Other-as-culture, are patently secularized or demystified versions of God. But it seems to me to make a difference just how one secularizes or demystifies God. Truth and other philosophical abstractions are obviously mystified reifications of political hegemony; but even "ideology" or "hegemony," conceived "structurally" as an underlying social belief structure with no sense of how it acts on and through individuals or of how it gets passed on from generation to generation, still seems mystified to me. Ideology works in mysterious ways. Grounding "ideology" or "hegemony" in an ideosomatic program that is transmitted as and by the double bind through the collectivized unconscious speaking of various actual human authorities (themselves definitively spoken by those collective voices) removes some of this mystery and makes it possible to discuss the operation of ideology in the simultaneously private and public, individuated and collectivized behavior of people.

2. The resulting tensions within bourgeois society began to be widely recognized in the teens and twenties of this century, the very period in which Lardner rose to popularity. Warren I. Susman, for example, quotes a telling passage from V. F. Calverton and S. D. Schmalhausen's introduction to the book they edited in 1929, *Sex and Civilization*: "Nature and culture . . . destroying each other marvelously. . . . The body and the mind hate one another in queer ways that run the gamut from tenderness to violence. Ambivalence poisons our human nature. We are scientific and superstitious; critical and credulous; conservative and radical; libertarian and autocratic; savage and charitable; intolerant and amiable; educated and shallow; prosperous and empty" (quoted in Susman 114).

3. I am drawing here on Norbert Elias's discussion of the civilization process in *Power and Civility*. Perry Anderson also traces the transition from medieval feudalism to the modern state in *Lineages of the Absolutist State*.

4. I am drawing heavily here, and throughout this chapter, on Terry Eagleton's ideological history of criticism from the eighteenth century to the present in *The Function of Criticism*. My reading of the bourgeois Other-as-culture's inclusivism is indebted to Eagleton's first chapter on the eighteenth-century public sphere; my later discussion of the need to assimilate the proletariat into the middle class owes to his second chapter on the way the rise of the proletariat pushed bourgeois criticism into transcendental universalism.

5. I follow Peter Stearns and Stuart Blumin here in distinguishing the "bourgeoisie" and the bourgeois Other-as-culture from the "middle class" (Blumin 304). The bourgeoisie is the massive merchant/banker/lawyer class whose emergence in the thirteenth and fourteenth centuries and increasing dominance in the seventeenth and eighteenth centuries mark what we call the "modern" era (as opposed to the Middle Ages). Bourgeois or "liberal" ideology, which dominates our thinking today, idealizes inclusivism and upward mobility, thrift and practicality, tolerance for difference, and so on. The middle class is a historically contingent social grouping, defined by its position in the middle between the ruling class and the poor. In the first centuries of its emergence, the bourgeoisie

was the middle class between the aristocracy and the feudal peasantry; but as its upper echelons increasingly displaced the hereditary aristocracy as the dominant class (throughout the eighteenth and nineteenth centuries), the middle class became a kind of social "shifter," an ideological ideal with varying empirical references: it could refer to "headworkers" as opposed to "handworkers" (the critical split engineered in the midnineteenth century right down the middle of the old artisan class), managers as opposed to clerks, clerks as opposed to drivers, and so on. What remains constant about the "middle class" is the normative bourgeois conception of it as classless, or what Anthony Giddens describes as its definitive form, the *"denial of the existence or reality of classes"* (quoted in Blumin 308). "Inclusion in the middle class" may have meant different things to different groups of people in different historical periods (different forms of professional advancement, social acceptance, patterns of consumption and speech), but it has always by definition meant the ideological "eradication" of class, which is to say the "forgetting" of class markers and the concomitant belief that one has now risen "above" class to membership in the great classless democratic experiment.

For a contrasting view that partly overlaps with that of Stearns and Blumin (and which he cites in support of his own), see Arno Mayer, who advances a two-tiered conception of the middle class, upper and lower, and argues for a continuity within each sector from the late Middle Ages to our own day: the upper middle class has always comprised the rich urban elite (as opposed to the landed aristocracy) that in one way or another has run things for eight or nine hundred years; the lower middle class includes everyone else that we would consider bourgeois, from skilled artisans and clerks to lawyers, doctors, and professors. Stearns, too, dissents from the consensus I artificially created in the preceding paragraph, arguing that there is nothing "bourgeois" about the industrial middle class: "The bourgeoisie is a preindustrial grouping, indeed a legal entity in the system of estates or orders. The term is quite properly applied to pre-1789 Europe (though less so to England and North America)" (387), but is not synonymous with the middle class; he calls for a moratorium on its use (386).

I would argue that, despite specific social discontinuities between what Stearns calls the "old" and the "new" middle class, there is an ideological continuity that makes the term "bourgeois" still useful. To rephrase Stearns's argument in my terms, the bourgeois Other-as-culture continued to speak the new middle class created by the upheaval of the French Revolution in hegemonic ways, adapting its speaking to changed conditions, changing with the conditions, but without the kind of absolute rift or break that Stearns portrays in middle-class demographics. Stearns himself sees ideological persistence across the gap — "Elements of the bourgeoisie persisted, viewing the world as logically divided into a hierarchy of which they were a docile middle segment" (387) — but seems to believe that these "elements" are really nothing other than individual human beings whose "views" died with them. He also argues that the survival of a bourgeois ideology of cleanliness and sobriety is inconclusive proof of the survival of the bourgeoisie, since "cleanliness standards . . . altered dramatically with time" and "many middle-class elements who might claim such virtues were in practice perfectly capable of being drunk and disorderly misfits" (388). This is a peculiar confusion: as if actual social deviation from a dominant ideology somehow proved that the ideology wasn't truly dominant, as if continuing deviation or "unruliness" weren't structurally built into the esemplastic norm or rule.

Throughout this chapter I will use "bourgeois" to refer to the dominant ideology of the modern (postmedieval) West—a term that might be replaced in specific contexts with "liberal" or "capitalistic" but not, say, with "entrepreneurial" or "mercantile"—and I will use "middle class" to refer to a specific class configuration within that ideological construct, a class neither rich (and in control of social norms, political activities, and economic production) nor poor (and excluded from the cultural and monetary rewards of middle-class membership). Thus the bourgeois Other-as-culture will attempt to bring as many people as possible into the "classless" middle class.

6. More specifically, what took place was a division of the artisan class into a proletariat of "handworkers" (manual laborers, later to be called "blue-collar workers") and a clerical and managerial calss of "headworkers" (nonmanual laborers, later to be called "white-collar workers"). Stuart Blumin details the changes this division entailed, from modifications in the workplace—whereas earlier artisan tailors both sewed and sold, for example, by the mid-nineteenth century "the manual work of sewing, pressing, and cutting is confined to one room, while the well-dressed master tailor measures a customer in a separate room" (323)—to changes in patterns of consumption.

7. For further discussion, see Stuart Brandes, *American Welfare Capitalism*, especially his third chapter on the evangelists of welfare capitalism.

8. On the English Only movement, see Edward George Hartmann, *The Movement to Americanize the Immigrant* (1948), and Dennis Baron, *The English-Only Question* (1990). For a useful overview of the public library movement in America from the late nineteenth to the midtwentieth century, see Evelyn Geller, especially ch. 4 on the perception of a crisis in bourgeois society requiring the civilizing ministrations of public libraries; ch. 5 on free access to books; and ch. 6 on censorship. For a closer look at forbidden books in public libraries during this period, see Dee Garrison. In *No Place of Grace* and "From Salvation to Self-Realization," Jackson Lears has explored the broad social context of this process in terms of what he calls a "therapeutic antimodernism," an attempt to "recover" a self perceived as lost to or destroyed by rampant mechanization and dehumanization. In light of Lears's argument one might say that the incorporation of the working class into the middle class was "therapeutic" for the latter: that the middle class attempted to recover or restore a threatened bourgeois self by (among other things) expanding it to encompass the working class.

9. For a good discussion of one specific case, see ch. 5 of David Nye's *Image Worlds*, where he traces the efforts of General Electric to "discipline and control" (76) a culturally heterogeneous work force drawn largely from the burgeoning immigrant artisan population in the late nineteenth and early twentieth centuries. Finding that direct attempts to make workers submissive, passive, and inured to

the tedium of repetitive work backfired and led only to open confrontation, GE founded a magazine for their workers called *Works News*, and began to reshape the work force "culturally" through ideologically potent imagery. Nye notes that *Works News* rarely portrayed workers on the shop floor, in large groups; when they were shown at work, the image was carefully constructed to show a single worker engaged in an interesting, rewarding task (no group solidarity, no repetitive work). And far more prevalent were photos that had no connection to work at all:

> Surprisingly inside the magazine were virtually no photographs of this type [the individual worker at work]. Instead the articles and the images concentrated on a vision of the factory as a community where workers took vacations, played on sports teams, mutually contributed to pension plans, got married, held dances, celebrated Christmas, bought and sold household goods, and took a wide variety of evening courses. The photographs act as a series of visual proofs of the actuality of welfare capitalism. (83)

10. For further discussions of this tradition and Lardner's place in it, see Rourke, *American Humor* (esp. 227–29); Yates, *The American Humorist* (165–93); Bier, *The Rise and Fall of American Humor* (esp. 211–12); Duffey, "Humor, Chicago Style" (also articles by Holman [250–51] and Rubin [400–401] in the same collection); Blair and Hill, *America's Humor* (esp. 413–16); and DeMuth, *Small Town Chicago* (87–106).

11. See also Douglas Waples on reading preferences in a predominantly working-class area of South Chicago in 1933 (148): 90% read newspapers, 50.2% read magazines, 17.4% read books, and 8.2% read nothing. In an analysis of the relative amount of reading in books and magazines in the same area, Waples found that around three-fourths of the 6,850 subjects read more magazines than books and the remaining fourth more books than magazines, and that this proportion was roughly the same for all social groups studied, including the small group (816) of professionals—with the sole exception of students, 56.4% of whom read more magazines than books and 43.7% more books than magazines. The significant differences lay in the kind of magazines and books read: more unemployed (33.5%) and unskilled (24.4%) men read more detective and adventure magazines than skilled men (8.9%), shopkeepers and salesmen (6.6%), stenographers and clerks (8.8%), and professional men (1.2%); more lower-middle-class men (shopkeepers and salesmen 25%, stenographers and clerks 23.5%, skilled trades 22%) and professional men (19.9%) read more five-cent weeklies than unemployed (8%) or unskilled men (11.4%). Among women readers, more unemployed (18.8%) and unskilled (44%) women and housewives (16.5%) read movie, radio, and love magazines than skilled women (7.3%) or professional women (2%). Book reading showed fewer variations: women in all social categories read more "good fiction" (which Waples does not define; he also has a category called "literature") than men, in fact from two to four times more women than men; but reading in "other fiction" was more uniform, with only a few percentage points of difference between male and female readers in all social categories.

12. This congruence between vernacular humor and street literature is perhaps clearest in Shepard's introductory comments, where he describes the relationship between "sophisticated literature" (books) and street literature in terms that strongly resemble the relationship between, say, Fitzgerald's and Lardner's work:

> Sophisticated literature merely provided, as it were, chapter-headings for the real story of ordinary people, whose own sub-literature of ballad-sheets and pamphlets provided news, diversion, inspiration, fantasy, and political stimulus. It is precisely because of its faults and deficiencies that it is of greater significance historically than the more polished works of sophisticated writers, for that sub-literature was linked to the fierce energies of the crowds that created history, rather than to the culture of its rulers or manipulators. The crude half-truth of a slogan has always been more powerful than a reasonable truth. (13–14)

13. Cf. Shepard:

> Histories of books and authors give a very one-sided view of the growth and development of literature as a cultural and political force. Books were produced by professional writers for the privileged few who could afford them, and the themes and language of books, like their fine bindings, generally reflected the outlook of sophisticated society. In the first four centuries of printing, books were mainly for church dignitaries, noblemen, scholars, merchants, and gentlemen with private libraries, not for the masses. (13)

14. For a good overview of this development, see ch. 7 of Warren I. Susman, *Culture as History*, especially 112 on the *Reader's Digest* and the Book-of-the-Month Club (also 125 on Bruce Barton's promotional campaign for the *Harvard Classics*). For more detailed analysis, see, e.g., Janice Radway, "The Book-of-the-Month Club and the General Reader: On the Uses of 'Serious' Fiction."

15. For a brief history of the *Saturday Evening Post*, see Frank Luther Mott's discussion (4:671ff.).

16. In Shepard's words: "This is, in every sense, an ephemeral literature, since readers use the books as waste paper afterwards, often tearing up the pages for paper to roll cigarettes" (139).

17. Waples reports on a study done by Jeannette Howard Foster in 1935, classifying the 250 most widely read authors in five American communities according to fifteen subject categories and six "cultural levels" (social class, level of education) of about 15,000 readers. Foster notes that "it is the immature, whether they be fourteen or forty, who will shun the better and crave the more wish-fulfilling fiction. Moreover, they will seek those stories in which they can most creditably identify themselves with the successful character" (quoted in Waples 158).

In genre fiction (detective, adventure, romance, love), reading preferences are clearly weighted heavily in the bottom three social categories—although in adventure Foster finds authors like Edgar Rice Burroughs preferred in the bottom category, Zane Grey and Rider Haggard in the second, Jack London and Jules Verne in the third, Rudyard Kipling in the fourth, Daniel Defoe and Robert Louis Stevenson in the fifth, and Herman Melville—alone—in the sixth or top category. The "top-heavy" subject categories are "character" (Maupassant and

Jane Austen in the sixth, Eliot and Hemingway in the fifth, Balzac and Dreiser in the fourth, and so on), "psychological" (Joyce, Conrad, and Woolf in the sixth, Wharton in the fifth), and "philosophical problems" (Tolstoy and Hardy in the sixth, Hawthorne in the fifth).

Lardner's name does not appear in Foster's list, which was compiled shortly after his death; she has one category for humorous writers, with five names distributed fairly evenly through the first, second, third, and fifth categories (Twain, canonized by the early thirties, stands alone in the fifth category), and another for satiric writers, with thirteen names, also distributed fairly evenly across all six categories.

18. For a different approach to his clash, see my article "The Trivialization of American Literature."

19. For a similar discussion of popular writing in England, see Terry Eagleton, *The Function of Criticism*, 57–67: "Dickens, for example, required no middleman between himself and his public; the popular authors were themselves assuming one of the critic's functions, moulding and reflecting the sensibility by which they were consumed" (57). As V. S. Pritchett points out in his 1959 article on Lardner, however, vernacular humor never really caught on in England: "There was a moment, in Kipling's stories, when we clearly pre-dated the modern American school; he is our earliest vernacular writer, but he does not sustain the vernacular style for long because there is no general one to sustain; it falls away into tribal pockets" (580). Pritchett sees a resurgence in English vernacular humor in Joyce, but a writer like Joyce clearly does not have the "moulding" power of a Dickens or a Kipling—or of a Twain or a Lardner. Pritchett goes on to insist that the new "modernist" use of the vernacular "will not last unless it comes close to the way people naturally think and wish to go on thinking and it is noticeable that they do not altogether wish to go on in the lazy, native way. Common speech in English at the moment is a comic mixture of the incurable and the new gentility, and is too socially nervous to sound like an assured and single habit of mind—which has been the strength of the American tradition" (580). This seems to me to confuse the cart and the horse: the American vernacular of Lardner and others is socially nervous, too, but it is transformed in its very social nervousness into what *sounds* like an "assured and single habit of mind" by the "moulding" power of these writers (and the American Other-as-culture that speaks them). My sense is that the English Other-as-culture is less dedicated to the appearance of classlessness than its American counterpart— that the long centuries during which an aristocratic Other-as-culture dominated England left a sedimented legacy that damps out "upward" mobility, mobility particularly from the working class into the "classless" middle, far more effectively than anything in America, and thus has damped out the assimilative drive of vernacular humor as well.

Beyond that, of course, Kipling did not predate the modern American vernacular tradition at all: he was born in 1865, the year Twain published "The Celebrated Jumping Frog of Calaveras County," and was four years old when *Innocents Abroad* appeared. Pritchett's conception of the "modern" tradition is anachronistically short. Dickens, the proletarian boy turned realistic novelist, predates Twain (and Ward and the other nineteenth-century vernacular humorists born in the 1830s) by some twenty years; but of course Dickens frames the vernacular speech of his humorous characters with proper middle-class speech, and so does not have the same effect on proletarian readers as the American humorists.

20. For a useful discussion that makes many of the connections at which I am only hinting—the social utility of "culture" as reflected in industry, advertising, and sports—see ch. 8 of Warren I. Susman's *Culture as History* on Henry Ford, Bruce Barton, and Babe Ruth, three culture heroes of the twenties who are collectively and complexly representative of the assimilatory process I describe. Barton comes from a respectable middle-class background (a preacher's son), Ford from a rural background (a farmer's son), and Ruth from the urban underclass (the son of poor immigrants), and each brings to his particular area of cultural heroism—advertising and inspirational writing for Barton, mass production for Ford, baseball for Ruth—a characteristic social slant largely derived from that background. Barton transforms the middle-echelon businessman into the quintessential American, the truest good citizen, the ideal Christian; but his genteel moralism provides little cultural space even for the emergent lower middle class, let alone the rural and urban poor. Ford is the welfare capitalist who pacifies and unifies his work force by keying raises to social conformity, and who produces a luxury item like an automobile cheaply enough to transform workers into consumers; but his peasant mentality (his father's willingness to toil mechanically and repetitively on the farm, which Henry himself overtly rejected but ideologically transformed) blinds him to assembly-line workers' desire for variety and color in their work and lives, and he never understands the need for labor unions or advertising. Ruth is the eternal boy whose flair for style and color (much more than his undeniable athletic talent) wins him an immense salary and an astonishing following far beyond the bounds of baseball, because he gives lower-middle-class Americans what neither Barton nor Ford could— pizzazz and razzmatazz; but his "boyish" lack of discipline and self-control (his underclass "incorrigibility," his refusal or inability to conform to middle-class norms of proper behavior) prevents him from channeling his proletarian "color" in esemplastic ways. What esemplastic force Ruth exerted was mainly due to the genius of his agent Christy Walsh, who developed what Susman calls a "ghostwriting syndicate" for the publication of articles and books by sports heroes (146), got Ruth product endorsements and movie and vaudeville appearances, and so on, all anticipating the commodification of sports (and above all of the sports hero) that we now take for granted.

It is instructive to note that, while Lardner deplored Babe Ruth and everything he stood for, his own Jack Keefe ("ghostwritten" by Lardner, another syndicated writer) had very much the same kind of impact on American society as Ruth did.

21. For further discussion, see John Berger's remarks on publicity in *Ways of*

Seeing; Jackson Lears, "From Salvation to Self-Realization"; and ch. 7 of David Nye, *Image Worlds*. Nye's remarks are particularly germane to my reading of the assimilation of the proletariat: following Lears, he criticizes the scholarly practice of analyzing advertisements one at a time, in isolation from the corporate management of a media campaign. Nye writes:

> The corporation creates patterns of meaning wholesale and sells them to the public. It divides society into markets while ignoring fundamental divisions between workers and white-collar personnel, between regions, and between ethnic groups. The forms of mass culture, including world's fairs, magazines, advertising, corporate photography, commercial radio and television, and public relations, present a systematically controlled image of American society. These forms of communication and the large companies that control them must be linked to any investigation. (133)

Since Nye has just shown how carefully General Electric tailored its advertising campaigns to different audiences — how "under Barton's leadership, General Electric placed quite different advertisements in different periodicals" (124) — his claim that the corporation ignores "fundamental divisions between workers and white-collar personnel" seems strange. The different markets themselves reflected class and regional divisions: the magazines that Barton's advertising agency classed as "review" periodicals are clearly aimed at a white-collar audience, while many (not all) of the "general" periodicals are aimed at workers, "farm" periodicals are aimed at rural regions, and so on. In addition, the three GE house organs he analyzes in detail, for engineers, workers, and managers, were themselves advertising media.

22. See also his *Madness and Civilization*, especially ch. 6, "Doctors and Patients."

23. In this connection note also the congruence between Lardner's voicing of the proletariat in the vernacular stories and columns and his voicing of the mad — his experiments with schizophasic discourse — in the nonsense plays.

24. Indeed, given the epistemological hazards of empirical research, there is little more that we can do with specific writer-reader dialogues even when we do have controlled empirical data on them. Janice Radway was still forced, after gathering data on romance readers through observation, interviews, and questionnaires, to generate an imaginary dialogue between the readers she studied and the books they read — a dialogue shaped powerfully by her empirical evidence, but just as powerfully by her own dialogues with those books and with theoretical texts like Nancy Chodorow's *The Reproduction of Mothering*.

25. I am drawing here on Pierre Bourdieu's conceptualization of taste in *Distinction*.

26. See also Clifton Fadiman's elitist position, the first sentence of which I quoted in my epigraph to this chapter:

> These stories convey simultaneously two different impressions, one for the *Saturday Evening Post* reader and one for the civilized reader. The *Post* reader gets his laugh out of his sense of superiority — very slight — to the bushers and prize fighters whose

asininity Lardner cleverly shows up. But behind this asininity lurk a conceit, a selfishness, a brutality which the more sophisticated reader easily perceives; and as he perceives it he is bound to realize that the Ring Lardner who is apparently writing funny stories for the amusement of yokels is really drawing up an indictment of large areas of American society. (316)

27. Another moralistic reading of Lardner in this period is less professional: in 1966 John Wheeler, who had syndicated Lardner's "Weekly Letter" for years, sentimentalized Lardner as "a man of decency and integrity" and "a devoted family man" (115) who "believed in the old-fashioned standards of turn-of-the-century, small-town America" (116). He wrote this for *Reader's Digest*'s "My Most Unforgettable Character" feature.

28. An interesting variation on this theme in Lardner criticism is the moralism of Maxwell Geismar in *Ring Lardner and the Portrait of Folly*, which manages to be both elitist-intellectual and boob-moralist at the same time. He has all the elitist intellectual's rage at the banality of modern life, and indicts the twenties with all the fervor of an H. L. Mencken or a Clifton Fadiman, but he addresses his indictment to what sounds like an auditorium full of junior high school students:

Life in that earlier American scene was very different from life today. There were no automobiles, and dad did not rush off every morning to catch the 8:05 train for work. (5)

Well, this is the early Ring Lardner's version of a typical American couple on an expensive vacation, having what they call fun; and it is pretty ghastly and perhaps closer to the average citizen than we'd like to believe; or do you disagree? (30)

I could go on and on quoting from these Lardnerian rules for a happy marriage, and I only hope you will get hold of them and read them for yourself, just for fun. (55)

It is really the way you and I talk, isn't it? unless and until we are taught better. It is the way we naturally think, until we learn to use a kind of formal logic to break up this endless streaming of association with grammar or rhetoric, which are formal — in a sense, false — ways of presenting the natural material in the human mind. (90–91)

It is a *den* — the room which some of you may have been brought up with or in, and which you now take for granted, but which was an absolute novelty in the American home of the mid-twenties. (92)

Now I am sure the ornaments in *your* den may be a little more modern than the Garrisons' were. I'd imagine the conversation in your den (if you do happen to live in the suburbs) is a little more grammatical. (95)

Does it sound silly to you? A whole generation grew up with this refrain, which is still in our heads as a memory, even while we listen to rock or soul music today. (112)

The extract on the use of formal logic to break up the streaming of association is characteristic, I think, of the double binds stretching Geismar's rhetoric: he knows, like a well-trained elitist intellectual, that formal logic is a falsification of "natural" associations, which he tacitly ties to William James's theory of the stream of thought; but he still insists, like a good low-church moralist, that we talk this way until we are taught *better*. Which is it: the formal logic of normative middle-class grammar as "false" or as "better"? Geismar wants to have it both ways, just as he wants to have both his scathing condemnation of modern life and his cloying address to thirteen-year-old middle-class kids living in the midst of that life.

29. If anything, in fact, the people spoken least by the Other-as-culture are those at the very bottom and those out on the furthest fringes of society: the poor, the homeless, the mentally handicapped, the insane, and peripheralized minorities and immigrants. The Other-as-culture does reach this "underclass," often through television, but characteristically fails to "speak" it in any systematic and therefore effective way. Everybody else, a fortiori those who wield the most power in society, those whose voices are most persistently heard, is constituted as a decent, upright citizen, as a loyal "subject" of the democracy, by his or her subjection to the Other-as-culture.

30. In *The Rhetoric of Fiction* Wayne Booth also implies, although much more indirectly, Whitey's moral superiority to Jim Kendall (156).

31. Other readings of the story did appear in the interim. In 1975 Charles S. Holmes refers to it in passing, but in terms so reminiscent of the traditional reading that he probably had not seen May's note: "In 'Haircut' there are decent people, to be sure, but they are hapless victims, not potential antagonists" (36). In 1977 Jonathan Yardley sidesteps the debate in an interesting way that does leave open the possibility that he is aware of it (though May's note does not appear in his bibliography). He quotes Fitzgerald's dismissal of "Haircut" in a letter to Max Perkins, discusses that dismissal as partly due to Scott's hurt feelings over Lardner's recent criticisms of *Gatsby* in page proof, then suggests that Fitzgerald was in some sense right: "The use of the village idiot to take revenge on Jim Kendall is indeed a cliché, and the story as a whole is just a little bit too pat; . . . It may have seemed to readers of a popular magazine to have been a brutal portrait of small-town hypocrisy and callousness, but those readers probably were unfamiliar with Sherwood Anderson's *Winesburg, Ohio*, published six years earlier and far superior" (288–89). Yardley's treatment implicitly links these "readers of a popular magazine" with the complacent moralism of the traditional reading and explicitly argues that a more sophisticated reader would not be so easily impressed (or reassured). But he does not take a stand on what *is* going on in the story: is the "small-town hypocrisy and callousness" that he refers to primarily Jim's or the town's? If it is Jim's, he leans toward the traditional reading; if it is the town's, he leans toward May's reading; but Yardley does not make it clear which he means.

Hal Blythe and Charlie Sweet also published a critical note on the story the year after Gilead's article appeared, in 1986, but did not substantially alter May's reading, merely offering additional evidence for it.

32. I am indebted here to Terry Eagleton, *The Function of Criticism*.

Chapter 6

1. Whitey's unreliable or problematic narration is portrayed by Blythe and Sweet as unwillingly or unwittingly self-revelatory: Whitey wants to keep the town's secret but is too stupid to maintain adequate control over his storytelling, and so reveals to us, trained literary critics, what really happened. In Freudian terms, Whitey's narration is like a dream or a parapraxis, a distorted return of the repressed that for the attentive listener voices the silenced message. In this sense the literary critic is like the psychiatric "doctor" in Foucault's essay who attempts to "cure monsters" through an attentive silence that is attentive to silence.

2. My discussion of sacrifice here and throughout this section is indebted to René Girard, *Violence and the Sacred.* For another application of Girard's theories to literary texts, there in terms of the diacritical impetus of ethical doubling vs. eschatological splitting, see my *American Apocalypses*, ch. 7.

3. See also Klaus Theweleit's brilliant first volume of *Male Fantasies*, especially the long first chapter on "Men and Women," where he explores the ideological program that coaches the German Freikorpsmen to at once idealize and violate women—"the games they play with the threat of rape from which most of these women only narrowly escape" (100). Theweleit's analysis shows among other things how the displacement of violence against the mother or her avatars into war only perpetuates the ideological pressure toward rape—how the "plundering of the castle may then function as a means of maintaining the threat of rape as an ever-present possibility" (100). The doubly bound implication is that rape is ideologically normal only when the attempt is repulsed, but the repulsion of rape becomes a faked image of repression which repeatedly presents the possibility of a renewed attempt.

4. DuPlessis deals with these three novels on 16, 17, and 88–89 (Chopin), 184–86 (Piercy), and 239, n. 49 (Walker; the novel was just out when DuPlessis was finishing her book).

5. I develop this reading of Fish at greater length in "Trivial and Esoteric Pursuits," especially 210–16.

6. The pieces in this collection by Bleich and Holland are proof of this claim: in place of the largely individuistic analyses of specific readers' interpretations that typified their work of the seventies, Bleich and Holland both meet the challenge obviously posed by the editors by making powerful connections between individual readings and the shaping ideological power of gender. This shift is perhaps most striking in the collaborative piece Holland did with Leona Sherman; they present their interpretive interchange on Ann Radcliffe's *Mysteries of Udolfo* in dialogue form, and Sherman's feminist sensibility frequently pushes Holland face to face with the ideological construction of gender:

HOLLAND: For me, both identifying with a female and imagining being penetrated call into question my male identity. Both raise the threat posed by the castle and the gothic machinery to a pitch where I no longer wish them relevant to me, the male me, and I sense myself relegating gothic to an alienating category, "women's fiction." Perhaps this is why I am acutely aware of another property of the castle — its flinty hardness. I want those stones to be inert, neither hurt nor hurting, whatever threats and penetrations go on between villain and victim. *They* cannot be penetrated, and if not they, then not I. (220)

"Identity" for the Holland who speaks here has lost the reassuring Freudian stability it had back in his works in the seventies: it can be called into question by a problematic gender identification. Holland still clings to the "way he is," his "normal" masculine desire to be rocklike and impenetrable, and he extrapolates that desire into interpretive strategy; but note, in the next passage, how he moves beyond that fundamentally conservative strategy into the first stage of reading beyond the ending:

Conversely, I can shape from my ambivalent feelings about the penetration *in* the novel an ambivalence toward my penetration *of* the novel. I want to penetrate its mysteries, yes, but I do not want to be penetrated by the book — I do not want to relax and let this kind of book happen to me like other novels. In the same way, my ambivalent absorption in the book, my feeling that *Udolfo* creates a stereotyped and artificial reality with which I am nevertheless involved to the exclusion of the real world, can let me imagine an ambivalent wish to escape in the plot. From my own mixed feelings toward the novel, I generate the heroine's mixture of eagerness to get out of danger and hesitation to enter the unknown outside. Out of Mrs. Radcliffe's failure to provide enough human aggression for me in the character of Emily, I supply it: Why doesn't she face up to Montoni? Out of the aggression I have supplied to the sequence of events, I shape my dissatisfaction with the novel: Why doesn't *it* give me a firm resistance to Montoni? (230)

7. This dictum applies, it seems to me, to Elizabeth A. Flynn's own contribution to the collection, "Gender and Reading," which attempts to show, to put it crudely, that women make better readers than men because they are more empathetic and better able to balance "detachment" and "involvement" in their responses to literature. This *is* a crude summary, since Flynn really only claims to be analyzing a selective sample of her students, not all men and women; but her ethnographic methodology is too vaguely outlined to determine just what kind of claim she is making about that sample, and what possible applications it might have to the generalities of "gender and reading."

Her conclusions are also vitiated by her normative approach to interpretation: invariably, the "best" students (usually the women) are those who "were successful in making sense of the story, usually because they came to a satisfying interpretation of its ending" (276) — an interpretation, that is (though Flynn will not come right out and say this), that satisfies her, the professor. Flynn has none of the dialogical openness to interpretive response of a Holland or a Bleich; there are right and wrong interpretations, and the right ones are the ones she likes, ostensibly because they balance dominant and submissive responses. That is, she conceals her complicity in what Fish calls the authority of the interpretive community to enforce conformity behind apparently objective criteria, thus revealing in her interpretations of her students' responses (especially those of her male students) precisely the dominant pole that she claims makes for bad reading.

8. This is very close, in fact, to Jameson's project in *The Political Unconscious*:

> Such is then the general theoretical framework in which I would wish to argue the methodological proposition outlined here: that a Marxist negative hermeneutic, a Marxist practice of ideological analysis proper, must in the practical work of reading and interpretation be exercised *simultaneously* with a Marxist positive hermeneutic, or a decipherment of the Utopian impulses of these same still ideological cultural texts. (296)

9. Ellen is referring here to my first draft of this chapter, to the section I wrote on the first draft of her article almost immediately after reading it, and then read to her over the phone. Since I have since replaced that section with this dialogue, let me quote the relevant passage here:

> Hence the importance, it seems to me, of dealing opening with Tom Cannon's and Ring Lardner's alcoholism in chapters 1 and 3 — with the disease that most of Lardner's critics pass over in silence, and others (Yardley, for example) dismiss as taking a few drinks to overcome your inhibitions. More important still, however, would be to follow the AA and admit publicly: "I am an alcoholic." This is the embarrassing fact that the Other-as-culture teaches alcoholics to silence ("sure I like to take a few drinks, but I can stop any time I want"), and as the AA insist, the silencing of that embarrassing fact is the greatest obstacle to health, or even to taking the first step toward health.
>
> Since I am not an alcoholic — my addictions lie elsewhere, in eating, for example — I did not take that tack in my discussions of Tom's and Lardner's alcoholism. Indeed, since I have had little luck getting confessional criticism past editors and external evaluators, I have woven my critical confessions of the "I am an alcoholic" variety as subtly as I can into the fabric of my "objective" readings — the only way, in the current academic climate, to get that sort of confession published. (Woven into the fabric of chapter 1, for example, was "I feel trapped by my mother"; one of the crucial confessions of all masculist criticism is "I am a sexist"; etc.) In the same way, Ellen Gardiner wove a confession on the order of "I am a melancholic" into her reading of Tom's wife's melancholia, and read revenge on Tom and Lardner and male critics out of her own feelings of enforced inferiority. If playing badly is the narrator's best revenge, reading "badly" is Gardiner's best revenge: reading against the grain, against authorial intention and the critical decorum founded on that rock, reading beyond the ending to the narrator's divorce from Tom and the feminist critic's divorce from the patriarchal marriage of author and reader, intention and interpretation. By admitting, in effect, that she is a melancholic, by giving full rein to her initial discovery that she identifies powerfully with Lardner's hurt monologist, Gardiner fights the hegemonic author-reader dialogue that would trap her in stupidity and inferiority and generates out of it an emancipatory image of revenge and divorce.
>
> These are, of course, still largely negative images: getting back at Tom, and getting out. But negative images are vitally important first (or second, or third) steps in the movement toward emancipation. Articulating one's incarceration in hegemonic structures — whether material or somatic or both — and one's angry desire to destroy those structures and those who maintain them is the indispensable preface to actually dismantling them.

10. For a discussion of the NAS's tactics, see Jacob Weisberg's *Lingua Franca* article, "NAS: Who Are These Guys Anyway?"

11. In his otherwise scurrilous "Ideas" piece in the April 1, 1991, issue of *Time* magazine, for example, William A. Henry III cites disturbing evidence that the loyalty of some oppositional academics is less to freedom, equality, and human dignity than to "pay-back," to an equally authoritarian reversal of traditional discriminatory behavior: "The University of Wisconsin at Parkside suspended one student for addressing another as 'Shaka Zulu'; yet the university's Madison campus held that the term red-neck was not discriminatory" (67), when it obviously is — just against conservative whites. Henry cites a number of such cases around the country, most of which are tainted as evidence by gross oversimplifications: "Several schools have punished students for expressing religious objections to homosexuality or, as at the University of Washington, questioning a professor's assertion that lesbians make the best mothers" (67). What kind of punishment? What kind of objections? What kind of assertion? Such fine-tuning is irrelevant in NASville.

What is most telling about the article is that it replicates rhetorically the closed-mindedness it attacks. Henry's only response to "deviant" ideological analyses patently spoken by various minoritarian Others — "the theme that organized crime 'is a metaphor for American business as usual'" (66), the notion that the liberal arts are "prone to 'a fetishized respect for culture as a stagnant secular religion'" (66), a course on "White Male Writers" (67), the assertion that ancient Greece derived its philosophical, mathematical, and scientific achievements from black Egypt (68), a minor in Gay and Lesbian Studies (69) — is one of hegemonic toxic shock, a repressive shudder that shuts down all possibility of dialogue and learning. This sort of openness to cultural diversity is just as bad, in Henry's book, as the tendency to impose new forms of closed-mindedness on students by force.

One might even say that the Other-as-culture has moved on and left people like William A. Henry III and the NAS behind, or that what we are witnessing is a pitched battle between two Others-as-culture, conservative and progressive, old and new, because when it is fought on these terms the battle clearly seems to be over naked social power — over who is to decide what is to be included and what is to be excluded, who is to be punished and who is to be praised. Another way of thematizing this battle is by noting that the Other-as-culture may shift ground, may even play two sides off against each other, but as long as it retains and wields on both sides the power to silence, to repress, to exclude, to punish deviants, the Other-as-escape-artist has been co-opted, hired by the warden to lead would-be escapees into another wing of the prison block and teach them to call it "freedom."

12. The instructor can, for example, allow the class to decide upon an alternative to the traditional final exam; grades can be drastically inflated, so that mostly A's are given, with a few F's for those who never come to class or do any of the work but forget to drop the course officially, and the group can discuss the criteria for lowering a final grade from an A to a B.

Appendix B

1. I borrow this term from Judith Fetterley's discussion of "Rip Van Winkle" in *The Resisting Reader* 1.

2. In fact, our conversations about this story, oral and written, have been the shaping force of my argument through all its stages. I would also like to thank Doreen Fowler, Deborah Barker, Ann Fisher-Wirth, and Thomas E. Maresca for responding to early drafts of this essay; all have provided much encouragement and support.

3. All page references to "Who Dealt?" will be to appendix A of this book.

4. Bowlby found that in some patients, particularly women, melancholia does not arise from the loss of an attachment to a love object, but rather from the inability of the sufferer to fully attach to another. For Bowlby, melancholia signifies the isolation felt when an attachment is found to be fragmentary, when a relationship has been fabricated in the imagination of the sufferer, when it has no "real" substance. Research like Bowlby's relates most particularly to women because studies have shown that it is most often women in culture whose "sense of self is built around being able to make and then maintain connections with others" (see Gilligan et al. 10–11). For women like the narrator, therefore, a "loss of relationship is experienced . . . as tantamount to a loss of self" (Gilligan et al. x).

5. Women also do not have an important economic role within the American family. As Anne Oakley points out, in industrialized societies "married women [are] 'engaged in unpaid home duties . . . not regarded as retired, but [are] treated as "others economically inactive"'" ("What Is a Housewife?" 78). While housework is work, it is low-status work. Society devalues women's role in American family life and women internalize society's devaluation. Furthermore, because her work keeps her in the home, she has little chance of developing relationships outside of it.

6. According to Chodorow, a daughter's relationship with her father also prepares her to idealize her adult relationships with men. While her mother teaches her to seek connections with others, the daughter's relationship to her father is critically important in her socialization to heterosexual relationships. Psychoanalysts argue that during the oedipal period the father offers the daughter a partial escape from maternal omnipotence. She turns to her father for a sense of separateness from her mother, but also wants desperately to be loved by him. Says Chodorow, "She (and the woman she becomes) is willing to deny her father's limitations (and those of her lovers or husband) as long as she feels loved, and she is more able to do so because his distance means she does not really know him" (72).

7. In a book that assumes the woman's role to be the hostess, it is also apparently ideologically "normal" for the woman to be the dummy. Sheinwold describes the proper etiquette of the dummy as follows:

> When you are the dummy, don't look at either opponent's hand. Don't ask your partner to pass his hand across the table so that you can follow what he is doing.

Above all, don't get up from your chair and stand behind the declarer while he plays the hand.

However, if you get up, when dummy, to bring refreshments to the players, nobody will hate you for sneaking a quick look at your partner's hand before you go off to do your chores. (442)

8. The question of why it is the narrator, rather than Tom, who can resolve her melancholia might be answered by again referring to recent studies of the way women were socialized in the 1920s. As a woman in this culture, the narrator is economically dependent on men for financial support. Studies in fact indicate that men tend to fall in love romantically, while women do so sensibly and rationally (Chodorow 74). Given the narrator's discussion of money in the text, her allusions to her own thriftiness, one suspects that part of the reason the narrator married Tom is her economic dependence, that her decision to marry Tom was not purely a romantic one, but a rational calculation to provide for herself. For this reason she is on one level more capable than Tom of developing distance to her marriage.

Works Cited

Althusser, Louis. "Ideology and Ideological State Apparatuses (Notes Toward an Investigation)." Trans. Ben Brewster. In Althusser, *Lenin and Philosophy and Other Essays*, 121–73. London: New Left Books, 1969.

Anderson, Perry. *Lineages of the Absolutist State*. 1974; rpt. London: Verso, 1986.

Anderson, Sherwood. "Four American Impressions." *The New Republic*, October 11, 1922: 171–73.

Bakhtin, Mikhail. *Discourse in the Novel*. Trans. Caryl Emerson and Michael Holquist. In Holquist, ed., *The Dialogic Imagination: Four Essays*, 259–422. Austin: University of Texas Press, 1981.

_____. *Rabelais and His World*. Trans. Helene Iswolsky. 1968; rpt. Bloomington: Indiana University Press, 1984.

Bannister, Robert C. "Gender and American Culture: The Masculinization of American Thought, 1910–1950s." Unpublished book manuscript.

Baron, Dennis. *The English-Only Question: An Official Language for Americans?* New Haven, Conn.: Yale University Press, 1990.

Barthes, Roland. *The Pleasure of the Text*. New York: Hill, 1975.

Bateson, Gregory. *Steps to an Ecology of Mind*. 1972; rpt. New York: Ballantine Books, 1985.

Berger, John. *Ways of Seeing*. Harmondsworth: Penguin, 1972.

Berryman, John. "The Case of Ring Lardner: Art and Entertainment." *Commentary* 22:5 (November 1956): 416–23.

Bier, Jesse. *The Rise and Fall of American Humor*. New York: Holt, Rinehart & Winston, 1968.

Blair, Walter, and Hamlin Hill. *America's Humor: From Poor Richard to Doonesbury*. New York: Oxford University Press, 1978.

Blake, William. *The Marriage of Heaven and Hell*. In David V. Erdman, ed., *The Complete Poetry and Prose of William Blake*, 33–45. 1965; rev. ed. Garden City, N.Y.: Doubleday/Anchor, 1982.

Bleich, David. "Gender Interests in Reading and Language." In Flynn and Schweickart, eds., *Gender and Reading*, 234–66.

————. *Subjective Criticism*. Baltimore: Johns Hopkins University Press, 1978.

Blumin, Stuart M. "The Hypothesis of Middle-Class Formation in Nineteenth-Century America: A Critique and Some Proposals." *American Historical Review* 90 (April 1985): 299–338.

Blythe, Hal. "Lardner's HAIRCUT." *The Explicator* 44:3 (Spring 1986): 48–49.

Blythe, Hal, and Charlie Sweet. "The Barber of Civility: The Chief Conspirator of 'Haircut'." *Studies in Short Fiction* 23 (Fall 1986): 450–53.

Booth, Wayne. *The Rhetoric of Fiction*. Chicago: University of Chicago Press, 1961.

Bordewyk, Gordon. "Comic Alienation: Ring Lardner's Style." *Markham Review* 11 (Spring 1982): 51–57.

Bourdieu, Pierre. *Distinction: A Social Critique of the Judgement of Taste*. 1979. Trans. Richard Nice. London: Routledge and Kegan Paul, 1984.

Brandes, Stuart D. *American Welfare Capitalism, 1880–1940*. Chicago: University of Chicago Press, 1976.

Brod, Harry, ed. *The Making of Masculinities: The New Men's Studies*. Boston: Allen & Unwin, 1987.

Brooks, Cleanth, and Robert Penn Warren. *Understanding Fiction*. New York: Appleton-Century-Crofts, 1959.

Buber, Martin. *I and Thou*. Trans. Walter Kaufmann. New York: Scribner's, 1970.

Burke, Kenneth. "A Dramatistic View of the Origins of Language." In Burke, *Language as Symbolic Action: Essays on Life, Literature, and Method*, 419–79. Berkeley: University of California Press, 1966.

Caruthers, Clifford M. *Letters from Ring*. Flint, Mich.: Walden Press, 1979.

————. *Ring Around Max: The Correspondence of Ring Lardner and Max Perkins*. Dekalb: Northern Illinois University Press, 1973.

Chodorow, Nancy. *The Reproduction of Mothering: Psychoanalysis and the Sociology of Gender*. Berkeley: University of California Press, 1978.

Cochrane, James, ed. *The Penguin Book of American Short Stories*. Harmondsworth: Penguin, 1972.

Cockburn, Cynthia. "The Material of Male Power." In Terry Lovell, ed., *British Feminist Thought*, 77–83.

Corneau, Guy. *Absent Fathers, Lost Sons: The Search for Masculine Identity*. Boston: Shambhala, 1991.

Deleuze, Gilles, and Felix Guattari. *Anti-Oedipus*. Vol. 1 of *Capitalism and Schizophrenia*. 1972. Trans. Robert Hurley, Mark Seem, and Helen Lane. Minneapolis: University of Minnesota Press, 1983.

————. *A Thousand Plateaus*. Vol. 2 of *Capitalism and Schizophrenia*. 1977. Trans. Brian Massumi. Minneapolis: University of Minnesota Press, 1987.

————. *Kafka: Toward a Minor Literature*. Minneapolis: University of Minnesota Press, 1986.

DeMuth, James. *Small Town Chicago: The Comic Perspective of Finley Peter Dunne, George Ade, Ring Lardner*. Port Washington, N.Y.: Kennikat Press, 1980.

Denning, Michael. *Mechanic Accents: Dime Novels and Working-Class Culture in America*. London: Verso, 1987.

Douglas, Ann. *The Feminization of American Culture*. New York: Knopf, 1977.

Dubbert, Joe L. "Progressivism and the Masculinity Crisis." In Pleck and Pleck, *The American Man*, 303–20.

Duffey, Bernard. "Humor, Chicago Style." In Rubin, ed., *The Comic Imagination in American Literature*, 207–16.

DuPlessis, Rachel Blau. *Writing Beyond the Ending: Narrative Strategies of Twentieth-Century Women Writers*. Bloomington: Indiana University Press, 1985.

Eagleton, Terry. *The Function of Criticism: From "The Spectator" to Post-Structuralism*. London: Verso, 1984.

Elder, Donald. *Ring Lardner*. Garden City, N.Y.: Doubleday, 1956.

Elias, Norbert. *Power and Civility*. Trans. Edmund Jephcott. Vol. 2 of *The Civilizing Process*. 1939; New York: Pantheon, 1982.

Evans, Elizabeth. *Ring Lardner*. New York: Frederick Ungar, 1979.

_____. "Ring Lardner's Bridge-Playing Spoil Sports." *Notes on Contemporary Literature* 11:1 (January 1981): 5–8.

Fadiman, Clifton. "Ring Lardner and the Triangle of Hate." *The Nation*, March 22, 1933: 315–17.

Fetterley, Judith. *The Resisting Reader: A Feminist Approach to American Fiction*. Bloomington: Indiana University Press, 1978.

Fiedler, Leslie. *What Was Literature? Class Culture and Mass Society*. New York: Simon & Schuster, 1982.

Filene, Peter Gabriel. "In Time of War." In Pleck and Pleck, *The American Man*, 321–35.

Fish, Stanley. *Doing What Comes Naturally: Change, Rhetoric, and the Practice of Theory in Literary and Legal Studies*. Durham, N.C.: Duke University Press, 1989.

_____. *Is There a Text in This Class? The Authority of Interpretive Communities*. Cambridge, Mass.: Harvard University Press, 1980.

Fitzgerald, F. Scott. *The Great Gatsby*. New York: Scribner's, 1925.

_____. "Ring." *The New Republic*, October 11, 1933: 254–55.

Flynn, Elizabeth A. "Gender and Reading." In Flynn and Schweickart, eds., *Gender and Reading*, 267–88.

Flynn, Elizabeth A., and Patrocinio P. Schweickart, eds. *Gender and Reading: Essays on Readers, Texts, and Contexts*. Baltimore: Johns Hopkins University Press, 1986.

Forward, Susan, with Craig Buck. *Toxic Parents: Overcoming Their Hurtful Legacy and Reclaiming Your Life*. New York: Bantam Books, 1989.

Foucault, Michel. "The Discourse on Language." In Foucault, *The Archaeology of Knowledge*, 215–37. Trans. A. M. Sheridan Smith. New York: Pantheon, 1972.

_____. *Madness and Civilization: A History of Insanity in the Age of Reason*. Trans. Richard Howard. 1961; New York: Random House, 1965.

_____. "What Is an Author?" In Josué V. Harari, ed., *Textual Strategies: Perspectives in Post-Structuralist Criticism*, 141–60. Ithaca, N.Y.: Cornell University Press, 1979.

French, Warren, ed. *The Twenties: Fiction, Poetry, Drama*. DeLand, Fla.: Everett/Edwards, 1975.

Freud, Sigmund. *The Interpretation of Dreams*. Trans. James Strachey. 1900; New York: Avon Books, 1965.

_____. *Jokes and Their Relation to the Unconscious*. Trans. James Strachey. 1905; New York: Norton, 1960.

_____. "Mourning and Melancholia." In John Rickman, M.D., ed., *A General Selection from the Works of Sigmund Freud*, 124–40. Garden City, N.Y.: Doubleday, 1957.

Friedrich, Otto. *Ring Lardner*. Minneapolis: University of Minnesota Press, 1965.

Frye, Northrop. *Anatomy of Criticism: Four Essays*. Princeton, N.J.: Princeton University Press, 1957.

Garrison, Dee. *Apostles of Culture: The Public Librarian and American Society, 1876–1920*. New York: Free Press/Macmillan, 1979.

Geismar, Maxwell. *Ring Lardner and the Portrait of Folly*. New York: Crowell, 1972.

_____, ed. *The Ring Lardner Reader*. New York: Scribner's, 1963.

Geller, Evelyn. *Forbidden Books in American Public Libraries, 1876–1939*. Westport, Conn.: Greenwood Press, 1984.

Gilead, Sarah. "Lardner's Discourses of Power." *Studies in Short Fiction* 22 (1985): 331–37.

Gilligan, Carol, Janie Victoria Ward, Jill McLean Taylor, with Betty Bardige, eds. *Mapping the Moral Domain*. Cambridge, Mass.: Harvard University Press, 1988.

Girard, René. *Violence and the Sacred*. Trans. Patrick Gregory. 1972; Baltimore: Johns Hopkins University Press, 1979.

Goldberg, Herb. *The Hazards of Being Male: Surviving the Myth of Male Privilege*. 1976; rpt. New York: Signet, 1977.

_____. *The Inner Male: Overcoming Roadblocks to Intimacy*. New York: NAL, 1987.

_____. *The New Male: From Self-Destruction to Self-Care*. 1979; rpt. New York: Signet, 1980.

_____. *The New Male-Female Relationship*. 1983; rpt. New York: Signet, 1984.

Goren, Charles. *Goren's Hoyle Encyclopedia of Games*. New York: Greystone, 1961.

Graham, Bessie. *The Booksman's Manual: A Guide to Literature*. 3rd ed. New York: Bowker, 1928.

Griffin, Susan. *Woman and Nature: The Roaring Inside Her*. New York: Harper & Row, 1978.

Gugliemo, Wagner J. "Ring Lardner and 'The Battle of the Century.'" *Markham Review* 14 (Fall/Winter 1984–85): 12–15.

Hantover, Jeffrey P. "The Boy Scouts and the Validation of Masculinity." In Pleck and Pleck, *The American Man*, 285–301.

Harpham, Geoffrey Galt. *The Ascetic Imperative in Culture and Criticism*. Chicago: University of Chicago Press, 1987.

Hart, John E. "Man as Thing: Ring Lardner's *You Know Me Al*." *South Dakota Review* 23:1 (1985): 114–22.

Hartmann, Edward George. *The Movement to Americanize the Immigrant*. New York: Columbia University Press, 1948.

Hasley, Louis. "Ring Lardner: The Ashes of Idealism." *Arizona Quarterly* 26 (1970): 219–32.

Heidegger, Martin. "Language." Trans. Albert Hofstadter. In *Poetry, Language, Thought*, 189–210. New York: Harper & Row, 1971.

Hemingway, Ernest. "Defense of Dirty Words: A Cuban Letter." *Esquire*, September 1934: 19, 158B, 158D.

Henry, William A., III. "Upside Down in the Groves of Academe." *Time*, April 1, 1991: 66–69.

Hirsch, E. D., Jr. "Objective Interpretation." *PMLA* 75 (1960). Reprinted in Hirsch, *Validity in Interpretation*. New Haven, Conn.: Yale University Press, 1967. Reprinted in Hazard Adams, ed., *Critical Theory Since Plato*, 1177–94. New York: Harcourt Brace Jovanovich, 1971.

Holland, Norman. *5 Readers Reading*. New Haven, Conn.: Yale University Press, 1975.

_____. *Poems in Persons*. New York: Norton, 1973.

Holland, Norman, and Leona F. Sherman. "Gothic Possibilities." In Flynn and Schweickart, eds., *Gender and Reading*, 215–33.

Holman, C. Hugh. "Anodyne for the Village Virus." In Rubin, ed., *The Comic Imagination in American Literature*, 247–58.

Holmes, Charles S. *The Clocks of Columbus: The Literary Career of James Thurber*. New York: Atheneum, 1972.

_____. "Ring Lardner: Reluctant Artist." In Louis Filler, ed., *A Question of Quality: Popularity and Value in Modern Creative Writing*, 26–39. Bowling Green, Ohio: Bowling Green University Popular Press, 1976.

Ingram, Forrest L. "Fun at the Incinerating Plant: Lardner's Wry Waste Land." In French, ed., *The Twenties*, 111–22.

James, William. *The Principles of Psychology*. 2 vols. 1890; rpt. New York: Henry Holt, 1908.

Jameson, Fredric. *The Political Unconscious: Narrative as a Socially Symbolic Act*. Ithaca, N.Y.: Cornell University Press, 1981.

Jardine, Alice, and Paul Smith, eds. *Men in Feminism*. New York: Methuen, 1987.

Kimmel, Michael. "The Contemporary 'Crisis' of Masculinity in Historical Perspective." In Brod, ed., *The Making of Masculinities*, 121–54.

Kristeva, Julia. "Place Names." In Kristeva, *Desire in Language*, 271–94. Ed. Leon Roudiez. Trans. Thomas Gora, Alice Jardine, and Leon Roudiez. New York: Columbia University Press, 1980.

Kuehl, John, and Jackson R. Bryer, eds. *Dear Scott/Dear Max: The Fitzgerald-Perkins Correspondence*. London: Cassell, 1973.

Lacan, Jacques. *Ecrits: A Selection*. Trans. Alan Sheridan. New York: Norton, 1977.

_____. *Speech and Language in Psychoanalysis*. Trans. Anthony Wilden. 1968; rev. ed. Baltimore: Johns Hopkins University Press, 1981.

Lardner, Ring. "Alibi Ike." *Saturday Evening Post*, July 31, 1915. In Lardner, *Round Up*, 35–52.

_____. "Allie Bobs Oop Again." *New Yorker*, July 30, 1932: 24, 25–27.

_____. "The Battle of the Century." *Saturday Evening Post*, October 29, 1921. In Lardner, *Some Champions*, 134–49.

_____. *The Big Town*. Indianapolis, Ind.: Bobbs-Merrill, 1920.

_____. "Bob's Birthday." *Redbook*, November 1933. In Lardner, *Some Champions*, 167–73.

_____. "A Caddy's Diary." *Saturday Evening Post*, March 11, 1922. In Lardner, *Round Up*, 393–409.

_____. "Champion." *Metropolitan*, October 1916. In Lardner, *Round Up*, 109–28.

_____. "Contract." *Harper's Bazaar*, March 1929. In Lardner, *Round Up*, 129–39.

_____. "Cured!" *Redbook*, March 1931. In Lardner, *Some Champions*, 158–66.

_____. "A Day with Conrad Green." *Liberty*, October 3, 1925. In Lardner, *Round Up*, 159–70.

_____. "Dinner." *Harper's Bazaar*, September 1928. In Lardner, *Round Up*, 141–48.

_____. "A Frame-Up." *Saturday Evening Post*, June 18, 1921: 14–15, 65, 68, 71.

_____. "The Golden Honeymoon." *Cosmopolitan*, July 1922. In Lardner, *Round Up*, 221–36.

_____. *Gullible's Travels, Etc*. New York: Scribner's, 1925.

_____. "Haircut." *Liberty*, March 28, 1925. In Lardner, *Round Up*, 23–34.

_____. "Harmony." *McClure's*, August 1915. In Lardner, *Round Up*, 181–98.

_____. "Horseshoes." *Saturday Evening Post*, August 15, 1914. In Lardner, *Round Up*, 249–70.

_____. *How to Write Short Stories*. New York: Scribner's, 1924.

_____. "Hurry Kane." *Cosmopolitan*, May 1927. In Lardner, *Round Up*, 87–108.

_____. "I Can't Breathe." *Cosmopolitan*, September 1926. In Lardner, *Round Up*, 13–22.

_____. "I. Gaspiri (The Upholsterers)." *Chicago Literary Times*, February 1924. In Lardner, *What Of It?*, 45–47.

_____. "Insomnia." *Cosmopolitan*, May 1931. In Lardner, *Some Champions*, 91–98.

_____. *Lose with a Smile*. New York: Scribner's, 1933.

_____. "The Love Nest." *Cosmopolitan*, August 1925. In Lardner, *Round Up*, 199–210.

_____. *The Love Nest and Other Stories*. New York: Scribner's, 1926.

_____. "Lyricists Strike Pay Dirt." *New Yorker*, November 19, 1932. In Lardner, *Shut Up, He Explained*, 252–54.

_____. "The Maysville Minstrel." *Cosmopolitan*, September 1928. In Lardner, *Round Up*, 3–12.

_____. "Mr. Frisbie." *Cosmopolitan*, June 1928. In Lardner, *Round Up*, 75–86.

_____. "My Roomy." *Saturday Evening Post*, May 9, 1914. In Lardner, *Round Up*, 327–46.

_____. "Old Folks' Christmas." *Cosmopolitan*, January 1929. In Lardner, *Round Up*, 171–80.

_____. *The Real Dope*. Indianapolis, Ind.: Bobbs-Merrill, 1919.

_____. "Rhythm." *Cosmopolitan*, March 1926. In Lardner, *Round Up*, 347–56.

_____. "Ring Lardner's Letter on Neglected Husbands." *Wheeler's Magazine*, 1922.

_____. *Round Up: The Stories of Ring Lardner*. New York: Scribner's, 1929.

_____. *Shut Up, He Explained*. Ed. Babette Rosmond and Henry Morgan. New York: Scribner's, 1962.

_____. *Some Champions: Sketches and Fiction by Ring Lardner*. Ed. Matthew J. Bruccoli and Richard Layman. New York: Scribner's, 1976.

_____. "Some Like Them Cold." *Saturday Evening Post*, October 21, 1921. In Lardner, *Round Up*, 357–74.

_____. *The Story of a Wonder Man*. New York: Scribner's, 1927.

_____. "Sun Cured." *Cosmopolitan*, January 1927. In Lardner, *Round Up*, 437–46.

_____. "There Are Smiles." *Cosmopolitan*, April 1928. In Lardner, *Round Up*, 271–82.

_____. "Travelogue." *Cosmopolitan*, May 1926. In Lardner, *Round Up*, 305–16.

_____. *Treat 'Em Rough*. Indianapolis, Ind.: Bobbs-Merrill, 1918.

_____. *What Of It?* New York: Scribner's, 1925.

_____. "Who Dealt?" *Cosmopolitan*, January 1926. In Lardner, *Round Up*, 317–26.

_____. "Women." *Liberty*, June 20, 1925. In Lardner, *Round Up*, 149–58.

_____. *You Know Me Al: A Busher's Letters*. 1916; rpt. New York: Vintage Books/Random House, 1984.

_____. "The Young Immigrunts." *Saturday Evening Post*, January 31, 1920. In Lardner, *What Of It?*, 221–56.

_____. "Zone of Quiet." *Cosmopolitan*, August 1925. In Lardner, *Round Up*, 65–74.

Lardner, Ring, Jr. *All for Love*. New York: Franklin Watts, 1985.

_____. *The Ecstasy of Owen Muir*. Melbourne: Sun Books, 1966.

_____. *The Lardners: My Family Remembered*. New York: Harper & Row, 1976.

Lears, T. J. Jackson. "From Salvation to Self-Realization: Advertising and the Therapeutic Roots of the Consumer Culture, 1880-1930." In Richard Wightman Fox and T. J. Jackson Lears, eds., *The Culture of Consumption: Critical Essays in American History, 1880-1980*, 1-38. New York: Pantheon Books, 1983.

_____. *No Place of Grace: Antimodernism and the Transformation of American Culture, 1880-1920*. New York: Pantheon Books, 1981.

Lentricchia, Frank. *Ariel and the Police: Michel Foucault, William James, Wallace Stevens*. Madison: University of Wisconsin Press, 1988.

Leverenz, David. *Manhood and the American Renaissance*. Ithaca, N.Y.: Cornell University Press, 1989.

Lipsitz, George. *Time Passages: Collective Memory and American Popular Culture*. Minneapolis: University of Minnesota Press, 1990.

Littell, Robert. ". . . And Other Stories." *The New Republic*, September 29, 1926: 147-49.

Long, Elizabeth. "Women, Reading, and Cultural Authority: Some Implications of the Audience Perspective in Cultural Studies." *American Quarterly* 38 (Fall 1986): 591-612.

Lovell, Terry, ed. *British Feminist Thought*. Cambridge: Blackwell, 1990.

Lynn, Kenneth S. "Bush-League Swift." *Reporter*, February 14, 1963: 60-62.

Matthews, T.S. "Lardner, Shakespeare and Chekhov." *The New Republic*, May 22, 1929: 35-36.

May, Charles E. "Lardner's HAIRCUT." *The Explicator* 31:9 (May 1973): #69.

Mayer, Arno J. "The Lower Middle Class as Historical Problem." *Journal of Modern History* 47 (1975): 409-36.

Mencken, H. L. "Lardner." In Mencken, *Prejudices: Fifth Series*. London: Jonathan Cape, n.d.

_____. *Letters of H. L. Mencken*. Ed. Guy J. Forgue. New York: Knopf, 1961.

Miller, Alice. *For Your Own Good: Hidden Cruelty in Child-Rearing and the Roots of Violence*. Trans. Hildegarde Hannum and Hunter Hannum. 1980; New York: Meridian/NAL, 1983.

_____. *Thou Shalt Not be Aware: Society's Betrayal of the Child*. Trans. Hildegarde Hannum and Hunter Hannum. 1981; New York: Meridian/NAL, 1986.

Moseley, Merritt. "Ring Lardner and the American Humor Tradition." *South Atlantic Review* 46:1 (January 1981): 42-60.

Mott, Frank Luther. *A History of American Magazines*. 5 vols. Cambridge, Mass.: Belknap Press of Harvard University Press, 1938-68.

Nevins, Allan. "The American Moron." *The Saturday Review* 5 (1929): 1089-90.

Nye, David E. *Image Worlds: Corporate Identities at General Electric, 1890-1930*. Cambridge, Mass.: MIT Press, 1985.

Oakley, Anne. "What Is a Housewife?" In Terry Lovell, ed., *British Feminist Thought*, 71-76.

Osherson, Samuel. *Finding Our Fathers: The Unfinished Business of Manhood*. New York: Macmillan/Free Press, 1986.

Olsen, Paul. *Sons and Mothers*. 1981; rpt. New York: Ballantine/Fawcett Crest, 1982.

Patrick, Walton R. *Ring Lardner*. New York: Twayne, 1963.

Pleck, Elizabeth H., and Joseph H. Pleck, eds. *The American Man*. Englewood Cliffs, N.J.: Prentice-Hall, 1980.

Pleck, Joseph H. "Men's Power with Women, Other Men, and Society: A Men's Movement Analysis." In Pleck and Pleck, *The American Man*, 417–33.

Pritchett, V.S. "The Talent of Ring Lardner." *New Statesman*, April 25, 1959: 580–81.

Pynchon, Thomas. *The Crying of Lot 49*. 1966; rpt. New York: Bantam, 1967.

Radway, Janice. "The Book-of-the-Month Club and the General Reader: On the Uses of 'Serious' Fiction." *Critical Inquiry* 14 (Spring 1988): 516–38.

_____. *Reading the Romance: Women, Patriarchy, and Popular Culture*. Chapel Hill: University of North Carolina Press, 1984.

Robinson, Douglas. *American Apocalypses: The Image of the End of the World in American Literature*. Baltimore: Johns Hopkins University Press, 1985.

_____. "Dear Harold." *New Literary History* 20 (Autumn 1988): 239–50.

_____. "Henry James and Euphemism." *College English* 53 (April 1991): 403–27.

_____. "No Less A Man: Masculist Transformations in Post-Feminist Popular Culture." Unpublished book manuscript.

_____. "Ring Lardner's Dual Audience and the Capitalist Double Bind." *American Literary History* 4 (Summer 1992): 264–87.

_____. *The Translator's Turn*. Baltimore: Johns Hopkins University Press, 1991.

_____. "Trivial and Esoteric Pursuits: The Power Politics of Interpretive Communities." *Southwest Review* 72 (Spring 1987): 203–23.

_____. "The Trivialization of American Literature." *American Quarterly* 20 (June 1988): 205–23.

Rosenberg, Charles E. "Sexuality, Class and Role in 19th-Century America." In Pleck and Pleck, *The American Man*, 219–54.

Rourke, Constance. *American Humor: A Study of the National Character*. Garden City, N.Y.: Doubleday/Anchor, 1955.

Rowan, John. *The Horned God: Feminism and Men as Wounding and Healing*. London: Routledge and Kegan Paul, 1987.

Rubin, Louis D., Jr. "'The Barber Kept on Shaving.'" In Rubin, ed., *The Comic Imagination in American Literature*, 385–405.

Rubin, Louis D., Jr., ed. *The Comic Imagination in American Literature*. New Brunswick, N.J.: Rutgers University Press, 1973.

Saussure, Ferdinand de. *Course in General Linguistics*. Trans. Roy Harris. 1916; London: Duckworth, 1983.

Schwartz, Delmore. "Ring Lardner: Highbrow in Hiding." *Reporter*, August 9, 1956: 52–54.

Schweickart, Patrocinio P. "Reading Ourselves: Toward a Feminist Theory of Reading." In Flynn and Schweickart, eds., *Gender and Reading*, 31–62.

Searle, John. *Speech Acts: An Essay in the Philosophy of Language*. Cambridge: Cambridge University Press, 1969.

Seldes, Gilbert. "Editor's Introduction." *The Portable Ring Lardner*, 1–19. New York: Viking, 1946.

Sheed, Wilfrid. "Introduction" to Ring W. Lardner, *You Know Me Al: A Busher's Letters*, 11–18. New York: Vintage/Random House, 1984.

Sheinwold, Alfred. *Five Weeks to Winning Bridge*. New York: Pocket Books, 1964.

Shepard, Leslie. *The History of Street Literature: The Story of Broadside Ballads, Chapbooks, Proclamations, News-Sheets, Election Bills, Tracts, Pamphlets, Cocks, Catchpennies, and Other Ephemera*. Detroit: Singing Tree Press, 1973.

Smith, Leverett T., Jr. "'The Diameter of Frank Chance's Diamond': Ring Lardner and Professional Sports." *Journal of Popular Culture* 6 (Summer 1972): 133–56.

Spatz, Jonas. "Ring Lardner: Not an Escape, but a Reflection." In French, ed., *The Twenties*, 101–10.

Stearns, Peter. "The Middle Class: Toward a Precise Definition." *Comparative Studies in Society and History* 21 (1979): 377–96.

Stein, Allen F. "This Unsporting Life: The Baseball Fiction of Ring Lardner." *The Markham Review* 3:1 (October 1971): 27–33.

Susman, Warren I. *Culture as History: The Transformation of American Society in the Twentieth Century*. New York: Pantheon, 1984.

Theweleit, Klaus. *Male Fantasies*. Vol. 1, *Women Floods Bodies History*. Trans. Stephen Conway, in collaboration with Erica Carter and Chris Turner. Minneapolis: University of Minnesota Press, 1987.

Tiverton, Dana. "Ring Lardner Writes a Story." *The Writer* 45:1 (January 1933): 8–9.

Tobin, Richard L. "The Writer." *Saturday Review* January 25, 1964: 6.

Van Doren, Carl. "Beyond Grammar: Ring W. Lardner: Philologist Among the Low-brows." *Century* 106 (July 1923): 471–75.

Voloshinov, V.N. *Marxism and the Philosophy of Language*. Trans. Ladislav Matejka and I. R. Titunik. New York: Seminar Press, 1973.

Waples, Douglas. *People and Print: Social Aspects of Reading in the Depression*. Chicago: University of Chicago Press, 1938.

Webb, Howard W., Jr. "The Development of a Style: The Lardner Idiom." *American Quarterly* 12 (Winter 1960): 482–92.

———. "The Meaning of Ring Lardner's Fiction: A Re-evaluation." *American Literature* 61 (January 1960): 434–45.

———. "Ring Lardner's Idle Common Man." *The Bulletin of the Central Mississippi Valley American Studies Association* 1 (Spring 1958): 6–13.

Weisberg, Jacob. "NAS: Who Are These Guys Anyway?" *Lingua Franca* 1.4 (April 1991): 34–39.

Wheeler, John. "Unforgettable Ring Lardner." *Reader's Digest* 89 (October 1966): 113–17.

Wilden, Anthony. "Lacan and the Discourse of the Other." In Lacan, *Speech and Language in Psychoanalysis*, 159–311.

Wilkinson, Rupert. *American Tough: The Tough-Guy Tradition and American Character*. New York: Harper & Row, 1986.

Wilson, Edmund. "Ring Lardner's American Characters." 1924; rpt. in Wilson, *A Literary Chronicle: 1920–1950*. Garden City, N.Y.: Doubleday/Anchor, 1952.

Wimsatt, W.K., and Monroe C. Beardsley. "The Affective Fallacy." In Wimsatt, *The Verbal Icon*, 21–39. Lexington: University of Kentucky Press, 1954.

Woolf, Virginia. "American Fiction." *Saturday Review*, August 1, 1925: 1–3.

Yardley, Jonathan. *Ring: A Biography of Ring Lardner*. New York: Random House, 1977.

Yates, Norris W. "The Isolated Man of Ring Lardner." In Yates, *The American Humorist: Conscience of the Twentieth Century*, 165–93. Ames: Iowa State University Press, 1964.

Index